MRS. ASTOR REGRETS

Mrs. Astor Regrets

*The Hidden Betrayals
of a Family
Beyond Reproach*

Meryl Gordon

HOUGHTON MIFFLIN HARCOURT

Boston · New York

2008

Library of Congress Cataloging-in-Publication Data
Gordon, Meryl.
Mrs. Astor regrets : the hidden betrayals of a family beyond reproach /
Meryl Gordon.
p.   cm.
Includes bibliographical references and index.
ISBN 978-0-618-89373-7 (alk. paper)
1. Astor, Brooke.   2. Socialites—New York (State)—New York—Biography.
3. Philanthropists—New York (State)—New York—Biography.
4. New York (N.Y.)—Biography.   I. Title.
CT275.A847G67 2008
974.7′043092—dc22   [B]   2008034893

Book design by Melissa Lotfy

Printed in the United States of America

DOC 10 9 8 7 6 5 4 3 2 1

To Walter
Now more than ever

To my parents
Adventurous, passionate, supportive

Contents

Mrs. Astor Regrets

Prologue

Trial by Tabloid

WHEN GOD CREATED TABLOIDS, that Tuesday after Thanksgiving was surely the kind of day he had in mind. On the morning of November 27, 2007, New York City's two leading practitioners of that irreverent style of newspapering were thirsty for blue blood. Though the *New York Times* maintained judicious restraint, both the *Post* and the *Daily News* bannered the latest twist in the most talked-about high-society scandal in years, the saga of the late Brooke Astor and her only child, Anthony Marshall. She was, of course, the glamorous socialite and philanthropist who had transformed herself, thanks to cranky Vincent Astor's charming fortune, into a beloved philanthropist and influential American icon.

Her son, a clubbable war hero, former ambassador, and award-winning Broadway producer, had been transformed at age eighty-three from the epitome of WASP rectitude to a handcuffed suspect facing an eighteen-count indictment. Tony Marshall's fall from grace was abetted by his mother, his son, his attorney (who was charged in the same indictment), and the tabloids (which were just doing their thing). Charged with grand larceny, falsifying business records, conspiracy, and possession of stolen property, Marshall was looking at the specter of a quarter-century behind bars. "BAD BOY," scolded the *News*. "CROOK ASTOR," snarled the *Post*.

The headlines referred to his alleged scheme to swindle his mother's millions from her favored cultural institutions (including the Metropolitan Museum of Art and the New York Public Library) into his own accounts. But the case was always as much about family as it was about money. It began sixteen months earlier with the seismic jolt from charges by Tony Marshall's son Philip, a college professor, who alleged that his 104-year-old grandmother had descended from Park Avenue splendor to gentrified squalor (despite eight squabbling servants). Taken up with lynch-mob ferocity by the tabloids were such allegations as Tony's seemingly selfish refusal to allow his mother to visit her country estate, his inexplicable sale of her favorite painting, and the claim that Mrs. Astor (yes, Mrs. Astor) was spending her declining days lying on a dog-urine-stained couch.

So began this upper-crust reality soap opera. Here in a nouveau riche age was America's true aristocracy, the arbiters of society, the twenty-first century's link to the New York of Edith Wharton and Henry James. But in this world of emeralds and Astors, things were not always what they seemed. Resentments seethed just below the surface, and ambition was cloaked in polished manners. The hired help, from the butler to the social secretary to Mrs. Astor's nurses, would be drawn into the fray, testing their loyalty and discretion.

Past and present intertwined during the final reels of the Brooke Astor story, harking back to her failures as a mother and to the girl she had been, a teenage bride married off to a dashing millionaire whose acts of violence would haunt her for more than eighty years. This family drama involved a son whose mother, father, and succession of stepfathers left him with no sense of how a loving parent might behave. And then there was the money, nearly $200 million, a ruthless American fortune built on the lust for fur pelts and Manhattan real estate.

At 7:58 A.M., Tony Marshall arrived at the Manhattan district attorney's office at One Hogan Place to turn himself in. White-haired and courtly, he wore a dark, well-tailored suit with his Marine Corps tie and clasp, clinging defiantly to these symbols of accomplishment and propriety. In the grim squad room on the ninth floor, Marshall was given paperwork to fill out — the business of being arrested. With its fluorescent lights, beat-up furniture, stacked water-cooler bottles, and jail cell with rusted metal bars, this setting must have seemed a harsh rebuke to a man accustomed to antiques, fine art, and regularly freshened floral arrangements.

In the upper reaches of society, it is not enough to acquire wealth; it must be protected from interlopers, some of whom are family members. As a young man in his twenties, Tony Marshall made his first court appearance, nearby in another Foley Square building, when his biological father unsuccessfully sued him in an effort to wrest away Tony's trust fund. Brooke Astor had been taken to court over money as well, battling to protect her full share of Vincent Astor's millions and fend off claims from one of her husband's aggrieved family members.

But these squabbles had been mere civil matters, quarrels among family members without the involvement of the authorities. Tony Marshall was handcuffed when detectives escorted him downstairs for his mug shot and fingerprinting. The latter proved surprisingly complicated. Modern fingerprinting machines are not calibrated for aging digits, which leave indistinct markings. Several attempts were made before the detectives finally resorted to the ink method. Back in the squad room, Marshall was offered a nutrition bar, orange juice, and a banana, but declined. A member of the Knickerbocker Club, the New York Racquet Club, and the Brook Club, on a normal day he would have been lunching among the city's elite.

By the time he was paraded in full perp-walk fashion across the street to the courthouse at 111 Centre Street, his face was ashen and his hair disheveled. Here was another photo opportunity in the unrehearsed spectacle of New York, seized on by the mobs of cameramen and journalists who had been staking out the building for six hours, eager to capture Tony Marshall's downfall in time for the news at five. A news vendor hawking a stack of newspapers yelled out, "The rich stealing from the rich, find out what happened." Spying the defendant, the vendor cried out, "Mr. Marshall, why did you do it? Do you have anything to say?"

Walking slowly into the courtroom, Tony appeared to have aged dramatically in just a few hours, the portrait of Dorian Gray. His alarmed wife, Charlene, hurried up the aisle and wrapped her arms around him, covering his face with kisses. As she ran her hands through his mussed hair, Tony wiped tears from his eyes. Grasping his arm in support, Charlene walked down the aisle by his side, repeating, "We'll be okay, we'll be okay." Moments later he joined his lawyers at the wooden table and faced Justice A. Kirke Bartley, Jr., a former prosecutor known for trying mob boss John Gotti.

Rising to her feet as the hearing began, the prosecutor Elizabeth Loewy solemnly told the judge, "Despite his mother's generosity when she was well, he used his position of trust to steal from her." Handed a copy of the indictment accusing him of fraud, conspiracy, and theft, Tony Marshall read through it slowly, as if having trouble comprehending the words. When asked to respond to the charges, he whispered, "Not guilty."

Three months earlier, at the age of 105, Brooke Astor had passed away at her Westchester country home, Holly Hill. For nearly a century she had presented herself to the world as a woman with a good-natured and witty persona, keeping her secrets and sorrows at bay. But as her life began to draw to a close, her dreams grew more vivid and disturbing; imaginary intruders pursued her. In her last year, she was dangerously fragile and afflicted with a *Merck Manual* of ailments. A voracious reader and the author of four books, she had lost the ability to speak in full sentences but could still communicate using gestures or facial expressions. Each morning the nurses would hold up a choice of outfits (mostly from Eileen Fisher) and Mrs. Astor would point to indicate her preference. "She could make her will known," says her social worker, Lois Orlin. "If she didn't want something or she liked something, you could tell." Even near the end, keeping up appearances still mattered, as she clung to her sense of dignity.

As Brooke drifted through the days, gazing idly out the picture windows at the trees and gardens of her estate, her staff devised ways to remind her of the glory of her life and past good times. A favorite tactic was propping up on a lectern the photo album with pictures from Brooke's one hundredth birthday party. "She really loved them," recalls her physical therapist, Sandra Foschi. "She looked in closely." The staff paged quickly past the photographs of Tony and Charlene, fearful that Mrs. Astor might find the sight upsetting. Sometimes Brooke would smile in recognition of the faces of her friends. Other times, overcome with memories, she would weep. "It was very emotional for her," says Foschi. "She would tear up, she would hang her head down. It brought great joy but also great sadness."

Perhaps her reaction reflected change and loss. But maybe in some corner of her mind she sensed the troubles that were tearing apart the family that she had come to care about too late.

1

The Astor 100

THE SMALL WHITE NOTECARD was a whisper of understatement, its simplicity suggesting how unlikely it was that anyone would forget this particular invitation: "Mr. David Rockefeller expects you on Saturday, March 30th for Dinner at 7 P.M. The Playhouse. Black Tie." The *New York Times* later took the unusual step of printing both a partial list of invitees to this evening at Kykuit, the sprawling Rockefeller estate in Pocantico Hills, New York, and the names of those who had sent their regrets. Those unfortunates who had not made the cut were faced not only with the original humiliation but a second reminder in a very public place.

The luster of the evening stemmed from the honored guest and the occasion. Brooke Astor was celebrating her one hundredth birthday on March 30, 2002. Thanks to Vincent Astor's largesse, she had made herself indispensable in New York's five boroughs, using his foundation's millions to help revive the New York Public Library, create a serene Chinese courtyard at the Metropolitan Museum, underwrite an expansion at the Bronx Zoo, preserve historic Harlem houses, and endow innumerable worthy causes.

She had married well, but her real accomplishment had been taking a storied but fading American name and adding luster to it, rebranding the Astor image with a newfound glamour and respect. "She took on the Astor Foundation and made it something to be proud of," says Viscount William Astor, the head of the British branch of the family and her nephew by marriage. "She did a lot for my family's name and reputation in America."

The daughter of a Marine Corps general and a status-obsessed southern belle, Roberta Brooke Russell was bred to ascend to the highest ranks of society. Her ambitious mother, Mabel, tutored her in the art of flirtation, pulled her out of Washington's Madeira School for fear that she was becoming too intellectual, and married her off at the age of seventeen to the heir of a New Jersey fortune, John Dryden Kuser. "Mrs. Russell was a very material-minded woman," says Louis Auchincloss, the novelist, who knew both mother and daughter. "She spent her life in the Marine Corps without any money at all. She wanted to set Brooke up, certainly persuaded her to do it."

That early marriage produced, in 1924, Brooke's only child, Tony. But Dryden Kuser turned out to be an alcoholic with a dangerous temper and a penchant for adultery. He left his young family for another woman, and Brooke headed to Reno in 1930 to obtain a divorce. Her second marriage, to Charles "Buddie" Marshall, a socially connected stockbroker with middling financial means, was more successful. The former first lady Nancy Reagan recalls, "Buddie was the love of her life." But at age fifty, Brooke was suddenly widowed and went on to beat her Social Register contemporaries at their own game.

A mere six months after Buddie Marshall's funeral, in November 1952, Brooke received a marriage proposal from Vincent Astor. Whether she chased him or he set out to win her remains a matter of dispute, although Brooke admitted later that her primary motivation for her marriage in 1953 was financial security. "She always said Vincent was difficult. I don't think she ever loved him," says Barbara Walters, a close friend, recalling Brooke's account of the marriage. "But she did respect him and did her best to make him happy."

When the moody and possessive Astor died at age sixty-seven, a mere five and a half years later, Brooke Astor was left with a famous surname, an intense desire for liberation from a claustrophobic existence, and a trust fund of more than $60 million. Luxury was hers for life. Her forty-two-person staff included a social secretary to manage her schedule, a French maid to choose her wardrobe, a chauffeur kept busy day and night, a French chef to create delicacies for her dinner parties, a butler, and seven gardeners, all to attend to her needs on Park Avenue and at her country homes in Northeast Harbor, Maine, and Briarcliff Manor, New York.

After a lifetime of being an accessory to men, she hungered for meaningful work and the chance to be valued on her own merits. With the well-endowed Astor Foundation, she shrewdly turned herself into a celebrated philanthropist and a sought-after social arbiter. The ability to dispense millions made her popular and powerful, and Mrs. Astor reveled in her long-running starring role, savoring the accolades.

"She always wanted to be in the limelight," says Philippe de Montebello, the director of the Metropolitan Museum, who fondly recalls Mrs. Astor's regal need to be paid her due. "At a cocktail party, if you were paying too little attention to her, she noticed and she let you know. She would regularly arrive one minute late at all our board meetings to make sure that everyone noticed the grand entrance." Brooke Astor was a narcissist, but a beguiling one, admired and admiring, good-hearted in her deeds and her public persona. "She was terrified of boredom," de Montebello adds. "So she arranged not to be bored."

Mrs. Astor — an instantly recognizable lady in white gloves, an ornate hat, pearls, and a diamond pin — became a symbol of aristocratic beneficence over the course of four decades. No stranger to Harlem and Bedford-Stuyvesant before gentrification, she supported programs for summer education for Puerto Rican teenagers, gave money to Catholic Charities to maintain a residence for the elderly, and paid for equipment for the Knickerbocker Drum and Bugle Corps. Instead of just writing checks, she went out to see how her money was being spent and to meet the recipients. Her involvement in a cause was the equivalent of the Good Housekeeping Seal of Approval. "It always really helped to say the Astor Foundation is one of your backers," recalls Peg Breen, the president of the Landmarks Conservancy. "The reaction was, 'If Brooke Astor thinks this is a good idea . . .'" Howard Phipps, the veteran president of the Wildlife Conservancy, adds, "Once Brooke began giving major grants to the zoo, others followed. We named an elephant after her, and when baby Astor died, she was very upset."

At night Mrs. Astor turned her home into an elite salon where big ideas were discussed and connections were made. Bending the rules with her guest lists, she mixed the school chancellor with a curator, society ladies with an up-and-coming movie producer, an acclaimed writer with a Wall Street upstart or a venerated politician. Vernon Jordan, the civil rights leader and Clinton confidant, recalls meeting her in the early 1970s; soon he was a regular at her table in an era when Park Avenue dinners were not integrated. Mrs. Astor did not require a Mayflower genealogy or an eight-figure bank balance. The ticket to admission was being accomplished, interesting, and fun. "The worst thing she could say about someone was, 'He was a dud,'" recalls Linda Gilles, the executive director of the Astor Foundation, who often got the morning-after report from Mrs. Astor about her dinners. "The best thing was, 'He's got plenty to say.'" Mrs. Astor expected amusement and witty banter with cocktails. Her dutiful son was a quiet fixture at her larger parties. Brooke would sometimes complain that he was "boring," although he was widely perceived as conducting himself with aplomb. As Nancy Kissinger recalls, "Tony was always very nice and polite to me, a good conversationalist."

Mrs. Astor boasted about dropping two or three dull friends every year. She was very loyal to her inner circle, but she did have a habit of moving on, replacing dour faces with young and frisky newcomers. "She didn't like the same people to take her around," recalls Vartan Gregorian, the president of the New York Public Library. "Brooke told me the rule of longevity is 'Don't speak to the same people all the time, otherwise I finish your sentences, you finish mine.'" This attitude created anxiety whenever major events like the hundredth birthday party came around. Freddy Melhado, a money manager who was thirty years her junior and her dance partner for decades, notes, "She was determined to have younger friends because she thought it was life-giving."

In the kingdom of Astor, there was a flurry of pre-one-hundredth-birthday-party activity in the sixteenth-floor aerie at 778 Park Avenue where Mrs. Astor had entertained royalty, a president named Reagan, first ladies from Jacqueline Onassis to Lady Bird Johnson to Nancy Reagan, and a succession of mayors and governors. The fourteen-room apartment had been decorated by Sister Parish with Albert Hadley and updated by Mark Hampton. Visitors often admired the pearl-inlaid black wooden Chinese cabinet in the imposing entrance hall. Off to the right was Mrs. Astor's famous red-lacquered library, which housed Vincent Astor's collection of leather-bound first editions and showcased his widow's favorite and most valuable painting, Childe Hassam's *Flags, Fifth Avenue*, which hung over the eighteenth-century French marble fireplace.

The sumptuous central living room, with Louis XVI furniture, overlooked Park Avenue; to the left, the green dining room was decorated with eighteenth-century French scenic panels and billowing curtains designed by Hadley "to look like ballgowns." An eclectic collector, Mrs. Astor scattered valuable jade figurines, dog paintings, and bronze and vermeil animal sculptures around her rooms, along with an inexpensive but eye-pleasing array of teapots. She had recently added a new off-white ceramic version from Swifty's; a mere admiring glance had had the restaurant's owner, Robert Caravaggi, reaching for a gift bag. "She was talking so nicely that I gave her four, for her residences," he recalls. "She seemed so happy." People delighted in giving her presents, for the reward of her radiant smile.

Of course Mrs. Astor needed a new dress for her party, and of course Oscar de la Renta, the designer husband of her best friend, Annette de la Renta, had offered to create a couture gown. "Brooke loved dressing up," recalls Annette. "What else could you get her?"

Brooke and Annette, Annette and Brooke — the two were inseparable, despite a thirty-seven-year age difference. They spoke on the phone every day. They served on the same boards (the Metropolitan Museum, Rockefeller University, the Morgan Library, the New York Public Library) and presided over countless charity galas. The society queen and her protégé were so in sync that observers often remarked that they seemed like mother and daughter. Tom Brokaw says, "It was kind of genetic between them, as if they had the same DNA."

Brooke had initially been close to Annette's mother, Jane Engelhard, a formidable woman known for her beauty and her awesome wealth, which she had gained through her second marriage, to the metals titan Charles Engelhard. An art collector and a Democratic Party power broker, Charlie Engelhard owned a string of racehorses and was said to be the model for the James Bond villain Goldfinger. (*Forbes* estimated Jane Engelhard's fortune, including trust funds for her five daughters, at more than $365 million in 1986.)

Annette was the only child from her mother's brief first marriage. Adopted by her stepfather, she had transformed herself from a self-described "huge" adolescent into a slender, much-photographed epitome of style, perfectly dressed and groomed. She met Brooke through her parents when she was a teenager, recalling, "I inherited her." When Annette, at age twenty, married her first husband, Samuel Reed, in 1960, Brooke attended the wedding and began inviting the newlyweds to her dinner parties. As Annette says, "She was incredibly nice to me as a young married woman in New York, when she didn't need to be." Under Brooke's affectionate tutelage, the once-shy Annette became a power player in board rooms, admired and even a bit feared. "Brooke looked upon Annette as the next Brooke Astor," says Philippe de Montebello. "It was a very conscious mentoring process that she was passing the baton on to Annette."

The relationship between the women had gradually altered in the past decade, as the preternaturally energetic Brooke reached her nineties and began showing her age. Annette had become Brooke's defender and protector, attentive and thoughtful, ever eager to please. She always sat next to Brooke at the Metropolitan Museum's board meetings, helping her follow the agenda and even reaching over to turn pages.

As was her custom, Brooke was wintering at a $45,000-per-month rental house by the ocean in Palm Beach when Annette rang to say that Oscar wanted to make her a dress. When Brooke returned to New York, she eagerly met with the tailors, who went to her apartment for several fittings. Even approaching one hundred, she still cared about her looks and worked with a physical trainer to stay fit. "Brooke always felt it was her duty to enchant everybody," says Oscar de la Renta, who adds that for her special day, she was determined to attract admiring eyes. "In her flirtatious way," he goes on, "she used to always tell me that she could wear a deeper neckline than other ladies of her age." De la Renta's elegant gown was nonetheless age-appropriate, with a neckline high enough for the convent. Brooke was absolutely thrilled by the elaborate concoction, with ruffled long sleeves and a bow at her waist. Even the color had a pedigree; it was called Natier blue and was associated with the eighteenth-century painter Jean-Marc Natier.

Birthdays could be a dilemma, for Brooke Astor loathed acknowledging her age but did love a good party. Vartan Gregorian had orchestrated one celebration for her and instructed the guests not to mention her age. But his warning did not deter Henry Kissinger, who got up and gave a toast, saying, "For an eighty-year-old woman, you look great." Gregorian recalls the upset look on Mrs. Astor's face, saying, "She didn't like that. Because in many ways she was ageless."

Ten years later, on her ninetieth, she had allowed the Citizens Committee for New York City, which she had helped launch with an early donation of $50,000, to hold a fundraiser in her honor. The vast Seventh Regiment Armory was transformed into a rose-covered gazebo and confetti was shot out of a cannon, raining down on the more than 1,500 revelers, including Jacqueline Onassis and Mayor David Dinkins. The entertainment included three musical groups: the Peter Duchin Orchestra, the Marine Corps Band (in honor of her father, the general), and the Illinois Jacquet Big Band. "She had a ball that night," says Oz Elliott, the former *Newsweek* editor, who was then president of the Citizens Committee. Mrs. Astor loved to foxtrot, and even at ninety she danced nearly all night.

Yet she also let her mask slip that evening, revealing her vulnerability in a five-minute videotaped interview that was broadcast at the event. Speaking about a recent dream, Mrs. Astor described a nighttime vision in which her long-dead grandmother, so gaunt as to be initially unrecognizable, materialized on the street. "I ran back and threw my arms around her," Brooke recalled. "She pushed me off. I said, 'Granny, I didn't recognize you, you were so thin.' She said, 'Do you know why? Because the dead live off the thoughts of the living. And nobody is thinking of me.'" It was an odd story to evoke at this celebration of her life, but at ninety, Brooke was worrying about her legacy and wondering how or if she would be remembered.

The *New York Times* treated Brooke Astor's birthdays with the civic reverence granted to holidays on which alternate-side-of-the-street parking is suspended. Every year the event was commemorated with a story or a photograph. "I don't feel old. I can walk as fast as anybody. I got a new driving license this year," Brooke told the *Times* at age ninety. "I don't hear as well as I used to, have to wear a hearing aid, which I hate." She went on to add, "But I can't sit there with an open mouth when people are telling me some dreadfully wonderful story."

Peter Duchin played at so many parties that Mrs. Astor either gave or attended over four decades that the events had all become a blur. As a teenager, Duchin had known Vincent Astor and his second wife, Minnie Cushing, and recalls a raucous New Year's party at their country home where guests jumped into the pool. Valets stood by to press their sopping clothes. Duchin still remembers the ancient gossip about how Brooke became the third Mrs. Astor. "Vincent was a very difficult, overly possessive man," he says. "Minnie was great, she just got fed up with him. She and Babe Paley and Slim Keith got together and decided that Brooke Marshall would be the perfect bride for Vincent — that's the story I always heard."

Even in gala-fatigued New York, Brooke's ninetieth birthday party was a roaring social success, and it netted $892,741 besides. The Citizens Committee was eager to replicate the evening and celebrate one hundred years of Mrs. Astor's benevolent rule. "I went to Brooke, and she semi-agreed," recalls Elliott. The gossip columnist Liz Smith even ran a save-the-date item in her column on June 12, 2001, promising that a Broadway theater had been booked and Shakespearean actors would perform in honor of Mrs. Astor's centennial. "Then it got more iffy and Brooke backed out," says Elliott. She sent a note to her friend George Trescher, the public relations mastermind who had burnished her reputation and served as her social gatekeeper. Although Trescher died in June 2003 of emphysema, his second-in-command, Vincent Stefan, can still recite parts of Mrs. Astor's candid note from memory: "I'm old and I'm tired. I would like this birthday to be fun for me, instead of being on display for some organization."

Plans for a private celebration were already under way. On New Year's Eve 1999, Brooke had been a guest at a party given by David Rockefeller at the Playhouse at Kykuit, when her host turned to her and asked whether she would let him give her a dinner-dance right there. Of course she accepted. Brooke Astor had been friends with the Rockefeller family since her marriage to Vincent Astor. David Rockefeller, the youngest member of the family and her junior by thirteen years, recalls, "I think the first time I met her was in 1958, on a boat off Providence, Rhode Island. My uncle Winthrop Aldrich, who was the former ambassador to the Court of St. James's, took us out for a day sail on his boat, the *Wayfarer*."

Brooke became extended family to David Rockefeller and his brother Nelson. But her true confidant in the family was another brother, Laurance, the conservationist and philanthropist. They were so enamored of each other in public that rumors circulated for decades that Brooke and the long-married Laurance were having an affair. Whether amour or friendship, the feelings were powerful and long-lasting. In the closing hours of her ninety-fifth birthday party at the Carlyle Hotel, a girlish Brooke turned to her date, a prominent younger businessman, and said, "I hope you don't mind, but Laurance has asked to see me home."

Five years later, in 2002, Laurance was ninety-two, a widower, and in frail health, so it fell to the youngest Rockefeller brother, David, then eighty-six and also a recent widower, to host Mrs. Astor's festivities. The retired Chase Manhattan chairman and Brooke had much in common, from philanthropy to overlapping social circles to homes near each other on the Upper East Side, in Westchester County, and in Maine. "Laurance was in many ways the one of us that she saw the most of," says David Rockefeller. "I got to know her really well in the last twenty years, and saw a great deal of her." He took her out for horse-and-carriage rides in Westchester and Maine. When climbing into his carriage became difficult for her because of her advancing age, he bought her a two-step lift. "That made it easier for her," he says, "especially an elderly lady with a tight skirt."

Several months before her birthday, Rockefeller went to Brooke's apartment to discuss the arrangements for the party. The two old friends sat in her corner library, sipping tea in front of the fireplace, contemplating the momentous occasion. The seemingly insurmountable challenge would be to keep the guest list small enough for everyone to fit in the room where the dinner would be served yet allow plenty of space for dancing. Caroline Schermerhorn Astor, Vincent Astor's status-conscious grandmother, had been renowned in the 1890s for entertaining "the Astor 400," the precise number that fit in the ballroom of her grand Fifth Avenue mansion. But Brooke Astor's fete had to be smaller and thus even more exclusive. Since Brooke was turning one hundred, Rockefeller suggested having one hundred guests. Asked whom she would like to invite, she replied, "Ninety-nine men would be nice."

She loved to flirt, to be provocative and even naughty, and it did not matter whether the men were straight, gay, married, or many decades younger. "There were rotating men in her life, which made it work," says the movie producer John Hart, who was fifty years her junior. He had joked with her one evening: "'The reason I have you at Café Daniel is I'm going to propose to you.' She looked at me and said, 'Why? Do you need money?'"

In the end, there were surprising omissions from the guest list. When the historian Barbara Goldsmith called Mrs. Astor's home to RSVP, she got an earful from the social secretary, who confided, "You can't believe what's going on. All these people are calling and saying, 'Of course I'm included on the list, and I have to say, 'I don't know.'" As Goldsmith puts it, "People were lobbying to get in."

For twenty-three years, Linda Gillies had accompanied Brooke Astor to libraries in the South Bronx and renovated historic row houses in Harlem. As a child, Gillies had been visiting her grandparents in Paris when the famous Mrs. Astor showed up at a Sunday lunch wearing bracelets encrusted with diamonds, sapphires, and rubies. They had met again in New York when Gillies was working at the Metropolitan Museum, and Brooke had hired this granddaughter of friends to run the Astor Foundation, where she served from 1974 until Brooke decided to give away its assets and dissolve the foundation, in 1997. Brooke had often praised Gillies, telling an interviewer that her deputy had transformed the place: "When I got Linda to come here, we had a marvelous time." But Gillies was not on the guest list. Several friends attempted to intervene on Gillies's behalf to wangle an invitation. John Dobkin, then the head of Historic Hudson Valley, says, "Brooke was human and she was jealous. Linda was her sidekick and confidante for all those years. Linda was fifty-five, Brooke was one hundred — I think she was jealous and peeved. It was a huge mistake." But once the foundation closed its doors, the axis of their relationship shifted. "Once something was over, it was over for her," Gillies says. "There were several friends of the heart who died while I knew her, and once that happened, you never heard about that person again. I think for her I represented something that was over."

The developer Marshall Rose, who had been a guest at Brooke's ninety-fifth birthday celebration at the Carlyle Hotel, had been banished too. He and Brooke had bonded as fellow board members of the New York Public Library. Rose and his wife, Jill, were guests at Brooke's home in Maine, and after Jill died, Brooke tried to cheer him up by including him at dinners in her home and asking him to escort her to her nightly round of parties. Their friendship ended when Marshall began dating the actress Candice Bergen, whom he married in 2000. Eager for Brooke to meet his new love, he arranged for them to have tea at the Astor apartment. "We walked in, and the conversation was decidedly cold. Ice cold," remembers Rose. The couple made their excuses after a tense forty-five minutes. Brooke called him the next morning at 9 A.M., uncharacteristically early for her, to inquire, "Are you going to marry that woman?" Rose thought the phone call revealed a touching display of jealousy. "I laughed, because isn't it wonderful that that could enter her mind as an issue?"

Tom and Meredith Brokaw had been seated at the head table at the ninetieth birthday celebration but were among those passed over a decade later. "Brooke was a big flirt," says Nancy Reagan, whose mother introduced her to Mrs. Astor more than a half-century ago. "I remember when she had this huge crush on Tom Brokaw. She was so cute in her flirtations." Did she have a crush on President Reagan? "Not that I know of," the former first lady replied, laughing. Brokaw was succeeded by his professional competitor, the ABC News anchor Peter Jennings. "She had an infatuation at the time for Peter as well," recalls Brokaw, who says that Mrs. Astor tried to create a rivalry between them. "Peter and I talked about it. Brooke would say to me, 'Peter works in this homeless shelter.' I'd say, 'I know he does, Brooke.'" But Brokaw relished her company, saying, "She had this great spirited cackle." (Peter Jennings was among the guests who had every reason to believe they would outlive their hostess. Jennings died of lung cancer in August 2005 at the age of sixty-seven; nine other partygoers, all younger than the honoree, would pass away in the next five years while Brooke, remarkably, lived on.)

At an age when few people are healthy or even ambulatory, Brooke Astor was still in the thick of high society and had just hired a new social secretary, Naomi Dunn Packard-Koot, a blond and lithe Princeton graduate then in her early thirties. She was charged with sorting through the dozens of invitations that continued to arrive each month and to organize Mrs. Astor's appointments. "She could have kept every single minute occupied," marveled Packard-Koot. "She was still doing a lot." But the nonagenarian's memory was fading, and her friends were graciously trying to find ways to help her out.

"We had a little game," says Gregory Long, the president of the Brooklyn Botanic Garden, who had known Brooke Astor for thirty years, dating back to his first job at the Metropolitan Museum. "She'd say, 'I went to see these people last night — you wouldn't believe what happened.' I'd say, 'What people?' She'd say, 'Oh, you know,' and I'd say, 'No, you have to tell me.' So she'd say, 'Jewelry designer.' I'd come up with a list of designers whom she might know, and she'd tell me when I hit the right one." Several days before Brooke's hundredth birthday, she and Long had lunch at her favorite spot, the Knickerbocker Club, an exclusive private men's club founded in 1871, where she retained widow's rights after Vincent Astor died. "She was very excited about the party, thrilled that David was doing it," says Long, but he worried about whether she was up to the event. "She didn't say she was nervous, but I wondered. Things seemed hard for her."

Mrs. Astor had a lifelong ability to rise to the occasion, however, and appeared in perfect command that week in an interview conducted over afternoon tea at her apartment with Alex Kuczynski of the *New York Times*. Although she came from a genteel generation that shied away from seeing their names in the newspapers, she was a master of public relations and used the press to publicize her causes, consistently providing great copy for generations of journalists. She recalled playing tennis with Ezra Pound (he was "terrible to the ball boys" she told *USA Today*), viewing Mussolini at a reception held at a grand Italian palazzo on the eve of World War II, and even meeting Henry Adams. Once again she did not disappoint, giving a performance that seemed to promise many more years of perfect bons mots. She slyly pointed out a statue of a young nude and claimed that it was her younger self. "Darn, I can't lie about my age any longer," she joked about her birthday.

Mrs. Astor ended the interview with a favorite conversational gambit, bringing up the topic of plastic surgery. "I have never had any work done," she said, and then asked, with the perfect timing of a honed punch line, "Tell me honestly. Could I use some?" Even at one hundred, she delivered the goods. In truth, she had made a similar remark a few years earlier to Marian Heiskell, a member of the Sulzberger family, who had reacted with a skeptical smile. Brooke had then admitted, "Well, maybe just a little around the eyes."

Kuczynski walked away impressed at Brooke Astor's stamina and well-maintained lifestyle. "She was pretty much all there — she was compos mentis. The apartment had a sweet smell, the smell you find in well-run homes. It has something to do with fine cotton and high-grade linen." (A few years earlier, a journalist from the *Toronto Globe and Mail* had described the odor as "that fine smell of beeswax and money.") But contemplating the aroma of old money can get a reporter only so far. Kuczynski needed another voice for her story, so she turned to Brooke Astor's son, Tony Marshall, for the expected filial quote.

2

A Little Night Music

⚜

TONY MARSHALL had a secret, and it was a secret that appeared to be nagging at him in the weeks prior to his mother's one hundredth birthday. Brooke Astor had begun behaving erratically in recent years, from getting lost on her property in Westchester to lashing out with displays of temper and frustration that were out of character. Her staff members had quietly confided their concerns about her behavior to Tony and repeatedly asked for his guidance. A little more than a year earlier, he had arranged for his mother to see a neurologist in December 2000. She was so furious at her son's effort to intrude and fearful of what might be learned that she delayed getting dressed on the day of the appointment, in order to be deliberately late. Tony accompanied her to the physician's office and subsequently received the dreaded diagnosis: Alzheimer's disease.

Protective of his mother and her image, he did not want her friends or the public to know that her occasional slips masked a serious condition. But he and his third wife, Charlene, could not carry this burden alone. Tony informed his twin sons, Alec, a freelance photographer who lived just a mile from Brooke's country house, and Philip, a professor of historic preservation at Roger Williams University in Rhode Island. While the brothers had seen their grandmother only intermittently as children, now, in their forties, they had developed a genuinely warm relationship and a determination to bask in the time they had left with her.

"It was obvious that she was having problems," says Alec Marshall. "There were gray areas. I'd have tea with her; she'd repeat herself and get confused." Nonetheless, Philip Marshall remembers that his father was adamant about keeping the news confidential. Philip got the word during a weekend family visit to Holly Hill. "My father took me into the library and said, 'I have something important to talk about. Your grandmother has Alzheimer's. This is hush-hush, a big secret.' I thought to myself, what else is new?"

In the early stages of the disease, people can often carry on, albeit with moments of disorientation. Brooke was still able to finesse most situations with her well-practiced charm and a century's worth of favorite anecdotes. She had handled herself quite well with the *Times*. But interviews offered the potential for danger. When *Newsday* called Tony to comment for a story on his mother's hundredth birthday, his careful facade cracked slightly, as if he could not help referring to the truth, even if obliquely. "Her health is pretty good, but with age comes the aging process," he told the newspaper. "She does have a little problem with her memory. She knows she's having the problem and it irritates the hell out of her when she can't remember someone's name." Tony acknowledged that his mother was unsteady, noting that she had recently lost her balance, fallen, and cut her leg, so she now needed a cane.

Brooke had always been extremely independent and was used to ruling her fiefdom of servants. She resented any interference from her son. But as Mrs. Astor's only child, Tony felt obligated to become more involved in supervising her household. At least it was convenient. He lived only a few blocks from his mother, in a second-floor duplex at Seventy-ninth and Lexington Avenue which was modest compared to his mother's apartment. Decorated with chintz-covered furniture, a spinet piano, an antique globe, and objects such as a carved giraffe and elephant, his apartment was a testament to his well-traveled life. Brooke Astor bought her son this co-op after he married his third wife, Charlene, and in 1999, his mother gave him $3.9 million to allow him to buy the apartment from her, a sum that also covered the gift tax. Tony had lived off his mother's financial generosity virtually all his life.

His last name often confused people, since he was the product of his mother's first marriage, to Dryden Kuser, but took the last name of her second husband, Buddie Marshall.

Tony had been managing his mother's money as a full-time job since 1980, after an action-filled early career. Enlisting in the Marines during World War II, he led his unit in the assault on Iwo Jima and was wounded in the leg and arms by shrapnel and was awarded a Purple Heart. He joined the CIA during the height of the cold war, spent a few years on Wall Street, and then, apparently thanks in large part to generous family donations to Richard Nixon, landed ambassadorships to Madagascar, Trinidad and Tobago, and Kenya during the Watergate years. Brooke was so committed to helping her son's career that she was willing to be cynical about her politics. She met Nixon shortly after he left office, at the California home of the media tycoon Walter Annenberg. Ashton Hawkins, the counsel for the Metropolitan Museum and her escort that evening, recalls, "Nixon didn't know who Tony was, or who she was. Afterwards, she told me, 'I supported Nixon not because I believed in him but because Tony got appointments.'"

Over the years, from time to time Brooke lamented to friends — and even made indiscreet remarks to her staff — that her son always seemed to need a helping hand. Leaving Maine for a quick trip to Manhattan one summer weekend in the late 1970s, she told her veteran gardener, Steve Hamor, "I've got to go get my son a new job."

Tony was indeed at loose ends after his government career ended with the Democratic takeover of the White House in the 1976 election. His mother's financial portfolio was stagnating, so she offered him a chance to manage it. His record as an investment adviser appears to have been decidedly mixed in the view of financial experts. Tony would later boast that he increased his mother's assets from $19 million to $82 million between 1980 and 2006, which works out to a compound growth rate of 5.9 percent a year. During the same period, the Standard & Poor's 500 grew by 11 percent per year.

This new life, in which his annual compensation for managing his mother's money reached $450,000 by 2004, left Tony with ample time for leisure pursuits. He wrote a guidebook to American zoos and aquariums and in 2001 he self-published a novel, *Dash,* about financial hijinks. Tony also served on numerous boards, including those of the Wildlife Conservancy, the public television station WNET, and the Metropolitan Museum, where he assumed his mother's seat.

Despite his comfortable livelihood, Tony was dependent on his mother's good will. He had hoped to succeed her in running the Astor Foundation, and she dangled that as a possibility but then decided to spend down the assets. She loved her son but often acted as if she did not like him. As hard as he tried to please her and earn her affection, she did not make it easy. It is difficult for any child of a famous parent to establish a separate identity, and in the eyes of New York, he was known by all as Brooke Astor's son.

On the day in 2002 that the *Times* contacted him, Tony may have been tired of talking about Brooke Astor or nervous about letting his secret slip. Reporters never inquired about his own accomplishments, and sometimes his frustration showed. "He was cool in a frigid way, very unlike his mother," says Alex Kuczynski, the *Times* reporter, adding that he appeared annoyed by the mere fact of her call. Failing to elicit useful anecdotes, the reporter asked what Tony planned to say in his toast at his mother's birthday party, and the *Times* printed his solemn reply: "I think I'll talk about how I have loved and admired my mother for more than three-quarters of a century."

The television and radio news reports on the morning of the party, March 30, 2002, highlighted the sad changing of the guard across the Atlantic: the Queen Mother, aged 101, had died. Brooke Astor had been befriended by the royal family and had made a tradition of visiting London at least once a year. When Tony Marshall called to break the news to her, she was sleeping in at Holly Hill, so he asked her longtime butler, Christopher Ely, to pass it along. Ely was extremely reliable about Tony's requests, but this time he decided that he would "forget" the message. On Brooke's day, nothing should ruin her pleasure, or remind her of her own mortality. A former footman at Buckingham Palace, Ely, thirty-nine and single, never hesitated to stand up for himself when necessary. He had declined Brooke's request that he wear a uniform, in preference for a professional dark blazer and slacks. A slender, balding Englishman with an impish sense of humor, he had asked to be referred to as Chris rather than by his last name.

When Mrs. Astor woke up on her birthday, she was in an anticipatory mood. Though the staff advised her to rest, she was too keyed up to take a nap, and besides, company kept arriving. First a beautician made a house call to administer a facial and a manicure. Then Viscount William Astor, a member of the House of Lords, arrived from London. The handsome Astor, then fifty, had often been Brooke's host in England and had known her since he was a child. "I came up at lunchtime," he recalls. "She was very excited — she was looking forward so much to the party." He was shown to the Cardinals' Room, a lemon yellow sanctuary decorated with portraits of cardinals (religious figures, not birds). When Freddy Melhado and his wife, Virginia, arrived, they were given a large chocolate brown bedroom with a red carpet and a water view. When Tony and Charlene arrived, they were directed to a second-tier room at the back of the house. Brooke had made the sleeping arrangements, but Ely carried them out, a job that did not always make him popular.

Philip Marshall and his wife, the artist Nan Starr, who had driven from their home in South Dartmouth, Massachusetts, were housed in a guest cottage. Ferrying the revelers to the party at Kykuit, a fifteen-minute drive, presented a logistical problem. The Marshall brothers and Nan had already arranged to go together, and the Melhados planned to take their own car. Viscount Astor was amused when Brooke asked him to escort her to the party. "Brooke had a mischievous streak," says Astor. "I think she did it to irritate her daughter-in-law, so they'd have to take a separate car. She said, 'Thank God you're here. I don't want to go with them.'"

Brooke had never gushed over either of her son's first two wives — no one would ever be good enough for her boy — but she had particularly taken umbrage over Charlene. "Brooke never liked any of her daughters-in-law," says Vartan Gregorian. "Who she had in mind for Tony, I don't know, but she never became close to any of them." Gregorian felt a certain amount of sympathy for Mrs. Astor's son, saying, "He's a very private, reticent, sometimes humorous, earnest man. It's not easy to be Brooke's son, always in the shadow."

Charlene met the Astor family when she was married to Paul Gilbert, the rector of St. Mary's-by-the-Sea, in Northeast Harbor, Maine. Brooke attended the church, which was just a few blocks from her summer home. The ensuing affair between Charlene and Tony and their decision to leave their spouses for each other had been a village scandal. Brooke complained to friends that she was embarrassed to show her face in church. Even ten years after the couple wed, with Brooke in attendance, the matriarch still opted for the periodic passive-aggressive gesture toward Charlene, as if just for sport.

Her friends had witnessed Brooke's enmity. Shortly before her birthday party, Brooke gave a small dinner at her home, and Annette de la Renta arrived without jewelry. The hostess went into her bedroom and returned with a sparkling gold and diamond necklace and matching earrings, insured at $75,600, for Annette to wear, and later she insisted that Annette take them home as a gift. As Annette left the room in search of a mirror, Brooke turned to Nancy Kissinger and announced, "I don't want Charlene to get it."

Mrs. Astor knew that all eyes would be upon her tonight. How much more advantageous to arrive on the arm of the attractive and aristocratic viscount than on that of her watchful son. Chris Ely drove the pair of Astors over to the party in a forest green Mercedes Benz. David Rockefeller, aware of the butler's devotion, had personally invited him to be one of the hundred guests at tonight's party. But Ely begged off because he did not feel that it was appropriate for him to cross this social boundary.

During the brief ride, Mrs. Astor, eager to make a good impression and fearful of appearing forgetful, worried out loud about the evening. "She was in quite a nervous state," Lord Astor recalls. She instructed him to 'hold my arm, take me in. Every time someone comes up to say hello to me, whisper in my ear who it is, in case I don't recognize them.'"

At dusk the black town cars and limousines crept slowly up the long, twisting drive to Kykuit. The estate, which once belonged to John D.

Rockefeller, who founded Standard Oil, is now operated by the National Historic Trust as a tourist site. The gracious stone palace was built in 1906 on 250 acres of pristine land and has an incomparable view of the Palisades. Perfectly situated on the broad expanses of lawn are enormous sculptures by Picasso, Alexander Calder, and Gaston Lachaise collected by Nelson Rockefeller, and visitors can glimpse the artworks through the trees. On the evening of Mrs. Astor's party, the main house, with its oriental rugs and eclectic art collection (a roomful of Ming ceramics, a Rodin sculpture, and paintings by John Singer Sargent, Gilbert Stuart, and Robert Motherwell), was closed for the evening. But just down the hill, the large Playhouse, built to amuse the Rockefeller children with a bowling alley, squash court, and tennis court, was invitingly lit. The swimming pool had been boarded over for dancing. The tuxedoed waiters were on standby; the musicians were in their places. It was a stage set, ready for action to begin.

And oh, what a famous cast began emerging from the vehicles. There was Kofi Annan, the secretary-general of the United Nations; a trio of TV anchors (Jennings, Walters, Mike Wallace), the former *New York Times* editor Abe Rosenthal; Henry and Nancy Kissinger; Vartan Gregorian and his successor at the New York Public Library, Paul LeClerc; the political widows Happy Rockefeller and Casey Ribicoff; the writers George Plimpton, John Richardson, and Barbara Goldsmith; the jewelry designer Kenneth Jay Lane; and a full cadre of socialites, philanthropists, and officials from various museums (the Metropolitan, the Frick, the Museum of Natural History). The Duke and Duchess of Devonshire had declined, and the Marquis and Marchioness of Salisbury had sent their regrets, but Annette and Oscar de la Renta had flown back from their getaway in the Dominican Republic.

As Lester Lanin's band played Cole Porter and George Gershwin favorites, songs written as Brooke was just starting her ascension to American royalty, the guests mingled and joked and reminisced. Brooke was a wisp of a woman, but she had been a towering influence on the lives of her friends. She had ignited their careers, introduced them to new worlds, made them laugh, given their lives sparkle. There were so many memories: Brooke flirting with every man in the room, marching energetically up mountains, entertaining on a rented yacht in the Caribbean, helping friends in trouble, reading from *The Wild Party* to liven up a dull dinner. She sent plane tickets so intimates could visit her in Maine or Palm Beach, lost her emeralds (repeatedly), wrote poetry that was published in *The New Yorker,* discussed novels in a highbrow book group, and sent elegant thank-you notes, a lifetime of meaningful and memorable gestures.

For Gregorian, entrusted in 1981 with reviving the moldering New York Public Library, she had opened her home, giving dinners to introduce him to her moneyed world, making calls with him to try to wring donations from tough targets such as Donald Trump, whispering amusing asides. For Emily Harding, she was Aunt Brooke, who had swooped in to help when Emily's mother, Alice Astor — Vincent Astor's sister — suddenly died. Brooke and Vincent offered to adopt Emily, who was then fourteen, and when Emily declined, Brooke toured boarding schools with her. Even after Vincent died, Brooke worked with his two ex-wives to give Emily a coming-out party at the St. Regis, the hotel that Vincent had owned. "The three aunties did it together," Harding recalls. "It showed there were no hard feelings among them."

Henry Kissinger remembers Mrs. Astor's spark when they all spent Christmas holidays together at the de la Rentas' luxurious Dominican Republic vacation home. "We always took a walk at the end of the day, on the golf course — Annette, Brooke, myself, Barbara Walters," Kissinger says with a smile. "We had a rule that on walks you could not talk about any subject, only people, and you could not say a good word about anybody. Brooke lived up to it."

Among the guests at the party were several family retainers who had now become old friends: George Trescher; Dr. Rees Pritchett, who oversaw Brooke's physical care; and Henry "Terry" Christensen III, the third generation of Sullivan & Cromwell partners to handle her legal needs and estate planning. Brooke had been loyal to the white-shoe firm since 1959, when a partner had successfully fended off a challenge to Vincent Astor's will on her behalf. Fond of the debonair Christensen, a Harvard Law School graduate who had taken over her legal affairs in 1991, she had put him on the board of her foundation.

At 778 Park Avenue, Christensen was a familiar face. He often went by to discuss his and Brooke's favorite author, Anthony Trollope, the chronicler of Victorian mores. But literature was a side topic. Brooke relished updating her will, rewarding or downgrading friends and family members via gifts of artwork and jewelry and cash, revising bequests to museums and charities. Considering that she had personal assets of $120 million plus a charitable trust worth more than $60 million, the contents of her will would have made for gripping reading. She often dropped hints about her decisions, but only Christensen, her son, and her daughter-in-law were aware of the details. Just two months before her birthday, on January 30, 2002, Brooke had approved the most recent draft.

Christensen had established a relationship with Tony as well, having referred him to a lawyer for Tony's second divorce. When Tony turned seventy-five and gave a party for himself in Turkey, Christensen was among the guests. On that occasion Christensen met Tony's new friend Francis X. Morrissey, Jr., a Boston-born lawyer whose father, a municipal judge, had been one of Joseph Kennedy's cronies. When Morrissey Sr. was nominated to a federal judgeship by Ted Kennedy, the *Boston Globe* won a Pulitzer Prize for exposing his lack of qualifications.

The younger Morrissey, who summered in Maine, had befriended Charlene back when she had been the rector's wife. A fixture in society, he was the frequent escort of wealthy widows. Although he had been suspended from practicing law for two years over a fee dispute with a client, this inconvenient fact was not well known. Christensen felt confident enough about his relationships with both Mrs. Astor and her son that he did not consider Francis Morrissey, Jr., a potential threat. Besides, he knew Morrissey's younger brother, Richard, a partner in Sullivan & Cromwell's London office; it would have been ungentlemanly for Francis to poach a client from his sibling's firm. But Morrissey had begun to ingratiate himself with Mrs. Astor through visits and flowers. Although he had not been invited to the birthday party, he had joined Tony and Charlene in taking Brooke out for a celebratory lunch a few days earlier.

Several of the birthday guests speculated that Mrs. Astor was already starting to deaccession. Her Childe Hassam painting was no longer hanging in its honored place in the library and had been replaced by a portrait of her father. Brooke had loved the color and patriotism and

Manhattan vibrancy of the Hassam, which she had purchased in 1971, and had vowed for years to donate it to the Metropolitan Museum as her legacy. "She lived with that painting," says Florence Irving, a museum trustee. "Whenever she had people over, she had cocktails or coffee in the library so they could see the painting. It was New York City, it was her." But now the artwork was on display in the country home of its new owner, the billionaire George Soros. "I didn't want to sell it," Brooke confided to a friend. "But Tony said I needed the money." This odd comment was taken by her friend as a sign that Brooke must be joining the ranks of elderly widows who worry unnecessarily about their finances.

As observant social insiders scanned the crowd for amusing indiscretions or faux pas, two men strolled around the party aimlessly, looking out of their depth. Philip and Alec Marshall, then forty-nine, had met a few of these important guests before, but they had not grown up in their grandmother's Upper East Side world. "We hardly knew anyone," says Philip. Only nine years old when their parents divorced, they had left Manhattan with their mother, Elizabeth Cryan, after she married the geneticist Craig Wheaton-Smith and moved to the Boston suburbs and then to Vermont. Their father had presented the twins with two stepmothers: Tony was married to his former secretary, Thelma Hoegnell, known as Tee, for more than twenty-five years before he left her for Charlene. For the twins, weekends and summer vacations with Tony often took them into the company of their grandmother, whom they called Gagi. "We did not grow up in my grandmother's world," says Alec. "We were raised by my mother and stepfather." Since their last name was Marshall, most of their classmates and adult friends were unaware that they had a connection to the Astor family.

"Brooke was fond of them and felt sorry that they had gotten short shrift as children," says Ashton Hawkins. "Alec was a bit of a lost soul, very nice, very well-intentioned." John Hart had a similar take, recalling that "Philip was very nice, but seemed out of place. It was not their world. He was happy to be there."

Some pairs of twins are eerily similar in personality and appearance, but the Marshall twins scarcely seemed to come from the same gene pool, or, as their paternal aunt, Suzanne Kuser, puts it, "They could not be more different." They share deep-set, piercing blue eyes and identical rakish smiles, but there the similarities end.

Alec, a good-looking man with a full head of dark brown hair, is a photographer who specializes in lifestyle magazine and architectural assignments. "I am more conservative," he says. Quiet and reserved like his father, Alec is listed in the Social Register but does not have the luxurious life of his contemporaries in that aristocratic breeding book. Twice divorced, with a daughter, Hilary Brooke, Alec supports himself as a freelancer, living in a small apartment on the second floor of an aluminum-sided 1915 Sears, Roebuck kit house in Ossining, New York.

Philip, the firstborn, is taller than his brother by several inches, athletically wiry, and has shaved his balding head. Exuberant and outgoing like his grandmother, he has no interest in claiming his place in the Social Register. Philip had been the family rebel, rejecting his Episcopalian background to become a practicing Buddhist. As a teenager he had visited his father in Trinidad, where Tony was serving as ambassador, wearing his long hair in a ponytail, which provoked the predictable reaction. At Brown University, Philip purchased a one-dollar suit at a thrift shop and wore it for formal occasions, including parties given by his grandmother. By the time of the hundredth birthday party, he had settled into a comfortable life as a tenured professor with a free-wheeling, charismatic style. "Philip's courses aren't very structured, but he knows so much and he really cares," says Kevin Clark, who was his student in 2007. "He e-mails us all on our birthdays." Philip and his wife, Nan Starr, a painter from a wealthy Philadelphia family, have two children, Winslow and Sophie, and her inheritance supplements his academic income.

The Marshall twins were not rich, or even close to it, despite their link to one of America's great fortunes. For all her generosity to philanthropic causes, Brooke was not a financially doting grandmother. Her clothes were couture — she spent $25,000 twice a year, fall and spring, at Chez Ninon, a Manhattan dressmaker — but she did not establish trust funds for her grandsons. She provided a $30,000 down payment to help Philip buy his first house, and she underwrote part of Alec's rent during his first years after college and paid for half a used car. Otherwise she restricted her gifts to her grandsons to $10,000 or so per year, most likely less than the sum of her Christmas bonuses to her staff and doorman. Money was not the currency of her relationship with Alec and Philip. She apparently viewed her son's financial dependence on her as crippling and wanted her grandsons to be self-sufficient. But she was happy to use her contacts to help their careers. When Alec left a staff job as a medical photographer at New York's Mt. Sinai Hospital in 1983, Brooke wrote to the editor of *Architectural Digest* and asked that he be given a chance. As Alec now says, "They have been my steadiest client."

A handful of Brooke's friends had met the twins over the years. "She wasn't a grandmother who wanted to sit around and chuck babies under the chin, but she wanted to know them," says Gregory Long. "She was proud of her grandsons. They were very attractive. Alec is very quiet, shy, sweet, very handsome." In recent years she had become closer to Philip and Alec, welcoming their visits and afterward even joking with friends, saying, "Now you know I don't like children" and then proudly showing off pictures of her three great-grandchildren.

In the whirl of the birthday celebration, Tony and Charlene greeted guests, acting as unofficial hosts to Brooke's friends. Surrounded by women for whom thinness was a religion and a competition, Charlene stood out for her normal-size figure, closer to a size 12 than a 2. With a playful, earthy, and emotional personality, she was her husband's opposite, all heat and impulse to his cool, starched demeanor. The Marshalls had their own social circle but were familiar with the guests from previous occasions. They extended the occasional invitation to Brooke's friends, who felt obliged to accept. "I liked Tony. I went to a couple of dinners he gave," says Barbara Walters. "I can't say I felt sorry for him, but I felt something like that." Fiercely protective of her husband and sensitive to her mother-in-law's all-too-frequent slights, Charlene was eager to play a central role this evening. "Tony and Charlene seemed very keen on having their pictures taken with Brooke," says one guest, putting his own amused spin on it all. "You could see them hovering."

Brooke radiated happiness, although her friends kept a watchful eye, given her emotional and physical frailty. "She wasn't totally there, but she was there enough," says Henry Kissinger. "David Rockefeller did an extraordinary job of very delicately taking her around." Brooke perched regally on a sofa in her gown, accepting compliments. "Oscar did this phenomenal dress for her, this exquisite blue taffeta, all these ruffles, a work of art. She knew how fabulous it was. She took great pleasure in being attractive," recalls Paul LeClerc. "She put herself forth as an object of pleasure for other people, by virtue of being Mrs. Astor and never abandoning the glamor of that." At dinner she was seated at a table which included Laurance and David Rockefeller, Kofi Annan and his wife, Nan, Viscount Astor, Walters, and the de la Rentas. Tony and Charlene were seated at another table that was near and yet so far — the equivalent of being in Siberia in a Brooke-centric universe.

The waiters served an appetizer of trout mousse with sautéed spinach and a caviar beurre blanc sauce, followed by poussin, asparagus with hazelnuts, and pureed potatoes and pears. Tony stepped up to the microphone and announced that Charlene would be presenting his mother with an arrangement of flowers that had been sent by Prince Charles. If the crowd had been surveyed at the moment, the collective sentiment would have been taken straight from Bette Davis: "Fasten your seatbelts. It's going to be a bumpy night." Robert Pirie, the former chairman of Rothschild Inc., recalls, "Everybody knew that Brooke did not like Charlene, and Tony did it to try to establish the impression of a relationship." All eyes went to the centenarian, who looked dismayed. As Walters says, "Charlene brought over the flowers to Brooke, who made a terrible face. The pleasure of the flowers coming from Prince Charles was taken away by the fact it was Charlene delivering them."

A wave of discomfort drifted through the room at this obvious rebuff, as guests registered the hurt look on Charlene's face. "Brooke had some kind of altercation with Charlene," says Liz Smith. "She thought Charlene was horning in on her big moment. I was just horrified." Smith's sympathies were with Charlene, who was humiliated in front of her mother-in-law's famous friends. Brooke had always had a reputation as a gracious hostess; she might raise a quizzical eyebrow, but she never revealed exasperation. As Pirie puts it, "This time, her feelings got shown in public."

The moment passed, the champagne flowed, and everyone oohed and ahhed over the desserts, extravaganzas of vanilla cake with plum filling, each one topped with a fantastical marzipan hat, in honor of Brooke's signature accessory. "The cakes were gorgeous," recalls Alec.

Chris Ely slipped into the back of the room to listen to the speeches. Summoning her energy and wits, Brooke rose to her feet to speak. She echoed her mother's advice never to get above herself and repeated the line "I guess I can't lie about my age anymore." She sweetly reached out to urge the two Rockefeller brothers to stand up with her, as she wanted to acknowledge their importance in her life. David Rockefeller read aloud a letter sent by President George W. Bush, lauding Brooke as a "trailblazer." Bush wrote, "You have served your community, your friends, and the people of New York in at least one hundred generous ways . . . May you continue to bring joy to those around you."

Tony Marshall had prepared in advance for his turn, crafting a formal speech and memorizing his lines. At his mother's ninety-fifth birthday party, he had started off his toast by saying with a poker face, "I am not my mother's only child. There was Freddy" — and he glanced over at Freddy Melhado — "and Sandy and Daisy and Siegfried," running through the names of all his mother's dogs, to much laughter. His dry wit softened his reserved demeanor. Tonight his mother had exchanged his arm for a viscount's and then behaved hurtfully to his wife. Long skilled at repressing his feelings, he graciously continued as planned with his affectionate toast.

Tony wanted to do something "innovative and pixyish," so he ran through the things that had happened during his mother's lifetime. "My mother was born a year before Orville Wright's . . . Kitty Hawk flight. She missed that flight but in recent years has been a passenger on the Concorde at Mac 2 speed," he said. He added that she was born before five states had been admitted to the union, nine years after the invention of the zipper, six years before the Model T Ford. "Fortunately, she was born two years after the invention of the telephone." (Everyone chuckled, but in truth Alexander Graham Bell patented the telephone in 1876, twenty-six years before Brooke Astor's birth.) Next Tony spoke of a recurring childhood memory of taking long walks with his mother. "Her loves have always been books, people, and her dogs, although sometimes I've gotten stuck with the dogs. Once when my mother, Buddie, and I were hiking in Switzerland in September 1939, we went for a walk but were overly ambitious and ended up walking twenty-four miles. I carried an exhausted dachshund named Fafner in my rucksack for the last ten miles. When we returned to the hotel, we were told that the Germans had moved into Poland."

It was a child's-eye view of Brooke's passage through life and the history that she had personally experienced. But the toast also included the image of a blithe mother oblivious of her stalwart son's discomfort. One guest recalled being struck by the poignancy of his words: "There would be Brooke swinging along and Tony carrying a dog, bringing up the rear, panting and puffing."

After the toasts, guests lingered for dancing, and as the music played on, the spring evening took on a special quality. "It was a magical night, her life in review," says Gregorian. John Dobkin agrees: "You looked around and everyone was there. She was beautiful, and she was engaged. It was a great place for her to say hello — and if things had been different, to say goodbye to everyone." As a keepsake, the evening's guests were given a beautifully bound book of Vincent Astor's love letters to Brooke. The guest of honor was tired and left early; Chris Ely drove her home, with Lord Astor.

Brooke Astor's birthday and the party got the royal treatment in newspapers around the globe. The *Hartford Courant* effusively called Mrs. Astor a "precious asset"; the *New York Times* said that "she has had everything to do with making New York a greater city than it would have been without her." In the *Times* of London, a columnist wrote, "On Saturday, the day that Britain began mourning Queen Elizabeth the Queen Mother, her near-equivalent in New York, Brooke Astor, was celebrating her 100th birthday." Queen Brooke still reigned, in all her dignified glory.

But as she left that evening, many of her friends wondered if they had seen the last of Brooke Astor, the epitome of society, or at least the Brooke Astor they had known and loved. As tenaciously as she clung to the world, her faculties were going. She had been a public person for so long, but now her social circle was shrinking and she belonged to a few devoted friends, her family, and her servants. That night the velvet curtains were starting to quietly close, but her final act would continue — offstage.

3

Disaster for Mrs. Astor

AT HOLLY HILL the morning after the party, Philip Marshall and Nan Starr felt so queasy that they could scarcely get out of bed in the guest cottage. A roadside stop for food the previous day had been a mistake. By the time the couple made their way to the kitchen in the main house for coffee, Tony and Charlene had already left to drive back to New York. The chef was startled when Philip inquired about his father's whereabouts and blurted out, "I can't believe Mr. Marshall just went off without saying goodbye."

It was typical. Father and son had scarcely spoken the previous evening. Their relationship had been on a downhill slide, and Philip had begun to despair about making things right, as his father seemed committed to turning each encounter into a grudge match.

Philip dated the beginning of the problem to a trip nearly two years earlier, when he and Nan and their children, Winslow and Sophie, had spent five days with Brooke in Maine. Her estate in Northeast Harbor, Cove End, included a large house and a separate two-story cottage by the water, where the Marshalls stayed. Delighted by her great-grandchildren, Brooke offered on the spot to give the cottage to Philip, and she even called Terry Christensen to get the paperwork in order. Tony Marshall had expected to inherit the entire property and was upset to learn that his son would be a partial beneficiary. He urged both his mother and his son to maintain the status quo. The mansion was not winterized, and Tony argued that he wanted to be able to take advantage of the cottage off-season. As Philip recalls, his father told him, "'Philip, you don't want the cottage. It'll be a burden — you'll have to keep it up, you'll have to pay taxes. You can visit anytime and use it.'" Both Brooke and her grandson acceded to Tony's wishes. But ever since then, Tony had appeared wary of his son.

Open hostilities had erupted five months before Brooke's one hundredth birthday. Philip drove to Brooklyn in late October 2001, just six weeks after the September 11 attacks, for a historic preservation conference at Floyd Bennett Field. He ventured into Manhattan briefly to see the damage at Ground Zero but did not call his father. Heading home, he stopped in Westchester to spend the night with his brother and to visit Brooke at Holly Hill.

His conversation with his grandmother took a strange turn that day, since Brooke was dwelling in the past. The collapse of the Twin Towers had been so wrenching that she preferred to discuss traumatic incidents from her own youth, particularly her 1919 honeymoon with her first husband, Dryden Kuser. Philip was in the awkward position of hearing intimate details of his grandmother's wedding night. "She kept saying that he didn't know anything about sex," Philip remembers, "that it was difficult for her."

A few days later Philip received a call from his father, who had learned of his son's trip from Brooke and was perturbed that Philip had not made time to stop by to see him and Charlene. Tony appeared to be even more annoyed that Philip had spent an afternoon with Brooke without alerting him in advance. "In any other family, it would be, 'Oh, you saw your grandmother, how nice,'" says Philip. Instead, his father made saying, "You visited my mother" sound like an accusation. Philip thought his father's tone was possessive: "He didn't call her 'your grandmother.'" Philip regretted hurting his father's feelings but wondered why he suddenly needed a permission slip and a chaperone to see Brooke. "I thought, maybe I need therapy on this one."

The estrangement deepened several weeks later when Philip, Nan, and Alec attended a New York Public Library gala honoring Brooke as a "Literary Lion." The three of them were standing together in Astor

Hall, just inside the library's Fifth Avenue entrance, when Tony and Charlene swept past without a handshake or a nod. "I'll never forget their faces when they saw us and their smiles disappeared," recalls Nan. Philip adds, "They didn't say a word to us, not even to my brother. I thought, 'What's the big deal?'"

Brooke left the Literary Lions party early, escorted by David Rockefeller, so she was unaware of the family tensions. Nan was so upset that she brooded on the four-hour train ride home the next day, remembering, "I was so hurt and confused." She then wrote Tony a letter asking what she and her husband had done to offend him and Charlene. This caused Tony to become even angrier. He called Philip and asked, "Why is your wife writing me a letter?" Philip explained that Nan was troubled by her in-laws' behavior and hoped for a conversation to air things out. Nan never did get a response from Tony, and she now says of her father-in-law, "It was the beginning of the end of any relationship I had with him. It was brutal." Next Alec got a call from his father apologizing for the cold shoulder. As Alec recalls, "He said he did not intend it towards me."

Tony and Philip were now antagonists. Even though they made sporadic attempts at the rituals of reconciliation, such as exchanging gifts at holidays, beneath these gestures was an Oedipal struggle. But neither of them could have imagined that this family rupture would lead to Tony's being in a holding cell at One Hogan Place.

New York City was engulfed in a heat wave in late July 2006, with sweltering temperatures and humidity. Mrs. Astor's apartment lacked central air-conditioning, so its owner and her nurses, who now worked round the clock, were confined to a few air-conditioned rooms. Tony and Charlene Marshall, however, had decamped to Northeast Harbor to spend the summer at Cove End, with its cooling breezes off the harbor. Vincent Astor had purchased the seven-acre estate in 1953, and for nearly a half-century Mrs. Astor had been in residence during the summer. Now the Marshalls had taken the place over, making changes to fit their tastes. Picture windows had been enlarged, and gardeners had plowed over Mrs. Astor's magnificent flower garden and installed its aesthetic antithesis, a lawn with a series of oversized plastic black and white chess pieces on it.

In the four years since Brooke Astor's one hundredth birthday, Tony and Charlene had flourished in new careers as Broadway investors, producing two Tony Award–winning plays, *A Long Day's Journey into Night* and *I Am My Own Wife*. Mimicking his mother's rotating array of famous houseguests, Tony and Charlene now entertained theater friends, including the actors Frank Langella and Jefferson Mays and the couple's coproducer, David Richenthal. Martha Stewart, who owned a home in nearby Seal Harbor, and the painter Richard Estes were dinner guests. Family members were welcome too: Alec Marshall had visited just a few weeks earlier with his fiancée, Sue Ritchie, and now Charlene's pregnant daughter, Inness Gilbert Hancock, was staying in the large cottage. A weekend at the Marshalls' typically included a sail on the couple's luxurious new 55-foot, $900,000 boat, the *General Russell*, named after Tony's maternal grandfather. The couple had hired a full-time captain, putting him on Mrs. Astor's payroll along with the gardeners, the housekeeper, and other Maine employees.

On Monday morning, July 24, the serenity of Tony and Charlene's Maine vacation was shattered. First Brooke Astor's doctor, Rees Pritchett, called to say that his 104-year-old patient had been taken by ambulance early that morning to Lenox Hill Hospital, suffering from pneumonia. Then Philip Marshall called. He and his father had not spoken at all for a year or seen each other for two years. "I said, 'Gagi is in the hospital,'" recalls Philip. "My father said, 'I know.' He was livid that I had found out first. I said, 'Well, things have changed.'"

And then Philip made such a startling announcement that his father, who wears a hearing aid, just kept saying, "What?" as if he could not believe Philip's words. Philip had to repeat himself three times to get his message across: he had filed a guardianship petition in court to wrest the control of Brooke Astor's care and, perhaps more important, her fortune away from his father. Twisting the knife, Philip told Tony that he had powerful backers: David Rockefeller, Annette de la Renta, and Henry Kissinger had joined him in this legal action. Tony, furious, told his son, "I can't believe this. I'll never talk to you again." Then he hung up. Charlene, who had been listening on an extension, remained on the line. Philip kept talking, saying, "I am sorry I had to do this." He recalls her sarcastic reply: "I'm sure you are."

Charlene's tone of voice irked Philip and he let loose, criticizing his stepmother's sense of entitlement to Brooke's money. A staffer in Mrs. Astor's office had confided to him that Charlene had recently demanded $25,000 for a new truck and then complained about the expense of having two of Brooke's nurses overlap on a shift. "I'm sorry you made me have to do this, because of your actions," Philip told his stepmother. He accused her of "trying to deny my grandmother health care while you're buying yourself a truck."

Tony promptly called his other son, Alec, to ask whether he knew about the lawsuit. Alec had sailed and dined with his father and Charlene in Maine recently but had given no hint that anything was amiss. "Yes," said Alec, admitting that his twin had confided in him. Tony followed up by asking, "Do you agree with Philip?" "No," Alec replied. Tony sounded relieved, and wrapped up the brief conversation by saying, "That's all I wanted to know." Alec thought afterward that the conversation had gone as well as it could have under the circumstances. But his father had a different reaction. As Tony brooded over it, he became enraged that Alec had not warned him but had chosen brotherly loyalty over filial obligation.

The phone rang again in Northeast Harbor. This time it was the Marshalls' friend Daniel Billy, Jr. Billy had trained with Charlene to be lay ministers at St. James' Church, an Episcopal bastion on Madison Avenue, and their religious commitment had evolved into friendship. With managerial expertise from running a small foundation, Billy had been hired ten months earlier by the Marshalls to supervise Mrs. Astor's staff, and he was now working out of an office in her apartment. He told Tony that he too had just received a call from Philip, with instructions to take his personal effects, lock up, and leave the keys. Billy recalls, "I offered to barricade myself into the office." But Tony told him to go home — it would all be sorted out.

Next Tony tracked down his friend Francis X. Morrissey, Jr., in Paris to tell him about the lawsuit. Two years after Brooke's hundredth birthday party, Tony had fired his mother's attorney, Terry Christensen, and replaced him with Morrissey, who immediately presided over two codicils to Brooke Astor's will. While Tony needed legal advice to deal with this sudden crisis, Morrissey was not a courtroom litigator. In fact, Morrissey would soon find himself embroiled in the case, with the need to hire his own lawyer.

Frantic to understand what had happened, Tony summoned Steve Hamor, his mother's gardener, who had been working out in the yard, into the library. Hamor had worked for Mrs. Astor in Maine since 1965; his wife, Pat, laundered her linens, and his two sons were employed as full-time gardeners on her estate in Maine. "Tony asked me, 'Have you been talking to Philip?'" recalls Hamor. "I said, 'I haven't spoken to Philip for two or three years.' Tony said, 'Philip is accusing me of wrongly spending my mother's money.'" Hamor adds, "That afternoon Tony boarded a plane and went to New York. He seemed very upset."

Tony and Charlene left so abruptly that they neglected to alert Sam Peabody, a Manhattan philanthropist who was en route to stay for a week with the couple. "I drove up the driveway, got out and took my bags and rang the bell, and the housekeeper said that Mr. and Mrs. Marshall had been called to New York on an emergency," says Peabody. "I thought, 'Oh, thank goodness, poor Mrs. Astor has finally died.'"

With each phone call that Monday, the news of the lawsuit spread. But the warring parties all believed, naively, that this would remain a private family battle, conducted behind closed doors. Unbeknown to those personally affected, events that would soon make the lawsuit notoriously public had already taken place. Three days earlier, Ira Salzman, Philip's lawyer, had filed a copy of the lawsuit with the Manhattan clerk's office to get a docket number and then walked the original file to Justice John Stackhouse's office. The lawyer requested in writing that the judge seal the papers. "Ira asked us not to talk about it," says a courthouse employee.

Salzman expected to leave Stackhouse's office with the order to seal the lawsuit and take it directly to the clerk's office. But the judge decided to hold on to it temporarily. Salzman called repeatedly to find out when he could pick it up. Late on Friday, Salzman finally took a photocopy of the order to the clerk's office, but the clerk declined to accept it, insisting on having the original. Thus the case, "Index No. 500096/06: PHILIP MARSHALL for the Application of Guardians of the Person and Property of BROOKE ASTOR, an alleged Incapacitated Person," was left in the public record.

On Monday afternoon, Helen Peterson, a *Daily News* reporter, received a tip that guardianship papers involving Brooke Astor had been filed. In light of Peterson's six years of covering the legal doings at 60 Centre Street (and twenty-three years at the *Daily News*), her source was probably a courthouse employee, although all Peterson will say is, "It was not Ira Salzman." While reporters routinely check the records room at 4 P.M. each day for new lawsuits, from slip-and-fall cases to business disputes, guardianship files are not typically requested. By the time Peterson got the tip, the record room was closed for the day.

At 10 A.M. on Tuesday, the reporter went to the musty basement office and asked for the Astor file. The clerk handed it over. "I started reading it and my hands started shaking," Peterson recalled. "I knew it was a huge story." Philip Marshall had charged his father with "elder abuse" of Brooke Astor. According to the document, Mrs. Astor, the city's most beloved philanthropist, was living in squalor amid peeling paint and was being deprived of medical care. Peterson took out a roll of quarters and photocopied the hefty file — constantly looking over her shoulder in fear of rival reporters — and then took the subway to the *Daily News* headquarters. Her editor, Dean Chang, was in a meeting. "I have to talk to you," she said. He waved her off; she went back twenty minutes later to interrupt again. "You don't understand," she said. "I have to talk to you right now. I have tomorrow's front-page story."

Late in the day she called Tony Marshall at his Upper East Side co-op for a comment prior to publication. He was so thrown by the situation that he did not immediately defend himself. "He sounded sad," she says in retrospect. "Sometimes people start screaming at me. He was well brought up. He wasn't rude — he was very polite." Tony Marshall informed her, "No, I don't want to comment." Peterson told him that she found the allegations shocking. Tony's reply, quoted the next day in the *Daily News,* was, "You said it is shocking, and I agree. It is a matter that is going to be coming up in a court of law and it should be left to the court."

That night Philip Marshall, the instigator of it all, stayed in Queens with Tenzing Chadotsang, a Tibetan friend who worked for the Landmarks Preservation Commission. As they were driving back to the Chadotsang family's modest brick home after dinner at a Korean restaurant, Philip's cell phone rang. The *Daily News* wanted a comment. Philip was startled, since Salzman had assured him of privacy. As Chadotsang says, "I knew that Philip had filed the suit, but he expected it to be a quiet thing. Philip got off the phone and said, 'Oh my God, it's going to be in the newspapers.'" Philip contemplated calling Annette de la Renta but decided not to ruin her evening. "At that point," he said, "I didn't know Annette well enough to call her at ten-thirty or eleven at night."

Annette is an early riser, and at 5:30 the next morning she took her three rambunctious dogs for a walk, strolling down quiet Park Avenue, contemplating the day ahead and a visit to Brooke in the hospital. When she got back to her building, the doorman handed her the *Daily News,* delivered just minutes before. Annette was horrified by the sight of the huge black words on page one: "DISASTER FOR MRS. ASTOR: Son forces society queen to live on peas and porridge in dilapidated Park Avenue duplex."

The story inside — "Battle of N.Y. Blue Bloods" — made for mesmerizing reading for the city's entire five boroughs, with special double-takes all over the Upper East Side. "The sad and deplorable state of my family's affairs has compelled me to bring the guardianship case," Philip had written in his affidavit requesting that his father be removed as Brooke Astor's legal guardian and replaced by Annette de la Renta. "Her bedroom is so cold in the winter that my grandmother is forced to sleep in the TV room in torn nightgowns on a filthy couch that smells, probably from dog urine." Philip charged that his father "has turned a blind eye to her . . . while enriching himself with millions of dollars."

Detailed affidavits about the alleged abuse had been signed by three nurses (Minnette Christie, Pearline Noble, and Beverly Thomson) and by Chris Ely, who had been fired by Tony eighteen months earlier.

"The apartment is shabby and poorly maintained. It always has a foul odor because her two dogs are obliged to live enclosed in the dining room," wrote Annette de la Renta in her affidavit. "Because of the failure of Mrs. Astor's son, Anthony, to spend her money properly, the quality of life of Mrs. Astor has been significantly eroded." David Rockefeller seconded this concern about Brooke's "welfare," and Henry Kissinger attested that Mrs. de la Renta would make an "excellent guardian" for Mrs. Astor.

By the time the *Daily News* published its story, Justice Stackhouse had already taken action to remedy the situation. The judge named two temporary guardians for Mrs. Astor, Annette de la Renta and JP-Morgan Chase, the bank that Rockefeller had headed for decades. With the stroke of a pen, Tony Marshall lost responsibility for his mother's care as well as his hefty salary for managing her money. The judge named a court evaluator, the lawyer Susan Robbins, an outspoken former social worker with expertise in guardianships. All this happened without a hearing, which the judge then scheduled for several weeks in the future. Tony Marshall had been stripped of his powers without the chance to offer his version of events and defend himself.

New York is a city that virtually, under civic charter, requires a summer scandal, and the Astor affair fit the bill. This was not just another family feud but a sprawling saga involving society figures, millions of dollars, appalling charges, and backstage intrigue. A media war erupted. The *New York Times* assigned a battalion of reporters and ran stories with eight different bylines in the next few days. Television and print reporters staked out the Marshalls' Manhattan apartment as well as Alec's place in Ossining and Philip's forest green shingle-style home on a corner lot in Massachusetts, taking pictures of Winslow mowing the lawn. As Nan recalls, "That's when I knew our lives would never be the same."

At Lenox Hill Hospital, extra security guards were hired to keep interlopers such as reporters pretending to deliver flowers away from Mrs. Astor, who was recovering from a near fatal bout of pneumonia.

"Reporters were outside my parents' home," recalls Dr. Sandra Gelbard, who was in charge of her care. "I don't know how they got the address."

On Northeast Harbor's tiny Main Street, reporters from the *Daily News*, the *New York Post*, and the *Boston Globe* went from door to door, trying to dig up dirt. Bob Pyle, the town's librarian, says, "We felt like we had to pull down our shades at night to escape the paparazzi." Charlene's daughter Inness, staying on at Cove End, was so distraught by the press attention and the gawkers that she called her mother to say she felt ill and was worried that her pregnancy would be endangered. "I thought the *New York Post* was going to give my daughter a miscarriage," says Charlene Marshall. "But she went to the hospital and they saved the baby."

The unfolding saga was polarizing Brooke Astor's friends and the Marshalls' social circle. People felt forced to take sides. In Washington, D.C., Suzanne Kuser, Tony Marshall's half-sister and a former State Department intelligence analyst, got a call from her nephew Philip explaining the situation. Kuser says, "I thought he had a case." Kuser had a distinct theory about the psychological underpinnings of her half-brother's behavior, saying, "Tony has a lot of problems. Some of them are mommy issues. There's a whole history."

In California, Nancy Reagan was saddened but not entirely surprised to read of the scandal. "I felt terrible, just terrible, that this could happen to Brooke," she told me. "We all knew that something was wrong up there. But nobody knew quite how wrong it was." Mrs. Reagan called Annette de la Renta to inquire about the details. "Annette explained to me that she wasn't supposed to talk." Even to you? "Even to me."

Viscount William Astor was on holiday in Scotland when the story hit the newspapers. He admitted that he had been worried about Brooke in recent years. "I'm just appalled by the way she's been treated," he said. "Annette de la Renta has done the right thing, and we've all been encouraging her to do something for a long time. It's all about money."

Indeed, nearly every day for the following six months Tony and Charlene Marshall were pilloried in the press. They were accused of finagling millions from Mrs. Astor, including diverting money to invest in their theatrical company. They were attacked for firing Mrs. Astor's longtime staff — Chris Ely, her chauffeur, her French chef, her social secretary, and her Maine housekeeper — and denounced for preventing friends from visiting in order to isolate her. There were ominous reports that Tony had shredded eighty boxes of documents. He was criticized for selling the Childe Hassam painting for $10 million and taking a $2 million commission, and there was an uproar when he admitted that he had erred in filing his mother's taxes, resulting in a huge underpayment of capital gains tax on the transaction.

The Marshalls protested their innocence in quaintly old-fashioned terms. "My mother has always emphasized the importance of good manners," Tony said in a statement that he passed out to the press. "Those who have associated their names with this action taken against me and my wife Charlene have not only exercised bad manners but total disrespect and a lack of decency." He charged that Rockefeller and Kissinger "have given undeserved credence to my son Philip's charges against me and stirred up a massive media campaign."

Tony was stunned by the betrayal of these people he knew — or at least thought he knew. As an ambassador in the Nixon administration, he had reported to Kissinger, then the secretary of state. Through his mother, Tony had known and socialized with the entire Rockefeller family for decades. He and Annette both served on the board of the Metropolitan Museum, and they were often thrown together at Brooke's larger parties. "I thought they were all friends," Tony later told me, and then, without prompting, he conceded, "Of my mother's."

Rockefeller and Kissinger, who have spent their lifetimes in the public eye, serenely took the high road, declining to respond to Tony Marshall's criticisms and authorizing Rockefeller's veteran public relations adviser Fraser Seitel to handle the media. Even more than a year later, when Rockefeller and Kissinger spoke with me, they avoided directly criticizing Tony and pointedly praised Philip. In a lengthy conversation in his art-filled office on the fifty-sixth floor of Rockefeller Center, Rockefeller insisted that he became involved because he was concerned about Brooke's "personal comfort and happiness." He added, "I don't know Philip well, but I felt his motives were totally unselfish and caring for his grandmother. I've been very impressed." Kissinger, speaking at his Park Avenue office several blocks away, explained, "Nobody said, 'Let's get all these names together and really do a job here.' When we were caucusing among ourselves, it was entirely on the issue of how can we make life better for Brooke in her final years?"

Thanks to the star power arrayed against the Marshalls, only a few of their friends were willing to support them openly. David Richenthal, the lead partner in Delphi Productions, the couple's theatrical venture, was their staunchest vocal defender. He lashed out at Philip, calling him "a disturbed attention-getting young man who is acting irrationally." The CBS newsman Mike Wallace, who had met the Marshalls when he profiled Brooke Astor for *60 Minutes,* issued a formal statement saying, "I am perplexed by the attacks leveled against Anthony. I believe they are completely undeserved." Wallace later told me, "When I read about it, I said, 'This is horseshit.' I've spent time with these people. They seemed reasonable and not greedy." At St. James' Church, Rector Brenda Husson was convinced that the Marshalls were innocent of all charges. "I was dumbfounded," she says. "It just did not line up with anything I knew either about them or about their relationship with Brooke. I'm very aware of regular visits and ongoing care."

The controversy dominated conversations and created schisms. Eleanor Elliott, a former *Vogue* editor who had attended Brooke's hundredth birthday party, wrote a note of support to the Marshalls, declaring that she was not a fair-weather friend. But her brother-in-law Oz Elliott thought the charges were probably credible, saying, "If David Rockefeller got involved, there must have been more fire than smoke."

For a son to take his father to court is a stunning act of familial disloyalty. William F. Buckley, Jr., Brooke's neighbor at 778 Park Avenue, described Philip's lawsuit in his syndicated newspaper column as a "parricidal intervention." Tony told close friends that he could not fathom his sons' behavior. As Daniel Billy, Jr., says, "What they've done is biblical in their betrayal." Alec did not join in the lawsuit, but in his father's eyes he was as culpable as Philip. As Billy adds, "By not taking sides, he's taken sides."

The Marshalls descended into a nightmarish existence in which everything they had ever said or done was scrutinized by the press. They were villains in the tabloid drama, and they confided to friends that strangers called in the middle of the night with death threats. Virtually every newspaper story featured lovely old photos of Mrs. Astor decked out in her finest jewels and hats and smiling benignly, alongside unattractive new photos of an enraged Charlene snarling at the cameras like Cruella de Vil, with a baffled and somber Tony at her side.

It seemed that the story would rival *The Fantasticks* as Manhattan's longest-running show, setting off a chain reaction of efforts to capitalize on the explosive charges. In Washington, the U.S. Senate was prompted to hold a hearing on exploitation of seniors, inviting testimony from Philip Marshall's lawyer, Ira Salzman. Oregon's Republican senator Gordon Smith declared, "As we have learned from the highly publicized Brooke Astor case, no matter your age, finances or social status, none of us in this room today are beyond potential abuse." And the television show *Law & Order: Criminal Intent* filmed a episode called "Privilege" in which an elderly character resembling Brooke Astor, played by the actress Doris Roberts, appears delirious after being denied medical care. She is forced to sign financial documents by her scheming son and his trophy wife. The phrase "urine-stained sheets," which was close to the wording in Philip's affidavit, was worked into the dialogue.

The foibles of the rich have always made for great copy, but Brooke Astor's prominent role in the life of New York City added an underlying note of poignancy to the tale. Adorned with diamonds, sapphires, and emeralds, she had perfected an image of herself as Lady Bountiful with a common touch, ever accessible to the admiring strangers who stopped her on Madison Avenue or shook her hand at a housing project in Queens. "She never went out at night with less than a million dollars around her neck," says Louis Auchincloss. "Someone once said to her, 'You might lose that,' and she said, 'So what? Be in the safe all night? Don't be ridiculous.'" She was unapologetic about her lavish lifestyle, which is why the charge in the lawsuit that expensive floral arrangements had been replaced by cheap Korean market bouquets seemed like such an insult. Auchincloss adds that Brooke once told him, "I know what people have. I know that Jayne Wrightsman [a wealthy widow and Metropolitan Museum trustee] could buy and sell me several times over, but look at the way she lives. I've got about fifty people in my employ and I know how to spend it. Jayne's got much more money, but she doesn't dare."

Yet Brooke Astor could also be obliviously obtuse about money and social class. In a *New York Times Magazine* profile in 1984, the reporter Marilyn Berger trailed her to the South Bronx to visit homes being constructed for poor families. During a lunch break, Berger wrote, Mrs. Astor noticed mustard and lumpy Russian dressing for sandwiches in little plastic containers and exclaimed, "Look at the marvelous sauces."

If her last name had remained Russell or Kuser or Marshall, Brooke would never have been quite so famous, even with a similar fortune. But a few names have held the American public in thrall for two centuries. In 1960 the writer Cleveland Amory published his bestseller *Who Killed Society?*, about the downfall of the American aristocracy, which highlighted the Astors as the epitome of privilege gone to seed. The Astor history was rife with destructive marriages, scandals, and embarrassing peccadilloes. "The American Astor Family in its fifth generation would have made the original John Jacob turn in his grave," Amory wrote, before concluding that by 1958 the Astors had "proved that by six generations an American family is about ready to start all over again."

Brooke Astor, newly widowed when the book was published, had saved society, rescuing the Astor name from ignominy and making it fashionable again. Mrs. Astor combined her noblesse with oblige, which won the hearts of jaded New Yorkers. At the depth of New York's fiscal crisis in 1975, she flamboyantly stepped up as a leader by doubling her foundation's giving, passing out $6.4 million to keep the doors of libraries and museums open. She loved chatting with museum curators, librarians, and security guards, even making a point of memorizing the doorkeepers' names. At the Metropolitan Museum, she funded a Christmas lunch for all the employees to boost morale, and she proudly showed up every year. "She loved to get to know the people who did the work," recalls Gregory Long. "She was endlessly interested in people. She wanted to know people high and low."

Brooke Astor was hardly a saint. She was mercurial, she made promises that she did not always keep, and her charming public persona vanished at times when she dealt with her family and employees. She could be imperious and hurtful to those near and dear and was a master of the devastating putdown. Caught up in being Mrs. Astor, she brooked no complaint. That said, many, many people shared the view held by Tom Brokaw: "She was irresistible."

The feud over Brooke Astor laid bare the schisms in a storied Manhattan clan. There is something spellbinding about the sight of a family falling apart in public, and there's a special schadenfreude to be had when tens of millions of dollars are at stake. The public and the press become voyeurs, everyone has an opinion, and the real people at the center of the drama are reduced to caricatures.

Once the headlines faded away, the New Yorkers who thought they knew Brooke Astor — as well as Tony and Charlene Marshall — retained a haunting curiosity about what had actually happened, and why. At Park Avenue dinner parties, guests offered up theories as if playing an adult game of Clue with a lineup of suspects and motives. Had Mrs. Astor somehow brought this all on herself? Was Tony seeking revenge for his mother's lifelong detachment? Did Philip Marshall have ulterior motives, ranging from a simmering hatred for his father to old-fashioned greed? Was the real culprit Charlene Marshall, twenty-one years younger than her husband and acting to protect her own financial future? Was Annette de la Renta trying to displace Brooke Astor as the leader of society, as Tony and his supporters loudly claimed, or was she truly selfless? What if there had been a rush to judgment and the Marshalls had been wrongly accused?

Truth is elusive. But maybe the simplest answer is that it had all begun long before, so long before that Woodrow Wilson was in the White House. Perhaps it had begun with Brooke's marriage to her first husband, John Dryden Kuser.

4

"I Married a Terrible Man"

⚜

GUARDED BY TWO stone lions, Patience and Fortitude, the main branch of the New York Public Library is an imposing marble Beaux Arts landmark at Fifth Avenue and Forty-second Street. Its cornerstone was laid in May 1902, two months after Brooke Astor was born. On a wintry December day nearly a century later, Mrs. Astor ascended the stairs to accept yet another in a long series of public service awards.

The library had been a second home for her in the past two decades. A bookish child who had turned into an insatiable reader, she had written two poignant autobiographies, *Patchwork Child* and *Footprints,* and two well-reviewed novels, *The Bluebird Is at Home* and *The Last Blossom on the Plum Tree,* which was deemed "a lovely summertime entertainment" by the *New York Times.* Her career as a writer began with a book review in *Vogue* in 1926; her most recent offering had been an essay in *Vanity Fair* in 2000 on the lost art of flirting. "She took books with her to the hairdresser's, in her car — there was always a book by her side," says Linda Gillies, of the Astor Foundation. "Mrs. Astor used to say that you can never be lonely if you read."

The occasion at the library on December 10, 2001, was the inaugural awarding of the Andrew Carnegie Medals of Philanthropy. Mrs. Astor was being honored for spearheading the revival of the library, and her talk was preceded on the luncheon program by a series of yawn-inducing speeches from fellow honorees. The financier George Soros intoned, "We need better and stronger international institutions," and then David Rockefeller observed, "We all have the responsibility for the well-being of our society and its citizens."

Dressed in a blue suit and a large navy hat, and overwhelmed by three large strands of pearls, a huge diamond pin, diamond earrings, and a gold bracelet, Mrs. Astor appeared unsteady on her feet as Vartan Gregorian took her arm and escorted her to the podium. She gazed with pleasure at the audience and then, in a raspy aged voice still tinged with patrician pronunciation, she launched into a rambling speech that was rivetingly personal.

"My mother used to say to me, Brooke, don't get beyond yourself. I am beyond myself in two ways," she began. "The first is all of you being so nice to listen to me, since I have practically nothing to say. And the other, frankly, is that I'm still alive." Mrs. Astor smiled tremulously, and the audience laughed in support. "I was an only child and I had my father, who was very sensible, and my mother, who was insensible," she continued. "So here I am, a very mixed-up person who has had a wonderful life, and also a hard life at times."

Then she spoke of an early mistake that had become a badge of shame. "I married a perfectly terrible man," she recalled, harking back to her wedding at seventeen. "They were not what you call interesting people, but they had a lot of money. I was pushed into marriage, and in those days I thought if a man kissed you, a baby popped out of you. I didn't know what it was all about."

Then she suddenly looked disoriented, as if she had lost her bearings. Mrs. Astor became incoherent in the middle of a sentence. There were nervous titters; as Annette de la Renta recalls, "No one knew what to do." After a moment, Mrs. Astor valiantly carried on, trying to wrap up with her views on dealing with her fellow men, albeit with an odd coda: "Don't hurt them — always try to help them. If they're absolutely nuts and stupid, stay away from them." The protective Gregorian then whispered in her ear, and she replied, her words captured by the microphone, "You say I've said enough? All right, I think I've said enough."

. . .

In a life that spans more than a century, innumerable events and memories compete for mental space; there are hours that linger for years and years that pass in a flash. Brooke Astor outlived three husbands and defined her life by those marriages. She was grateful to Vincent Astor for giving her the opportunity to become an influential member of society. Charles "Buddie" Marshall provided marital happiness. But Brooke's first husband, John Dryden Kuser, cast a long and troubled shadow that haunted her until her dying day. Kuser materialized in her nightmares. Events occurred during their time together that she could neither forgive nor forget.

Her feelings toward her son were blunted by her rage toward his father. She knew it and felt guilty, but she could not help herself. Brooke Astor grew up in an era when psychoanalysis had yet to penetrate the straitlaced remnants of Victorian America. There was no such thing as a self-help aisle in the legendary Scribner Book Store. Rather than ruminate over traumatic experiences, Brooke forged ahead, determined to keep busy every single minute of the day. She accepted more engagements than anyone could possibly keep and then berated her social secretaries when she was late or forced to cancel at the last minute. If she could just stay in motion, she could avoid unpleasant thoughts. But the past caught up with her when she spent time with her son. "Keep in mind, Tony is the son of Brooke's first husband, who treated Brooke abominably," says Robert Pirie. Ashton Hawkins adds, "Part of the problem is that Tony always reminded her of Dryden. It's not his fault, but he did."

On April 27, 1919, the *Washington Post* featured a lengthy story on its society page about the wedding of Roberta Brooke Russell to John Dryden Kuser at St. John's Episcopal Church. The ceremony was noteworthy because the daughter of Colonel John Russell of the Marine Corps was marrying into a wealthy and well-connected family. "Mr. Kuser is a grandson of the late Senator John F. Dryden of Bernardsville, N.J.," the *Post* wrote, noting that the senator's District of Columbia residence "was the scene of some of the most brilliant and elaborate of official entertainments which made up the social history of Washington in the past 20 years."

Brooke was accompanied by eight bridesmaids in the lavish wedding. As the *Post* noted, "The little bride wore a girlish graceful gown of soft white satin" and a veil trimmed with orange blossoms. Brooke's mother, Mabel, who had encouraged the match, "wore gray chiffon with a blue hat veiled in tulle and trimmed with ostrich feathers." The newspaper pointed out that Brooke was young for marriage. The bride and groom would head off by train for a wedding trip to the palatial Hotel Greenbriar in West Virginia, "after which they will go to Princeton, where the bridegroom will complete his courses at the university where he graduates in June."

Brooke would later tear up her wedding pictures in a fury. She had grown up as a sheltered only child, traveling the world with her parents as her father moved from her birthplace, New Hampshire, to Hawaii, Panama, Newport, and China with the Marine Corps. The Russells were a patriotic family with a tradition of military service; Brooke's paternal grandfather, Admiral John Russell, had been praised by President Lincoln for defeating Confederate warships during the Civil War. Her mother's parents, the lawyer George Howard and his wife, Roberta, a society belle, had been disappointed by Mabel's decision to marry a military man without significant independent means. Although Mabel opted for love, she came to appreciate her parents' concerns and was determined that her own daughter would make a more financially advantageous union.

Although Brooke was not always a reliable narrator in chronicling her life in her autobiographies, she showed a keen eye in describing her parents' expatriate social life in China — and her mother's provocative flirtations and the resulting family quarrels. Brooke learned her social skills from a self-confident master of the art. When the *New York Times* profiled her father, newly named as commandant of the Marines, in 1934, the Washington bureau chief, Arthur Krock, went out of his way to compliment Mabel as "extraordinarily able and attractive." An acquaintance who knew Brooke's mother in the 1940s says, "Mrs. Russell was divine. She was charming beyond belief. She would say, 'It's so lovely going to a party when you know you're going to make the evening for some young man.'" According to Ivan Obolensky, Vincent Astor's nephew, "Mrs. Russell was jolly, intelligent, the perfect commandant's wife. The problem was, the family had influence but was without money. Brooke was brought up in penury, but with all the accoutrements."

John and Mabel Russell lived well overseas, with a household of servants, thanks to the strong dollar and officers' perks. But after the couple and their daughter moved to Washington, D.C., money became a problem. Brooke was forced to drop out of school, not for financial reasons but because her mother feared that a good education might hurt her marital prospects. "I revered Miss Madeira, but Mother took me out when I wanted to learn Greek and Latin," Brooke told *Women's Wear Daily* in 1991. "She thought I would become a bluestocking — a bore and not attractive, someone who wouldn't flirt at all."

Brooke was only sixteen when her life was upended by a phone call. A friend was supposed to attend a Princeton dance but had the measles; Mabel Russell encouraged Brooke to step in as a substitute. Brooke later wrote that she went to the dance against her will. Wearing borrowed clothing (a white and silver chiffon dress from an aunt, her grandmother's red mohair cape, and her own silver high-heeled slippers), she was on the dance floor when Dryden Kuser took her in his arms. He was a clumsy dancer, but in the following weeks he began to court her with visits and gifts, including a blue leather-bound copy of *The Oxford Book of English Verse*, and she was flattered.

The managing editor of the *Daily Princetonian*, the president of a debating society, and already the author of a modest book, *The Birds of Somerset Hills*, Dryden Kuser looked great on paper. And his family was rich — fabulously rich. His mother, Susie Dryden, was the daughter of the founder of Prudential Insurance Company, and his father, Anthony Kuser, was a New Jersey tycoon. The son of German and Austrian immigrants, Kuser had started out as a pants presser, found success as a wholesale dealer for a brewery, and gone on to become the founding stockholder in Fox Films and president of the local power company.

Mabel Russell was thrilled when it became clear that her daughter had the opportunity to marry into the Kuser family, an emotion shared by Brooke. She had not even come out as a debutante but was skipping straight to the engagement ring. During the entire whirlwind romance, Brooke's father was stationed in South America, and her mother decided to act quickly lest the moment pass. By the time John Russell returned to Washington to meet the groom, his daughter's engagement had been announced and wedding plans were under way.

The marriage was a disaster right from the wedding night. Brooke later complained that her mother had never explained to her precisely what happened during sex, and as a new bride she was horrified by Dryden's marital expectations. "We were a totally miscast pair," she wrote in *Footprints*. "Dryden was oversexed and completely inexperienced, and I was hopelessly ignorant and unprepared in any way for this great adventure." During the honeymoon, Dryden also displayed an ardor for alcohol that was a harbinger of future problems. Even half a century later, Brooke frequently recounted how she begged her parents to help her arrange for a divorce. A daddy's girl, she blamed her mother for getting her into this mess. As Liz Smith recalls, "She told me that she ran and jumped in her father's lap — she worshiped him. She was so unhappy. Whatever happened on her honeymoon, the guy was brutal. She was shocked by sex." But Brooke was married. The deed was done, and in that era it was not something easily undone.

Many of Brooke's friends speculated that she never did enjoy sex, although she wanted to be perceived by men as alluring. Whether this was a reaction to her wedding-night trauma, no one knew. She once confided to a close male friend that a Catholic bishop had made a pass at her and she had been so upset that she experienced several days of hysterical blindness. Brooke reveled in flirtation and the feeling of conquest and certainly had lovers through the years, but she gave the impression that the actual act was not for her the climax of romantic liaisons. Nonetheless, she played the part of sexy woman to the hilt. "She was naughty," recalls Philippe de Montebello. "She would deliberately say almost off-color things." In her novel *The Bluebird Is at Home*, written when she was sixty-three years old, an aging woman says, "When I can't sleep, instead of counting sheep I try to remember my lovers." Mrs. Astor loved that line so much that she often used it in conversation. Vernon Jordan laughs affectionately as he recalls how even in her dotage she was still vamping. At a conference in Bilderberg, Germany, he and the financier James Wolfensohn escorted Mrs. Astor, then in her nineties, back to her hotel room after a dinner, and she turned at the doorway to say, "If only I were younger, I'd invite you both in."

But as a teenage bride, Brooke was thrust into an alien environment. She and Dryden moved in with his parents and his younger sister, Cynthia, at Faircourt, the family's grandiose Italianate villa in Bernardsville, New Jersey. Perched on a hillside, the mansion sported a red-tiled roof, marble floors, and elaborate wood-paneled rooms finished with gold leaf. Nearly a century later, it is still considered one of the great historic houses of this moneyed enclave. Back then the landscaped grounds sprawled over 250 acres, and the colonel, a bird lover, kept a huge flock of pheasants. While Brooke was initially awed by the grand lifestyle — the Kusers employed sixteen servants — she thought the family had terrible taste and she felt ill at ease, like a caged bird. Her father-in-law was so domineering that he kept his watch on the dining room table, and if Brooke and Dryden were late for dinner, he docked their allowance by $100 per minute.

Brooke had been dazzled during her courtship by Dryden's accomplishments. But in her autobiography, she paints her ten years with him as a long stretch of misery. Colonel Kuser used his clout as a major shareholder with Lenox China to get his son a job with the company, based in Princeton, New Jersey. During his year with the firm, his bride was so unhappy that she gorged herself, briefly weighing ten pounds more than her husband. Brooke and Dryden moved back in with the Kusers again and had the bad luck to be on the premises during a notorious robbery in 1921. The robber broke in late at night, chloroformed the family, and stole $20,000 worth of jewelry, most of which belonged to Brooke. (Her mother-in-law's jewels were in a safe deposit box.) Brooke later downplayed the incident, saying that she had been pleased to receive the insurance money, but it must have been frightening to be rendered unconscious while her engagement ring was slipped off her finger.

The couple eventually moved to their own large stucco home, just down the hill from Faircourt. From the master bedroom on the second floor with its wrought-iron balcony, Brooke could look out and see a regal corridor of maple trees flanking the long driveway. Her dressing room was adorned with a beautiful crystal chandelier and a full-length mirror. But even with a generous stipend from Dryden's parents, the couple never had enough money and quarreled constantly. Dryden was a gambler; he lost $36,000 in bets at the nearby Somerset golf club in one afternoon. "Dryden was fast drinking, fast smoking, fast women, and an incredibly calculating, fast, brilliant mind," says his nephew, Andrew Kravchenko. "He wasn't great at making fortunes like his father, Colonel Kuser. He was great at spending them."

Dryden Kuser gravitated to the perfect career for a man with his spendthrift ways — politics. He was elected as a Bernardsville city councilman and moved on to the New Jersey legislature as an assemblyman and then a state senator. He never built a career as a distinguished lawmaker; his major accomplishment was the passage of a bill that designated the eastern goldfinch as New Jersey's state bird, a gesture meant to please his father the pheasant fancier.

Brooke and Dryden's marriage contained dark secrets. Brooke remarked in her autobiography, regarding the news from a doctor that she was pregnant with her first and only child, "Having not participated very willingly in this future event, I was perturbed." Given the implication that her son was conceived during a marital rape, it is hardly surprising that Brooke dreaded motherhood.

Later in life Brooke repeatedly dropped hints to friends and even mere acquaintances about her problems with Dryden Kuser. In the summer of 1967 she was parked near the fire station in Northeast Harbor when she spotted Bob Pyle, who had recently graduated from soda jerk to summer police officer. As he recalls, Mrs. Astor walked over, put her hand on his forearm for emphasis, and said, "Now, Bob dear, don't be influenced by name or social position in dealing with domestic abuse. Wealthy people can be bastards too." Pyle was taken aback and says, "I thought to myself, who beat her?" Similarly, Sandra Graves, who worked as a summer cook for Mrs. Astor in Maine, interviewed her employer for a college class and says, "She wanted to talk about the husband who beat her. Tony's father."

It was not until Brooke was eighty-two years old that she publicly revealed what she had been hinting at for so long: she had been a battered wife. In an interview with Marilyn Berger for the *New York Times Magazine* profile in 1984, Brooke said of Kuser, "One day he knocked me down and broke my jaw. Father wanted me to leave him, but I said I couldn't because I was having his child." She was six months pregnant with Tony. The abuse was apparently not a one-time event; she told friends that when Kuser got drunk he hit her, and he drank early and often.

Brooke remained married to Dryden for five years after she gave birth, on May 30, 1924, to Anthony Dryden Kuser, named after his paternal grandfather and his father. She dealt with her anger toward her husband by spending as much time as possible in Manhattan with friends, avoiding her home. She professed to love her son but handed off his daily care to nannies, which was typical for women of her social class in those days. When she visited her parents in Haiti for several weeks on her own, Brooke justified her absence by saying that Tony would ultimately benefit from her improved mood.

Even in a marriage where the joy has long since vanished for both parties, it often takes an external event to trigger a divorce. The death of Colonel Kuser in February 1929 proved to be the catalyst. En route home after the funeral, Dryden asked Brooke for a divorce. He wanted to marry Vieva Fisher Banks, a married woman with three daughters, with whom he had been having an affair. (She too promptly filed for divorce.) Just as Brooke's marriage made the society pages, so did its demise. The *New York Times* carried a story on February 16, 1930, with the headline "Mrs. Kuser Files Suit; Gets Custody of Son." The story noted that the couple's problems had begun early in their union. "Mrs. Kuser complained that a year later her husband began to embarrass her in social activities, that he told her he no longer loved her, and that their marriage was a failure." An Associated Press story noted that Mrs. Kuser said her husband "was critical of her dress and upbraided her because of alleged extravagance."

Brooke won a substantial settlement and custody of Tony. In a letter discussing the family's finances, Dryden Kuser's second wife, Vieva, later disclosed that Dryden paid Brooke about $680,000 for an apartment and alimony, which included "a trust fund that brought $90,000 per year." Brooke agreed that if she remarried, her alimony would go into a trust for Tony until he turned twenty-one. She would come to regret this clause.

Once the divorce was finalized, Brooke moved to an apartment at Gracie Square in Manhattan, uprooting her six-year-old son from his pony and country life. Dryden Kuser remained in the Bernardsville house, and he and his new wife had a child, Suzanne, in 1931. Tony was not a regular visitor to the household, and he and his half-sister, known as Sukie, got to know one another only as adults, when both worked at the State Department. Dryden Kuser walked out on his second marriage two years later, after becoming enamored of another married woman, a secretary to a committee that he chaired in the state legislature. The revelation of this affair ended his political career. "I hardly ever saw my father," says Sukie Kuser. "He moved to Reno, where he could divorce his various wives. He had a drinking problem and a gambling problem." Dryden Kuser eventually married three more times. Although he inherited $600,000 when his mother died, sold real estate, and worked as a columnist for the *Nevada State Journal,* he was perpetually short of cash. As his nephew recalls, "He once created a manifesto about why everyone who owed him money should give him more, and they did. He was incredibly charming."

Before her divorce from Kuser, Brooke had been quietly seeing a married stockbroker, Buddie Marshall, a Yale graduate from a well-to-do family, whom she had met on a fox hunt. She was discreet for many years but conceded in an interview with the author Eileen Simpson in 1996: "I had an affair with him while we were each still in our marriages. My father, who heard the gossip about it, told me to break it off." She followed his advice. Buddie Marshall finally left his wife, with whom he had a daughter and a son, to marry Brooke in 1932, in a small ceremony at her apartment. Brooke had apparently been living above her means. "I was quite shocked when Brooke called Dryden and asked for a couple of thousand to pay off her debts so she wouldn't have to ask Buddy [sic] for it," Vieva Kuser wrote in a letter to her daughter many years later. "Of course, he obliged."

Tony, who was eight years old when his mother remarried, was very attached to his nanny, Madame Grumeau, who had been the one constant in his domestically tumultuous life. But Buddie Marshall disliked the woman, so Brooke fired her. When the newlyweds moved into a luxurious penthouse at 10 Gracie Square, Tony was exiled to a room built on the roof. But after a year or two, his mother decided that he was still too close for comfort. Abruptly announcing that Tony had become spoiled, she shipped him off to the Harvey School, in Westchester County, with her new husband's enthusiastic blessing. With typical understatement, Tony told me, "I didn't like it very much. I went downhill on a sled and ran into a tree. It put me back a bit." The accident nearly killed him; he suffered serious internal injuries, and the event left his mother with intense guilt.

Tony was starved for affection and attention. He was sent off to stay with Brooke's parents for months on end, and at least his grandfather always appeared happy to see him. Those memories were so important that when Tony was eighty-one years old, he regaled a roomful of Marine generals with a luncheon speech stressing his recollections of General Russell. "At the age of six I visited my grandfather when he was commanding general of the Marine Corps base at San Diego and flew my kite from the garden of Quarters One," Tony said. "The following year I spent Christmas with him and my grandmother at Quarters One at Quantico and he toured me about the base."

Brooke did not want more children and took steps to avoid having a larger family. "I'm totally for abortion," she told the *Guardian* in a 1988 interview. "In my day we said we didn't have it, but of course we just called it curettage." She was even more candid in a conversation with three women friends during a walk in Palm Beach. When the conversation turned to abortion, Brooke announced, "In my day, we called it a D & C, and I had three of them."

As a teenager, Tony attended the Brooks School, in North Andover, Massachusetts. Sam Peabody, a fellow Brooks alumni, recalls, "He was very shy, somewhat isolated, a middle-of-the-road student." Peabody remembers meeting Brooke and Buddie Marshall when they came to visit Tony at school. "I must admit, I'd never seen such an attractive mother. I think Tony was very lonely," Peabody recalls. "My impression was that he was incidental to his parents."

Tony did not see much of his biological father, and in 1942 he decided to change his last name to Marshall, though his stepfather did not legally adopt him. ("I did not have a very happy relationship with my father," he later explained to me. "I did have a good relationship with my stepfather. I admired him a great deal, so I decided to change my name.") A few months later he enlisted in the Marines. He had intended to finish high school and then go into officer training school, but after he consulted his grandfather, his plans changed. "My grandfather said, 'You're a poor student — the right thing for you to do now is to go on active duty,'" Tony recalls. "So he telephoned to Washington, and a week later I was in boot camp." General Russell also called the Brooks School and successfully pressured the headmaster to give his grandson a diploma, since as a dropout he would not have been eligible for officer training. This was the first of many times in Tony Marshall's life when family connections meant everything.

Tony went to war armed with military heirlooms from his grandfather: a machete crafted at the turn of century from a carriage spring, and a silver-barreled, pearl-handled .38 Smith & Wesson pistol. When his father learned that he had enlisted, he asked Tony to take out life insurance for $250,000, making him the beneficiary if Tony died in battle. For Tony, it seemed that he was more valuable to his father dead than alive.

Assigned to the Third Marine Division, Tony attended boot camp at Parris Island and was stationed in Guam, where he contracted dengue fever. After he recovered, the young second lieutenant led his Marine unit in the brutal assault on Iwo Jima in 1945. His company arrived on D-Day plus 2, the third day of the attack. After several days of fighting, Tony was wounded in the leg and the arm by shrapnel, narrowly escaping the fate of the 6,800 American soldiers who died on that island. "I led a platoon, and half of them were killed and the others were wounded when I landed my platoon at Iwo Jima," he said. "Because I was wounded, I was evacuated. I had shrapnel in my leg — I could hardly walk. I was put on a hospital ship, and then in a hospital in Guam."

Back in New York, Brooke worried out loud about the fate of her son.

As Louis Auchincloss recalls, "Brooke was in a dither. She was very emotionally fired up." Tony recuperated physically, but his mother wrote that he had nightmares for several years thereafter (though Tony brushes that off, saying, "My mother sometimes exaggerated").

After the war ended, Tony Marshall left the Marines. "I didn't really want to go to college. I had in mind writing, but I decided it would be better to get a degree," he told me. He enrolled at Brown University, in Providence, where he fell in love with eighteen-year-old Elizabeth Cryan, a pretty, lively freshman at Brown's sister college, Pembroke. They shared the bond of growing up in a one-parent family: Tony had an absentee father, and Liz had never known her father, who had died of a heart attack shortly before she was born. Liz and her two brothers had been raised by their mother in Switzerland, an upbringing that gave her a more cosmopolitan flair than her classmates. Four years older, Tony was a good-looking war hero with family money and an aloof persona. Liz later told friends that it was his loneliness that hooked her: she thought maybe she could fill that void.

In March 1947, General Russell died suddenly of a heart attack at age seventy-four, leaving an emotional emptiness for his grandson. Although Tony had known Liz for only six months, he vowed to marry her, and she accepted his proposal. She began to have doubts as her wedding day approached, but her mother pressed her to keep the date. Brooke vehemently opposed the marriage, arguing that the couple was too young. Tony, uncharacteristically, stood up for himself. His wedding ceremony took place in June 1947 in suburban Philadelphia.

Tony entered into his marriage with a substantial trust fund, believed by family members to consist of several hundred thousand dollars, a legacy stemming from his parents' divorce. When Brooke married Buddie Marshall, her alimony went into an account for Tony. She still thought the money should have been hers; she had earned it with bruises and a broken jaw. Buddie had an income from a family trust as well as a career as a stockbroker, but when he suffered a series of financial reversals, Brooke used guilt to induce her son to help out. Tony gave his mother a monthly allowance, paid to put in a swimming pool at Brooke and Buddie's country home in Tyringham, Massachusetts, and even bought his mother jewelry from Cartier and Tiffany. "She got a lot of money out of him," says someone who knew Tony well in that era. "She made him feel that this is money that she should have gotten."

In the flush of his new marriage, Tony attempted a rapprochement with his father, arranging a lunch at the Biltmore Hotel in Providence to introduce his bride. Dryden showed up drunk. And then the phone calls began, with Dryden harassing the couple for money. Dryden finally took Tony to court, suing over his trust fund. His argument was that since Tony had rejected the Kuser name, he did not deserve to have Kuser money. Tony won the lawsuit, but this was such a painful topic that he turned stone-faced when I asked him about it, saying, "I won't discuss this."

Both Brooke and Tony later wrote novels that included fictionalized elements of their emotionally complex relationship. In *The Last Blossom on the Plum Tree*, Brooke describes the conflicts between a rich widow, Mrs. Shrewsbury, and her ne'er-do-well son, Joe, who wants to be a writer and depends on his mother's handouts. "The boy was another of her problems. They had never wanted a child. When he was seven, they shipped him off to boarding school, and from then on, it had been school in the winter, summer camp in Maine, and finally, Princeton." When Mrs. Shrewsbury's lawyer, Wendell Ponderosa, suggests that she revise her will to leave money to a foundation for her son to run, the widow reacts with horror, saying, "Heavens! For Joe to run? You must be out of your mind, Wendell!" (Brooke Astor closed the Astor Foundation rather than pass the reins to Tony.) Mrs. Shrewsbury grudgingly comes to respect her son when she discovers that he has a knack for managing money, a task that Tony was performing adequately for his mother when she published this novel.

In Tony's self-published 2001 thriller, *Dash*, the sad-sack protagonist, Mark, is the solitary scion of a rich British family with a distant mother and a tyrannical, cruel father. "From his first spanking as he exited his mother's womb, Mark Baldwin Wynwhip was expected to live up to his heritage of near-royal lineage, a confusing agenda for the tot," Tony wrote. "As the infant developed into childhood he was regarded in both physique as well as in manner as a hereditary mistake." After the fictional father arranges to have the beloved nanny murdered, the young boy is sent off to boarding school. Tony writes of his forlorn hero: "He was lonely, friendless, forever hungry and physically exhausted when he rose each morning after a night in the clutch of terrifying nightmares."

Even after Dryden Kuser lost his lawsuit against his son, he was incorrigible. As Tony's first wife, now Elizabeth Wheaton-Smith, recalls, "Dryden used to call only when he needed money. It went on and on. He'd invent these stories — 'I'm in the hospital, I can't pay the bill.'" And Tony would obediently write a check. Yet another attempt at a father-son reconciliation was made in the late 1950s, when Dryden, newly sober, took his fifth wife to meet his son and daughter-in-law. "They came for dinner," recalls Wheaton-Smith. "Dryden was offered a drink, and he said, 'No, can I have some coffee?'"

Most children expect their parents to provide for them financially. But Tony's Kuser trust fund was a toxic lure for his divorced parents. Instead of fending them off, Tony tried to win their love by writing checks. Despite their patrician pretensions, Dryden and Brooke, both with a sense of entitlement, set an avaricious standard of behavior for their son. They used Tony, sending him the message that all tactics are fair, from emotional blackmail to legal wrangling, in grabbing for a family's fortune.

By the early 1960s, Dryden Kuser, ill with emphysema, had been reduced to a sinecure as caretaker at High Point State Park, more than 10,000 wild acres that his father had donated to New Jersey back in 1923. He went to see Mrs. Astor at her Park Avenue apartment to beg for money. Brooke savored the moment — the man who had ruined her youth was groveling, and now she held power over him. Despite her bitter memories, however, she chose to be magnanimous. "Brooke was supporting him at the end, and did she enjoy it," says Louis Auchincloss. "It's the ultimate satisfaction, supporting a person who has been mean to you. He was destitute. She couldn't let her son's father starve when she had millions." Kuser died on March 3, 1964, at age sixty-six. Neither Tony nor Brooke went to the sparsely attended funeral.

Colonel Kuser's once glorious mansion in Bernardsville fell into disrepair after changing hands several times. The place had degenerated into a Jersey version of *Grey Gardens* by the time that Clive Meanwell, a British pharmaceutical executive, and his wife, Cynthia, bought the house in 2001. During the renovation, a black luxury car with New York plates pulled up in front of the secluded property and a couple got out. "Who the hell is that man wearing an ascot?" Mrs. Meanwell exclaimed to her husband. Tony Marshall introduced himself and Charlene, explained that this had been his grandfather's home, and requested a tour.

Tony and Charlene walked through the rooms, lingering in the forty-foot wood-paneled ballroom and walking past the intricate bronze and iron stairway and the living room with its marble fireplace. For historical reasons, the new owners had retained elements of the old intercom system, which included Dryden's name on a button. Recalling his visit later, Tony smiled wistfully as he described the house's layout to me, saying, "They've changed things around, but if you go to the left, there's the room where my grandfather kept stuffed pheasants. I remembered that room."

Perhaps that house represented Paradise Lost to Tony, harking back to a time when his parents, although battling, were still together and a cherished nanny cared for him. Shipped off to boarding schools, disdained by his father and stepfathers, and frequently ignored by his ambitious mother, Tony Marshall never had the security of unconditional love. Only at age sixty-eight did he finally find happiness, when he married Charlene.

5

An American Romance

BROOKE ASTOR was never the kind of woman who traveled light. When she went to Palm Beach every winter, she chartered a Gulfstream to accommodate her extraordinary amount of luggage, and before her arrival in Maine in the summer, her staff would drive up a station wagon or two full of her possessions. Her red T. Anthony suitcases trimmed with black leather contained ball gowns packed in tissue paper, a dozen pairs of shoes, Chanel suits, and silk nightgowns. Her maid would carry the black case containing her jewelry. In addition to her female finery, Brooke always took along two gold-framed photographs, which she propped up on her bedside table wherever the bed might be. These mementos reminded her of who she had been and who she had become. The photos were of Buddie Marshall and Vincent Astor.

Mrs. Astor was not a self-reflective person, but her life was full of might-have-beens. Just a quick glance at those pictures offered a constant reminder of how her life had changed in an instant and the bargain she had made. She was Mrs. Marshall for twenty years, and then, bereaved and panicked, within a year she married a man she did not love. She stood by Vincent Astor for five and a half years, until his death. But the title Mrs. Astor was then hers for life, another half-century, with tens of millions of dollars as her due, and that had made all the difference. Faced with tragedy, she had forged a new identity, yet she still needed to keep Buddie's image close at hand, a reminder of what was lost.

His death had come without warning, on Thanksgiving weekend in 1952. Buddie and Brooke, along with her widowed mother, Mabel, were spending the holiday at their weekend spread in Tyringham, a hilly rural village in western Massachusetts. As she often described that day, the morning began with a cozy romantic scene, as she and her husband woke together and watched the sunrise from bed. He then went off to spend the morning hunting, bagging several pheasants. During the afternoon friends came by, and Buddie kept complaining that he felt cold, although the room was overheated. The family was sitting by the fire reading that evening when Buddie got up to let the dog out onto the back porch. Minutes later Brooke heard a sound, got up, and went into the kitchen. Her husband was lying on the floor, motionless. Whether he had had a heart attack or a stroke is unclear, but his death had been instantaneous. She cradled him in her arms until the doctor arrived and gave the official verdict.

To lose the love of your life is devastating. But Brooke soon learned that she had also lost her financial security. Buddie Marshall's family trust fund reverted to his two children, and his divorce settlement granted his first wife a one-third interest in his estate. Brooke was left with approximately $525,000, according to Frances Kiernan's book *The Last Mrs. Astor.* At a time when the average American family earned $4,500 a year, gas was 27 cents a gallon, and a loaf of bread cost 16 cents, this sum guaranteed an upper-middle-class existence. But to stretch that sum for the rest of a normal lifespan — what fifty-year-old could have imagined fifty-five years still to come? — would have required Brooke to change her lifestyle radically. She had been working as an editor at *House and Garden,* but that did not bring in enough to underwrite the country house, the New York apartment, the staff, the trips to Europe, and the designer clothes. Now that Tony was working at the State Department, he was dipping into his capital, so she knew that he could not solve her long-term problem. As someone who knew her well then recalls, "She was feeling poverty-stricken."

Enter Vincent Astor, one of the wealthiest men in America. He was descended from John Jacob Astor, a butcher's son from Waldorf, Germany, who came to Manhattan in April 1780 and hit it big as a fur trader, then plowed his profits into New York real estate. By the time his great-great-grandson Vincent inherited the bulk of the family fortune in 1912, Astor's sprawling real estate empire was worth $87.2 million and included luxury hotels, apartment buildings, office buildings, and slums.

But Vincent Astor's unhappy childhood had left emotional scars. His depression and suspicious nature proved a trial for all those who tried to love him, including Brooke Marshall. Never far from his mind was the memory of being locked by his imperious mother into a cedar dressing-room closet, where he wept for hours before he was rescued by a butler. He confided to Brooke that when he was four, his nanny had dressed him in a sailor suit and taken him to see his mother, who was having tea with friends. She reacted by saying, "Nanny, take him away, he looks perfectly horrid."

From birth Astor was portrayed as a poor little rich boy in the press. A *Washington Post* story in 1904 began: "Always Kept Under Guard: The boy has heaps of money, loads of toys, but cannot eat candy and peanuts and never plays like other children." Vincent, then thirteen, was described as a "captive" attended by five employees (tutor, valet, groom, bodyguard, chauffeur) and fed a bland diet. When he contracted the mumps, the event merited a newspaper story, as if the fate of the nation rested on his health.

His parents battled for years and finally ended their union with an acrimonious divorce, amid rumors that their daughter, Alice, was the product of Ava Astor's illicit affair. Vincent's formidable mother then married a British lord and became Lady Ribblesdale. Even as adults, Vincent and Alice Astor were frightened of their mother. "She was a tigress," says Ivan Obolensky, Alice Astor's son. "They were terrified of her. Things had to be perfect."

After attending St. George's School in Newport, Vincent Astor went off to Harvard with twenty suits, ten pairs of shoes, and six trunks. But his college days did not last long. His father, John Jacob Astor IV, had celebrated his freedom from a difficult marriage by marrying a teenage debutante, Madeleine Force, in 1911, and the newlyweds had headed off to Europe. When the couple learned that Madeleine, then nineteen, was pregnant, they decided to come back to New York. Sparing no expense, Astor purchased first-class tickets on a luxury ship boasting a squash court, a Turkish bath, and three libraries — the *Titanic*. Astor went down with the ship on April 14, 1912, but Madeleine survived, and four months later she gave birth to a son, John Jacob Astor VI, known as Jack. She had signed a prenuptial agreement that limited her inheritance to $5 million; her son received a $5 million trust fund. The bulk of the estate, more than $60 million, went to the firstborn son, Vincent, who was only twenty. He dropped out of Harvard to take over the family business and begin public life.

Besieged by women, he received thousands of letters from female admirers with dollar signs in their eyes. Uniformed police had to intervene to rescue him from hordes of women while attending a social event at the Seventh Avenue Armory. "The perils of being young, unmarried and very wealthy were emphasized tonight when Mr. Astor almost was mobbed by throngs of maids and matrons," wrote the *Washington Post*. For a shy, gawky, six-foot, four-inch man, this was torture. Eager for stability, Vincent married a childhood playmate, Helen Dinsmore Huntington, telling reporters, "She is a typical American girl. She has no foolish notions or new fads. Horseback riding and tennis are her favorite recreations."

Despite his sheltered background, Vincent Astor had developed a social conscience, and he was mortified when he saw the housing that had been built on Astor-owned property. Developers had put up shoddy buildings that had quickly deteriorated into slums known as "Astor Flats." "Mr. Astor was shocked at the conditions he found in houses on Astor land and decided to get rid of slum properties," a *New York Times* story recounted. Astor sold the bulk of those buildings to the city for a nominal amount.

That was a generous act, and there would be others in his career. "It is unreasonable to suppose that because a man is rich, he is also useless," said Astor, who established a well-endowed foundation "for the alleviation of human misery." But despite his magnanimous moments, he developed a reputation as a loner who favored machines more than people. He raced and wrecked automobiles; built and sailed one of the largest private yachts; installed a miniature railroad, Toonerville, at his Rhinebeck estate; supported early aviation; and was a director of a railroad corporation and a shipping company. He served honorably as an ensign in the navy in World War I, where his lungs were damaged by fumes during a trip home via submarine.

One childhood friendship that endured was with his neighbor Franklin Delano Roosevelt. When the president-elect wanted privacy to choose his first cabinet, he took his advisers for a cruise on Astor's 263-foot yacht. (After the boat docked in Miami, Astor and the others accompanied FDR when he went to give a speech. As the group piled into cars to leave, Astor, in the car behind FDR, turned to his companions and said, "Any crank might take a shot at him. I don't like this." Minutes later a deranged man, Joe Zangara, shot at FDR, missed, and killed Chicago's mayor, Anton Cermak.) Astor's close relationship with FDR merited a *Time* cover on April 9, 1934, entitled "Fun with Friends." The newsmagazine sniffed that the multimillionaire lacked "social confidence" and referred to his "awkwardness."

But Vincent Astor's lineage and bank balance proved to be powerful draws for the opposite sex. Astor and Helen, a classical music enthusiast, discovered that they had little in common, and the childless couple began to lead separate lives. At a Washington dinner party in 1935, Astor met Minnie Cushing, the oldest and most intellectual of the three renowned Cushing sisters, daughters of a prominent Boston surgeon. (The sisters married well and often: Babe Cushing paired off with Standard Oil heir Stanley Mortimer, Jr., and moved on to CBS founder Bill Paley; Betsey Cushing's first husband was James Roosevelt, the president's son, and her second spouse was John Hay Whitney.)

The still-married Vincent Astor began traveling all over the world on his yacht with Minnie, not bothering to conceal the relationship. In 1940, Helen Astor asked for a divorce. Three weeks after the decree was final, Vincent married Minnie in a small, secret ceremony on Long Island.

After five years of amicable companionship, the tensions between the couple started to show. The hypersocial Minnie liked to spend time in Manhattan with artists and writers; Vincent preferred a solitary life on his boat. In *The Sisters: The Lives and Times of the Fabulous Cushing Sisters,* David Grafton makes a persuasive case that Minnie Cushing Astor was a lesbian, citing a list of her likely lovers (the department store heiress Kay Halle, a French actress named Annabella, and another French actress, Valentina.) But Astor was apparently besotted, and the couple stayed together for thirteen years.

During World War II, Astor enlisted in the navy again, at age fifty, and worked in intelligence. He was named commodore of convoy. But despite this achievement, he was a hypochondriac who smoked and drank relentlessly, and after the war his drinking escalated. "The word got out that if you wanted to do business with Vincent, you had to do it before eleven A.M.," says his nephew Ivan Obolensky. Astor even scared off the neighborhood children. "I was terrified of him," says Reinaldo Herrera, a contributing editor at *Vanity Fair*. As a teenager, Herrera visited Alice Astor's daughters, who lived next to Vincent's Rhinebeck estate. "We'd be in the pool, and the butler would come and say, 'Get out, Captain Vincent is coming.' He was a scary gentleman."

But even the gloomiest personality can sparkle when combined with an awe-inspiring bank account and a touching dose of ardor. Six months after Buddie Marshall's death, when Brooke was panicked about her future, she attended a dinner where the guests included Vincent and Minnie Astor, both of whom she knew slightly. "I thought he was difficult. Everybody said he was," she told Charlie Rose in a 1994 television interview. "I made [up] my mind we were going to hit it off." At the end of the evening the Astors invited Brooke to their country home, the fabled Ferncliff, for Memorial Day weekend.

What a sophisticated and civilized pair they were, Vincent and Minnie, out shopping together for a replacement wife for Vincent. As Brooke later described the weekend, Vincent whisked her away for a drive in his Mercedes and proposed. He told her that Minnie had asked for a divorce and he had resisted, but now that he had met Brooke, he would be willing to go through with the divorce. Brooke always insisted that she resisted this snap proposal but was won over by Vincent's letters, which she found "beguiling." Decades later she would frequently pull out these letters and read them aloud to friends as proof that she had not married merely for money. "If you have the slightest doubt of my love of Brooke, I wish that you could at this moment look inside my head or wherever it is that emotions lie," Astor wrote in a letter included in the set given to guests at Brooke's hundredth birthday party. Barbara

Goldsmith says, "It was important to her to believe that Vincent loved her. I don't think she would have married someone if she didn't think she could have a relationship."

Vincent Astor's family welcomed Brooke's arrival on the scene. But Ivan Obolensky is convinced that Brooke's tale of the couple's courtship omitted an earlier meeting. "Vincent would go to this sanitorium to dry out, Silver Hill," said Obolensky. "She was one of the companions to jolly people up. She met him there. When you get a guy worth two hundred million dollars under your thumb, that's an opportunity. She was predatory." (Obolensky was a major beneficiary of his uncle's wills before Brooke entered the picture, but Vincent Astor subsequently wrote him out, which may explain his jaundiced view of the third Mrs. Astor.)

Did she love him? Louis Auchincloss, who knew and heartily disliked Vincent Astor, has repeatedly insisted that Brooke embarked on the union for purely mercenary reasons. "If she married him for his charm, I'd have said she ought to be put in an asylum," says the novelist, who has long chronicled the mores of Upper East Side aristocracy. "Vincent was an enormously unattractive, bullheaded man, no fun to have around whatsoever. He was mad for her. The people who say that marriage was not consummated are crazy. I just know that randy old goat certainly looked after himself." But Auchincloss was impressed at how well Brooke behaved once she married Vincent Astor. "It was a bargain, and she kept it. She was the only one of his three wives who made him happy. That was quite a job, but she did it."

Vincent Astor made a hobby of perpetually changing his will. In the Poughkeepsie, New York, courthouse, several file cabinet drawers bulge with versions of his last wishes. Less than four months after meeting Brooke, he wrote a new will, on September 24, 1953, which gave his "prospective wife Brooke Russell Marshall" the sum of $5 million plus ownership of Ferncliff. This was the equivalent of a prenuptial agreement, and her payout only improved over time.

When Vincent Astor and Brooke Marshall married, on October 8, 1953, the *New York Times* mentioned that "only a few relatives and friends attended the ceremony." The hastily scheduled wedding took place at Joseph Pulitzer's home in Bar Harbor, Maine, a remote location chosen to avoid the paparazzi of the day and minimize attention to the unseemly haste with which the widow was remarrying.

Brooke had been a social nobody, a well-to-do matron on the edges of the aristocracy. But now she was Mrs. Astor, with all that the name implied. Her husband owned the St. Regis Hotel and *Newsweek* magazine, and he was a major shareholder of the premier shipping firm, the United States Lines. A wedding day photo shows the newlyweds boarding Astor's plane to return home. Brooke is grinning happily, while Astor, a boutonniere in his lapel, is posed awkwardly, almost shyly, by his new possession.

Tony, then twenty-nine, was among the wedding guests, but his wife, Liz, did not make the trip to Maine. She was home caring for the couple's twins, Alec and Philip, who had been born prematurely on May 14. The babies were so small that the doctor warned they might not survive, especially firstborn Philip, who had a heart murmur as well as a partial harelip (which was surgically corrected, leaving a faint scar). Later, as fun-loving and affectionate toddlers, Brooke's grandsons proved an asset to her new marriage, as Vincent Astor became enamored of the boys. But he took an instant dislike to his new stepson.

Despite the tensions between the two men, they had interests in common. Proud of his war record and his role as one of FDR's advisers, Vincent was a patriot who believed in government service. After graduating from Brown in 1950, Tony had gone to work at the State Department as an intelligence analyst. His first government job paid a paltry $3,100 a year, but thanks to his trust fund, he and Liz were able to buy a nineteenth-century row house in the heart of Georgetown. Tony hoped to enter the foreign service but failed the arduous entrance exam, so he went to see General William "Wild Bill" Donovan, the founder of the Office of Strategic Services, the World War II spy agency that was the predecessor of the CIA. "I asked him what I should do. I wanted to get into civilian government, and I was a reserve officer," recalls Tony. Donovan arranged for Tony to take a job with the CIA as a roving recruiter.

The early days of the cold war were a heady time to be a CIA operative, and Tony, with his Ivy League background and sterling war record, had the perfect pedigree. After two years as a recruiter, he took the opportunity to become a special assistant to Richard Bissell, a rising star who would become the head of clandestine operations. Bissell had been put in charge of developing the U-2 spy plane, and one of Tony's assignments was to fly to Pakistan to obtain the government's permission for the U-2 to use an airstrip. He later recalled his time in the CIA as the peak of his career, according to Frances Fitzgerald, the Pulitzer Prize–winning writer, whose father, Desmond, was a major figure at the CIA. "Tony clearly loved those days," recalls Fitzgerald. "You got the feeling that he was a man of action, slightly frustrated by not having made it all the way."

Vincent Astor showered his new wife with jewels, and Brooke found herself spending time with his famous friends, including the *Time* magazine founder Henry Luce and his wife, Clare Boothe Luce; the Wrigleys, of the chewing gum fortune; and the three Rockefeller brothers. But the new Mrs. Astor was not universally welcomed by society. Winthrop Aldrich, now the deputy New York State commissioner for historic preservation, remembers that his grandmother Margaret Chandler, an Astor cousin, banned Brooke from her home. "She did not approve of the remarriage," Aldrich says. "Vincent drove by the home with Brooke and said, 'That's a place where you'll never be able to go.'"

Just as Vincent's grandmother Caroline Schermerhorn Astor had been in the 1890s, Brooke was eager to make her mark in society as a hostess. But although Vincent grudgingly allowed her to give one dinner-dance at the St. Regis for 275 people during their first year of marriage, he then drew the line. He made it clear that his fantasy evening was a quiet night at home with Brooke playing the piano for him. The marriage proved suffocating for Brooke, who later described her husband as so possessive that he asked her not to talk on the phone when he was at home. He wanted to see only his friends, not hers, and urged her to limit contact with her emotionally needy son. Brooke chose to appease her wealthy husband. "I saw very little of Tony," she wrote in *Footprints*. "I concentrated on Vincent. It was what he longed for and needed desperately, and what I had to give." She later described her married life as Mrs. Astor with a simple refrain: "I was lying fallow."

Brooke's first husband's alcoholism had been a problem, but this time she chose to ignore the fact that Vincent drank too much. At least Vincent was only a morose drunk, not a violent one. When Tony and Liz went to Ferncliff for a rare weekend visit, Brooke's daughter-in-law was astounded to witness the alcohol intake. "At ten-thirty A.M. the sherry came out. Before lunch the martinis came. Wine with lunch. At five o'clock the scotch came out, and then everyone went and changed for dinner. Dinner was martinis and wine, and liquor afterward," says Liz. She adds, "I was appalled, because Vincent was on a million medications. I remember looking in the bedroom once, and he had this chest of drawers, and the entire top was covered with medicines."

The Astors spent winters in Phoenix, and at Brooke's behest, Vincent purchased Cove End as a warm-weather retreat. The Rockefeller clan was based nearby, in Seal Harbor, and Brooke worked hard to fit in among the summering aristocrats. "Vincent had a boat called the *Little Nourmahal*," says James McCabe, a Philadelphia money manager whose father, a former chairman of the Federal Reserve, socialized with the Astors. "Vincent drank a lot. I don't think he felt comfortable being social."

But he could be kind when it mattered. After his sister, Alice, died suddenly, in 1956, Vincent and Brooke took two of his nieces to Maine for the summer. "He was tall and gruff and bearlike, but that was his appearance. He really did try to be nice to me," recalls Emily Harding, who declined the couple's offer to adopt her, choosing her older sister, Ramona, as her guardian. "He was always trying to joke with me and bring me out of my shell. He and Aunt Brooke seemed happy together."

Vincent also took Brooke's grandsons, Philip and Alec, to Maine for a summer of sailing, and welcomed them for weekend visits at Ferncliff. He sometimes took the twins on his private train, Toonerville, or hoisted them onto his donkey. Photographs from that era show Vincent smiling as he roughhouses outdoors, in suit and tie, with Philip and Alec. Brooke, sitting on the ground, maternally cuddles one of the boys in her lap. "Vincent had one of the early VWs, and his idea of fun would be to throw us in the back and drive around," recalls Philip. "He really liked croquet, and the professional rigors of croquet. He would teach us to play, and afterwards we'd go to the teahouse." Vincent Astor was so fond of the boys that on May 15, 1957, he revised his will to give Alec and Philip $100,000 each. He did not leave a penny to Tony Marshall.

Through their words and deeds, both Brooke and Vincent Astor created a family dynamic that gave Tony good reason to resent his own young sons.

Vincent Astor half seriously suggested to Brooke that they consider adopting her two grandchildren, whose parents were not getting along. Tony had come to regret marrying so young. Liz lamented that she had dropped out of college at Tony's insistence, and confided to friends that her husband had a wandering eye. He confessed to one affair, and Liz suspected several others. But they patched things up enough so that in 1958, when the CIA sent Tony to Turkey as vice consul for economic affairs, they decided to go together, with the twins.

Just before they left, Tony and Liz paid a farewell visit to Brooke and Vincent at Ferncliff. Brooke usually put on a good front about her life with Vincent, but on this weekend she chose to be honest. She took a walk on the grounds with her daughter-in-law and confided, "I don't think I can stand being married to him anymore. I don't think I can take it. He never wants to go anywhere — he's so antisocial."

Vincent Astor suffered from serious cardiovascular problems, a legacy of his damaged lungs and his smoking and drinking habits, and his health was deteriorating. There was a constant parade of doctors and nurses on the premises. Brooke's feelings about that grim period were reflected in the advice she later gave to Barbara Goldsmith, a fellow trustee of the New York Public Library. When Goldsmith's husband, the filmmaker Frank Perry, was diagnosed with terminal cancer, he reacted by asking for a divorce. In a heart-to-heart at the Four Seasons restaurant, Brooke announced to her friend: "You are the luckiest person in the world." The stunned Goldsmith replied, "I beg your pardon?" Brooke explained, "You had a very good marriage. I know you would have stuck with it until the bitter end, and it will be a bitter end. This way, you're forgoing all the nurses around the clock, the bedpans, all the craziness. You can walk away with your head held high."

If Lloyd's of London had taken bets on the longevity of the union between Vincent and Brooke Astor, who had five marriages between them, the odds would not have favored a silver jubilee. Rumors circulated that Vincent had also tired of Brooke and was on the verge of asking for a divorce shortly before he died. Ivan Obolensky heard that Vincent had gone so far as to contact his lawyer, Roland Redmond, to say, "I've had it — I want to divorce Brooke." Frances Kiernan writes in *The Last Mrs. Astor* that that conversation occurred while Vincent, Brooke, and Redmond were crossing the Atlantic by ship. In Kiernan's version, upon arriving in London, the remorseful Astor ordered an elaborate emerald necklace for his wife. Whatever the timing, he did not follow up on his threat.

Vincent Astor died of a heart attack at the couple's apartment at 120 East End Avenue on February 3, 1959, at the age of sixty-seven. His funeral, attended by four hundred mourners, took place at St. James' Episcopal Church on Madison Avenue. The coffin was covered with yellow jonquils and ferns, and the altar was obscured by 140 floral arrangements. A Who's Who of dignitaries attended, and a fifty-person choir sang Astor's favorite hymn, "Oh God, Our Help in Ages Past." Brooke later requested that the same hymn be sung at her funeral.

The contents of Vincent Astor's will were splashed across the newspapers. His estate was worth $127 million, $60.5 million of which had been left to his foundation. Astor gave $827,500 to other beneficiaries (including $100,000 to Emily Harding, $25,000 to his first wife, Helen, and $2,500 to each of his servants). Brooke became a rich woman, with $2 million in cash, $60 million in a trust for her benefit, and valuable real estate, including the couple's New York apartment, Ferncliff, and the houses in Maine and Arizona. She also received her husband's blessing to run the Astor Foundation. When Vincent had rewritten his will on June 26, 1958, he had eliminated the $100,000 bequests to her grandsons, Alec and Philip Marshall. Perhaps he assumed that the boys would inherit money from Brooke, or his initial affection had waned.

Brooke always insisted that she was not involved in Vincent's decision to revise his will in her favor. "He used to change his will constantly. It was a game with him — almost a social event — and it always put him in a merry mood," she wrote in *Footprints*. "I did not know or care about the will."

Other Astor family members had suspicions, however. Vincent's half-brother, Jack, promptly sued Brooke for a half share, insisting that Vincent had been mentally incompetent when he had signed his June 1958 will, during a stay at New York Hospital. Jack Astor charged that

Brooke and the estate's executors had used "undue influence" and that Brooke had taken liquor to her husband while he was in the hospital. Brooke hired as her defender David Peck, a partner at Sullivan & Cromwell, which was the beginning of a four-decade relationship with the firm.

Brooke's first act as the Widow Astor was to take the witness stand in pretrial hearings in a Poughkeepsie courtroom. She admitted that Vincent drank but insisted that he had been fully competent. She later recalled that Jack Astor's lawyer snarled at her: "'Vincent drank so much that he had a bottle of liquor in the hospital. Did you know that?' And I said, 'Of course I did, I took it to him.'" Jack Astor hired a forgery expert to examine the will. The sensational trial was treated by the press as a joke. "Please Help Poor John Jacob Astor" read the headline in the *Washington Post,* and the columnist Charles Van Deusen mocked the plaintiff's three marriages and his 270-pound girth. Just before a jury was about to be picked, Jack Astor settled for a paltry $250,000.

This was an awkward beginning for Brooke's new life as a woman on her own, although a touch of scandal had its allure. Now wealthy and free, Mrs. Astor celebrated with a classic symbolic gesture: she called in a decorator to change her sleeping arrangements. "Vincent Astor had died, and she wanted a new bed," recalls Albert Hadley. "It was my first commission for her." He designed a headboard upholstered in lettuce green silk, a color inspired by that season of renewal, spring. Mrs. Astor could now lie down alone between soft sheets on her new double bed and daydream about her fresh start.

6

White-Glove Philanthropy

WHEN BROOKE ASTOR showed up for work at the Vincent Astor Foundation at 405 Park Avenue, she had a surprising reaction: she became angry. Assuming that she could not possibly be serious about taking over, the men in charge treated her with disdain. She later singled out as her nemesis Allan Betts, the foundation's director, who expected to continue in his pleasant sinecure. "Vincent told me before he died, 'You're going to have a hell of a lot of fun with the foundation,'" Brooke told Peg Breen, the president of the Landmarks Conservancy, in a 1996 interview. "The people who were then running the foundation said to me, 'You can go on having a good time, take a trip around the world.' 'No,' I said, and sat down at this desk. 'I'm going to stay here.' Well, they didn't like that." In this prefeminist era (Betty Friedan's book *The Feminine Mystique* arrived four years later, in 1963), Mrs. Astor did not see herself as a pioneer, yet she acted like one. "I don't know whatever possessed me that I stood up to these two men — they wanted to run it. People came here to the office and asked for money, and they gave it," she continued. "I said, 'I don't want to do that — I want to see what I'm giving to. Maybe it's good or maybe it won't be good.'"

Philanthropists have varied motivations, from humanitarian concern to guilt over their riches to the social-climbing benefits of being on the "right" boards. Brooke Astor had at times regretted marrying for money;

the foundation offered her a chance to redeem herself, plus a way to make her own mark. Over the years, she had turned herself into the ideal cultured wife. "Brooke was perfectly aware that if she was going to circulate in the world of men, she needed to know about the things that interested them," says Philippe de Montebello, the director of the Metropolitan Museum. "So she learned about finance and international diplomacy. She could talk about art, about any subject. She read assiduously and avidly." Now she could build on that store of knowledge and use it for purposes beyond dinner-party chitchat.

Mrs. Astor started by giving relatively small grants that reflected her personal interests: literature and art, architecture and historic preservation. Since the Astor money came from New York real estate, she decided that it should go back to the city. Given Manhattan's role as the nation's media capital, this strategy also gave her foundation more visibility. A conscientious newspaper reader, Brooke Astor was engaged in the issues of her times, from the fledgling civil rights movement to Lyndon Johnson's War on Poverty. As someone who felt that she had been deprived of a good education, she was a soft touch for any grant proposal related to reading. In 1961, the first year that she was in control of the foundation, her grants ranged from $15,000 to the Boys' Club to $1 million to the United Neighborhood Houses of New York. In 1962 she gave $500,000 to convert the Arnold Constable department store to the Mid-Manhattan Library. In 1963 she contributed $25,000 to the Legal Aid Society to pay for lawyers to represent indigent teens. During the city's newspaper strike that year, when Robert Silvers, an editor, asked Brooke for backing to launch the *New York Review of Books,* she dipped into her own funds to invest $50,000.

Influenced by Jane Jacobs's book *The Death and Life of Great American Cities,* Mrs. Astor was inspired to improve slum housing by turning a concrete courtyard into a park and convinced city officials to let her experiment at the low-income George Washington Carver public housing development at East Ninety-ninth Street. A landscape architect was hired to install plantings, chess tables, and benches. This new gathering place was lauded as a success, and the foundation went on to underwrite a series of similar "outdoor living rooms." Soon Mrs. Astor was getting national attention for her efforts. "Brooke really came into her own after Vincent died," says Howard Phipps, the chairman of the Wild-life Conservancy, who served on the board of the Astor Foundation for eighteen years. "There hadn't been an Astor for a long time associated with philanthropy. She loved playing Mrs. Astor when she went out on her visits."

A lifelong Republican, Mrs. Astor crossed party lines to become friendly with Lady Bird Johnson and served on the first lady's beautification committee. "Mrs. Astor came frequently to see Mrs. Johnson," recalls Marie Ridder, Mrs. Johnson's liaison to her husband's Great Society programs. "She was enchanting. I encountered her once in the airport, coming to dinner at the White House. She said, 'Of course I'm coming — Lady Bird asked me herself.' She looked so chic."

Mrs. Astor did not believe that she had to dress down to be taken seriously. She was a regular patron at the weekly fashion shows at Chez Ninon, the custom couture shop. "She had this wonderful personality — she never came in with a sour face. She loved suits and hats, and she liked little sexy things," recalls Elizabeth Corbett, who began working at the store in 1960 as a model and eventually bought out the owners. "She would bring her mother. Her mother was a very elegant woman. She used to wear a hat with a veil and smoke her cigarette through the veil."

The rhythm of Mrs. Astor's life mimicked the Preston Sturges comedy *Sullivan's Travels:* Wealthy Park Avenue matron goes to Kenneth's salon to have her hair styled, meets friends for lunch at the Colony Club or the Knickerbocker, and then ventures in her chauffeured car to housing projects in East Harlem or the Bronx. The Mercedes pulls up, and Mrs. Gotrocks alights in a Chanel suit, white gloves, a hat, and a flash of pearls or sapphires. "I thought it was wonderful the way she was always perfectly dressed when she went to see all the places she was thinking of giving money to," says Nancy Reagan. "Brooke always said, 'They want to see Mrs. Brooke Astor — they didn't want to see me schlepping there in slacks.'" Mrs. Astor explained her sartorial philosophy again and again, with slight variations in the wording. "If I go up to Harlem or down to Sixth Street and I'm not dressed up or I'm not wearing my jewelry, then the people feel like I'm talking down to them," she told Marilyn Berger of the *New York Times.* "People expect to see

Mrs. Astor, not some dowdy old lady, and I don't intend to disappoint them."

As word spread that Mrs. Astor was eager to write checks for good causes, she was deluged with letters and new friends. With more than seven hundred grant applications per year, the Astor Foundation gave its blessing to about one hundred groups, although sometimes the checks were for nominal amounts. Mrs. Astor could pick up the phone and meet anyone in New York. "Brooke, to her ever-loving credit, figured out that the foundation could be a vehicle not only to do good for people but to make a name for herself," says Peter Duchin. "I think she really liked the name Astor."

In 1964, Mrs. Astor received the ultimate recognition that she had arrived when she was invited to join the Metropolitan Museum board, an exclusive old-money bastion where Jews and African Americans were persona non grata for decades. Trusteeships were typically passed down within families as sacred heirlooms. (Tony Marshall later joined the board, at his mother's behest.) The previous Mrs. Astor, Minnie Cushing Astor Fosburgh, was already a member. "There was consternation among people who worried about whether they could have two Mrs. Astors on the board," recalls Ashton Hawkins. But Brooke had the support of her predecessor. As Hawkins recalls, "Minnie told me later that she liked Brooke and supported her coming on the board."

At the Metropolitan, Mrs. Astor's interests were unconventional for the times. A member of the acquisitions committee, she was intrigued by Asian art, thanks to her childhood time in China, and she worked to expand the museum's collection. And she was genuinely eager to befriend the museum's staff. "She was not a snob," says Philippe de Montebello. "She went to the curatorial departments, and she knew the guards by first name. She was a people person. When other trustees talked about bricks and mortar at the board meetings, she'd bring them back to the staff."

Self-promotion is as ubiquitous in New York City as divorces once were in Reno. Brooke hired George Trescher to ensure that her good deeds and outings did not go unnoticed by the *New York Times* and the society columns. Liz Smith, whose items for the "Cholly Knickerbocker" column helped her launch her own syndicated column, recalls how things worked in those days. "I went to things, and George would put me in Brooke's way," she says. "He thought I'd be good for her."

Mrs. Astor never met a reporter she did not like, and she played the press game adroitly, often emphasizing how hard it was to get people to take her seriously. "If you are an Astor, people expect you to be silly and jangling bracelets," she told the *Washington Post* in 1966. She insisted that she felt an obligation to her former husband to do the right thing with the Astor money. "Vincent was a very suspicious man," she later told the Associated Press. "The fact that he had total confidence in me to run the foundation made me want to vindicate him, show him — wherever he is — that I could do a good job."

Although she always had a man on her arm, Mrs. Astor never expressed an interest in marrying for a fourth time. As she said to the Associated Press, "People have asked me to marry them, but I couldn't. The foundation was more important to me." After one happy marriage and two troubled experiences, she did not want to be tied down again. Watching two husbands die was enough, and she told friends that she did not want to wind up pushing an old man in a wheelchair. However, she was frequently infatuated with someone, and she confided in friends about her flirtations and romances: Laurance Rockefeller, a mysterious European, and, later in life, former treasury secretary Douglas Dillon, who shared her appreciation for Asian art. She told the writer Caroline Seebohm that she had turned down a proposal from Adlai Stevenson while they were hiking in Maine. "I knew he was hard up," Brooke was quoted as saying in Seebohm's biography of Marietta Tree, *No Regrets*. "I told him he did not love me. He agreed, but said that we were good friends and he hoped we might take it a little further." Brooke remembered the moment fondly, adding, "I still walk past the rock where he talked about it."

But Mrs. Astor cherished her name and her independence and kept serious suitors at bay. For company, she frequently turned to gay men. There was an endless supply of young men in the art world who were happy to escort her in the evening, board a chartered yacht, or take a gallery-hopping trek through Europe. Her secretary would send plane tickets; expenses were discreetly paid.

It was liberating for Mrs. Astor to be able to splurge on herself without having to ask anyone for permission. She sold Vincent Astor's apartment at 120 East End Avenue and bought two floors at 778 Park Avenue, taking the sixteenth-floor aerie with a terrace for herself and installing her mother on the floor below. She had long since forgiven her mother for marrying her off to Dryden Kuser and was committed to Mabel Russell's care, hiring the actor Frederic Bradlee (the newspaperman Ben Bradlee's brother) to read aloud to her (Mrs. Russell died in 1967). To decorate her new flat, she hired Sister Parish; Parish and her junior partner, Albert Hadley, later found a nineteenth-century British painting of black whippets for the wall, a discovery that launched Mrs. Astor on a quest to collect dog paintings and helped inspire a high-society trend.

Unable to have much of a social life while she was with Vincent Astor, Brooke made up for lost time by entertaining constantly at all her homes. "She made a big effort to be Mrs. Northeast Harbor," recalls James McCabe. In New York she was equally busy. To make her dinner parties distinctive, she instructed her chef to reverse the usual progression and serve hot appetizers and cold main courses. Potential guests were shrewdly assessed as she sought to mix the city's up-and-comers with the social elite. She was always subtle, but the nouveau riche couples who donated generously to her favorite charities were often graciously rewarded with an invitation to her home. To be able to say that one had dined with Mrs. Astor gave one cachet.

In the glory days of New York society, she made all the rounds. Of course she attended Truman Capote's masked Black and White Ball, given at the Plaza Hotel in 1966 for Katharine Graham, the *Washington Post* publisher. She loved making an entrance, and was once described in a society column as appearing "bathed in a glow of emeralds." Brooke Astor was even cited as a guest at Leonard Bernstein's notorious party in 1970 for the Black Panthers. She wrote an annoyed letter to the *New York Times* afterward, stressing that this was not her kind of scene: "I was invited to the party, as I imagine a whole list of New Yorkers were, but I did not attend."

As Brooke was becoming the fabulous Mrs. Astor, her son, Tony, was also reinventing himself. After returning from Turkey for Vincent Astor's funeral, he decided to leave the CIA for a more lucrative career in New York. He and Liz were still bickering. She relocated to Philadelphia with the twins to stay with her mother, but the separation was temporary, and the family soon joined Tony in New York. The couple bought a large fourth-floor apartment, with three bedrooms, a library, and an enormous living room, at 1030 Fifth Avenue. The Marshalls enrolled their sons at the Allen-Stevenson School and then the Browning School. Buddie Marshall's brokerage firm, Butler, Herrick & Marshall, took Tony on for a while, and he then set up two companies to do business in Kenya and Nigeria. Like so many ex-CIA employees, he had severed his formal ties but remained on call. "The CIA never lets you go," says someone who knew Tony well during this period. "After he left, they always kept in touch."

In 1961 Tony's fragile marriage with Liz finally broke down. Announcing that he wanted a divorce, Tony moved out. "I was desperately upset for the first six months," Liz says, "and then I realized that it was a blessing. We were wrong for each other." Liz went to Mexico for a divorce, accompanied by the twins and her mother, who suggested a side trip to visit relatives with a ranch in rural New Mexico. It's odd to take a trip to end a marriage and fall in love again en route, but at the ranch Liz became enamored with her second cousin, Craig Wheaton-Smith, an Oxford-educated geneticist.

The Marshall twins were eight years old when their parents divorced. "I don't think we saw it coming," says Philip. "One day Dad wasn't around, and then we were hanging in his new apartment. He saw quite a bit of us for the first few years. He'd take us to the park, and we'd go up to Rhinebeck with him for weekends and spend time there with him and our grandmother. My mother never talked about the divorce with us — she didn't want to drag us in. She never dissed my father — it wasn't painted as a 'mean dad' kind of thing."

When Tony married his former secretary, Thelma Hoegnell, known as Tee, in 1962, the wedding was held in Brooke Astor's living room, with the twins in attendance. But Philip and Alec scarcely spent time with their father after that event, even though he lived nearby; according to Liz's appointment calendars, the twins saw Tony only eight times in 1964. The next year Liz married Wheaton-Smith, who was divorced with two children of his own. The twins then led a schizophrenic life. Vacations with their father and stepmother involved trips to luxury spots such as Beverly Hills or stays with Brooke in Maine. "Visiting my father and my grandmother was a formal situation — it always required a tie and jacket," Alec recalls. Liz and Craig had less money and a rugged concept of family fun: driving cross-country with the twins to Wheaton-Smith's New Mexico ranch, with cooking equipment in the car and roadside picnics to save on expenses. The private-school boys spent summers mending fences and herding cattle.

The Wheaton-Smiths abandoned Manhattan for a suburb outside Boston and ultimately, in search of a cheaper and more rural lifestyle, relocated to Dorset, Vermont. The boys went off to separate boarding schools. In 1967, Philip, then fourteen and with a strong academic record, began attending Vincent Astor's prestigious alma mater, St. George's School in Newport. Toby Hilliard, a classmate from Texas, recalls, "Philip was artistic — he was well-liked and looked up to. He didn't have an agenda." At school he painted, and his interest in art became a bond with his grandmother. When Brooke visited friends in Newport, she would arrange to see Philip, and when he went to Manhattan, she would take him to museums and introduce him to curators. "For a lot of years, family didn't come first — she was busy with New York," Philip says. "My grandmother and I connected through art."

His twin, Alec, had a harder road. Alec struggled with dyslexia and had repeated second grade, so he was a year behind his brother in school. But at the Proctor Academy in Andover, New Hampshire, he thrived. Tony Marshall, a talented amateur photographer, presented the teenage Alec with an Agfa camera and showed him how to use the speed and aperture control settings. It was an insightful and influential gift. Alec is shy, and the camera gave him a new way to see the world, to quietly observe events rather than participate. Alec snapped family photographs that intimately captured candid moments, and he spent hours in Brooke's gardens creating Monet-like images of her glorious flowers, an adolescent hobby that later became a career.

Tony Marshall lacked role models for a father, and his upbringing led him to value proper behavior over displays of emotion. He has such a formal demeanor that he told his boys that hugging and kissing were not manly, a lesson that did not take. But he made an effort to stay involved with the twins, writing and calling and conveying interest. As Philip puts it, "I've got to give my father credit for trying hard, since he wasn't with us all the time."

While Americans reeled from the assassinations of Martin Luther King, Jr., and Bobby Kennedy in the spring of 1968, the society pages marched on. On June 16, just ten days after Kennedy's death, the *New York Times* ran an article headlined, "The Goal of Brooke Astor: Easing Misery of Others." The writer, Judy Klemesrud, described Mrs. Astor as "svelte, sixtyish, a swinging blonde grandmother with bright blue eyes that sparkle." Her two dachshunds, Benny and Judy Montague, leapt repeatedly onto Mrs. Astor's lap during the interview, as she complained about being treated as a dilettante. "I think I have to overcome quite a lot," she said. "Being Mrs. Astor, a lot of social workers are against you. They think you're a silly Lady Bountiful, who doesn't know a thing. When that happens I try to be as attractive as possible and win them over."

To stress her relevance, she brought up her interest in politics and race relations. She was that rare upper-crust Manhattanite who had actually been north of Ninety-sixth Street and to the South Bronx. She admitted to the *Times* that as finance cochairman with John Hay Whitney of Nelson Rockefeller's presidential campaign, she had advised the candidate: "Having a Whitney and an Astor on a finance committee for a Rockefeller seemed a bit much, but he didn't mind." She noted that she had recently accompanied Nelson and Happy Rockefeller and Laurance and Mary Rockefeller to Martin Luther King's funeral in Atlanta and described marching in the cortege. Klemesrud's piece ended by naming Mrs. Astor's favorite designers (Valentino and Mila Schön) and describing her relaxing weekends at her country home, where she "plays croquet [and] romps with her twin 14-year-old grandsons."

Mrs. Astor, who had given the reporter a Rockefeller button, worked hard for her Hudson Valley neighbor. If Rockefeller had won the GOP nomination and the presidency, a post in the new administration might have opened up for Tony. Tony had joined the board of his mother's foundation, but he had higher aspirations. Once Richard Nixon became the Republican standard-bearer, Brooke, according to her friends, made generous contributions to his campaign on her son's behalf. A year after Nixon took office, the president named Tony Marshall as ambassador to Madagascar, a volatile former French colony off the coast of Africa. "I'm sure that her contributions were a factor," says Henry Kissinger. Tony's half-sister, Sukie Kuser, who spent her entire career at the State Department, is blunter, saying, "Brooke bought the ambassadorship for him."

Just how much Mrs. Astor contributed to the Nixon campaign cannot be determined: full and accurate record-keeping began only after the Federal Election Commission was established in the wake of the Watergate scandal. According to transcripts of the White House tapes, Richard Nixon instructed his chief of staff, H. R. Haldeman, on June 17, 1971, "Anybody who wants to be an ambassador must give at least $250,000." As Louis Auchincloss recalls, "Brooke used to say that he was a great ambassador to Madagascar. I said, 'Have you ever heard of a bad ambassador to Madagascar?' She said, 'That's enough out of you.'"

Tony Marshall has a more elevated view of his diplomatic career. "I was a friend of Dick Nixon, I helped him in '64 and '68," he told me. "After he won the election, he asked me where I wanted to go to be an ambassador. I did not want to go to Europe. I wanted to go to Africa." After Common Cause, a public-interest group, successfully sued for information about Nixon donors who became ambassadors, it was revealed that Tony Marshall contributed $20,000 to Nixon's campaign in 1968.

"Suzy Says," the syndicated gossip column by Aileen Mehle, made mention of Tony's new job, with the assumption that readers had no idea who he was but might be interested because of his mother. The item referred to "Anthony [Tony] Marshall, Mrs. Vincent Astor's son." He could not escape that comma after his name.

William Fulbright, then the leading Democratic critic of the Vietnam War, held a confirmation hearing on Tony's nomination before the Senate Foreign Relations Committee on December 12, 1969. The senator lobbed softballs, inquiring how long it would take to travel to Madagascar ("You can make it if you hurry in about four days," Tony replied) and asking what language the natives spoke (French, Tony replied, noting his own "brushing knowledge" of Swahili). Tony's résumé, provided to the committee, seemed almost a parody of a clubbable man, listing eighteen memberships in organizations and private societies, including the Brook Club and Explorers Club in New York, the Metropolitan Club in Washington, the Chevy Chase Club in Maryland, and Buck's Club and the Royal Geographic Society in London. Asked about his occupation, Tony told the committee that "my principal interest was in food manufacturing in Nigeria using locally available raw materials." When pressed, he acknowledged that he ran a company that used cocoa, yams, plantains, and potatoes to make doughnuts and chips in Nigeria. He listed his apartment as his office address.

"Madagascar was not one of our critical posts," said David Newsom, who was then the assistant secretary of state for African affairs. "He had some Africa experience, and therefore he wasn't totally the new boy on the block." Pamela Walker, whose husband, Peter, a career foreign service officer, spent six months as Tony's deputy in Madagascar, recalls, "We wondered what Tony Marshall would be like, given his background, but he turned out to be a very good friend and a good ambassador." But she came away with the impression that there was tension between Tony and his wife, Tee. "They both were only children and both had difficult mothers," Walker says. "Tee's mother was constantly sick and needed to be cared for. I don't think Tee cared much for Mrs. Astor."

While Brooke rarely spent time alone with her grandchildren, she made an effort during those years, taking the teenage twins to Europe on a ski trip. They flew to Paris, where she took them to a cocktail party with Jackie Onassis and Sargent Shriver, and then went on to St. Moritz. "I had brought my ratty clothes, and my suitcase was lost on the flight," recalls Philip. "She took me to Pierre Cardin — I wasn't used to shopping. She got us each our own personal ski instructor, and would meet us back at the chalet for lunch."

After eighteen months, Tony's tour in Madagascar ended abruptly under mysterious circumstances. On June 1, 1971, local officials asked that he be sent home, and Tony left the country five days later. "He was persona non grata with the Malagasy government," recalls Sukie Kuser. "They said he was a spy — he had been with the CIA." A 1971 *Wall Street Journal* article titled "Little Black Lies: Spy Groups Increase Use of False

Material to Put Enemy on the Spot," led with the tale of Tony Marshall's ouster. The Malagasy government claimed to have received a secret document that implicated Tony "in a supposed coup planned against President Tsiranana," according to the *Journal*. The U.S. government dismissed the document as a hoax. The *Washington Post* noted that Tony Marshall "aggressively attempted to attract American business and ranching investment to Madagascar."

Getting booted out of Madagascar, even if the charges were fraudulent, did not boost Tony's stock at the State Department. His next diplomatic appointment was a distinct step down: ambassador to the tiny Caribbean islands of Trinidad and Tobago. Languishing in the tropics on an ambassador's yearly salary of $31,000, Tony donated $48,505 to the Committee to Re-Elect the President (CREEP) between January 1971 and March 1972. In January 1974, Nixon named him ambassador to Kenya, a post that he held until Jimmy Carter took office in 1977. "I suspect the influence of Mrs. Astor in the White House was not an insignificant factor," Newsom said drily.

Kenya was unquestionably Tony Marshall's most challenging diplomatic assignment. A former British colony, the country won independence in 1963 after the violent Mau Mau uprising and was led by President Jomo Kenyatta, whose regime was marred by charges of corruption and brutality. With American companies eager to invest and a large Peace Corps contingent in the country, Tony had his hands full representing U.S. interests.

"Tony was competent," says Henry Kissinger. On a visit to Kenya, Kissinger, Nixon's secretary of state, met with Kenyatta to discuss U.S. military aid, accompanied by Tony, and posed for the cameras on a safari, telling reporters that he had borrowed Tony's bush jacket. Declassified cables and news stories show Tony negotiating over American aid, protesting the expulsion of American businessmen, helping a high-ranking African leader get medical treatment in the United States, and flying back to Washington to brief the White House national security adviser, Brent Scowcroft.

During his time as an ambassador, Tony scarcely saw his sons, and he was furious when Philip ridiculed Nixon in a cartoon for the St. George's School magazine in the wake of the Kent State shootings. But after the twins went off to college — Philip attended his father's alma mater, Brown University, while Alec went to the University of Vermont — they visited him in Kenya. Brooke wrote to Tony during this period expressing her concerns about Philip and Alec and urging her son to be more involved as a parent. She was particularly troubled by Philip's rebelliousness and the lack of an authority figure in his life.

After the Democrats took over in Washington, Tony Marshall and his wife returned to New York, in the spring of 1977. He did some consulting work for Amoco and United Technologies, but ended up dependent on his mother once he took on managing her money in 1980 as a full-time job. "I was very glad to do it," Tony told me. "I discovered things were being mismanaged badly. The trouble was that a bank had all of my mother's money, which wasn't very much at the time, and banks, in my opinion, don't manage money well."

At the Vincent Astor Foundation, Tony took over an office right next door to his mother's. He placed some of her money with Freddy Melhado's firm and also invested in bonds, options, and stocks. Over the next twenty-five years, his rate of return lagged significantly behind the Standard and Poor's index. Monitoring these investments was not a nine-to-five job, so he had ample time for long lunches and to dabble as a writer. Linda Gillies recalls that Brooke was happy to have her son on the premises: "You could often hear them laughing together." As the secretary of the Vincent Astor Foundation, Tony kept an eye on the budget, but he never joined his mother on her trips to the slums or weighed in on grant proposals.

By then Tony was accustomed to seeing his sons sporadically. After college, Alec moved to New York to study medical photography, and at the last minute his housing arrangements fell through. "My father had plenty of room, but he didn't take me in," Alec says. "It would have disrupted his life." First as children and then as adults, the twins learned that if they wanted to see their father, they needed to make an appointment. As Alec puts it, "He told us when to arrive and when to leave."

During the years that Tony had been overseas, Brooke had been running the most famous salon on the Upper East Side. She had tepid feelings toward her son's second wife, Tee, which became more of an issue once the couple was back in New York. "The wives couldn't get along with her," says Sukie Kuser. "It got so that when he was married to Tee, they had separate holidays, he with his mother, she with her mother."

The publication of Brooke's autobiography *Footprints* in 1980 led her to grant another interview to the *New York Times*. She coyly told the newspaper that in the twenty-one years since Vincent Astor's death, she had received "lots of proposals" but preferred single life. "I'd have to marry a man of suitable age and somebody who was a somebody, and that's not easy," she said. "Frankly, I think I'm unmarriageable now. I'm too used to having my way." She mentioned her affection for her grandsons. "They were hippies to begin with," she said. "But now they've emerged and they both have paying jobs." Alec was then working as a medical photographer for Mt. Sinai Hospital, while Philip had just received his master's degree in historic preservation at the University of Vermont.

Even though the seventy-eight-year-old Mrs. Astor was reflecting back on her life, she was then in the midst of creating her crowning achievement at the Metropolitan Museum — Astor Court, a courtyard crafted in Soochow, China, and installed on the second floor at the museum. She had lived in China from 1911 to 1914 and devoted much of her memoir *Patchwork Child* to those years. She would often reminisce about a peaceful summer spent with Buddhist monks. Under Mrs. Astor, her foundation spent nearly $10 million to install the courtyard, which featured a skylight, a koi pond, and Ming Dynasty furniture, at the museum.

The *New York Times Book Review* described *Footprints* as "delightful" and "bubbling," but avid readers in Brooke's social circle thought her portrayal of Tony was cruel. She described him as a "spoiled" boy and an emotionally wounded war veteran who would "cry out in his sleep," and she admitted that she had not been a good mother. "A lot of us knew there had been difficult times between Brooke and Tony and he legitimately could have felt a little bit hurt by her autobiography," said Howard Phipps. In the closing pages of the book, she did write that "one of my great delights is my son Tony." But that did not atone for the pages that came before.

However, there were perks associated with being Mrs. Astor's son.

She used her clout at the Metropolitan Museum, the Wildlife Conservancy, and the New York public television station, Channel 13, to help Tony win seats on those boards. "She asked all of the boards to take him on as a trustee," says Ashton Hawkins. "They did it, swallowing hard."

Ronald Reagan's election in 1980 boosted Brooke Astor's already high profile, as she reveled in her close friendship with the president and the first lady. She threw a celebratory party at her apartment right after the 1980 landslide victory over Jimmy Carter. Nancy Reagan now fondly recalls the evening as "the party where Ronnie was under the table looking for Brooke's earring."

Mrs. Astor had dined at the White House before, but during Reagan's two terms she took the shuttle to attend state dinners so often that she might just as well have left a toothbrush in the family quarters. "A lot of people wanted to sit next to Brooke — she was so much fun," says Mrs. Reagan. "She'd stay at the White House, in the Lincoln bedroom. She was more of a night owl than we were. Ronnie was tired and we would go to bed." In the morning the two women would dish. "We'd talk about who looked pretty and who didn't and who did what that they shouldn't have. I felt like I could tell her anything." Brooke Astor was reticent about personal matters but quietly conveyed her disappointment with Tony. "I did meet him," Mrs. Reagan says. "You got the feeling that all was not happy, but I never questioned her about him. They just didn't have a good relationship."

Mrs. Astor made a point of summoning many of the friends who attended her fete for the Reagans — the Kissingers, William Paley, Douglas Dillon, Liz and Felix Rohatyn, Victor and Betsy Gotbaum — back to 778 Park Avenue for another gathering almost exactly a year later. This was, in a sense, a revenge dinner. Always in denial about her age, she had been furious when officials at the Metropolitan Museum invoked the standard policy requiring board members to step down to nonvoting emeritus status when they reach age seventy-five. Mrs. Astor did not want to go quietly into the New York night. Now she was giving a dinner in honor of Vartan Gregorian, the newly hired president of the New York Public Library. For her, this was the equivalent of taking out a two-page ad in the *Times* to announce that she had chosen the library as her new philanthropic cause.

Gregorian was charmed when Brooke paraphrased Thornton Wilder to explain her approach to philanthropy: "Wealth is like manure — if you collect too much, it stinks. You've got to spread it around." He describes their relationship as friendship at first sight. "She could talk about books, about people, about issues, about nature, about gardens, about African Americans," he explains. "My wife told me that if Brooke were thirty years younger, she wouldn't have trusted me." The library was so cash-strapped during those days that books were moldering from neglect, the doors were closed on Thursdays to save money, and neighboring Bryant Park had become a haven for drug dealers. Mrs. Astor gave an influential grant of $10 million, urged her friends to join her, and created an annual fundraising gala for the library that became a sold-out event where socialites mixed with raffish authors.

There was something touchingly personal about Mrs. Astor's involvement in the library. Just walking into the building made her happy. She admired the underappreciated librarians and started a tradition of sharing lunch with the staff on her birthday. While she did not single-handedly save the library, she was profoundly involved in its renaissance. "By virtue of her prestige and influence and ability to inspire people, she brought a whole level of interest to giving to the library by New York's social-philanthropic-economic circles," says Paul LeClerc, the current library president. "She made the place."

But for all her warmth and generosity, Mrs. Astor had developed an imperious side. As her courtiers learned, attention had to be paid. Her elegant mask slipped at home, since no woman is a heroine to her social secretary. "You had to be tough to work for her, because she went after people," says John Meaney, her chauffeur from 1985 to 1995. "Her favorite thing was to say, 'I just took a hate on them.' She knew it was irrational, but she could be erratic and harsh. She needed to vent, and the only people she could vent with was staff. Familiarity breeds contempt."

Like her predecessor Caroline Astor, the twentieth century's Mrs. Astor believed that all guests, no matter how high their station, should abide by her rules. She was not subtle in expressing her feelings. When she hosted a lunch at her home for Nancy Reagan, she was not pleased when the guest of honor was late. She broke with protocol by seating her guests and telling the waiters to start serving the appetizer. As John Hart recalls, "It was Brooke's way of saying, 'You don't show up forty-five minutes late for a lunch, even if you are the president's wife.'" Mrs. Reagan still recalls the experience with mortification. "It was traffic," she explains, by way of apology. "She went ahead and started lunch. I was glad she did. I was upset because I was late — I didn't want her to be upset with me."

All was forgiven. And a few years later, when Mrs. Reagan was going through a difficult time, her friend reached out with memorable words of comfort. "After my mother died, Brooke said to me, 'Now Nancy, I know nobody can replace your mother, but I'd certainly like to try. Anything I can do for you, anything you want, just think of me as your mother.' It was so sweet."

In truth, a younger woman was already playing the role of Brooke's surrogate daughter. This intimate relationship had begun in the 1950s and lasted for nearly half a century, with powerful repercussions for both women.

Annette de la Renta was a central figure in the drama during Brooke Astor's last years, yet despite her rarefied social standing (or, perhaps, because of it), she has always been a reclusive figure to reporters. It was not until the early days of 2008, six months after Mrs. Astor's death, that I finally arranged my first formal interview with her.

A butler answers the door at the de la Renta apartment, which occupies an entire floor of a Park Avenue building in the east sixties. An enormous Edward Lear landscape of Kilimanjaro dominates the marble-floored foyer. The sixty-foot living and dining room, which encompasses the entire width of the building, is sumptuous, with eighteenth-century English furniture, an Aubusson rug, yellow walls, and cranberry drapes. The room is filled with so many beautiful objects — a collection of little leather boxes, a Saint-Gaudens sculpture of Diana, two severe portraits of Elizabethan women all in white, a Géricault painting of a nude man, ornate side tables, pink peonies in a vase — that one's eyes dart around trying to take everything in. On this wintry afternoon, both fireplaces are ablaze.

Wearing a simple brown wool sheath dress from her husband's designer collection and brown suede stiletto boots, the sixty-eight-year-old Annette enters the room accompanied by her three dogs. The dogs are mutts, rescued dogs, and they jump all over the valuable furniture while Annette smiles indulgently. She has four more dogs at the couple's home in the Dominican Republic. There's something about stray dogs — "those eyes," she says — that tugs at her emotions. She has a fierce public persona, so her attitude to the dogs reveals a surprisingly soft side. "I would have twenty more if Oscar would let me," she says. Oscar later described how his wife noticed a stray dog by the side of the road while racing to the airport in the Dominican Republic and then repeatedly called to beg him to find the stray. "How am I going to find that one dog?" he asked with a tone of puzzled affection. A love of dogs was one of the many things that Annette shared with Brooke Astor, although Brooke favored pedigreed dachshunds rather than roadside strays.

Perching on a wooden chair by the fireplace, Annette presides over the silver tea service brought by her butler, Hans Dreschel, a family retainer for forty-two years. "Brooke was always a friend. She gave sage advice," she says. Although many mutual friends likened their relationship to a mother-daughter connection, Annette balks at the description. "I never saw her as a mother figure. She treated me as a contemporary. I had a fantastic mother, but one was enough."

If Annette's family history were fictionalized, the result would be a Harold Robbins potboiler about the super-rich combined with an Alan Furst novel about prewar Europe. Small wonder that Brooke Astor, the general's daughter with pretensions, would be drawn to Annette, who grew up in a wealthy Social Register family shadowed by tragedy and who took delight in breaking the rules.

Wildly rebellious as an adolescent, Annette famously rode her horse, Next Chance, into the living room of her parents' estate in Far Hills, New Jersey. Her friend Betsy Gotbaum, New York City's public advocate, who has known Annette since she was thirteen, recalls, "She was a hellion. She was mischievous, a lot of fun, and she still has that." There is a core of steel within her too. As Betsy's husband, Victor Gotbaum, adds with a wry smile, "I'm glad Annette is my friend, because I wouldn't want her as my enemy."

Annette's father, the German Jewish financier Fritz Mannheimer, was the director of the Mendelssohn Bank of Amsterdam and has often been described as one of the richest men in the world, but he died several months before Annette was born. Jane Pinto-Reis Brian, her strikingly beautiful mother, was born in Qingdao, China, the daughter of a Brazilian diplomat and his American wife, Ignatia Mary Murphy. Jane's father died young, her mother remarried, and Jane was brought up in Paris as a convent-educated Catholic. The twenty-year-old was pregnant with Annette when she married Mannheimer, an art collector who had filled his homes with Rembrandts, Vermeers, and Fragonards, at a ceremony attended by the French finance minister Paul Reynaud. Already in poor health, Mannheimer died two months later, in August 1939, at the age of forty-nine. His death, on the cusp of World War II, unleashed havoc in the European financial markets. Although physicians listed a heart ailment as his cause of death, rumors still abound that he committed suicide. The day after he died, his bank went bankrupt.

A *New York Times* obituary described Mannheimer as a genius in currency manipulation and so influential that "when the Nazi regime made it impossible for him to live in Germany, he obtained Netherlands citizenship by act of Parliament." Based in Paris, Mannheimer, a grand officer of the Legion of Honor, made large donations to the French government's national defense fund. A *Time* obituary drew on anti-Semitic caricatures to portray him as brilliant and controversial, a "cigar-smoking German Jew . . . No one ever liked Fritz. He was too smart. During the War [World War I], barely out of college, he got a job in the German Government bureau directing the flow of raw materials through Germany. In no time, he headed it." The magazine noted, "His was the last Jewish-owned bank allowed to do business in Germany."

After Annette was born, with the patriotic given name of Anne France, in December 1939, Jane left the infant with her mother in Cannes and fled to Argentina and then New York. She retrieved her baby a year later, during the Nazi occupation of France. Jane Mannheimer had inherited a microfilm company that copied U.S. war records, and she joined the firm as a vice president for marketing. Her legacy was Mannheimer's extraordinary art collection, but she had to battle both his creditors and Nazi impounders to obtain a mere three paintings. By 1942, Jane had become a glamorous figure in New York society. Statuesque and exquisitely dressed, she was one of those rare women of whom it can truly be said that she walked into a room and conversations stopped.

Jane Mannheimer made a fortuitous marital match to Charles Engelhard, a globe-girdling industrialist who traded in precious metals. Engelhard, a man of large appetites, did everything in a big way. He owned a string of 250 racehorses, including the legendary Nijinsky, winner of the Triple Crown. He turned his family's business into a personal fortune worth more than $300 million. He evaded India's ban on gold bullion exports by making "pure-gold bracelets and other trinkets that were just as quickly melted back into bars once they arrived as such destinations as Hong Kong," according to the *Wall Street Journal.*

Settling down in the horse country of New Jersey where he had been raised, Charles Engelhard adopted his young stepdaughter, and he and Jane went on to have four more daughters. The former Jane Mannheimer behaved as if she had never had an identity before becoming Mrs. Engelhard in deference to her husband's wishes. Annette's half-sister Susan, seven years her junior, says, "I didn't know Annette wasn't a full sister until I was thirty or forty years old. We knew my mother had a previous life, but we never went there. Our mother never talked about it." Oscar de la Renta, ever protective of his wife, adds, "People think Annette is in denial about her father. But she never knew him, and her mother would not tell her about him." Expressing regret that Fritz Mannheimer will be forever unknown to her, Annette says, "As far as I was concerned, my father was Charles Engelhard."

Cragwood, the family's estate in Far Hills, was a Georgian brick manor house with a staff of twenty. *Town & Country* described the property as so extensive that "one could not infer the existence of another human settlement in the state of New Jersey." Charles Engelhard collected properties the way his wife collected Monets and Picassos. There was the fishing camp on the Gaspé Peninsula, an estate in Boca Grande called Pamplemousse, a seaside home in Dark Harbor, Maine, an apartment in London, and a game park in South Africa, where he had mining interests.

In New York during the 1970s, Brooke Astor and Jane Engelhard moved in the same world, from serving on the board of the Metropolitan Museum to regularly visiting Miss Craig, the fitness instructor at Elizabeth Arden. The two women could have easily been social rivals, but they chose to become friends (although the couture dressmaker Elizabeth Corbett admits that they checked with her to make sure they did not purchase the same gowns). With so much in common — childhood in China, a love of art, widowhood followed by marriage to a fabulously wealthy man, a desire to be influential rather than merely decorative — they came to appreciate each other's company. Robert Silvers, the editor of the *New York Review of Books*, recalls, "Brooke admired Jane, and she thought that Jane had created a little duchy in New Jersey."

Annette came of age with a strict mother who was the family disciplinarian and an indulgent father who gave her free rein. "Her stepfather adored her — he was fun and he let us do everything we wanted," recalls Gotbaum. "Her mother was quite formidable. She scared me." The Engelhard parents traveled constantly, and once their daughters were old enough for boarding school, they saw each other mostly during summers and school vacations. "We had the nannies and the tutors and the servants," recalls Susan O'Connor. "Our parents were very busy with their own lives."

With a mother on the best-dressed list and photographed by Cecil Beaton and Horst for *Vogue*, Annette rebelled via food, eating her way into plump adolescence. At Foxcroft, the exclusive girls' boarding school in Middleburg, Virginia, her roommate Elise Lufkin recalls, "She'd make everybody laugh in class, and teachers would be irritated. She looked very different than she does today. She got very thin when she was seventeen."

Annette slimmed down in time to be presented as a debutante in the 1957–58 season. After spending a year in Paris studying art, at age twenty she married Samuel Pryor Reed, a Trinity College graduate whose prominent parents, Joseph and Permelia Reed, had turned Jupiter Island, Florida, into an exclusive WASP retreat. As the ruler of the Jupiter Island Club, Permelia Reed was famous as a social arbiter and for being shamelessly anti-Semitic. "People practically committed suicide because she wouldn't give them the time of day," wrote Liz Smith in her book *Dishing*. But Annette was well equipped to deal with her imposing mother-in-law. "I loved her and she loved me," says Annette, who was raised Catholic. "You always knew where you stood with Permelia."

Charles and Jane Engelhard were devoted Democrats — Jane helped Jacqueline Kennedy redecorate the White House — and the couple's parties at Cragwood were legendary for their extravagance. Dinner guests still recall the stacks of gold Krugerrands used as table decor and given away as party favors.

Living in Manhattan, Annette and Sam, who worked for his father-in-law, attended a dinner at Cragwood honoring the Duke and Duchess of Windsor. Oscar de la Renta, then designing clothing for Elizabeth Arden, had been invited, along with his wife, Françoise, because they knew the royals. Oscar recalls, "They served this enormous chocolate cake for dessert, but no one touched it." He too declined, but he asked Annette what would become of the cake. "She took me into the pantry," he says, and they gorged like children. The Reeds and the de la Rentas were soon vacationing together and always seemed to be the best of friends.

As a society phenomenon, Annette was profiled by the *New York Times* in 1967 along with her friends Mica Ertegun and Chessy Rayner. "They Look Alike, They Dress Alike, They Like Each Other Very Much" read the headline. Looking radiant in a Maximilian mink coat, Annette, then the mother of two children (Beatrice and Charles, and later there would be Eliza), was described as living in a ten-room apartment, having a Swiss nanny, and boasting a size 6 figure. "They are among the current crop of switched-on young matrons," gushed the *Times*. "They know what to do before everyone does it, what to wear before it becomes popular, and where to go before the hordes descend."

When Charles Engelhard, who was morbidly overweight, died of a heart attack in 1971 at his Florida home, at age fifty-four, Annette lost the only father she had known. Jane Engelhard created the Charles W. Engelhard Court at the Metropolitan Museum in her husband's honor and forged on — just as the widowed Brooke Astor had — by taking on new challenges, such as serving as the first woman member of the Port Authority of New York and New Jersey. In the years ahead, Annette's four younger sisters chose to make their lives away from their mother's sphere of influence, but Annette stayed within her mother's social world.

Relationships often build slowly, as small moments accumulate. Brooke Astor had watched Annette grow up and was drawn to her tart-tongued wit. By the early 1980s, Mrs. Astor had begun to reach out a welcoming white-gloved hand, offering uncritical friendship. "Annette was unquestionably the brightest, most cultivated, most humorous and good-hearted of the ladies whom Brooke knew," says the writer John Richardson. As Florence Irving, a Metropolitan Museum board member, adds, "Brooke was a better mother to Annette than Annette's own mother. Brooke was available, she paid attention." Extremely shy, Annette, with Brooke, could allow herself to be both warm and mercilessly funny. Randy Bourscheidt, New York's deputy cultural commissioner in the 1970s, watched their friendship evolve and says, "They could be unguarded — they trusted each other. More than anything, they laughed together."

Their relationship intensified as Jane Engelhard began to withdraw from public life, resigning from her boards. Annette took her mother's place at the Metropolitan Museum in 1981. Jane began to spend more and more time in Nantucket and finally moved there full-time. "Jane gathered into herself," recalls Robert Silvers. "She had frail health and trouble getting around." Annette, then in her early forties, was ready to take on a more public role. "When my mother moved to Nantucket, Annette took her place as Mrs. Astor's friend," says Susan O'Connor, adding that her older sister also took on the family mantle in society and in philanthropy. "She stepped right into my mother's shoes in a big way."

Brooke encouraged Annette's election to the boards of Rockefeller University and the New York Public Library. Although Annette was not as diplomatic as her mentor — "She does not suffer fools gladly," says an acquaintance — she made herself indispensable at the Metropolitan Museum.

Oscar and Françoise de la Renta were regulars at Brooke's table during this time. All the ladies loved Oscar: his Latin warmth lit up a room, and his lush creations made their wearers feel sensuously elegant. When Françoise died of cancer in 1983, Oscar turned to Annette for comfort. "My wife died at four A.M. and I called Annette at six A.M. and she didn't leave my side for twenty-four hours," he recalls. It was an Upper East Side scandal when Annette left Sam Reed, a quiet man with the perfect pedigree, for this exuberant foreigner who had built a multimillion-dollar garment district company. The divorce was treated as a news story with major repercussions. In *Manhattan Inc.* magazine, Julia Reed outlined the resulting succession crisis in society: "Astor herself had chosen Annette Reed to carry the torch, but Reed left her husband, as well as her status as a serious contender, when designer Oscar de la Renta caught her eye."

That was a prediction that did not stand the test of time. Brooke loyally gave her blessing to her friend's divorce and remarriage. "It was unpleasant," Annette says. "It's always unpleasant when you leave your husband. Brooke was the first to come to call on me. She said that she was sorry that it had gotten into the papers. She was very supportive of me and Oscar."

Oscar and Annette, who married in 1990, treated Brooke as a beloved member of the family and always tried to think of new adventures when she visited them in the Dominican Republic. Betsy Gotbaum recalls Brooke's reaction when the couple arranged for houseguests to swim with the dolphins, saying, "I was a little nervous, but Brooke was the first one in the water." On another visit to the island, Oscar organized a helicopter trip to take Brooke to Santiago, where her father had been stationed as a Marine general. "Brooke was clinging to a portrait of her father when we arrived, and she started to cry," Oscar de la Renta recalls. What Silvers, who was also visiting, remembers is the army band in full red-uniformed regalia which magically appeared, as arranged, to serenade Mrs. Astor. As he recalls, "They were playing 1930s swing songs for her — 'It Had to Be You.'"

As Brooke Astor reached her nineties, she worked hard at remaining contemporary. During the 1992 presidential campaign, she summoned Tom Brokaw to lunch at the Knickerbocker Club to discuss his political coverage. As the anchorman recalls, "She leaned over and tapped me on the knee and said, 'Thomas, lay off on this stuff about Bill Clinton and his girlfriends.'" Brokaw told her that he was surprised she was taking such an interest. "It doesn't mean that I'm going to vote for him, but every man is entitled," she said. Then Mrs. Astor mischievously added, "Of course, he should be having affairs with Hillary's friends, not with that trailer trash." Arthur Schlesinger, Jr., quoted Mrs. Astor as saying to the Democratic powerhouse Pamela Harriman, "Why couldn't Mr. Clinton have stayed with girls of his own class?"

Brooke Astor did not object to other people's messy romantic lives, but her attitude was different toward her son's misadventures. She was genuinely upset by Tony's decision to leave his second wife for Char-lene Gilbert, whom he married in 1992. For decades she had dangled before her son the possibility that he would inherit her role as head of the Vincent Astor Foundation. Given her obsession with control, per-haps she never intended to let him take over, but Brooke's friends be-lieve that Tony's third marriage lowered the odds. Board members watched from the sidelines as Brooke and Tony struggled over his fu-ture role. "I think there was a moment when they were in real disagree-ment about what would happen with the foundation," says Howard Phipps. "It was not clear that she wanted to entrust Tony to manage things and advise her and play that role with the foundation forever."

She offered the job instead to Viscount William Astor. "She always wanted it to remain an Astor Foundation," Lord Astor recalls. "Tony was always trying to get a bit of it. She said to me, 'Would you take the foundation on?' I said, 'If you want it to be for things in New York, no.' I was in England. I told her to wind it up, which she decided to do."

Mrs. Astor had started to grow forgetful, which was becoming an in-creasing problem for those in her orbit and employ. "She unraveled to the point that I had to talk to her son," says John Meaney, dating the problem back as far as the early 1990s. "Tony was so intimidated by her: 'She's my mother, what can I do?' She was a mess, rattled, confused. She was clearly slipping, but then she willed herself back."

By 1996, however, even the indomitable Mrs. Astor, then ninety-four, was feeling her age. The Metropolitan Museum staff would meet her at the entrance with a wheelchair so she could avoid the long walks down the corridors. But she retained her competitive spirit. Awaiting the arrival of the ninety-nine-year-old Madame Chiang Kai-shek for a reception at Astor Court, she ordered Philippe de Montebello to scout out the situation, because she was worried about being upstaged. As he recalls, "Brooke said, 'Go out and see if Mrs. Kai-shek is in a wheelchair.' So I went around the corner, and came back and told Brooke, 'She's not.' The speed at which Brooke got out of her wheelchair was amazing."

But that autumn Mrs. Astor was finally forced to acknowledge her mental decline. For several months she and Linda Gillies had been discussing a major grant for an after-school program. But one Friday afternoon, when Gillies broached the topic, Brooke went completely blank and asked, "What project?" Gillies tried to finesse the situation, but Mrs. Astor was shaken by her lapse of memory. She spent the weekend at Holly Hill considering her options, and early on Monday morning she called Gillies and requested a meeting. Mrs. Astor arrived at the office and without pleasantries announced that she had decided to close the Astor Foundation. She would spend down the remaining funds in the next year, and the doors would shut in 1997. Making her decision public, Brooke explained her reason for closing the foundation in an interview with the New York Times reporter Geraldine Fabrikant in December 1996. "My son is not an Astor," Mrs. Astor said. "There is no family to leave it to. If you have children, like the Rockefellers did, you leave it to your children. If you have no children, I think it's a nice idea to close it." Her only child was sitting right beside her as she made these comments. Tony Marshall told Fabrikant that he supported his mother's decision, saying, "I would hate to second-guess 'Is this something that my mother would like to give to?'"

Without the foundation's work to keep her busy, Brooke Astor appeared unmoored. She continued to make her social rounds night after night, but she had lost her sense of purpose. As one of her staff members recalls, "I'd see her pull herself together and go out with people and maintain her graciousness, but at the end of the night, she'd empty out like a paper bag — she'd gotten through the evening."

For Tony, his mother's decision to close the foundation marked the end of his hopes of becoming a major New York philanthropist. He continued to manage his mother's money, signing the checks to pay for her expenses. Brooke Astor had always lived well, and her son looked askance at her extravagance. This was a theme in the mother-son relationship that Brooke's friends had been hearing about for years. "He was always giving her grief that she shouldn't spend so much money," recalls Robert Pirie. "She'd say to me, 'When Tony finds out how much I spent in England this trip, he's going to have a fit.'" Like many of Brooke's friends, he thought Tony's complaints were inappropriate. As he puts it, "Whose money was it? It wasn't his." But Tony knew that much of the money would eventually be his. It was just a matter of time. Given Brooke's remarkable longevity, however, each minute seemed to last an hour, and her son's life was ticking away too.

7

The Perils of Charlene

SUMMER MORNINGS in Northeast Harbor, Maine, have a quiet, magical feeling. The sun on the water, the birds in the trees, the profusion of blossoms in the gardens, make for an enchanting ambience. If the fog lingers, the salt-scented sea air and the swirling mist create a mysterious intimacy. Although Brooke Astor was a night owl in Manhattan, she always rose early at Cove End to savor the pleasures of island life — a morning swim, a walk with her dogs, or a stroll around her garden. But during her last summer there, in 2002, she slept in most mornings. She was, after all, one hundred years old. In her second-floor bedroom overlooking a quiet ocean cove, the floral drapes were closed to block out the sunlight, and she wore a sleep mask.

When Mrs. Astor awoke in her antique four-poster bed, usually around 9:30 A.M., she rang a buzzer to summon her maid. The maid would open the drapes, help her into a robe, and bring her breakfast in bed. She drank hot water with a sugar cube dissolved in it, but even though the cook tried to tempt her with fresh fruit or eggs or Cheerios, she never ate very much. Her dachshunds, Boysie and Girlsie, slept beside her at night, one under the covers, one by her feet, and in the morning she let them nibble from her plate.

Maine had been Brooke Astor's sanctuary for more than a half-century. She had visited nearby Bar Harbor during her marriage to Dryden

Kuser, then returned as a divorcee and fallen in love with the pines and the mountains and the ocean. The house that Vincent Astor purchased at her urging was modest for a man of his wealth, but the shingled cottage was on the water, with two separate guest cottages and space for a half-acre garden, and was about a five-minute stroll from the quaint Main Street.

Mrs. Astor had been summering in this tiny resort community for so long that three generations of local families had come to know her. Although she imported her own staff from New York and employed a few full-time Maine workers, each summer she hired extra cooks, maids, and gardeners. She wanted her constant stream of houseguests to feel cosseted — to have their clothes unpacked and pressed and to be served whatever special requests they had for meals. "Maine was perfect," recalls Judy Miller, a former *New York Times* reporter who visited several times with her husband, Jason Epstein, a highly respected Random House editor and one of the founders of the *New York Review of Books.* "Everyone in town knew her. You'd walk down the street, and it would be, 'Oh, Brooke,' every few steps." Adds Barbara Walters, "The house in Maine had the most glorious garden I've ever seen. Brooke and I would sit on the porch and read. She'd walk a great deal on the Rockefeller estate. She walked too fast for me."

Mrs. Astor was a local fixture in her straw hat and white gloves, marching proudly in the Memorial Day parade, popping into the library, visiting the shops on Main Street, and attending Sunday services at St. Mary's-by-the-Sea. Betty Halpern, a clerk at the Kimball Shop on Main Street, remembers watching her shop with Barbara Walters in tow. "They were fighting over who would buy this white embroidered negligee for the other," she says. Walters won, but Mrs. Astor then had the shop order and ship a duplicate to the anchorwoman. Mrs. Astor would also impulsively purchase gifts for her help. "She'd pick out something pretty for her housekeeper too," says Halpern. In the late 1990s she gave a party to thank the year-round townspeople, such as the assistant fire chief and the ambulance drivers. "This party was not for the big summer names but people who were precious to her," says Bob Pyle, the town librarian, who helped her draw up the guest list. "She used a different caterer, because her usual caterer was a guest."

Pedestrians and fellow motorists had been mesmerized and terrified by the sight of Mrs. Astor tearing down the streets in her gold Opel, "old pal," and its replacement, a fire-engine red Ford Escort. As Judy Miller puts it, "She was hell on wheels." After several fender-benders, the police chief, along with her anxious friends and staff members, finally dissuaded her from taking the wheel. "She was terrible — went a mile a minute, bounced off curbs," recalls Freddy Melhado. "When she turned ninety-five, I started inventing everything I could to keep her out of the driver's seat. I'd say, 'You don't want to drive, it's a bore.' She'd look at me, her fists clenched, and say, 'You would deny me the thing I like most in the world.'"

Mrs. Astor had prided herself on her vigor and had continued to hike up Parkman Mountain well into her nineties, but by 2002 even climbing a flight of stairs was difficult. In 1997 she had tripped and fallen in the ladies' room at the American Museum of Natural History in New York, breaking her hip. Tony and Charlene worried that Maine had become too difficult for her. "They wanted me to dissuade her from going," says Naomi Packard-Koot, Brooke's social secretary. "They said she wouldn't be able to get around the house. But I had tea with her in the library one day, and she kept talking about how much she loved Maine. So I made it my mission to make it happen." Packard-Koot arranged to have a chairlift installed on the Cove End stairwell prior to Mrs. Astor's summer visit.

In 1995 Brooke had sold her rugged, wild 100-acre Maine camp, August Moon, a painful acknowledgment that her hiking, rambling, and ocean swimming days were over. She added a lap pool to Cove End. She had always proudly boasted that she swam a thousand strokes a day, and even now she managed to get into the water in an effort to keep her aged limbs in working order. Fiercely independent, she still insisted on privacy when in the pool, but her staff tried to keep an unobtrusive watch on her.

Her mornings had a ritual quality these days. After breakfast, she would summon her housekeeper, Alicia Johnson, who loved animals as much as she did. "She would be sitting there with her dogs by her side," recalls Johnson. "I would go up and ask her plans for the day — was she going out, was she having friends for dinner, and if so, who would be seated by whom. Then she might go into the living room and read her mail." When Johnson had begun working at Cove End, ten years earlier, Mrs. Astor would arrive from New York with ten suitcases, and on many evenings there would be a sit-down dinner for as many as twenty-six people. The house was stocked with twenty complete sets of china — Wedgwood, Limoges, Valentino, and a precious gold-edged set that had been a gift from Nelson Rockefeller — and each season the Astor silver would be retrieved from a bank vault.

The phone rang all day long back then, with calls from friends near and far. The staff logged in the messages: "Mrs. de la Renta sends you lots of love." "Mr. Marshall arrived safely and will call in the morning." "Reverend Paul Gilbert called." "Patricia phoned to say the flowers you have sent for the church in memory of Captain Astor are wonderful." "Pamela Harriman is arriving." "Gregory Long said to tell you he loves you and will try again." "Philip Marshall called twice, please call." "Mr. Laurance called." "David Rockefeller asked if you might like to take a walk." "Mrs. Reagan called, please return the call." But now Cove End was quiet. Gregory Long, Charles Rhyscamp, and Freddy Melhado came up in the summer of 2002 to visit, but many of Brooke's close friends had died, and some New Yorkers had begun making excuses to avoid the trip to Maine. Brooke had put on an impressive public performance at her recent birthday party, but her wandering mind made conversation difficult. One of her most loyal friends, George Trescher, had visited the previous year but found the experience emotionally draining. "George went every summer, but he hated it in the later years," says his sister, Susan Trescher. "She was getting so addled, she kept repeating herself. It broke his heart." Paul Pearson, who had served as Mrs. Astor's butler from 1984 through 1997, had watched as Mrs. Astor's social life diminished. "By the time I left, the phone rang less frequently, which I found sad," he says. "She was someone who could make a difference for people — she'd give someone a push. But at the end they weren't doing their part for her."

His successor as butler, Christopher Ely, had an impressive resume: a stint at Buckingham Palace as a senior footman to Queen Elizabeth, several years with an Arab sheik, and five years in Los Angeles working for the movie producer Joel Schumacher. "Christopher is outstanding and perfect," wrote Schumacher in a job recommendation, adding that Ely was "loyal, honest, completely trustworthy, charming, extraordinarily well mannered and well dispositioned." He was also able to develop a comfortable rapport with Mrs. Astor. He was deft at playing the role of "veddy proper" butler, but he could make her laugh. John Hart recalls how he once came into the library in Maine to inform Mrs. Astor that a man invited for dinner that evening had sent over his butler in advance with a list of wines that he wanted to have served — Château Margaux and other rare vintages. Ely was straight-faced in passing along the presumptuous request, but his employer knew exactly what he thought of such impudence. "Brooke read it and rolled her eyes," Hart recalled.

In theory, Ely's job was to manage Mrs. Astor's households in Maine and at Holly Hill (she no longer had a butler in Manhattan), but in reality his job was much larger. The butler's responsibilities had expanded as Mrs. Astor faded. Ely spent quite a bit of time alone with her, and he tried to be inventive in helping fill her days. Long drives in the countryside, in Maine as well as Westchester, cheered her up and eased the claustrophobia of spending too much time at home. Ely had been one of the few people in whom Tony Marshall had confided about Brooke's mental condition. Discreet and concerned, the butler had bought a book to read up on Alzheimer's disease. Now he was in the awkward position of telling his frail employer what she could or could not do. Her moods had become unpredictable, and she was sometimes childish in her whims. As Alicia Johnson recalls, "She would get into this firing mode — maybe the maid wore the wrong dress. Chris would have to talk her out of it."

Self-aware enough to know that she was being impossible at times, Mrs. Astor was worried that Ely, now the central man in her life, might be tempted to leave, so she kept begging him to promise to stay with her as long as she lived. Of course he agreed — how could he not? Ely, who was single, had become emotionally attached to his employer, and his position had become much more than a job. Although he was careful not to overstep his place, Brooke's friends had gotten into the habit of calling him to ask after her and to conspire with him on her behalf. "Brooke couldn't talk on the phone anymore because she was so hard of hearing," said Emily Harding. "So Chris was the person you talked to. He was always very nice, and good with her."

Even with her hearing aids, Brooke had great difficulty following conversations. She would valiantly carry a notebook to jot things down. A friend had given her pills, vitamins that were supposed to help. "I need to take my memory pills," Brooke told her housekeeper one day, searching with annoyance for the bottle, and then added wryly, "They're not a lot of good, are they? I can't remember where I put them."

Her calendar that summer included frequent outings with Eben Pyne, a banker who had known Vincent Astor, and his wife, Nancy, one of Brooke's favorite traveling companions. "We were both nutty about dogs," says Nancy Pyne, who is proud of the antique dog paintings that decorate the stairwell in her Maine house. "Brooke loved coming into my hallway and looking around and saying 'I have sixty-eight dog pictures,' compared to my pitiful ten. She did it with such humor — she loved to rub it in." But Pyne, who had attended the one hundredth birthday party, adds, "She was fading that last summer. She wasn't the zippy, incredible conversationalist that she always had been."

Small-town admirers felt protective of Mrs. Astor, and in the summer of 2002, people politely tried to smooth over awkward moments. She had been one of a group of wealthy summer residents who banded together to save the town's financially beleaguered grand hotel, the Asticou Inn. Now, at the annual board meeting, she showed up overdressed — everyone else was in khakis and polo shirts — and appeared disoriented. As James McCabe recalls, she asked, "Is this another thing I'm supposed to give to?" before being escorted out. At a party, she plaintively told the philanthropist Gerrit Livingston Lansing, "I don't know why I'm living so long."

The deterioration was a painful sight. "She'd be right on top of things one minute, and then her mind would be gone and she'd have no idea what we were talking about," says Steve Hamor, her gardener, a lanky man with a New England drawl. "Mrs. Astor always said, 'You'll be well taken care of — you don't need a retirement plan,'" he adds. His son Steve Jr. recalls that when he joined her staff, Brooke told him, "'You'll have a job here as long as I'm alive, and five years after that, which will give you time to find another job.' When Mrs. Astor said that, you could take it to the bank. It would have insulted her to ask for it in writing."

The elder Steve Hamor was accustomed to giving Mrs. Astor's guests a tour of her flower garden, a riot of snapdragons and zinnias and roses. But that summer one tour took a sad turn. When a visitor asked him how long he had worked there, Hamor replied, "I've been here thirty-seven years." After Mrs. Astor escorted her friends to their cars, he heard the gate creak open again. "Mrs. Astor was coming up the main walk, and she was crying. I said, 'What is it, Mrs. Astor?' She said, 'You've been here thirty-seven years, and I can't even remember your name.'"

Yet there were also still good days and moments of lucidity, when she displayed her wit and legendary charm. Robert Pirie, who had known her for more than thirty years, accompanied Brooke and David Rockefeller to see the ocean liner *Queen Elizabeth II,* which had docked in Maine. "The high point came when the idiot who was taking us around turned to Brooke and said, 'Which of your relatives went down in the *Titanic?*'" Pirie recalls. Brooke replied, "It was my husband's father. His new wife survived, but fortuitously, the will leaving everything to her went down with him. My husband always used to say, 'It was a grand ship, the *Titanic.*'"

Mrs. Astor could often be found that summer dozing in her chair in the living room, with a yellow legal pad with scribbled notes in her lap, a blue pen leaking onto her clothes or the furniture. "Sometimes I lie down and daydream," she had once told Marilyn Berger of the *New York Times.* "Now and then I let waves of nothing sweep over me." Maine was a place with so many memories stretching back to her girlhood. "Brooke told me that the first time she came up here, she was sixteen and the war had just started," said the developer Marshall Rose. "She was talking about World War I." Her emerald engagement ring from Vincent Astor was still lying in the Maine waters; it had slipped off her finger a half-century before, when she and Vincent were stepping off his yacht onto Jack Pierrepont's dock. "I didn't understand then how expensive emeralds are," recalls Pierrepont's daughter Peggy, a child at the time, "but there were a lot of people trying to find it."

For Brooke, Maine had held out the promise of nature's beauty and rejuvenation for five decades. If she felt low, Cove End lifted her spirits, and she treated the townspeople like extended family. Ever eager to help, she embraced civic betterment, creating scholarships so school-teachers could take trips to Europe and underwriting library renovations. This was her town. But something wrenching had happened here, and she still brooded over the experience. Her long-rooted feelings of security had been swept away, leaving her embarrassed in front of the entire community. She blamed that humiliation squarely on the shoulders of Tony, and even more on his third wife, Charlene.

Mrs. Astor's church in Northeast Harbor, St. Mary's-by-the-Sea, was founded in 1882 by a visiting Episcopal minister and has always catered to the village's summer aristocracy. The picturesque unheated stone chapel with soaring wooden arches was built in 1902, the year Brooke Astor was born, and a smaller winterized chapel was later added a few blocks away from Cove End. In 1982 a new minister was hired: Paul Gilbert, a Wesleyan graduate and naval officer who had come late to his calling. The convivial Gilbert, whose previous congregation had been in the affluent New Jersey suburb of Short Hills, was an avid sailor. He and his wife of fourteen years, Charlene, concluded that Northeast Harbor was an ideal place for their three young children, Arden, Inness, and Robert. True, the salary was low — $18,000 a year — and the church-provided residence was cramped, with a tiny living room and mismatched furniture. But the job offered the prestige of preaching to and influencing one of the most elite congregations in America.

It was de rigueur that the minister and his wife join the summer social circuit, attending the cocktail parties and mingling at the village's private swimming club with the town's wealthy scions, academics, and literary lights. Northeast Harbor's nickname has long been Philadelphia-on-the-Rocks for its Main Line summer migrants, but New York, Boston, and Washington have also contributed their share of distinguished names listed in the Redbook, the indispensable seasonal phone book, which cites the owners' estate names, Lil Hope and Saltmeadow Farm and Pebble Beach and Windy Willows. Frankie Fitzgerald, a life-long summer resident and a descendent of the famous Episcopal rector Endicott Peabody, says that in order to succeed as pastor of St. Mary's,

"You have to provide pastoral care for the local people and really pay attention to them. Then you have these whiz-bang summers and you have to be a powerful preacher to keep those people in their pews. That's when you raise all your money."

Brooke Astor, who attended church every Sunday, was quickly captivated by the articulate minister, a fellow literature-lover who worked references to John Updike, Joseph Conrad, and even Winnie the Pooh into his sermons. For his part, Gilbert was pleased to discover that Mrs. Astor, despite her wealth and prominence, was unpretentious and approachable. "I liked the fact she was a straight shooter," he says. "She spoke her mind and functioned very well in a world of men. She was a good listener."

On a summer Sunday in 1983, Paul and Charlene Gilbert took the five-minute walk from the rectory to Cove End for afternoon tea, on a weekend when Tony Marshall was visiting without his wife, Tee. For Tony, who was not devout, the idea of chatting with the new minister and his wife may not have been high on his to-do list. But as his mother and the minister conversed, he found himself intrigued by Charlene, who was more than twenty years younger than he. She was alluring, with a raucous laugh and a risqué sense of humor. Several decades later, asked if it was love at first sight, he smiles and replies, "We admitted later that we saw something in each other's eyes." At the time, Charlene confided to a childhood friend that she was smitten. "Charlene told me that the moment she laid eyes on him, she knew," the friend recalls. "Charlene said, 'I walked in and I thought immediately, "One day I'm going to marry him."'" But despite the spark, the kindling did not immediately burst into flame. It smoldered quietly, for six years.

Charlene Detwyler Tyler grew up in Charleston, South Carolina, in one of those downwardly mobile southern families that had more pedigree than money; in the local shorthand, they were the kind of people who were "too poor to paint, too proud to whitewash." Charlene's ancestors are said to include the portrait painter George Inness and President John Tyler. The family home at 14 Rutledge Avenue, built in the 1890s by her paternal great-grandfather, was in a good location, a few blocks from the Battery and its Civil War cannons, with Fort Sumter across

Charleston Harbor. But whatever resources had once distinguished the Tylers were gone by World War II. During Charlene's childhood, Azile Brown Tyler, her widowed grandmother, still lived in the handsome Victorian home with the wraparound porch but rented out the top floor to make ends meet.

Charlene's mother, Marguerite, known as Meg, had been the Azalea Queen in a small town nearby and had been swept off her feet by the charming Charles Tyler, Charlene's father. But early in the couple's marriage, Charles was severely injured at the local navy shipyard when a piece of heavy equipment fell on him. According to family legend, he was pronounced dead at the hospital, but then, to the shock of the attendants, the white sheet placed over him began to move. Tyler was left permanently disabled. "He could walk, but it really affected his arm," said Oscar Johnson Small, Jr., a retired Charleston accountant distantly related to Charlene's family. Suffering from a lifetime of excruciating pain, Charles Tyler turned to alcohol to anesthetize himself, and his wife kept him company. The five Tyler children, four girls and a boy — Charlene, the second child, was born in 1945 — were terrified by their parents' boozy battles. As a friend of Charlene's recalls, "The father and mother were alcoholics and they fought like cats and dogs, and it affected the children. The girls got out as quickly as they could. The father came from a good background, a moneyed background, but he just couldn't make it."

Tyler nominally sold health and accident insurance. "He was a born salesman — he was like a comet and took off. But then he self-destructed because of alcohol, mainly to address his pain issues," said Paul Gilbert. Meg Tyler helped support the family by working as a lab technician at the Medical University of South Carolina and as a caterer. "Charlene had a childhood that was out of one of those southern novels — highly dysfunctional," says a woman who has known her for forty years. "Her mother was a beauty queen and a hard-drinking woman, but she was a great cook."

Sometimes Charles Tyler would set off to take the children to church on Sundays but would detour to the wood-paneled bar tucked into the back of the members-only Hibernian Hall, an imposing 1840 historic landmark with white Ionic columns, where he would drink while the children played. Family members call him an abusive drunk but refrain from detailing the particulars. A Charleston resident with an intimate knowledge of the Tyler home life explains, "What happened in that house was real, and it was horrible, and everyone in the family is still living with the repercussions. Those girls cannot have enough security or enough money to protect themselves."

From an early age Charlene took on the role of family peacemaker, using her charm to distract the adults. In search of a reliable parental figure, she turned to her grandmother. "Charlene would come by, and she was a great comfort to her grandmother — she did chores, the little things that you women need done," says Small. Charles and Meg Tyler uprooted their brood to Greenville, South Caroline, but the relocation did not change the sad realities of the marriage. Bravely fleeing toward safety, Charlene, then just twelve, got herself back to Charleston and showed up at her grandmother's door. "The grandmother saved Charlene," says one of Charlene's childhood friends. "Charlene was at a tender age — she needed to get out. Mrs. Tyler thought, 'At least I can save this child.' Charlene was always a loving girl."

Azile Brown Tyler set out to give her granddaughter the kind of education that would pave her way into Charleston society. The route in was Ashley Hall, one of the most prestigious girl's preparatory schools in the South, whose graduates include Barbara Bush, the novelist Josephine Humphreys, and the children's author Madeleine L'Engle. Founded in 1909, Ashley Hall exudes southern gentility. The administrative office is in a four-story 1816 Regency house with Oriental rugs, marble fireplaces, and antique chandeliers. Located in downtown Charleston, the school boasts elegant gardens and an aviary, the Shell House, which is decorated with conch shells and has been converted into a student gathering spot. Yet despite its finishing-school appearance, Ashley Hall was designed to offer a rigorous education; in Charlene's day, its students were required take Latin.

After she enrolled in 1960, when she was fifteen, Charlene blossomed. She sang in the glee club and performed on the varsity drill team. Anne Miller Moises, also in the class of '63, recalls that "Charlene was very funny and seemed happy and chipper. She had such rosy cheeks." Moises goes on to speculate, "Maybe she is the type who makes the best of everything, but she never let on that she had had a hard time." Charlene would ride her bike to school with her neighbor Gail Townsend Bailey. "I remember sitting with Charlene on her front porch, shooting the breeze," Bailey says. "She was very gregarious, great to be around."

Her high school years were a swirl of circle pins, pleated skirts, and dancing the shag. In the 1963 Ashley Hall yearbook, the *Spiral*, Charlene Detwyler Tyler is described as having "cheeks like apple blossoms in the spring." Her nickname is Rabbit, her favorite phrase is "Hey, babes!" She is slender and lovely in the picture, her dark hair in a flattering bob that comes just below her ears, and she has a shy smile on her unlined face.

For Ashley Hall girls, the standard path was to come out at the St. Cecilia Society ball, go to college or spend a year working at a socially acceptable job (in an art gallery or historic preservation), and then marry and move into a house in the narrow area south of Broad Street. Charlene could not afford college and went to work at the South Carolina National Bank as a teller, the job she had when she met her first husband, Paul Gilbert.

The year was 1967, the occasion was a boat race in Charleston Harbor, and a mutual friend invited both Charlene and Paul to crew on a sailboat. Faced with a low draft number during the Vietnam War years, Gilbert had entered navy officer training school and had just been stationed in Charleston. New to the city and a Yankee, he was pleased to encounter this popular local girl. "She was very outgoing, very charming, great sense of humor — a slim young woman with a lot of life to her," he recalls, wistfulness evident in his voice.

Charlene was still living at home with her devoted grandmother, sharing the downstairs quarters while boarders occupied the top floor. One night in November 1967, while at the movies with Gilbert, she suddenly had a feeling that something was wrong and insisted that they leave. The clocks in her grandmother's home had stopped, and her seventy-eight-year-old grandmother was dead. In her will, Azile Tyler left her home to Charlene, who was bereft at the loss of the woman who had raised her. A short time later, Paul Gilbert proposed. "I felt like I was doing the noble thing," he says, "but I was also in love with her." They were married at St. Philip's Church on August 28, 1968, with a reception afterward at the Hibernian Hall on one of the hottest days of the year. "There was no air conditioning," recalls Mary Lou Scott, Paul Gilbert's sister. "I have never seen so many drunk people."

A month later Gilbert was promoted to captain and became the commanding officer of a minesweeper, the USS *Meadowlark*, berthed in New Jersey. The couple spent a year in Perth Amboy. When his navy service ended, in late 1969, the Gilberts moved back to Charleston, where their first child, Arden, was born. Paul Gilbert worked at a series of unsatisfying jobs, including administrator at a local medical college and yacht broker. Charlene gave birth to another daughter, Inness, in 1972, and to a son, Robert, in 1976. Pursuing his interest in religion, Paul Gilbert enrolled in the Virginia Theological Seminary and took his family with him to Alexandria. "Faith was important to Charlene, and she supported me all the way through," he says. "I'm very grateful to her for that."

During the six years between Charlene's introduction to Tony Marshall and the encounter that would rupture both their marriages, she and Paul Gilbert became popular figures in Northeast Harbor. Like many resort communities, the town lives by the calendar, with a summer population of several thousand dwindling to fewer than five hundred people after Labor Day. To supplement the rector's income, Charlene became an event planner, first at the Mount Desert Island Biological Laboratory and then at the Maine Community Foundation. "Charlene and Paul were warmly received, very involved in the community and in activities supporting their children," says Bob Pyle. When the town's fire alarm went off, he says, "Charlene was one of the first people who would show up, with coffee and doughnuts."

One full-time local resident, Gunnar Hansen, a writer and actor who specializes in horror movies (he played Leatherface in the cult classic *The Texas Chain Saw Massacre*), spent two summers living with the Gilberts while he rented out his own house to vacationers to pay the mortgage. "Charlene was more talkative and social, but Paul to me was the caregiver at home," he recalls. "She was out the door in the morning. He had made the sandwiches and got up and made breakfast and got the kids off to school."

But Charlene took on the role of caregiver when her mother was diagnosed with inoperable cancer. Although her three sisters lived in Charleston, their mother chose to leave that city, where she had spent most of her life, to be with her once-rebellious daughter in Maine. Pattie O'Brien, Charlene's younger sister, recalls, "My mother died in Charlene's arms. I've always been grateful to Charlene, because I couldn't have done it. That's so hard, twenty-four hours a day, seven days a week." Paul Gilbert supported Charlene's desire to take in her mother at the end. "We converted our living room to her bedroom, and she died there," he recalls. "She reconciled with Charlene, which was quite beautiful."

As compensation for the difficult winter months in Northeast Harbor, the summers offered a constant cornucopia of invitations for the minister and his wife. "We had them to dinner a few times," says Frankie Fitzgerald. "They're both very smart. Charlene includes people in conversation — she makes a big effort towards everyone." The minister and his wife were also frequent summer dinner guests at the home of August Heckscher, a former New York City parks commissioner. At Heckscher's home, the couple met the erudite and entertaining New York lawyer Francis X. Morrissey, Jr., whose father was intimately involved in the life of the Kennedy family. Frank Morrissey benefited from that Camelot connection and moved in well-to-do circles. "Francis is very charming and worldly. Augie saw him as a third son," recalls Paul Gilbert. "He was so smooth, you wouldn't believe it. He reminds me of the movie *The Talented Mr. Ripley.*"

Important moments in life often arrive without a change in background music to signify a plot twist. For Tony Marshall, his annual visit to his mother in Maine had always been a pleasant interlude, especially once he stopped taking Tee, who did not get along with Brooke. Cove End was beautiful, the deferential staff looked after him, and his mother invited interesting people to visit, as she did in July 1989, when she gave a large luncheon for Katharine Graham, the *Washington Post* publisher.

May 1997. Brooke Astor, New York's most enduring philanthropist, at age ninety-five. She shut down the Astor Foundation that year but was still constantly out and about. *Serge J-F. Levy/AP Photo*

Dazzling in her custom-designed Oscar de la Renta gown, Brooke Astor celebrates at her one hundredth birthday party with intimates Laurance (left) and David Rockefeller.

Mary Hilliard/Courtesy of David Rockefeller

David Rockefeller welcomes Brooke Astor's son, Tony Marshall, and his lively wife, Charlene, to the festivities. *Mary Hilliard/Courtesy of David Rockefeller*

Nan Starr (left) with her husband, Philip Marshall, and his fraternal twin, Alec, with Brooke Astor. The twins, especially Philip, would grow closer to their grandmother during her last years.

Mary Hilliard/Courtesy of David Rockefeller

Philip and Alec Marshall at the grand birthday celebration. Philip had a difficult relationship with their father, but Alec was usually on good terms.

Collection of Philip Marshall

Brooke, age seventeen, and her new husband, Dryden Kuser, in Venice. The union was a disaster from the wedding night on.

Brooke and Buddie Marshall (husband number two and the man she considered the love of her life) at their country home in Tyringham, Massachusetts, in 1952. He died there unexpectedly later that year.

Collection of Philip Marshall

Dryden Kuser during a rare family visit with his two children, Suzanne and Tony.

Collection of Suzanne Kuser

Time's Vincent Astor cover, April 9, 1934. The twice-divorced millionaire misanthrope would marry Brooke nineteen years later. "If she married him for his charm," remarked the author Louis Auchincloss, "I'd have said she ought to be put in an asylum."

Time Magazine/Getty Images

Brooke Astor and Tony's first wife, Elizabeth Cryan Marshall, and the twins, who arrived in 1953.

Collection of Philip Marshall

Vincent and Brooke Astor, frolicking with her grandsons (whom he, uncharacteristically, adored) and a donkey at Ferncliff, Astor's country house. Vincent often took the twins for rides in his own train, Toonerville, which traveled through the estate.

Collection of Philip Marshall

Brooke Astor and her young grandsons. After the twins moved away from Manhattan with their divorced mother, Brooke saw them sporadically. She got to know and appreciate them later in life.

Collection of Philip Marshall

In 1960, shortly after Vincent Astor died, Tony Marshall, who had just left the CIA, visited his mother at Ferncliff. *Collection of Tony and Charlene Marshall*

Brooke Astor at the Astor Foundation in 1971. The philanthropist, always dressed to the nines, gave away $200 million to New York City organizations.

Mel Finkelstein/New York Daily News

Brooke Astor hiking in Maine in 1976 with her son, grandsons, and beloved dachshunds.

Photograph by Alec Marshall

Philip and Tony Marshall, son and father, during a happy day in Maine in 1986, two decades before their relationship went awry. *Photograph by Alec Marshall*

CHARLENE DETWYLER TYLER
1960   White
Charleston, South Carolina
"Cheeks like apple blossoms in the spring."
Rabbit . . . "Hey, babes!" . . . Boston Celtics . . .
captains outrageous . . .
Glee Club 2,3,4; Drill Team Varsity 2.

A teenage Charlene Tyler in her 1963 Ashley Hall yearbook. Fleeing a tumultuous background, she was raised by her grandmother in Charleston. After leaving her first husband, Paul Gilbert, the priest of Brooke's Episcopal church in Maine, Charlene married Tony Marshall in 1992. *Courtesy of Ashley Hall*

Cove End, Brooke Astor's waterside estate in Northeast Harbor, Maine, represented a second existence for the urbane Mrs. Astor. Brooke's desire to leave a guest cottage to her grandson Philip, rather than her son, Tony, exacerbated family tensions.
Collection of Philip Marshall

Brooke Astor in a seemingly contemplative mood at her rural Maine retreat, August Moon, 1975. Divorced and then twice widowed, she chose to remain single from age fifty-seven on.

Photograph by Alec Marshall

Brooke Astor, grandson Alec Marshall, and his daughter, Hilary Brooke, at Holly Hill, April 1997. Alec lived just a mile away.

Photograph by Alec Marshall

Tony and Charlene Marshall, on holiday in London in 2003, won two Tony awards as successful Broadway producers.
Collection of Tony and Charlene Marshall

During her last summer in Maine, in 2002, Brooke Astor relaxes with daughter-in-law Charlene. *Collection of Tony and Charlene Marshall*

Annette de la Renta, Brooke Astor, and Oscar de la Renta. Brooke's best friend for four decades, Annette would later be appointed her guardian.

Bill Cunningham/New York Times

Holly Hill, Brooke Astor's sixty-five-acre estate in Briarcliff Manor, New York.
Collection of Philip Marshall

The serpentine staircase at Holly Hill, decorated with paintings of dogs.
Photograph by Alec Marshall

Brooke Astor with her son, Tony, Charlene Marshall, and the star-crossed lawyer Francis X. Morrissey, Jr., at the Living Landmarks benefit, November 2002.
Ron Galella/Getty Images

Brooke with her longtime butler, Chris Ely. Fired by Tony Marshall in 2005, the devoted Ely was later rehired by Annette de la Renta and worked for Mrs. Astor until her death. *Collection of Philip Marshall*

At Holly Hill, Brooke Astor with grandson Philip, who would later instigate the suit against his father to improve his grandmother's living conditions. *Photograph by Alec Marshall*

November 27, 2007. Already in custody, Tony Marshall, accused of swindling tens of millions of dollars from his mother, arrives at court for arraignment on charges of fraud and larceny. *John Marshall Mantel/New York Times/Redux*

The last photograph of Brooke Astor, American icon, at Holly Hill with family members and nurses. The shot was taken on July 17, 2007, a month before her death. Girlsie, her beloved dachshund, is nearby. *Collection of Philip Marshall*

Brooke Astor in Maine, August 2000. Left: grandson Philip Marshall and great-granddaughter Sophie Marshall. Right: great-grandson Winslow Marshall and Nan Starr. *Collection of Philip Marshall*

She also invited the minister and his wife, seating Gilbert at her table with Mrs. Graham and Charlene next to Tony at another table.

Oh, the mischief that can arise out of a simple arrangement of place cards. Charlene and Tony quickly discovered they had interests in common: he loved opera, she played the piano; they were both amateur photographers; he had a wry sense of humor, she was a responsive listener. Suddenly they were laughing and flirting on a summer day, having a party of their own. It could have stopped there, but it did not. Tony, always a gentleman, is circumspect about the events that led to the breakup of two marriages. When I asked him about his second meeting with Charlene, he simply says, "It was a renewal. We fell in love, and got married."

There are few secrets in Northeast Harbor, a town so small that it does not even boast a traffic light. Sandra Graves, whose family runs McGrath's, the only newsstand on Main Street, was working as a cook for Mrs. Astor that summer. "I got to work a little before seven A.M.," she says. "The kitchen window looks out to the driveway, and you can see anyone who walks up. Charlene showed up early and rang the front doorbell. It might have only happened once or twice, but it was drilled in my head because it was so odd." Tony was waiting downstairs and slipped out to join Charlene for a walk. Graves and her companion in the kitchen, the housekeeper, Helen Dodge, found Charlene's appearance disturbing.

The walks quickly became local knowledge. There was the predictable tongue-wagging because Charlene left her sleeping family for an early-morning stroll with Mrs. Astor's married son. Dot Renaud, Sandy's mother and the newsstand proprietor, says, "If you're a minister's wife, you're supposed to conduct yourself, especially in a small town. She had children, and while they weren't babies, they were young." (Robert was twelve, Inness was sixteen, and Arden was nineteen.) In the next few weeks, other members of Mrs. Astor's staff noted jarring things. Tony, not known to venture far, was gone for twelve hours at a stretch. His new passion for bird watching, he told people, was keeping him busy.

Philip Marshall, visiting in August, was too wrapped up in his own romantic life to notice much else. Two weeks earlier he had attended a cousin's wedding in Canada and met a painter and filmmaker, Nan Starr, a Philadelphia native who was then living in Boston. "I was telling everyone that I had met this wonderful woman," recalls Philip, then teaching at Southeastern Massachusetts University. Armed with a basket of warm popovers baked by his grandmother's staff and a bouquet of basil from his grandmother's garden, Philip drove down to see Nan. Seven weeks later they were engaged. Nan, whose father ran a gourmet food company, came from an affluent family herself but had some trepidation about marrying into a family with such enormous wealth and public attention. As she puts it, "I was very much in love with Philip, who didn't have any money himself, but I was concerned about raising a healthy family in the shadow of his grandmother's fame and fortune. I've seen excessive wealth cause serious problems for some families." Only later, when Tony Marshall called Philip to say that he had left Tee, did Philip realize that he and his father had been falling in love at the same time.

Paul Gilbert may have been the last to know. He and Charlene had problems — "We were broke; we had nothing," he says — but the marriage seemed to be "on cruise control." When the summer ended and Tony returned to New York, Charlene told her husband that she had to take several out-of-town business trips on behalf of the Maine Community Foundation. One September Sunday, when Charlene purportedly was in Boston, the Episcopal priest invited parishioners to a communal coffee after services. A woman came over to chat with him and idly passed along a bit of gossip: "My cousin in Washington just saw your wife getting off a plane. She went up and hugged this older man. Was she going to see her father?" The priest managed not to drop his coffee. The marriage ended quickly. When Charlene came home, Gilbert confronted her, and she moved to a friend's house a few blocks away. Three weeks later she packed her clothes and headed to Manhattan.

Brooke Astor was aghast over the affair. Fond of Paul Gilbert, she was devastated that her hospitality had led to this fracture of two families. "Charlene's husband would call every single day, and they would talk while Mrs. Astor was having breakfast in bed," recalls Sandra Graves. "She swore to God that Charlene would never be allowed in the house. Mrs. Astor made all these comments about how she was going to disown Tony, not let him have anything, didn't want Charlene in his life — she was very, very angry. But I knew she would get over it. Charlene knows how to talk and get things around to her own way."

Charlene came back to Northeast Harbor several weeks later to visit her children. The streets of the small town were empty, and she and the rector took a walk. Charlene said that things seemed to be moving too quickly. As Gilbert recalls, he replied, "Quick? You moved out, you left your kids, you've taken up with an older man — what do you mean, quick?" The couple filed for divorce in the fall of 1989.

When the official decree came through, Gilbert felt obligated to talk about the breakup in a sermon. "He had to. Everyone sort of knew," says Nancy Pyne. "This winter was a particularly hard one for me," he told his congregation. "My marriage of twenty-one years came to an end in January. I thought that I knew what brokenness was, but this was a new and even deeper experience. Each day as I woke up to face this new situation, all I could say to myself was this: 'I am alive this day, and it will be a good day.' Some days were not good at all. Now the days are good again, and all I can say is that somewhere along the way my brokenness was mended. I have more of a limp than I did before, but I am walking once again."

Given Gilbert's role as the wounded party, left with two children still at home, the blame for the split fell on Charlene. But her friends argue that she had reasons for wanting to get out of the marriage. Sam Peabody explains, "She has said the marriage was very difficult, and Tony came along and she adores him."

Tony's wife, Tee, took the news as hard as Charlene's husband did. "One of the sad things about Tee is that she just couldn't get over the divorce," says Pamela Walker, who had befriended Tee in Madagascar. "You have to pull yourself together and go on, but she had a hard time doing that." The soon-to-be-ex Mrs. Marshall made anguished phone calls to Tony's sons. "I'd talk to her — I'd want to be polite and nice," said Alec. "I just felt that I didn't want to take sides, and blood is thicker than water." Philip, sympathetic to Tee's misery, found it difficult to welcome Charlene into the family. "It was hard because I knew Tee had been collateral damage of this new romance," he says. Yet he was also glad to see his father's spirits soar, adding, "Charlene is outgoing, fun — she really did bring a lot of great stuff into my father's life." Mortified by the scandal, Brooke could not stop complaining to her friends. Ashton Hawkins says, "She didn't go to her parish for a year because she felt so embarrassed."

Against this backdrop, the two women who dominated Tony Marshall's life embarked on a relationship fraught with mutual mistrust. Even though Brooke had a permissive attitude toward divorce, she could not believe that Charlene had walked out on her husband and children. Charlene presumably was not interested in hearing moral strictures about parenting from Brooke Astor. Just as Vincent Astor had once regaled Brooke with tales of his mother's cruelty, Tony was apparently honest with Charlene about his tangled relationship with his mother. Impressed by Tony's accomplishments, she loyally believed that his family should show him more respect. But she made a strategic error in voicing those complaints to Philip, who found her obsession with ancient family history to be self-serving. "Charlene was talking about 'Look what your grandmother has done to your father, sending him away to boarding school as a child,'" he says. "We always wondered why she was harping on that so much."

Tony Marshall was not a wealthy man by his mother's standards, but he was a millionaire with an apartment in the Carlyle Hotel (which Tee received in the divorce settlement), a hefty annual income, and the prospect of a staggering inheritance. As someone who had been living in a minister's modest quarters, Charlene was bedeviled by the same kind of gossip that had followed Brooke's marriage to Vincent Astor — that she was only marrying for money. Nan Lincoln, the arts editor of the *Bar Harbor Times,* recalls the speculation: "Was she a gold digger, or was this a romantic love story — the poor stifled parson's wife who finds the man of her dreams?"

The final judgment on docket number BAR89-DV-053, *Charlene T. Gilbert v. Paul E. Gilbert,* was entered into court records on January 26, 1990 — a divorce document with a poignant breakdown of the couple's assets. Charlene was ordered to pay her husband $113 per week in child support for Inness and another $73 a week for Robert. The Gilberts had a meager $720 in a money market account, $550 in a savings account, and $28 in a checking account, but jointly they owed $2,800 on credit cards. They did have one valuable asset; 4.4 acres of land in Bar Harbor, valued at $200,000, with a small mortgage of $22,000. Paul Gilbert kept three Persian rugs, a guitar, a bookcase, the stereo system, a cedar chest, his father's picture, a baby picture, and a thermos lamp. Charlene claimed as her property $20,000 worth of possessions: a 12-inch television, a brass tray, a portrait of her ancestor Judge Tyler, a Chinese plant stand, a piano, a wicker sewing basket, some silver and cut glass, a boudoir rocker, a brass fireplace set, a Zenith radio, a Duncan Fife couch labeled "broken," and a beer stein lamp.

Charlene spent more than two years in Manhattan waiting for Tony's divorce to be finalized. Living in a studio apartment (which Tony now describes as "a ratty hole"), she supported herself as the executive director of the Garden Club of America. "She had a miserable beginning in New York," says a Charleston confidante. "She was flat broke." (During this period, though, Tony did have something in common with one of his sons. Alec Marshall's first marriage had just broken up, and over lunch at the Racquet Club, he and his father would commiserate about divorce lawyers.)

Tony and Charlene were married in 1992 at St. Thomas Church on Fifth Avenue, in a service conducted by Father John Andrew. Reconciling herself to the inevitable, Brooke graciously played mother of the groom. The couple's five children from their previous marriages did not attend. "I was not invited. I would have gone," says Alec. "My father said, 'We've decided that either all of you go or none of you go.'" Charlene's version of her wedding day was passed to me via a note from her Manhattan friend Suzanne Harbour Kahanovitz. "When Tony and Charlene married, they wanted a small private ceremony," Kahanovitz wrote. "Mrs. Astor insisted on being the witness and then taking them out for a celebratory lunch at her favorite place, La Grenouille, so she could be the first to tell all her friends. Mrs. Astor also called the judge to make sure that Anthony's divorce from his prior wife went through in a timely manner." Sensitive to Tony's postdivorce financial situation, Brooke bought the couple a duplex apartment in a prewar building at Seventy-ninth Street and Lexington Avenue.

To friends, Brooke stressed that "Charlene makes Tony happy." As a mother, she appreciated how Charlene cared for Tony, whose health was not always robust. A few years after the couple married, Tony suffered a heart attack, and the doctors found scar tissue that indicated he had had a previous episode. Charlene told Philip and Alec that she had found the stricken Tony in the closet, searching for the right tie to wear to the hospital.

Tony would later insist that his mother and his wife enjoyed each other's company. But Brooke's friends said that she never warmed up to her new daughter-in-law. "Brooke was never hostile to Charlene in any way, never said anything unkind," says Freddy Melhado. "Charlene tried very, very hard, but they didn't speak the same language." Henry Kissinger is blunt in describing Brooke's attitude: "My impression was that Charlene set her teeth on edge."

Charlene did not begin to understand the rigorous rules of Brooke's social set in New York, and her faux pas endlessly irritated her ninety-year-old mother-in-law. For example, Charlene decided to take advantage of Tony's membership at the Knickerbocker Club to give him a birthday party there. The old-fashioned club, which discourages meetings and forbids guests from taking notes in the dining room, was Brooke's favorite lunch spot, and she relished its gracious atmosphere. But on the evening of Tony's party, she heard the strange sound of jangling bangles: Charlene had hired a belly dancer, whose bare stomach was undulating away. Brooke muttered to Marilyn Berger, who was seated next to her, "Can you believe this?"

Charlene admired Brooke's jewelry, but her compliments displeased her mother-in-law. "Charlene is one of those people who is in your face," says Viscount Astor, who recalls an evening when Brooke wore her sapphires and Charlene overdid it. "Brooke grabbed my hand and whispered, 'She only said that because she wants it.'" Brooke always sensed a subtext, whether it was present or not, when Charlene was around.

At Cove End, Brooke's houseguests were struck by the simmering tensions time and again. "Tony and Charlene would be staying in the cottage and Brooke would say, 'We have to go see them,'" recalls John Dobkin, then the head of Historic Hudson Valley. "Tony would have prepared little Ritz crackers with peanut butter and bacon chips. We'd be there half an hour, and Brooke would heave a deep sigh of relief when we left, apologizing." Even Mrs. Astor's staff felt uncomfortable watching how she treated Tony. "Mrs. Astor used to tell Mr. Marshall what to do all the time," says Alicia Johnson, the housekeeper. "That grated on Charlene. He tried so hard to please his mother. He used to see her every day — he was kind to her. He'd go through the mail with her, set up dinner parties."

If Tony and Charlene were visiting when prominent guests arrived, Brooke would order the couple to vacate the large cottage and exile them to less desirable quarters, a cabin without a water view. "Brooke assigned them to the little cottage — I stayed in the big one," recalls Ashton Hawkins. "We wouldn't see them for meals, only for big parties. Brooke was very embarrassed and very upset and did not conceal it from Charlene." When Liz Smith visited, she heard an earful of complaints from her hostess. "She thought Charlene was taking her jewelry. I said, 'Oh, Brooke, surely not.' I thought it was geriatric insecurity," says Smith. "Brooke wasn't very nice to them. I felt she didn't want them there, but she had no choice."

Everyone in Northeast Harbor was aware of Mrs. Astor's deliberate efforts to maintain a friendship with Paul Gilbert. When Gilbert married his second wife, Patricia Roberts, in 1994, she magnanimously gave the newlyweds the use of her Maine summer camp, August Moon, for their honeymoon. She also paid for the addition of an extra bedroom at the minister's church-owned housing. These gestures, especially the honeymoon stay, undoubtedly struck Charlene and Tony as deliberately hurtful. When Charlene and Paul Gilbert's oldest daughter, Arden, was married in Northeast Harbor, with a reception at the Asticou Inn, Brooke Astor made a point of spending time with Gilbert's second wife, who recalls, "I loved sitting next to Mrs. Astor." Paul Gilbert's derogatory nickname for Charlene was his "ball and chain." He would tell Roberts, "I can't believe the ball and chain is going to get that house."

Tony and Charlene arrived for their annual visit to Cove End on July 25, 2002, and stayed for nearly three weeks. Tony had always loved boating, and Charlene took a triumphant pleasure in returning to this village where her life had changed for the better. She did not mingle much with old friends. "She behaved like a summer person," says Gunnar Hansen.

"She'd be delighted to see me because I'm an old friend, but she would never invite me to the house. The summer community sticks with the summer community."

The Marshalls were solicitous of Brooke that summer, sharing at least one meal daily and taking her out to lunch at the Asticou or to dinner at the Bar Harbor Inn. They ferried her to cocktail parties and took her for a walk in the Rockefeller gardens. Now that she had fewer houseguests and was no longer such a formidable figure, she was more dependent on them for companionship — and Tony snapped a photo of Brooke and Charlene chatting amicably in the library.

Brooke had always told her son that he would inherit Cove End (valued at $6.2 million in 2004), but she had periodically considered giving the $850,000 waterfront cottage to someone else. She asked Vartan Gregorian if he was interested (he declined) and half offered it to the butler, Chris Ely, who became alarmed. As Hart recalls, "Chris said, 'Don't do that. I can't afford to keep it up, and Tony wouldn't be happy to have me here.'" She also told Steve Hamor Sr. that she might give him a portion of her Maine property for his own greenhouse — she even told Nancy Pyne about this plan — but she never followed up on that offer either.

These were the whims of an elderly woman. But to Tony, Brooke's effort to give her grandson Philip the cottage in 2000 may have represented a serious change in his mother's estate plan. In deference to Tony's objections, Brooke backed off from the gift, but she had not entirely abandoned the idea. In the most recent version of her will, dated January 30, 2002, she had written: "My grandson, Philip Marshall, has visited me in Maine with his wife and children to our common pleasure. I hope that he will keep visiting his father there after my death and that his father will leave him an interest in the Maine property upon his death, if Philip still would like to own and use my home in Maine when that time comes." For Tony and, more important, for Charlene, that wording had worrisome implications. If Brooke, now one hundred, were to outlive Tony, with his history of heart attacks, Philip would have a legal claim to Cove End. Under that scenario, Charlene would never reign at that shingled Maine retreat. At the time, though,

Mrs. Astor's will was a confidential document; only Tony, Charlene, and Terry Christensen had read the contents.

Unaware of his grandmother's wishes and his father's anxieties, Philip was still trying to be a dutiful son. He had sent his father a large fruit basket as a birthday gift in May 2002. Tony responded with a warm handwritten thank-you note, saying that he had been "delighted" to catch up during a recent conversation and was looking forward to seeing Philip soon. He signed the note "With much love, Father."

The Marshalls left Northeast Harbor in mid-August to return to Manhattan. Mrs. Astor spent a leisurely final few weeks at her cherished home. She took her entire staff out to dinner on Friday, August 30, as a gesture of gratitude. That Sunday she attended church at St. Mary's, and afterward, with plans to fly back to New York the next day, she spent the afternoon sitting in her backyard overlooking the water, soaking up the sun and the scenery.

"We went by and she was sitting in her chaise lounge," recalls Pyne. "My husband said, 'My God, Brooke you have the most beautiful ankles and feet.' She was known for that." Brooke was pleased but could not resist teasing her guests about their motives. As Pyne adds, "She paused and looked around at her possessions and said, 'What are you after?' It was so funny."

8

The Painting Vanishes

OF ALL THE ROOMS in Brooke Astor's Park Avenue apartment, the library was her favorite place to entertain visitors. The room gleamed with old-money elegance, from the red velvet Louis XV chairs to the walls shimmering with ten coats of oxblood lacquer, which the decorator Albert Hadley had used to replace fake wood paneling. Brass-accented bookcases showcased Vincent Astor's collection of three thousand first editions bound in Moroccan leather. For more than thirty years, the place of honor over the marble fireplace belonged to the Childe Hassam painting *Flags, Fifth Avenue.*

Mrs. Astor reveled in compliments about her painting, an astute purchase that had taken on a powerful emotional resonance. "An exhilarating picture it is, full of high hopes," wrote Brendan Gill in *The New Yorker*. Mrs. Astor was often identified with the 1917 painting, a vibrant image of the city awash in patriotic sentiment in the month after the United States entered World War I. The red, white, and blue flags of America, Britain, and France are draped on the B. Altman department store and neighboring buildings, with a busy street scene below.

Hassam, America's best-known impressionist, painted a series of similar flag pictures, and when he died, in 1935, he left most of them to the American Academy of Arts and Letters, which later sold the majority. The paintings slowly increased in value and renown. Mrs. Astor's

Childe Hassam (also known by art historians as *Up the Avenue from Thirty-fourth Street, May 1917*) had previously belonged to Irving Mitchell Felt, a sports impresario and the president of Madison Square Garden Corporation, who had snapped up the New York Rangers and the New York Knicks. Like many first-generation mega-rich New Yorkers, Felt wanted to enhance his social standing through philanthropy. Already a Metropolitan Opera board member and a founding patron of Lincoln Center, he targeted the Metropolitan Museum, where in the early 1970s a donation of $250,000 in cash or art would make him a benefactor. Felt sensed that the Childe Hassam would be his ticket, but the Met disagreed. As Ashton Hawkins, then the secretary of the Met's board, recalls, "The curator felt it wasn't worth that."

Hawkins, disappointed by the Met's decision, thought of Brooke Astor's zest for the city and the patriotism of her Marine general father. When he told her about the painting, Mrs. Astor eagerly sought it out, purchasing it for $172,000 in 1971 through Wildenstein & Company. She loved flags; the sight stirred something in her dating back to her expatriate childhood. In the belief that the Metropolitan Museum had undervalued the work, she decided to have the last word. "After she unveiled it, we talked about how she got it," recalls Hawkins. "She said 'It's going to go to the Metropolitan, along with certain drawings.'"

For decades Mrs. Astor repeated that verbal promise to museum officials. Philippe de Montebello says, "Every time I went to her house for dinner, she'd say, 'See that — that's for you someday.'" Dating from 1992 and perhaps earlier, her wills bequeath the Childe Hassam to the Metropolitan but feature a provision that was pure Brooke, insisting that the painting be kept on permanent display rather than risk the indignity of storage.

But then, in early 2002, Mrs. Astor suddenly sold her beloved painting to the Gerald Peters Gallery for $10 million, the highest price ever paid for a Childe Hassam flag painting. (The previous record, set at Christie's in 1998, was $7.9 million for *Afternoon on the Avenue*.) Even though she was still an emeritus member of the board and attended meetings, Mrs. Astor did not notify the Metropolitan; the bequest simply vanished from her most recent will. She could be capricious, but to many of her friends, the disappearance of the Childe Hassam seemed to reflect more than the whims of a one-hundred-year-old society matriarch.

Through much of 2002, Mrs. Astor was either in Palm Beach or in Maine or was enveloped in the pleasant haze of birthday preparations. Only when she returned from Cove End in September did the space where the Childe Hassam had hung seem hauntingly vacant, although the picture had been replaced by a portrait of her father, General Russell. David Rockefeller did not pry, but he was baffled by her decision to part with the Hassam. "It was a picture she always enjoyed," he said. "To have it removed from the apartment — I found it difficult to understand." Annette de la Renta was especially mystified when she heard Brooke's explanation for the sale. "I didn't even have to ask — Brooke volunteered," she recalls. "Brooke said, 'Tony wanted me to sell the painting because I'm running out of money.'" Annette found the notion of Brooke having to hock her possessions inexplicable, and said so. But Brooke repeated, "He says I'm running out of money. We sold it and got a very good price for it." Chris Ely would later tell many people involved in the Astor case that upon hearing that the painting had been sold for millions, Brooke plaintively asked, "Now can I buy a dress?"

For years Brooke had laughed with her friends about Tony's dreary efforts to force her to curtail her extravagance, but now she seemed genuinely frightened. No one knew whether this was a symptom of the sometimes exaggerated fears of the elderly or whether Tony was encouraging her to worry about money. Viscount Astor recalls a typical conversation, over dinner at La Côte Basque in the fall of 2002, with Brooke complaining, "'Tony says I have to sell this or that — I haven't any money.'" Alarmed, Lord Astor made surreptitious financial inquiries. "I finally looked into it, and discovered it was rubbish," he said. He learned that his friend was solvent enough to "keep anyone going for a long time, even at her level."

Four years later Tony offered his own explanation for the painting's sale. According to him, the triggering event occurred when his mother lent the painting to the Adelson Galleries for a Manhattan exhibition in the fall of 2001. "At the time the exhibition was arranged, we had some discussions about selling the painting if it generated interest," he wrote in a detailed chronology. "Not long after the Adelson exhibition ended, a potential buyer approached me . . . When I told my Mother how much was being offered, she decided to sell it, and to share some of the profit with me by paying me a 'commission' for arranging the purchase." That so-called commission was $2 million, but Tony has never explained how his mother settled on that figure. If she had taken a standard route and auctioned *Flags, Fifth Avenue* at Christie's for the same price, the fee would have been slightly more than $1 million. At the time, none of Brooke's friends or any Metropolitan Museum officials knew that Tony had profited directly from this transaction. "I remember her delight when she bought the Childe Hassam," Peggy Pierrepont recalls. "So when I heard the painting was gone, I thought, 'Oh, there's hanky-panky.' It just did not seem right."

Tony's chronology makes it seem as if the art dealer Gerald Peters aggressively pursued the painting. But Peters insists that Tony was the one eager to make a sale. "Tony Marshall was at a dinner sitting next to someone who works for me," Peters recalls. "He brought up the painting, and we took it on consignment, and after a period of time decided to buy it. He told us that he got the appraisal from the auction houses, and marked it up." Peters never dealt directly with Tony; everything was done through lawyers. But the gallery owner says that he was given the impression that everyone was being altruistic: "The implication was that we were helping Mrs. Astor and helping her philanthropy."

Peters resold the painting to George Soros, who kept the artwork in his country home. According to the *New York Times*, Soros bought the Childe Hassam for $20 million, twice the price that Peters paid to Brooke Astor and her agent, Tony Marshall. Peters will not comment on the price but says, with some justice, "It worked out well."

Like many people contemplating their mortality, Mrs. Astor had begun in recent years to shower her friends with gifts. In September 2002, she sent her string of René Boivin French estate seed pearls with a ruby clasp, insured for $29,000, to Van Cleef & Arpels to be cleaned and re-strung and then presented the necklace to Annette, who recalls, "I was touched." Most of the gifts were not that valuable but more in the na-ture of knickknacks to remember her by. Everett Fahy, a curator at the Metropolitan Museum and a friend for thirty years, says that Brooke called him at three o'clock one afternoon to say, "I want to see you." He replied, "Brooke, I want to see you too." She said, "I want to see you right now." So fifteen minutes later he was ushered into the red library, where Brooke presented him with a small Chinese jade figurine. He felt sad, knowing that "it was her farewell gift to me."

Whenever Vartan Gregorian visited, Brooke constantly asked, "What can I do for you, what would you like? You want my paintings, you want my rare books?" Gregorian, who gently pointed out to her that she had already promised the books to the library, worried about people who might take advantage of Brooke's generosity. He called Tony to warn him that visitors might feel "compelled to take things because they didn't want to offend her." As Gregorian recalls, "Tony thanked me for it."

Mrs. Astor was still keeping an active schedule of lunches and dinners. But in October her physician, Dr. Rees Pritchett, called to convey his concern for her safety, according to the staff's log of phone calls: "He stressed that you absolutely have to have someone on your elbow going to and from all of your appointments." She went to dinner twice in eight days at the home of Louise and Henry Grunwald, but as the hostess recalls, "She really didn't know that she had been here the week before." Oscar de la Renta laments that Brooke's advanced age and diminished hearing made chitchat awkward. "She always looked wonderful, impeccable, but it was very difficult to have a conversation," he says. "She wasn't really hearing. She was deeply embarrassed and would pretend she understood you. You could tell that she did not. It was her hearing, and old age." Yet Brooke could still summon up her vibrant personality enough to hearten her friends. According to her phone log, "You told Mr. Rockefeller that you were very upset about the nasty review of his Memoirs in The New York Times Book Review and that you had torn up a copy of it while speaking with him this morning!"

Tony Marshall dutifully called his mother every other day like clockwork and stopped by 778 Park Avenue once or twice a week, occasionally bringing Charlene along. The Marshalls had a complicated relationship with Mrs. Astor's staff. Tony had grown up with servants, and he was invariably pleasant and detached. The staff perceived Charlene as simultaneously overly friendly and oddly suspicious.

Tony and Charlene had hired Brooke's new social secretary, Naomi Packard-Koot, a statuesque actor-filmmaker trying to underwrite her artistic pursuits. A struggle over Brooke's care began almost immediately. Protective of Mrs. Astor, the new social secretary quickly realized that the ornate curving staircase connecting the fifteenth and sixteenth floors was a potential hazard. "A cook had fallen down years before and injured herself badly," Packard-Koot says. "Mrs. Astor was unsteady on her feet, and sometimes she'd wander around at night." She went to Tony and Charlene with a reasonable suggestion to install a gate at the head of the staircase. The social secretary was startled by the Marshalls' reaction: "They said it was too expensive and it would ruin the value of the apartment." Tony later conceded that he had turned down that request, arguing that his mother had an aide at night. But this was just a foreshadowing of the hostilities ahead. As Brooke's chauffeur, Marciano Amaral, puts it, "When Mrs. Astor began to lose her mind a little bit, they started to take control."

Tony knew that his mother was happiest with a man on her arm whenever she went out, and he had the ideal escort — Francis X. Morrissey, Jr. The charming Mr. Morrissey, with a gift for gab and an ingratiating manner, was someone almost everyone instantly liked. The cultured attorney knew how to curry favor without being obvious, sending Mrs. Astor books such as *The Diaries of Beatrice Webb* along with flowers and notes. She reciprocated with an autographed copy of her poem "Discipline," which had been published in *The New Yorker*. In years past she had frequently run into Morrissey at the home of Jack and Nancy Pierrepont, and she had presumably heard of the lawyer's kindness to the couple's retarded daughter, Mary Rutherford.

On November 6, 2002, Morrissey escorted Mrs. Astor to the annual black-tie benefit for the New York Landmarks Conservancy. In a photograph taken by Ron Gallela, she looks fashionable in her dark fur coat, black evening gown, and glistening diamonds — pendulous earrings and a necklace. But holding tightly on to Tony and Morrissey with her white-gloved hands, she appears frail and a bit bewildered, smiling faintly. Charlene, wearing a double strand of pearls, grins exuberantly, while Morrissey, a slender man with thinning hair and a tuxedo tailored to perfection, gazes with a look of concern and fondness at Mrs. Astor.

This must have been a moment of splendid vindication for Morrissey; a once disgraced attorney, he was on the arm of the Living Landmark Brooke Astor.

Francis X. Morrissey, Jr., is the man in the shadows of this story, and he is difficult to assess. The tabloids reduced him to a stock character out of a nineteenth-century melodrama, the swindler of the innocent, a con man whom the *New York Post* labeled a "shady lawyer." Yet some friends and relatives of former clients speak movingly of his care for and generosity to sick, elderly, and disabled people who had been neglected at times by their own families. The protracted debate over his character has been waged repeatedly in the Manhattan surrogate's court and takes up six boxes in the files of the New York State Appellate Division, with testimony from friends and foes. Rarely has a wills and estates lawyer been so loved and so loathed.

"You'd think he'd look like Sean Connery, that you'd swoon when you look at him — how could a lady resist? — but he's kind of a nonentity," marvels a lawyer who was involved in the battle over the estate of Elisabeth Von Knapitsch. Relatives of that Park Avenue widow claimed that Morrissey duped the dying woman into leaving him the bulk of her $15 million estate, including her apartment and two Renoirs.

"On July 17, 1997, decedent Elisabeth Von Knapitsch was not of sound mind or memory and was not mentally capable of making a will," charged her stepson Walter Von Knapitsch in his court complaint, insisting that she was the victim of "duress and undue influence" by Morrissey. According to court papers, she had previously been diagnosed with Alzheimer's. All sides agreed to settle the case out of court, with a confidentiality agreement. A similar case involving another one of Morrissey's elderly clients ended the same way. The attorney never testified, and the propriety (or impropriety) of his conduct was never determined by a court.

There is a mythic quality to Morrissey's background. His father, Francis Xavier Morrissey, Sr., one of twelve children of a stevedore, put himself through night law school and then took advantage of Massachusetts's Irish-dominated patronage system. Morrissey Sr. was working for Governor Maurice Tobin when he had his Horatio Alger moment. Joseph Kennedy snatched him up to work on the 1946 congressional campaign of his war-hero son Jack.

In an interview with the Kennedy Library, Morrissey reminisced, "It was my responsibility to put him to bed at night and that would be around one-thirty or two; then I had to get him up very early in the morning so we could start." After Kennedy's election, Morrissey helped run his Boston congressional office, worked on JFK's triumphant 1952 Senate campaign, and attended his 1953 Newport wedding to Jackie. Appointed a municipal court judge in Boston in 1958, Morrissey was widely regarded as a Kennedy family retainer. He was described by the *Washington Post* as a man "who never let Joe Kennedy's coat hit the ground."

His namesake was born in 1942, the second of seven surviving children. "Young Frank is a charming man," recalled Arthur Schlesinger, Jr. "He's a WASP version of his father." Morrissey attended Harvard and majored in English. His conversations today are peppered with references to Shakespeare, Plutarch, and Zola. Frederic Kass, the executive vice chair at Columbia University's psychiatry department, recalls being befriended by Morrissey at Harvard: "Frank appeared one day and he was like an older brother, extraordinarily bright and sensitive." As Kass, who remains friendly with Morrissey, puts it, "Frank has associated for all his life with people who are powerful and influential."

But Morrissey learned at a formative age the limitations of connections as he watched his father be humiliated as his reward for decades of service to the Kennedys. In 1961, John Kennedy told White House aides, according to Schlesinger, "Look, my father has come to me and said that he has never asked me for anything, that he wants to ask me only this one thing — to make Frank Morrissey a federal judge. What can I do?" Kennedy went through the motions but abandoned the effort after the American Bar Association issued a scathing report branding Morrissey unqualified. After the president was assassinated, Bobby and Teddy Kennedy tried again with Lyndon Johnson. As Schlesinger explained, LBJ gleefully nominated Morrissey, savoring the prospect of his least favorite family's near-certain embarrassment. Predictably, the

1965 nomination of Morrissey as a federal judge was greeted with outrage in the Senate, where he was denounced as a Boston political hack. The *Boston Globe* won a Pulitzer Prize for tracing his tangled path to practicing law after he repeatedly failed the Massachusetts bar exam, and Morrissey finally withdrew his name, telling LBJ in a letter that he wanted to "prevent further anguish to my family." Back in Boston, he remained a controversial figure and was later censured and fined $5,000 by the Massachusetts Supreme Judicial Court for failing to avoid the appearance of impropriety (he had sought information about a criminal case against a friend, who obligingly gave him a $4,000 gift). In the example he set for his son, the premium was on loyalty at all costs.

After Harvard, the younger Frank Morrissey acquired a continental patina and fluency in French by attending the Institute of Political Science at the Sorbonne. Turning his attention to a legal career, he attended the Hastings Law School at the University of California. Despite his gilt-edged education, he suffered from dyslexia, a problem that later affected his practice as a lawyer and had repercussions in his dealings with Mrs. Astor. Admitted to the New York bar in 1973, he had his choice of good offers and joined the blue-chip firm of Willkie Farr & Gallagher. As a friend puts it, "Kennedy's name opened doors — he met a lot of people in New York." Morrissey soon jumped to another top law firm, Cadwalader, Wickersham & Taft, then left with a partner to start their own boutique firm, representing the heirs of the founder of John Deere Co. "I'm one of the people who think Frank is a saint," says Nancy Colhoun, a descendent of the Deere family who was in her twenties when she met Morrissey in the mid-1970s. "I was raised on a farm. All of a sudden this gentleman was paying attention to me, giving me sweet little presents." Colhoun was particularly pleased when Morrissey introduced her to his family, recalling, "His father is the most delightful creature you have ever met, very short like a leprechaun, extraordinarily bright."

Colhoun stresses that Morrissey, who continued to represent her periodically after he established a solo practice in the General Motors Building, has never been a legal shark obsessed with fees and billable hours. "Frank lives very simply. He's not a bling-bling lifestyle kind of person," she says. "I believe that doing bad deeds would be against the fiber of who he is. However, I also know that money is a real tricky thing."

Indeed it is, and Morrissey's initial mistake may have been in trying to be too tricky in pursuit of it. The case that left a permanent blot on his legal record came his way in March 1980. A Spanish corporation, Mar Oil, owned a supertanker that had blown up and sunk. The firm's president, Carlos Garcia-Monzon, hired Morrissey to pursue a $10.6 million claim against the New Hampshire Insurance Company. With no experience in maritime insurance litigation, Morrissey brought in another law firm to handle much of the work. When the case was settled for $8 million, the money was paid into Morrissey's escrow account, and according to court records he withdrew $925,675, claiming that he was owed that amount in legal fees. Mar Oil sued Morrissey, charging that the lawyer had vastly overbilled, and won the trial. Morrissey was ordered to repay $1.388 million, which included interest. Brought up on disciplinary charges in 1994 before the New York Supreme Court's Appellate Division, he was accused of excessive billing and misleading Garcia-Monzon into signing a document approving the fee.

The New York University professor Stephen Gillers, who specializes in legal ethics, teaches the Mar Oil case as a classic example of untoward legal behavior. "It's blatantly improper for a lawyer to do what he did," Gillers says. "It has great value in teaching the students how not to behave. It's stark and dramatic."

Fighting disbarment or the lesser penalty of suspension, Morrissey submitted a stack of character references, from August Heckscher ("Of all men I know he is the least avaricious and the most caring"), the art book author Deborah Harding ("If you're in trouble in the middle of the night, he will be there"), his younger brother Richard, a partner at Sullivan & Cromwell ("I have long ago concluded that he is incapable of dishonesty, fraud, deceit"), and his favorite waiter at a New York deli, whom Morrissey had helped gain U.S. citizenship. Even Brooke Astor's name was dropped to convey his rectitude. Marcia Mehan Schaeffer, of the Youth Counseling League, wrote that Morrissey "was instrumental in soliciting a significant contribution from Brooke Astor for a special laboratory for children." Schaeffer also commended Morrissey for donning a bright pink stegosaurus costume to entertain children at a Halloween party at the Museum of Natural History.

The glowing testimonials presumably helped. Jay Topkis, who chaired the disciplinary panel, noted at the end of a two-day hearing in 1996 that his staff had recommended disbarring Morrissey. But the three-lawyer panel chose merely to suspend him from practicing law for two years. Granting that Morrissey had "in a deceptive manner obtained his client's signature" as well as billed for watching television while waiting for his client to call, Topkis nonetheless wrote that "we are not convinced he is a totally lost cause."

Then fifty-four years old and a legal pariah (although even during his suspension he earned a yearly income of around $150,000 for nonlegal advice), Morrissey could never have imagined how successfully he would recover, thanks largely to Tony and Charlene Marshall. "He was devastated and embarrassed," says Chuck Merten, a high school teacher who was then Morrissey's neighbor in South Salem, New York, where the lawyer had a weekend retreat. "He truly believed that he had not done wrong and he was being railroaded."

In order to be readmitted to the bar, Morrissey had to demonstrate contrition. At a disciplinary committee hearing on April 9, 1998, he was a portrait of remorse. His groveling became so overwrought that Charlotte Fischman, the special referee presiding over the case, asked him if he had sought psychiatric help. Morrissey claimed that during the terrible time he had gone to the Madison Avenue Coffee Shop and envisioned the neon sign "saying, Suicide, suicide." He admitted that he had seen a therapist but had been distraught at being given a prescription for antidepressants. According to the hearing transcript, the usually eloquent Morrissey launched into a hard-to-comprehend wail: "He frightened me too much and so I, I figured this pain, I won't say like Lady Macbeth, but I, I, figured I had to, I had to come to grips with it myself." Then he stopped long enough to declare, "I don't want anybody screwing around with my brain."

The lawyer also seemed genuinely mortified to have brought shame to his family. His father, then in his late eighties and teaching at an inner-city school, was the object of his concern, because "my name is the same as his." In his closing statement, Morrissey said, "I have to always watch these bad, these bad things inside me. I had to realize that I had not only breached ethics, but that something evil was inside me. I had to manage it." Convinced of his redemption, the panel allowed him to resume practicing law. But in an age of databases, Morrissey could not easily escape the stigma of his punishment. A simple Internet search turns up a 1993 article in the *New York Times* about Morrissey and the Mar Oil dispute, headlined, "A Modern Form of Tilting at Windmills: Try Filing a Lawsuit Against a Lawyer." The Mar Oil rulings and details of the lawyer's suspension are available on Nexis-Lexis. Morrissey was under no obligation to wear a scarlet *S* for suspended. The Marshalls later claimed that they had no idea that he had ever been disciplined for legal improprieties.

By the time Morrissey became Mrs. Astor's escort, he was embroiled in other legal controversies. He had developed a particular approach with elderly clients: wining and dining them if they were able, arranging nurses and caregivers if they were not, working on their estate planning, but rarely sending legal bills. Appreciative clients often left him substantial bequests in their wills, frequently making major changes in his favor right before they died.

Citing his dyslexia as a rationale for not doing paperwork, Morrissey often worked with two other lawyers, Peter J. Kelley and Warren Forsythe, who drafted the documents. "Frank can read and write but not as easily as the rest of us," says Kelley, who has worked on legal matters with Morrissey since 1984. "He relies on other people. He used me to draft a number of wills over the years. Frank would let me know what the parameters of the will would be. I would meet with the people only at the will signing."

A month before he died, in 1987, the art dealer José Garza, who was in the hospital, marked an agreement with an *X* to name Morrissey as an executor, apparently because he was too frail to sign his name. "The man was quite weak," explains Kelley. The lawyer insisted that Morrissey's clients have all been of sound mind and cognizant of what they were signing. "I would go over the will with them piece by piece to make sure that was what they wanted," he says. Kelley adds that Morrissey is thoughtful and compassionate to his clients, saying, "He treated elderly people and disabled people with more professionalism and insight than anyone I've ever met."

But as for Morrissey's legal billing practices, Kelley added, "I tried to tell Frank on more than one occasion, you have to be careful with your billing. You can't just wait and get all your rewards in the afterlife. It doesn't look good."

And angry relatives did pause in their grief to express their rage at Morrissey, charging the lawyer with using undue influence to benefit himself. Sam Schurr, an economist who had been felled by a stroke, signed a new will on March 3, 2002, the day before he died. The major beneficiary of the latest changes: Francis X. Morrissey, Jr. Schurr bequeathed to Morrissey a Diego Rivera drawing and his recently purchased $680,000 Manhattan apartment. But Schurr's nephew, New Jersey judge Stephen Rubin, contested the will. His lawyer, Donald Novick, pointedly noted that Schurr's signature on this will was "markedly different" from his signature on a will executed just a year earlier by his lawyer of twenty years, Michael Miller. The case was settled out of court.

The relatives of Elisabeth Von Knapitsch also settled out of court, on January 3, 2003, albeit with an amusing postscript. As noted, Morrissey had received two Renoirs from the widow. A friend of his arranged to have the paintings appraised, at his behest. It turned out that the Renoirs were actually department store reproductions, one valued at $300 and the other at $7.

To be fair, Morrissey also has his grudging admirers. Margot Adler, a National Public Radio reporter, came to know Morrissey well during the decade that he looked after her widowed aunt, Alexandra Adler Gregerson, who died at age ninety-nine in 2001. Gregerson, a psychiatrist, was the daughter of Alfred Adler, one of the pioneers of psychoanalytic theory. "There was no one to take care of Allie," says Adler. "Morrissey comes into this situation, he got these Irish ladies to give her round-the-clock care." The lawyer, a devout Catholic, was beside Gregerson's hospital bed for three weeks before she died. During that anxious time, he urged Adler and her husband to keep her aunt alive, even though she was on a respirator. "His attitude was, 'What would she want? What did we think?'" recalls Adler. "He had incredible respect for her." But the reporter was shocked to discover that her aunt's will, prepared under Morrissey's auspices, left him 40 percent of her estate — far more than previous wills. "The estate was 1.2 million dollars," Adler says. "My husband and I argued this thing. Should we fight it? Was it fair? Was he a crook? We said, 'No one else would have done what he did. He took care of her for ten years, and that's worth quite a lot.' He's a very complicated figure."

In the mythology of New York — from Lorenz Hart to Woody Allen — Central Park is the idyllic place, the urban Garden of Eden, where everyone from the poorest pushcart vendor to the richest . . . well, Astor can enjoy grass, trees, and sky. On a sunny November day in 2002, Brooke Astor, taking her usual walk in the park with Annette de la Renta, let go of Boysie's and Girlsie's leashes, and the two dogs took off. Annette went chasing after them and successfully caught up with the much cosseted pets. Despite the canine rescue, Brooke was in a querulous mood that day, complaining that Annette did not appreciate her. Annette took it in stride, assuming the mood would pass. But the next day, November 11, Brooke, worried that she had said something hurtful, poured out her heart to Annette in a four-page handwritten declaration of love, asking for forgiveness.

> Dearest, Darling Annette,
>   I had *the most* awful nightmare last night which continued until 11 o'clock this morning. It was *utterly terribly* stupid of me to have even thought that you did not love me (as a mother almost) . . . Frankly, there is no one in my life like you. My own dear Tony is so happy with at last a wife that loves him so that I hardly see them . . . Darling Annette, I love you dearly. You are *My* child — and I hope will always be so. Love, Love, Brooke

How rare, after nearly a half-century of friendship, to receive a note from a hundred-year-old woman that says it all. Still holding close to what remained dear to her, Brooke was staking her claim. This was one of the last notes that she wrote by hand on her monogrammed stationery, and these were words to cherish, words to hold on to, for the time when there would be no words at all.

Palm Beach was Mrs. Astor's favorite winter destination, although she preferred to rent rather than buy an oceanfront mansion. She scheduled her annual month-long visit to Florida for February 1, 2003, and arrangements were made for her to be met at the airport by Bunny du-Pont and Virginia Melhado, Freddy's wife. Four days before she left, David Rockefeller went by her apartment at 6:45 P.M. with his chauffeur to pick her up for a farewell dinner at Tony and Charlene's home. The other guests included Mike Wallace and his wife, Mary, and the theater producer David Richenthal.

The Marshalls had decided they wanted to try their hands as Broadway angels. Tony had first gotten the theater bug in 1982, when he signed on as a producer of a revival of Eva Le Gallienne's *Alice in Wonderland* starring Kate Burton. Investing $250,000 of his mother's money and $250,000 of his own funds, he also solicited his mother's friend Laurance Rockefeller for $400,000 and raised funds from WNET, where he was a board member. But after a scathing review in the *New York Times* ("miles of scenery sadly going to waste"), the $2 million show closed quickly, at a large loss. As Tony later told the *Times*, "I swore I'd never produce another one."

But now, at seventy-eight, Tony had been seduced again by the bright lights, and Charlene was also intrigued by the idea that the couple could become Mr. and Mrs. Opening Night. Richenthal, with a solid track record of producing Arthur Miller revivals, had convinced the Marshalls to invest in his upcoming version of *A Long Day's Journey into Night*. With the play opening in the spring of 2003, just in time to be eligible for the Tony Awards, the producer had lined up a stellar cast, with Vanessa Redgrave and Brian Dennehy. Richenthal's presence at the February dinner party at the Marshalls' home was fortuitous. If Tony and Charlene were going to be serious players on Broadway, it would be helpful to have Mrs. Astor's blessing and her financial wherewithal.

The theater was not Tony and Charlene's only stage in New York cultural life. As a member of the Juilliard School Council, a fundraising group created by the music school as a steppingstone to full trusteeship, Charlene had made a strong initial impression. Mary Rodgers Guettel, the daughter of the Broadway composer Richard Rodgers and a trustee of the school, says, "Charlene's a delightful person to talk to — I found her absolutely charming." But charm and good family connections only go so far up the hierarchy of New York cultural institutions, especially since the Marshalls had not been major benefactors at Juilliard. "The only thing we knew about them was that they didn't have a great deal of money," says Guettel, adding, "Everyone assumes they would, being related to Brooke Astor."

Brooke had always been generous to her son but kept him on a financial leash. When she died, however, everything would change. Tony was due to inherit her Park Avenue apartment (later valued at $46 million); Holly Hill, a sixty-five-acre property that could be developed; Cove End (worth $7 million); a $5 million bequest; and a yearly payment of $4.2 million for life, which represented a percentage of a trust. But for now he and Charlene were on an austerity program for people in their position.

Tony also had a real fear about the future and his ability to provide for Charlene. Apparently reflecting her ongoing pique at her daughter-in-law, Brooke had structured her will so that if Tony predeceased her, all of her bequests to him would go to charity rather than to Charlene. In her 2002 will, she left Charlene a spectacular diamond snowflake necklace with 367 round diamonds and matching earrings, but this generosity was coupled with the presumably insulting gift of two used fur coats, which had been tailored for Brooke's slender frame and were unlikely to fit her robust daughter-in-law. John Jacob Astor had originally achieved success as a fur trader in the 1780s, so for Brooke there may have been a mischievous poetry to leaving her old mink coat and often-worn chinchilla short coat to Charlene instead of giving her the means to buy her own coats from the celebrity furrier Dennis Basso.

Therefore, if Tony died before his mother, the Astor millions and real estate would be out of Charlene's reach — a nightmare scenario, and a very real one. Brooke had signed her most recent will just a year before, but she did have a lifelong habit of making revisions. It was not too late. Tony made a date to take his mother to lunch at the Knicker-bocker Club when she returned from Palm Beach in early March, along with her attorney, Terry Christensen.

On the night before Brooke's hundred and first birthday, Philip and Nan and their children, Winslow and Sophie, drove to Holly Hill for an early celebration. This was a stealth visit, designed to avoid over lapping with Tony and Charlene and arranged with the assistance of Brooke's obliging social secretary, Naomi Packard-Koot. She and Philip had become phone friends, and she was aware that the Marshalls frowned on his efforts to see his grandmother. "I always saw them bris-tle when Philip's name came up," Packard-Koot recalls. "It wasn't clear why. Philip and I really bonded on the phone — he wanted to know how she was, what he could do for her. I would try to get him in to see her without their knowing, because they would thwart it. It was a hor-nets' nest."

Philip had been going through an emotionally wrenching period. His much-loved stepfather, Craig Wheaton-Smith, had died a year ear-lier, leaving a poorly organized estate. Philip had been helping his griev-ing mother unravel her finances, which had turned into an unpleasant crash course in estate law. But although his grandmother was declining, there was still pleasure to be had in their relationship, and his children looked forward to the visits. "At Holly Hill, we'd sit in the library and Gagi would pick up pictures and tell us about them," recalls Sophie Marshall, who was ten years old the year her great-grandmother turned 101. "Everything she told me seemed so interesting, and very different from my life."

Brooke had written the family a series of affectionate notes in recent years. "I simply adore my Christmas presents, particularly the framed photographs of those two lovely children. It made my heart beat twice as fast, and I can hardly wait to see them," she wrote in one letter. In an-other she thanked Philip and Nan for returning copies of her poetry. "I was very glad to get them as I am now keeping all the things that could be read when I am on my way to heaven. I miss you both and I wish, wish, wish that we could all be together more often." With her friends either dying or drifting away, Brooke was seeing her family in a new light and was receptive to closer ties. After Nan crafted a ceramic artwork featuring dogs, Brooke wrote, "I adore my mantelpiece, I have it by my bed and sleep better."

For a birthday gift in 2003, Nan had created a collage of a family tree for Gagi, and dutifully included photos of Tony and Charlene. While Philip and his family usually took walks on the estate with Brooke, the family left promptly on the morning of her birthday. Tony and Charlene showed up a few hours later, along with Alec and his daughter, Hilary Brooke, for lunch and a second celebration.

That evening Brooke went off for dinner with the Rockefeller brothers, David and Laurance. Flirting with her two favorite men was the perfect way to cap the day. David Rockefeller gave her a diamond and emerald brooch. "I didn't give her important jewelry," he says, "but I gave her things I thought she would wear." There was still a fairy-tale aspect to her life, being given diamonds by a Rockefeller at age 101.

By late April, the Marshalls were excited about the upcoming opening night of *Long Day's Journey*. They had set aside tickets for Brooke to attend the play and the after-party at Tavern on the Green. It was an early curtain, 6 P.M. at the Plymouth Theatre, and Morrissey would escort her; everything had been arranged. But when the Marshalls asked Naomi Packard-Koot to put the event on Mrs. Astor's calendar, she expressed concern that her employer might be overwhelmed by large crowds. As she puts it, "Would you take a one-hundred-and-one-year-old deaf woman to a four-hour play?" Her words were dismissed as interference.

On opening night, May 6, Mrs. Astor was complaining about having to go. Awaiting Morrissey, she told her social secretary, "I don't like that man. He's not my friend, he's Tony's friend." But, unfailingly polite, she greeted the lawyer warmly, although she announced that her sciatica was acting up. Because she knew it meant a lot to her son, she would attend the first act, but she planned to skip the second act and the after-party. At intermission, Mrs. Astor and Mr. Morrissey adjourned instead for a quiet dinner at Swifty's, where they had a conversation that would have profound repercussions. Morrissey later said that Brooke had turned to him that evening and asked a simple question: "What can I do for Tony?" The lawyer replied, "Ask him."

It could be argued — and many of Brooke's friends took this position — that Brooke had done quite enough for her son already. But Morrissey took her at her word, detecting anguish in her voice. A deeply religious man, he later said that he believed that Mrs. Astor could not die in peace until she had made things right with Tony. When Morrissey submitted a bill for $15,455.76 to Brooke Astor's office ten months later, he dated his fees back to that night, actually charging for the dinner conversation.

The day after *Long Day's Journey* opened to rave reviews, Terry Christensen went by Mrs. Astor's home for tea. At that meeting, Brooke approved in writing a plan to speed up her bequest of Cove End to Tony. Christensen had assigned an accountant to research the tax consequences, and informed Tony by letter that there were three options. He recommended a scenario in which Brooke would give Cove End to Tony now and pay the $3,562,500 in gift taxes.

Although Brooke executed the transfer documents, it's likely that she had not entirely abandoned her hope that Philip would inherit at least part of Cove End. She did not change the language in her will that specifically expressed her desires, which she had repeated to several other people. Tony was aware of what his mother's wishes had been, at least in the recent past, regarding the property.

But in truth Tony had other plans for Cove End. For him, it was the romantic spot where his own life had changed for the better. What better symbolic gift for his third wife, as an expression of love and gratitude? Six months after Brooke signed the Maine estate over to Tony, he put the title in Charlene's name. In a memo to his files, he wrote of the transfer of Cove End: "I was very keen to have this accomplished during my lifetime so that, in the event BA might live longer than I, I would be able to leave the property to my wife."

Two days after *Long Day's Journey* opened, the Marshalls went to 778 Park to meet with Naomi Packard-Koot. They knew that Brooke had left a few hours earlier to go to Holly Hill for the weekend. At the start of the conversation, the Marshalls informed the social secretary that she was fired. "It was really sudden," she recalls. "I asked them why. Tony sort of fumbled and said that I didn't type quickly enough. First of all, I do type fast, but that wasn't part of my job anyway. My job was running her life and liaising with a lot of people and the staff." In a cruel twist, the Marshalls forbid her from returning to the apartment to say goodbye to Brooke.

By virtue of temperament and personality, Alec and Philip had developed very different relationships with their father. Alec was much closer to Tony emotionally, although Tony dictated the terms of their relationship, which was carried out at his convenience. Alec lived just a brief drive from Holly Hill, but even though Tony visited his mother there frequently, he had stopped by his son's apartment only a few times in a decade. Instead, he invited Alec into Manhattan for lunch every several weeks or so, usually at the New York Racquet Club or the Knickerbocker. Alec interrupted his workday and took the train in for the pleasure of his father's company.

For Alec, it had become troubling that his father and his brother did not get along, so he decided to play peacemaker, urging Philip to go into Manhattan alone, without Nan and the kids, to spend some time with Tony. The twins e-mail each other constantly and talk every other day, and finally, in early June 2003, Philip relented, agreeing to take his brother's advice and commit a few days to this exercise. The weekend that was good for him, unfortunately, was not ideal for his father. Still, when Philip arrived, his father proudly took him down to Times Square to see the theater where *Long Day's Journey* was playing. Tony had invited Philip to opening night, but the college professor had declined because of his teaching schedule. At least he could see the marquee, his father's bright lights, big city accomplishment.

Tony and Charlene had been invited to dine at Mike Wallace's apartment that evening and did not offer to take Philip along. Free on that first evening in Manhattan, Philip made a last-minute call to Naomi Packard-Koot — they had never met in person — and went out for what turned into a five-hour dinner at Island, on Madison Avenue. The former social secretary kept stressing her commitment to Mrs. Astor and voicing her concerns about Tony and Charlene's actions. Since Philip wanted his visit to improve family relations, he kept quiet the next morning at his father's apartment, where he had spent the night. But Tony had decided to cut the visit short. Announcing that it would be inconvenient for him and Charlene to host Philip for another evening, Tony reserved a room for his son at the Knickerbocker Club. As for dinner with Brooke, which had been scheduled, Tony said she was not feeling well and the get-together had been canceled.

Later that day Philip stopped by his grandmother's building to leave her a bouquet of flowers; when the doorman rang up, his grandmother's staff urged him to come up and see Brooke. She seemed in good spirits, although she chastised him for wearing shorts and sandals in the city. "I wasn't expecting to see her or I would have dressed up," he recalls. She did not look sick to him, nor did she mention an illness. That night, as Philip lay in bed in his room at the Knickerbocker, he mulled over his relationship with his father. Hurt feelings abounded on both sides. There had been Tony's seventy-fifth birthday celebration in Turkey: neither Philip nor Alec attended, duly noting that the invitation had arrived late and their father had not offered to subsidize the expensive trip. On the one hand, Tony kept saying he wanted to know his grandchildren, yet he and Charlene had last visited Philip in Massachusetts twelve years before, shortly after Winslow was born, in 1991. Invitations for return visits had been politely deflected. A reconciliation seemed to be nothing more than a shimmering mirage.

"I'm glad I made the effort, but I was disappointed," Philip later said about this trip. Nan Starr knew how much Philip longed for a connection to his father. "It felt to Philip that he was never accepted, that his father neither knew nor liked him," she says. "I think Tony had aspirations for his sons to follow in his footsteps or the footsteps of his own grandfather. But Philip chose a more bohemian academic life." She adds, "Philip could not let go of hoping that there was something more with his father in terms of unconditional love."

Mrs. Astor liked her privacy at night, and so she frequently ordered her aide to leave the room when she slept. But trying to get out of bed on the evening of June 24, she lost her balance and toppled to the floor, breaking her hip. Tony and Charlene met her in the emergency room at New York Hospital. After spending several days in the hospital, she returned to Park Avenue, and on July 15, Dr. John Lyden performed a hip replacement.

To be 101, disoriented, hard of hearing, suffering from insomnia, and now in intense pain was an ordeal. Her recuperation was slow, and Mrs. Astor became depressed and listless. This was the first summer in decades without Maine. At Holly Hill, Chris Ely had to wheedle and coax and finally argue with his employer, telling her that he was not going to let her rot in bed. He was on the phone continuously with her doctor, Rees Pritchett. Brooke did manage to walk again, but she would have nurses with her every day for the rest of her life.

Brooke was still recuperating at Holly Hill on August 13 when Terry Christensen arrived for a meeting. She was in her bedroom, seated on a sofa facing the Hudson River, when the lawyer was ushered in. Christensen had prepared yet another set of financial documents. This time Brooke magnanimously gave $5 million to Tony, ostensibly to take care of Charlene. Not long before, Brooke had been so frightened about her finances that she had agreed to part with her Childe Hassam. Now she was feeling profligate, sending her love and money in surprising directions.

Christensen had crafted a letter for her to sign:

Dear Tony,

Terry Christensen has reviewed with me again the terms of my Will, and of the charitable remainder trust which I establish for your life benefit under my Will. I am quite satisfied with that trust, except that I now realize that as the trust terminates on your death, there may not be enough to provide for Charlene.

I do want you to have enough money to provide for Charlene on your death.

I am therefore making an additional outright gift to you of $5,000,000. This should provide you with enough money to assure Charlene's comfort assuming that she survives you. You have my power of attorney, and I authorize you to transfer $5,000,000 of securities from my accounts to yours in order to effect the gift. I understand that there will be a gift tax payable on this gift, from my own assets (and not Vincent's trust), next year.

With my love.
Sincerely,
Brooke R. Astor

Who could say that Brooke Astor was not a good mother? In poor health, she had still remembered to make financial concessions to a woman whom by most accounts she loathed, and she volunteered to pay the gift tax too.

Unknown to Christensen, the walls had ears: his private conversation with Mrs. Astor was being overheard elsewhere in the house. Because Mrs. Astor kept demanding that the duty nurses leave her bedroom, a baby monitor had been unobtrusively installed to track her movements. As a result, every sound in her bedroom was broadcast to the room next door, where the nurses waited. A nurse's aide regaled the household staff with what she heard, claiming that Christensen mentioned a "rift between the Marshalls and Mrs. Astor" that could be resolved only by giving money to Charlene. The word *millions* got everyone's attention.

Chris Ely had been told by Tony twenty months earlier that Mrs. Astor had Alzheimer's disease. Now she was signing legal documents and giving away money? As Christensen was leaving, he stopped to chat with the butler. In a written account of the day, Ely acidly noted that Christensen "seemed to want me to agree with him that BRA [Brooke Russell Astor] was very well and in good mind. This comment coming from a man who could not look [at] me straight."

Mrs. Astor's mood changed after the lawyer departed. She told one of the nurses that she felt "foolish" and then retreated into silence. When she went down for dinner, she asked Ely what Christensen had wanted, as if she had no idea what had transpired. "I told her that I did not know, but as she had asked for a pen I thought she had signed something," wrote Ely. She asked to speak to Christensen, and the butler got the lawyer on the phone. But the conversation apparently did not alleviate her concerns.

The next morning Mrs. Astor, who believed that a lady should not be seen until fully dressed, broke tradition and summoned the butler to her bedroom. She "was not wearing make-up or her wig, she was lying flat on the bed without a pillow," Ely wrote. "I only see BRA like this in an emergency. She asked me what had happened the day before and what she had signed." At Mrs. Astor's request, the butler called both Tony and Terry Christensen's office and asked for copies of the paperwork; both declined to provide the documents. Unsure of how to resolve this impasse, Ely jotted down detailed notes describing the lawyer's visit and his employer's distress. It never hurt to keep a record.

Ten days later, John Hart went out to see Brooke at Holly Hill, and she told him wearily, "John, I'm gaga." Hart tried to reassure her and read out loud from *Patchwork Child*. "I'd show her pictures and say, 'Who's that?' and she would say, 'That's me!'" Once they moved from the sunroom to the living room, she had trouble carrying on a conversation and began to joke about the furniture. "She'd look at a chair and go, 'Way too big, way too fat,'" he recalls. "Inanimate objects became animate, they had personalities." His heart went out to his valiant friend. Hart says, "I cried when I left."

9

The Treacherous Codicils

BROOKE ASTOR had always rotated in new friends, like a stockbroker trying to beat a bear market. In the fall of 2003, the uniformed doormen at 778 Park Avenue watched as the latest group of regulars headed up to the fifteenth and sixteenth floors of Mrs. Astor's diminished world.

After Tony and Charlene set up a theatrical partnership, Delphi Productions, with David Richenthal, the gruff Broadway veteran moved into the handsome fifteenth-floor office that had previously been used by Naomi Packard-Koot. *Long Day's Journey* had not only made a substantial profit but won the 2003 Tony Award for best revival. Charlene also hired Erica Meyer, a friend of one of her daughter's, to take on the title of Mrs. Astor's social secretary.

Francis Morrissey, now entwined in so many aspects of the Marshalls' lives, had also become a regular visitor. The attorney joined Delphi's board of advisers and invested in upcoming shows. He also catered to Mrs. Astor, just as he had to many elderly friends and clients in the past. He brought cupcakes to her staff, going out of his way to be friendly. Catia Chapin, the wife of former New York cultural affairs commissioner Schuyler Chapin, was friendly with Morrissey and Mrs. Astor. She was impressed by the lawyer's thoughtful efforts, recalling, "He used to go visit Brooke every Wednesday. Every Wednesday, it was a joke, 'Where's Frank?' Of course, he's with Brooke. He'd go for tea in the afternoon, check in, see if she's all right." The lawyer told friends that he was honored to be close to Mrs. Astor and her son, and hoped to be as valued by this family as his father had been by the Kennedys.

In midtown, at 405 Park Avenue, Mrs. Astor maintained a separate business office with a two-person staff employed to pay her bills, for everything from the Chanel suits to the weekly arrangements of roses and lilies from Windsor Florist. Since 1993 the bookkeeper Alice Perdue had prepared checks, which Tony signed. A petite, animated woman with curly hair, Perdue was startled when Tony asked her to write two large checks in 2003 from his mother's accounts: $200,000 to Richenthal's company, Barking Dog Productions, followed by $250,000 to Delphi Productions. During the next two years, Perdue prepared two other theater-related checks at Tony's request: another $250,000 to Delphi and $200,000 to the Goodman Theatre in Chicago. Vincent Astor had so disliked the performing arts that Brooke, in keeping with his wishes, had given only minimal foundation grants in this arena. But now she became quite the Broadway supporter, parting with a total of $900,000.

Tony later insisted that his mother had authorized those checks because she was eager to support his new ventures. But Perdue recognized that supporting the theater was out of keeping with Mrs. Astor's usual behavior. "Everything was fine until Mrs. Astor broke her hip in June 2003," Perdue says. "But there was a definite change in everything after that. I saw things happening — I didn't know what to do."

Alicia Johnson, the housekeeper in Maine, noticed a curious item in her local newspaper, the *Ellsworth American,* that autumn: a fine-print listing of the property title transfer of Cove End to Charlene Marshall. Johnson sent a copy to Chris Ely, who lived at Holly Hill. The butler was on friendly terms with Philip Marshall and mentioned it the next time they spoke, assuming that Tony's son was already aware of what had happened. Philip was caught off-guard. "I knew there was no way my father was going to let me have it, after the conversation we'd had about the cottage," says Philip, but he adds that Tony's lack of candor was yet another blow. "I was mad at my father that he did not do this aboveboard." He also viewed his father's gift to Charlene as a harbinger of things to come, or, as he puts it, updating a witticism about bygone presidential politics, "As goes Maine, so goes the rest of the estate."

Although Charlene was now the lady of the house, the Maine expenses were still paid from Mrs. Astor's accounts. Tony expected his mother's bookkeepers to continue to pay for the gardeners, the housekeeper, the electricity, the cable TV, repairs, and taxes as they had before. "I did think it was odd. I didn't think it was right. I questioned a lot of things, but who was I going to talk to?" Alice Perdue says. "I didn't know Philip and Alec Marshall well. If I questioned Tony, I would have been out on the street."

For Mrs. Astor, her new reality was a New York life surrounded by nurses and aides. But she was still going out to see friends occasionally, and, ever conscious of appearances, she insisted that the nurses wear street clothes. They would accompany her in the car and help seat her at dinner parties, then retreat until it was time for her to leave. "All the nurses got dressed up for her, and she would tell us how nice we looked," recalls Minnette Christie, a stylish and slender Jamaican nurse with a passing resemblance to Angela Bassett. Christie had taken care of Mrs. Astor during her recuperation from her first broken hip, five years earlier, so this was a return engagement. The nurse noted that in her absence, the household staff had come up with a new nickname for Charlene, Miss Piggy.

Pearline Noble, another Jamaican, with an ebullient personality and a church choir voice, joined the staff as a nurse's aide with her friend Minnette's encouragement. Both women were in their forties, married, with three children each; they had met while caring for patients at Lenox Hill Hospital. Like a Broadway musical star who bursts into unexpected song, Noble sang to her patient through the day to cheer her up. "Suppose I'm taking her to the bathroom," Noble recalls. "I'd sing a kicky song and she'd pick up her nightgown and rock to the music and dance. She'd move faster."

Rounding out Mrs. Astor's primary team of nurses was Beverly Thomson, a gentle, friendly woman who had been living in Florida but who flew to New York when she heard about the job opening. "I started in Holly Hill just after she broke her hip," recalls Thomson. "She wasn't talking much, but she could hold a conversation. She told me about her grandchildren, who would come and play in the pool. She talked about her dogs, and food." These three women would be Mrs. Astor's constant companions for the next few years, with others rotating in and out as needed.

It is standard practice for nurses to jot down medical notes, but Mrs. Astor's caregivers kept unusually detailed accounts describing her activities, moods, nightmares, and reactions to visitors. Pearline Noble was the most prolific note-taker, with a vivid, descriptive writing style. "I just wanted to put down her state of mind — it wasn't meant for public knowledge," says Noble, who hoped her notes might be helpful to the next shift. In truth, there was a subtext here. Chris Ely kept hearing complaints from the nurses about events in the Park Avenue apartment. He urged them to write down anything unusual. If anyone ever asked, there would be a contemporaneous chronicle by eyewitnesses.

What the nurses captured in more than thirty voluminous notebooks over a four-year period was a portrait of a despairing woman who felt that she had lived too long. "She is dead set against eating, saying she wants to die," wrote Noble on September 25, 2003. "She said she is old and wanted the window shades down." The aide noted that Dr. Pritchett called that day to try to cheer her up and the housekeeper finally talked her into eating, but Mrs. Astor remained inconsolable. "She ignores us all and covers her face with the napkin." Mrs. Astor's emotions were even more turbulent three days later, as a night nurse wrote: "A very restless night. Had nightmares. Was not able to tell her dreams, only that someone was trying to kill her, and I showed her that the door was locked." The nurses took special notice of Tony's visits, writing that Mrs. Astor appeared "unhappy" after being in his presence.

Brooke had always appeared to be the last woman in need of Prozac or other mood elevators. Now she was tormented by panic attacks and nightmares. At 101 years old, perhaps she was fearful of being stalked by death, or was beset by the paranoia that often characterizes Alzheimer's. At times she appeared to be recalling Dryden Kuser and the beatings she had suffered. Like a mother trying to comfort a frightened child, Minnette Christie would pretend to search under her bed every night. "Mrs. Astor would tell me to use the cane to make sure," Christie recalls. "You know that no one is under the bed, but you do it to reassure her."

Mrs. Astor prayed at bedtime, asking Christie to get on her knees to join in the Lord's Prayer. Her worn Bible was her talisman against fear, and she took it with her to Holly Hill on weekends. (The car had to turn back one weekend when the Good Book was left behind.) But Christie's notes are heartbreaking: "Refused sleeping pill. Said she wants to be awake if anyone is trying to finish me. Reassured of her safety. Skin very dry, fragile." In order to hear the footsteps of her mythical tormentors, Brooke kept refusing to take her hearing aids out at bedtime, despite the nurse's protests.

Yet Mrs. Astor could still make a comeback, and there were moments when she appeared joyous — a contagious sight for her caregivers. Pearline Noble was delighted by her impulsive gesture as a friend departed, writing in her notes, "Mrs. A curtsied, she did it so gracefully, she's unbelievable!" One evening Mrs. Astor spent an hour trying to pass along her flirting techniques, literally teaching the nurses how to wink at men. Christie laughs as she recalls Mrs. Astor demonstrating her prowess and announcing, "This is how you do it."

As Brooke Astor faded, Tony, at age seventy-nine, was in the midst of an unexpected renaissance. The Marshalls were reveling in their roles as producers, thanks to Delphi's new play, *I Am My Own Wife,* a brilliant and innovative one-man account of a transvestite who survived in Nazi Germany. Richenthal discovered the property, by Doug Wright, but Tony and Charlene, his chief financial backers, revealed not only taste but artistic daring, since this show was unlikely to appeal to the suburban matinee crowd. The director, Moises Kaufman, was impressed by Tony's and Charlene's earnest and unpretentious attitude. "The first thing that struck me was how kind and unassuming they were," he says. "Usually producers walk into the theater with the sense of entitlement. This was a hard play to sell. They never wavered." He also enjoyed spending time with the third Mrs. Marshall. "Charlene has this kind of exuberance," Kaufman says. "I used to joke with her that she could talk to a wall and the wall would talk back to her."

For the first time in years, Tony was treated as more than his mother's escort. He was portrayed as an avant-garde producer in a profile on December 14, 2003, in *Variety.* The glowing account highlighted his service in the CIA and the battle of Iwo Jima. "The theatre is a little like going into battle. It is very tense," Tony said. "But you can't get killed, only wounded." Three days later he received the ultimate civilian medal — a gushing profile in the *New York Times* headlined "He Is His Own Producer, and Much More." Perhaps the most meaningful element of the article for Tony Marshall was that the story mentioned only in passing that he was Brooke Astor's son. How long had he waited to be acknowledged, praised, and recognized for his own merits? The *Times's* theater reporter, Jesse McKinley, wrote, "Even in an industry populated by moneyed eccentrics and grandiose credits, Mr. Marshall's resume stands out."

Although Mrs. Astor, her son's most important audience, would attend opening night, accompanied by Francis Morrissey again, she was not able to appreciate his triumph fully, given her declining health. On December 13 she was described in the nurse's notes as experiencing "periods of confusion and illusions. Continues to say being afraid and that someone is trying to kill her. Reassured of her safety. Did not want to be left alone. Pain in hip." The following day Mrs. Astor appeared to have lost the will to carry on. "Periods of confusion. Talks constantly about wanting to die. Involuntary tremors lasting 25–50 seconds." By December 17, as her deterioration accelerated, she could not complete full sentences or make her wishes understood. The day nurse wrote, "Paranoia, undecipherable words, disoriented after lunch." The night nurse noted, "Started conversations and then became incoherent."

The nurses saw Mrs. Astor unguarded, at her worst. Yet drawing on a lifetime of social skills, she could still pull herself together for guests, relying on snippets of recycled conversation. "She was on automatic pilot," recalls Barbara Goldsmith. "She would repeat favorite lines, like 'My mother always told me never to get above myself' or 'Vincent Always told me that I would have a lot of fun with the foundation.'" Annette, who went by at least once a week, marveled at Brooke's tenacity in clinging to social niceties. For a brief showing, Brooke could artfully perform like a wind-up doll who brightly repeats, "How nice to see you. How have you been? Would you like some tea?" But close friends were not fooled. They had spent too many years being entertained by, confided in, and bossed around by the genuine article.

Despite the incoherence and disorientation noted by the nurses on December 17, on the next day Mrs. Astor met with Terry Christensen, this time to change her will. Sometimes in recasting her bequests she would give in to whims, revising who got which piece of jewelry, but this was no minor modification. On this fateful day, Mrs. Astor agreed to the first substantial revision of her 2002 will. The change marked a radical shift in her attitude toward Tony: she was now passing along her avocation as a philanthropist. Christensen drafted the document, describing this as the "First and Final Codicil," as if he were giving Tony a message: This is it — no more changes.

Up until now Mrs. Astor had always left the bulk of her estate to charity, with a detailed list of beneficiaries. But under the new codicil she agreed to put 49 percent of the remaining assets left in a trust by Vincent Astor into a new entity, the Anthony Marshall Fund, to allow her son to give away the money. Now the Marshalls could be New York power brokers, able to pass out some $30 million, in total assets, to their favored entities. The codicil that Brooke signed reads: "I have enjoyed greatly the ability to help New Yorkers through Vincent's generosity throughout my long life, and I hope my son will obtain similar enjoyment and satisfaction, and find new ways to benefit the public." Under the provisions, Tony would be the sole trustee, but he could not be paid a commission or name future trustees. Any money remaining in the Anthony Marshall Fund at the time of his death would go to the Metropolitan Museum and the New York Public Library. Six years earlier, Brooke Astor had closed the Vincent Astor Foundation rather than turn it over to her son. Now she was making him a philanthropist for all the world to see.

Later that day, Brooke told the nurses that she was worried about being put in a nursing home. She had spoken of this fear repeatedly of late, and the staff did not know what to make of her anxieties. On December 18, the nurses' notes describing Brooke's mood read, "Wanted to know who was taking her to the nursing home or else she would die."

Mrs. Astor reiterated that thought in a slightly different fashion the next day, inquiring when "they are putting her away." According to the notes, she stated, "I want to live for at least six months but they told me I am going to die tonight." The night nurse added her own commentary: "Reassured that no one knows when she is going to die but God.

Appears to be in deep concentration. When asked if she was ok, said she has a lot on her mind but didn't want to talk about it."

When Louis Auchincloss, who practiced as an estates lawyer in addition to writing novels, learned about that 2003 codicil several years later, the date struck a chord. He and Nancy Pierrepont had taken Brooke to lunch just a week earlier at the Knickerbocker Club. Sadly, Brooke had had such a difficult time conversing that he had decided this would be their last encounter. "She knew me but had trouble coming up with my name," he says. He was astonished to learn later that his friend had been encouraged to sign legal papers. "She probably knew it was a codicil, but she didn't know what was in it," he speculates. "She was beyond it — she was in another world. Any son who took advantage of that to change a testamentary plan in any way was being a very bad person." Auchincloss has one other enduring memory from that last lunch, recalling, "The only time she flared up was when I mentioned something about Charlene. It was like watching a fire. God, she hated her."

The effect of Mrs. Astor's signature on this document was to put Christensen's reputation on the line. If she was competent on December 18, then presumably she would also be competent to make additional changes in the near future. By his unorthodox wording, Christensen appeared to be signaling that he would not be party to any more alterations to Mrs. Astor's will. If Tony wanted his mother to sign other codicils, he presumably would have to employ other lawyers. How fortunate for Tony that Francis X. Morrissey, Jr., had become so well versed in Brooke Astor's estate plans.

January 12, 2004, was a bad day to be Brooke Astor. That Monday was so memorable that several people immediately felt compelled to write down their version of events. Even the most self-serving accounts include details that are chilling. As legend has it, Brooke had once dissuaded a would-be thief on Fifth Avenue by politely extending her hand and saying, "I'm sorry, but I don't believe we've been introduced." But there was no way to charm the intruders on this day, who wielded a pen. In weak handwriting, Brooke Astor scratched her name on a second codicil, bequeathing $60 million directly to Tony Marshall and thereby disenfranchising the charities on whose behalf she had worked tirelessly for four decades. The new codicil enabled Tony to choose his fellow executors: he replaced Christensen with Charlene and the ever helpful Morrissey.

What was Mrs. Astor's mood on this fateful Monday? According to the lawyers dispatched by Tony, she appeared to be cheerful and sophisticated, dropping bons mots into conversation, discoursing on world events, and reading complex documents without her glasses. What the nurses described in their notes was a frightened old woman being dragged down a hallway against her objections to a closed-door meeting.

In Morrissey's account, Brooke was wearing a blue tweed suit and good jewelry and appeared pleased to see him when he arrived at the apartment at 4 P.M. to meet with her and Tony. "She extended her arm, and we both walked into the library side by side," he wrote. "She looked at me and said, 'We are here for something important.'" Morrissey, using Tony's favored honorific, wrote: "Ambassador Marshall explained to his mother that she had told him on Friday (1/9/04) that he should come to her with any problems. He said he found it difficult to work with Terry Christensen." In addition to Morrissey, the former ambassador had hired new lawyers in early January — G. Warren Whitaker and Robert Knuts of the firm Day, Berry & Howard — to draw up a new codicil.

Morrissey's chronicle goes on to describe an intimate mother-son moment: "She then said she loved him. She wanted to give him money. She turned to me and said you know Charlene and Tony have 'nobody,' they have to 'wash their own dishes.' She said she thought it was terrible and she wanted him to have the freedom to manage her affairs after her death . . . Mrs. Astor agreed that she wanted him to be happy and she didn't much care if Terry or Sullivan & Cromwell were disappointed. In fact she said jokingly, 'I don't give a damn. I'll be dead anyway.'"

The next step was to bring in the new team. "I then explained to Mrs. Astor that Mr. Knuts and Mr. Whitaker, both lawyers, prepared a second codicil to her will expressing her wishes so that it would be abundantly clear to everyone," he wrote. "Ambassador Marshall left and Mr.

Whitaker and Mr. Knuts came into the library and I introduced them to Mrs. Astor."

These strangers, who had shown up on her doorstep apparently unbidden, had drafted a document for her to sign, based on instructions from her son and Morrissey. "I gave her a pen," wrote Morrissey. "We were sitting on the sofa and there was not a hard surface for the pen to make a strong mark. She commented on the pen and said she would sign her middle name 'Russell' because Tony would like it." According to Morrissey, Mrs. Astor then looked at him directly and said, "How do you think things are going?" As Morrissey put it, "I knew intuitively and from past conversations with her that she was referring to world events." He added that she had gone on to regale him with stories of her girlhood in China. He wrote, "She demonstrated an acute awareness of the presence [present] as well as an awareness of what was going on everywhere in the world."

G. Warren Whitaker, who composed his own memo describing the signing ceremony for his files, was so concerned about getting the nuances right that he wrote four different versions, tweaking the language and description. He met with Mrs. Astor at 4 P.M., or at 4:05 P.M., or at 4:15 P.M. In one version he "reviewed" the changes in her will; in another he "explained" them to her. In one of the memos, Morrissey hands Mrs. Astor a document and tells her that this is "the codicil she had wanted prepared." In Whitaker's three other versions of the same scene, that line is missing and there is no indication that she knew anything about the codicil.

One vivid snatch of dialogue is contained in all of Whitaker's memos. Handed the codicil to read, she replied, "Good, I am not going to be around much longer." According to Whitaker, Morrissey explained that this codicil allowed Tony to leave property outright to his wife. "Mrs. Astor said, 'They are happy?' Morrissey replied that Tony and his wife were happy together. Mrs. Astor wryly replied, 'Are they happy in bed?' and everyone laughed appreciatively."

The nurses were not allowed into this meeting, but they saw Mrs. Astor before and after. Pearline Noble had started keeping a separate log, using easy-to-decipher pseudonyms for the characters: Brooke was Princess Polyanna, Tony was Golden Boy or Golden Retriever, Morrissey was Tutor, Charlene was Miss Piggy or Poor Little Rich Girl. Here's how Noble described that afternoon: "Golden boy & tutor took Princess Polyanna on each arm pulling her into the library . . . Mrs. Astor didn't know if she was coming or going. She told Mr. Marshall she don't want to be pushed in any business and she reiterated 'do you hear me' with a bang on the floor with her walking stick. She was having a hard time walking." Noble wrote that Mrs. Astor did not even recognize Morrissey and asked her son, "Who is that?"

Noble later confirmed her written remarks in an interview with me and then physically demonstrated, with her arms around me, how she usually helped Mrs. Astor walk, half carrying her. "They started to pull her," Noble insisted. "They are not holding her to balance her — it ended up being a drag."

That evening Minnette Christie wrote in the regular log that Mrs. Astor was frightened, saying that "four men are in the house who know everything about her and she doesn't know them. Also that the men want her to do things. Very hard on herself, referring to self as a 'dam[n] fool.' Reassured that no men are in the house and of her safety. Remained apprehensive and did not want to be left alone."

Someone had to break the news to Terry Christensen that his services were no longer needed. Christensen was in Florida on business when he got a series of urgent calls from Warren Whitaker. The Sullivan & Cromwell lawyer reacted with a mixture of fury and disbelief when he learned that he had been fired. He did not believe that Mrs. Astor had voluntarily agreed to do so. The lawyer called Tony, who insisted that the entire decision had been his mother's idea. Christensen asked to meet with Brooke; Tony refused.

While Christensen brooded, Tony arranged for his mother to host a lunch at the Knickerbocker Club on February 10 for her financial advisers, including her old dance partner Freddy Melhado, who ran a hedge fund, and Richard Thieke, a director of Deutschebank. Mrs. Astor spent that morning at the doctor's office, undergoing a battery of tests. Renowned for her spontaneous remarks, at this lunch she got up and read from a typed notecard: "It has not been easy to be my son. Tony has had to dance in back of me all of his life. He has proven himself to be a gentleman. He has never asked me for anything. I am proud of his service to our country as a decorated Marine — as was my father — and as an ambassador. I am grateful to him for what he has achieved while managing my affairs. He has done a magnificent job! Most of all, I love him and his wife Charlene and my great hope is for their continued happiness."

Lovely sentiments, to be sure. But Dr. Pritchett later stated that at this point in her decline, Mrs. Astor lacked the mental ability to write or dictate those thoughts. The purpose of the lunch appeared to be to display her in a public forum so that witnesses could see her looking mentally fit and praising Tony. The experience was so traumatic for Brooke that several weeks later, when a friend made a date to take her for lunch to the Knickerbocker, she became phobic outside the club, sitting in her car and refusing to enter the building.

The day after the Knickerbocker performance, Christensen met with Tony and Charlene at their apartment for a largely acrimonious fifty-minute meeting. Tony wrote a revealing letter for his files afterward, referring to everyone by initials: his mother is BA, Christensen is TC, Charlene is CTM, and he is ADM. As the memo states, "On entering our apartment, TC declared, 'I thought we were friends.' . . . With controlled anger, he declared that if it were to become known that he was no longer BA's lawyer he would be publicly humiliated." Then the conversation escalated, according to Tony. "TC went on to say that BA was incompetent (I interrupted saying that I completely disagreed with him) and that what Warren Whitaker, 'a second rate lawyer' did was unethical and that any respected firm would not have allowed him to do what he had done. TC told us that he had always looked out for our (ADM/CTM) interests. . . . TC commented that he had stood up for us when, he said, BA wanted to cut CTM out of her will some time ago."

Christensen has a different recollection. After being shown Tony's written account, Christensen, who had previously refused to discuss his relationship with Mrs. Astor, citing attorney-client privilege (which in New York continues beyond death), agreed to respond. "I did not describe Mrs. Astor as incompetent or believe she was incompetent," Christensen said. "She was old — her vitality had diminished. What I said to Tony was that given his mother's age and infirmities, it wasn't fair to ask her to make changes in her life, whether removing her counsel, or completely changing her estate plan." Christensen insisted that he did not personally attack Warren Whitaker.

As for Mrs. Astor's desire to cut Charlene out of her will, Christensen confirmed that that had indeed been the case. "I cannot break confidences of private conversations I had with Mrs. Astor, but it is fair to say — given what Mr. Marshall says in his memorandum — that I did urge Mrs. Astor from time to time not to remove Charlene, and some others, from her will." The lawyer adds that the session at the Marshalls' apartment "was sufficiently tense that at the end of the meeting, Charlene said she was worried about Mr. Marshall's health, given his heart attacks, and could we please terminate the meeting."

Whitaker sent Christensen a letter demanding Mrs. Astor's previous wills and codicils and pointedly reminding him of the December 18 codicil. "Presumably you determined at that time that she was competent since you signed the codicil as a witness," Whitaker wrote. "I do not believe you have seen Mrs. Astor since then, and therefore wonder what personal knowledge you have that would lead you to question her competence now." Worried about what Christensen might do, Tony consulted yet another lawyer, Kenneth Warner, an aggressive litigator who had worked for such high-profile clients as George Steinbrenner, the owner of the Yankees.

After debating the matter with his partners, Christensen decided against embarking on a public battle. "I considered publicly contesting Sullivan & Cromwell's removal as Mrs. Astor's counsel," he says, "but I decided that it was not in Mrs. Astor's interest to do so." He sent off the estate-planning documents, as requested.

This was unequivocally the moment when Tony, Charlene, and Francis Morrissey should have left well enough alone. Tony and Charlene's financial woes had been solved, and Morrissey had been guaranteed a very large payday. Day, Berry & Howard estimated that the executors' fees for handling Mrs. Astor's estate would be $4.89 million, shared among Tony, Charlene, and Morrissey. In addition, an estimated $3.38 million in legal fees would be divided between the law firm and Morrissey.

But the guiding principle of estate planning is "Avoid unnecessary taxes at all costs." For the Marshalls and Morrissey, their subsequent efforts at prudent tax planning would result in truly disastrous emotional and legal consequences. On March 3, Morrissey arrived at the Park Avenue apartment bearing a new document for Mrs. Astor to sign. Compared to the prior two codicils, which had totally transformed the terms of Mrs. Astor's will, this piece of paper had a modest intent. In order to save on estate taxes, the codicil instructed her executors to sell her real estate (the duplex apartment at Park Avenue and Holly Hill) and include the proceeds in the estate.

Since Morrissey had not brought witnesses with him this time, the lawyer recruited her social secretary, Erica Meyer, and the maid, Lia Opris, to certify that she had signed. Two years later, Meyer's lawyer told the *New York Times* that Meyer had no recollection of witnessing Mrs. Astor signing the third codicil. Opris, who is Romanian, told the *Times* that she had a vague memory of the meeting but added, "For me, English is a foreign language, and I am a little bit hard of hearing. It was not easy for me to follow the lawyer."

Morrissey sent a jubilant letter afterward to Tony Marshall, albeit with an odd admission. The lawyer pointed out that Mrs. Astor's signature on the third codicil appeared quite different from the frail strokes on codicils one and two. He offered a comforting rationale: "I agree with Charlene that the primary energy driving your mother's heart was to give you recognition, recognize Charlene's contribution to your happiness, achieve an independence for both of you and most of all, to thank you. I think the strength of her signature on the third codicil reflects these truths."

In the same letter, Morrissey warned that Terry Christensen might present a problem. "We still must be vigilant and careful because Terry's words to you and his letters to us reflect a treacherous and strategic mind which has not yet surrendered complete control over your mother's matters," Morrissey wrote. But they had nothing to fear. On May 17, 2004, Christensen submitted Sullivan & Cromwell's final bill, after forty-five years, to Mrs. Vincent Astor: $31,257.33, for services rendered from October 14, 2003, through February 2004.

Mrs. Astor's displeasure at being asked to sign more legal papers was duly noted in the nurses' notes. "Her son arrive with an unexpected guest. They all sat down to sign some papers. She got a book from the lawyer Morrissey. They left, she shook her head, saying what can I do." But social niceties still mattered to the centenarian. She learned that same day that Annette de la Renta's mother, Jane Engelhard, had died. As she was unable to write a personal note, her secretary typed a pro forma note, which Brooke signed. Annette had cherished and saved all of Brooke's handwritten notes, which provide a history of their friendship, but this one was so distant that it added to Annette's anguish, and she threw it out. Having just lost her mother, Annette simultaneously had to confront another sign that her dearest companion was fading fast.

Pearline Noble was so upset that she wrote in her notes a few days later that she and the chauffeur had promised Mrs. Astor that "me and the driver will protect her she's not signing anything else."

As the reigning authority figure in Mrs. Astor's employ, Chris Ely was the person whom everyone else looked to for advice, the keeper of confidences. Ever since the troubling sale of the Childe Hassam painting, he had been trying to signal to Brooke's friends that things were awry. But as a butler, he still had to practice indirection, dropping hints rather than saying anything outright.

Invited to lunch at David Rockefeller's country house near Holly Hill one weekend, Mrs. Astor got dressed up and went downstairs to depart. Then she told Ely to cancel — she did not want to see anyone. Knowing her devotion to the Rockefeller family, the butler insisted that she get in the car and express her regrets in person. When Rockefeller and two guests eagerly came out to greet her, she promptly announced that she was not staying for lunch. "It's okay," Ely said in a loud voice designed to be overheard by Rockefeller. "There's nobody here waiting for you to sign papers."

The butler's ruse worked. David Rockefeller went to dinner at the home of Henry and Nancy Kissinger and mentioned the strange episode. As Nancy Kissinger says, "She wouldn't get out of the car. David went up and said, 'Brooke, it's me, David.' She said, 'It's the men in blue suits, they make me sign things.'" Henry Kissinger adds, "David Rockefeller told me there was an incident where Brooke was afraid to go into a house." The story was burnished and embellished with each retelling on the Upper East Side. It was a sad but riveting piece of gossip. But no one knew what it meant, or ultimately how to respond.

Philip Marshall also had a scary moment in that March of 2004 that brought home to him how much his grandmother was losing her mooring in reality. He and Nan were in Manhattan with their children. Nervous about running into his father, Philip took the suggestion of Mrs. Astor's veteran housekeeper, Mily Degernier, that the family might be able to catch Brooke in her apartment lobby. They arrived just as she was being wheeled out of the elevator by a nurse. Brooke did not immediately recognize them and appeared to panic, unsure whether they were friends or foes. "She looked like a deer caught in the headlights," recalls Nan. "She got into the car, and the four of us leaned our heads in and began speaking to her soothingly. Philip started stroking her cheek, saying 'Gagi, it's Philip and Nan and Winslow and Sophie, we're all here and we love you.' Tears starting rolling down her cheeks."

Even though Mrs. Astor was not going out much anymore, her jewelry was. At the nationally televised Tony Awards that June, *I Am My Own Wife* won the award for best play. Charlene, Tony, David Richenthal, and Doug Wright proudly bounded up onstage to collect the trophy. Charlene was wearing a distinctive diamond necklace, which the members of Brooke's social circle recognized immediately as Mrs. Astor's prized snowflake necklace. Charlene later insisted that Brooke had graciously lent her the diamonds for the evening and that when she had tried to return them, her mother-in-law had told her to keep them. This jewelry was earmarked for Charlene in Brooke's will, but the sight of Charlene ascendant wearing Brooke's signature pieces raised eyebrows.

Brooke had begun to opt for passive resistance, pretending to be asleep when Tony and Charlene visited. "She played possum," recalls her chauffeur, Marciano Amaral. "After the son left, she would talk to the staff. She was powerless but trying to defend herself." Yet at 102 years old, almost in spite of herself, she showed an impressive will to carry on. The physical therapist Sandra Foschi, who worked with Mrs.

Astor three times a week starting in 2004, says, "She was always frail, petite, but with a real strength and strength of character to complete the task. She would express fatigue, but she always tried."

Even though Mrs. Astor dined alone at home most evenings, she still dressed for dinner. She wore her wig and full makeup, choosing among an array of gold, red, and blue silk caftans adorned with sequins and matching the outfit with a pair of custom-made Belgian flats. Jewelry was mandatory. Mrs. Astor made a ritual out of selecting her adornments: a large gold bangle, multiple diamond bracelets with sapphires or emeralds, her teardrop pearl and diamond earrings, and perhaps a three-strand pearl necklace. It did not matter that she was only going down the hall to the dining room or even eating at a tray in front of the television in the blue sitting room — she still carried a matching evening bag.

Whatever was hurting, however she was feeling, she was ready for dinner at 7 P.M. She had standards to meet, and it was in the small things, the manners and gestures, that she continued to rise to the occasion. One evening a temporary aide neglected to help her change for dinner. When Minnette Christie came in on the night shift, Mrs. Astor was furious. As Christie recalls. "She said, 'Ever since I was a little girl, I always dressed up for dinner.'"

Philip Marshall was traveling with a friend in Cambodia when he e-mailed his father to ask if they could meet in New York when he returned. Now fifty-one, he and Nan had started work on an estate plan for their family, and he wanted to know what he would inherit from his grandmother. With Cove End gone, he correctly assumed that his grandmother had left him a cash bequest. But with his father, money had always been a taboo topic. Looking back on his emotions in broaching the topic, Philip says, "To me, just writing this was 'Oh my God, this is so weird, it's such a simple question but so loaded. What is he going to think?'" He felt an obligation to try to get the information, adding, "I had a mother who had just lost her husband and was worried about money, and I had a brother who is a freelance photographer with no equity." Alec, in fact, had already asked Tony about his inheritance, and all his father had said was that the twins would be "comfortable." But what did that mean? Philip and Alec had never seen any of their grandmother's many wills, nor did they know that the bequests had changed direction in recent months.

Philip's meeting with Tony and Charlene was warmer than the Israeli-Palestinian peace talks, but not much warmer. All three of them came out of the meeting at the Marshalls' apartment with colossal misunderstandings. As Philip tells it, Charlene, who did most of the talking, was determined to present Tony as the good father who had recently persuaded Brooke to show a little generosity to her grandsons. "Charlene says my brother and I were going to get $10,000, and my father had been able to change it so it would be $1 million," Philip recalls. This was inaccurate, although Philip did not know it at the time. In a 1992 will, Brooke had indeed left Philip and Alec a comparatively modest $150,000 each (a far cry from the $10,000 mentioned by Charlene). In the will dated September 20, 1993, she had raised her bequests to the twins to $1 million each, and that figure remained unchanged in subsequent wills. If Tony had sweet-talked his mother into that seven-figure sum, he had done so eleven years earlier, but Charlene made it sound like this was hot-off-the-press news.

Tony later told reporters that Philip "acted strangely" after the $1 million bequest was revealed. This reaction, he argued, signified Philip's avaricious disappointment that he was not going to be showered with riches by his grandmother.

Philip admits that he was very upset by the conversation, but for an entirely different reason. He says that he "freaked" at the idea that his father had been able to "change" Brooke's will, since she had Alzheimer's disease. "I was thinking," he says, "if it happened in the last few years, it wasn't appropriate for my grandmother to have signed this. She didn't have the capacity." What else, he wondered, had been changed in his grandmother's will?

As Annette de la Renta headed out the door after a visit at 778 Park, she asked Pearline Noble what she could bring for Mrs. Astor the next time. "A man," Noble playfully replied. The following week Annette took that advice and turned up with one of Brooke's male friends, much to Brooke's evident delight. She became so engrossed in her gentleman caller that she completely ignored Annette. As Noble recalls, "I said, 'How you doing, Mrs. D?'" Laughing at her irrelevance, Annette replied, "Pearline, I'm toast."

Brooke was still alert enough to point with a mixture of amusement and horror every time Annette visited wearing designer jeans, much like an elderly mother who cannot stop criticizing her middle-aged daughter's clothes. As Annette says, "She thought I should be more feminine."

Affectionate, playful moments like these were recompense to Annette for more difficult days when Brooke was incoherent. Even though she was never certain what to expect, Annette frequently popped by for an hour or so. She would kneel on the rug so that Brooke, who had difficulty holding her head up straight, could see her. "Mrs. Astor would stroke her hair and kiss her head," recalls Minnette Christie. Noble concludes, "She was like a child in Mrs. Astor's eyes."

But many of Brooke's other longtime friends drifted away because it was so painful to behold her in her sad state. "I went to see her, and she had shrunk," Vartan Gregorian says. "I said 'Brooke, I'm here,' and she opened her eyes and grabbed my hand and said, 'I love you.' I kissed her hand and said, 'I love you too.'" Philippe de Montebello also gave up. "I would go to have tea with her with Annette, and Brooke would say, 'Who is that man?'" he says, grimacing with sorrow at the memory. "She wouldn't recognize me."

At the end of 2004, Brooke Astor's universe narrowed even further. Holly Hill, with its majestic view, landscaped gardens, and winding trails, was placed off-limits. Just before Thanksgiving, Brooke became seriously ill with a fever while visiting her Westchester retreat and spent several days in nearby Phelps Memorial Hospital Center. For Tony and Charlene, that was the breaking point — they decreed that Brooke was too fragile to ever go to the country again.

In February 2005, the Marshalls, accompanied yet again by Francis Morrissey, drove out to Holly Hill to tell Chris Ely (who lived in an apartment above the garage) that they were shutting down the property and his services were no longer necessary. The butler was not surprised — Tony and Charlene had always seemed to resent Brooke's reliance on him — but he was worried, since he felt that he had become

Mrs. Astor's sole protector. Brooke's closest friends were troubled by the firing too. "Chris was wonderful with Brooke," says David Rockefeller. "It was shocking to Annette and myself when Tony let Chris go."

From Holly Hill, Ely had long been his employer's conduit to the outside world. If Mrs. Astor seemed especially lonely, Ely would invite people over on her alert days. As Barbara Goldsmith recalls, "After Chris was fired, it became much more difficult to see her. You'd try and someone would say, 'There's not much point.'" The butler, who could be blunt and demanding, had not been universally loved by Mrs. Astor's staff. If he found a dust ball, he would reprimand the maids, and if he saw that the nurses had changed the channel on Mrs. Astor's television to watch a show they preferred — an evangelical program or Oprah — he would switch back to Mrs. Astor's longtime favorites, Turner Classic Movies or the Discovery Channel. But without Ely, who commanded respect in the household, there was no one the rest of the staff could talk to about their questions or problems.

Tony's glowing letter of recommendation complimented Ely for his "precise" fiscal accounting and entertaining skills and expressed gratitude for his solicitude. "During the past two years Mrs. Astor's strength and well-being has deteriorated," the letter said. "Chris was most attentive to Mrs. Astor's wishes and comfort and would frequently take Mrs. Astor for long drives along the Hudson River and through the countryside." Of course, Tony also was one of the few who knew the precise financial savings that followed termination of the butler's employment. Mrs. Astor had left Ely $50,000 in her 2002 will, but only if he was still employed by her at the time of her death.

Philip had always had warm feelings toward his grandmother's loyal butler. The next time he passed through Westchester, he took Chris Ely out for a meal. The butler was circumspect — after all, Philip was Tony's son — but he did take pains to mention the reports he had heard of lawyers traipsing through Mrs. Astor's apartment. "I thought it was a little late for her to be carrying on with lawyers," Philip says. "But no one told me about the codicils."

Although he listened to Chris Ely's concerns, Philip was too overwhelmed by other family problems to be receptive. His mother had recently been diagnosed with breast cancer; she was his priority. Still, with Naomi Packard-Koot and now Chris Ely gone, he was worried about who would watch out for his grandmother's interests. As he puts it, "I felt impotent."

For Mrs. Astor, the butler's disappearance from her life was traumatic. Several weeks after his departure, he called Mrs. Astor's nurses to say he wanted to visit. To jog her memory and give her something to look forward to, the staff had gotten into the habit of bringing out photographs of expected visitors. "We showed her a picture of Chris before he came," Minnette Christie recalls. "She wasn't talking much, but she asked, 'Is he dead?' She didn't believe me when I said no, so she asked Pearline, and she believed Pearline. She put her hand to her heart and said, 'I love him.'"

In Brooke Astor's addled mind, death was the only possible reason that Chris Ely would have abandoned her. But her son was either threatened by the butler's power over his mother or oblivious of the potency of their bond, since he soon banned Ely from visiting. "Chris called once and we put the phone to Mrs. Astor's ear," Christie recalls. "Tears ran down her face."

10

"I Didn't Know It Would Be Armageddon"

THE FIFTY-SIXTH FLOOR at 30 Rockefeller Plaza has been occupied since 1933 by the family that built Rockefeller Center. The elevators open to reveal a glass foyer on the south side, featuring a bronze bust of John D. Rockefeller, Sr., the dry goods clerk who founded the Standard Oil Company and eventually became the richest man in the world. A polite but firm security officer mans the desk, ensuring that no unwanted visitors intrude.

David Rockefeller, the grandson of the family patriarch and the last survivor of his generation of six siblings, operates out of a surprisingly small southwest corner office, albeit one with a panoramic view of the Empire State Building, the Hudson River, and the Statue of Liberty. Rockefeller Center was his father's crowning aesthetic achievement, but the influence of his mother, Abby, the artistic visionary who co-founded the Museum of Modern Art, is apparent on his walls. A Picasso cubist painting of a woman's head, a Gauguin (*Portrait of Jacob Meyer de Haan*), a large Signac of a man magically producing a flower, and a blue-and-yellow Dale Chihuly glass sculpture are among the $50 million worth of art in the office. Family photographs are scattered on the windowsills, including a picture of Rockefeller with Brooke Astor, beaming as recipients of the Presidential Medal of Freedom.

This is where the opening scene unfolded of what would become

Tony and Charlene Marshall versus the world. In late May 2005, when Brooke Astor was 103 years old, Rockefeller called Tony Marshall and asked him to come by his office to discuss what might be euphemistically called his mother's living situation but in reality was a joint effort by Rockefeller and Annette de la Renta to move Brooke back to Holly Hill. "I remember going to the Central Park Zoo with Brooke in May," Annette says. "It was hot — there were bus fumes in your face. I thought, 'What are we doing?'" Making matters worse was that 778 Park Avenue, for all its luxuries, lacked central air conditioning. Bob Silvers remembers accompanying Annette to see Brooke around the same time, on a day that Tony had told his mother once again that she could not return to Holly Hill. "Brooke was sitting there, all dressed up, wearing a hat, and she was crying," he says. "She looked up, tears coming from her eyes. She said, 'It's not right. I want to go.'"

Tony Marshall had recently received other pointed inquiries from Brooke's friends, who had heard that she had become a virtual prisoner of Park Avenue. Her care had been the topic of lunchtime gossip at the communal table at the venerable Brook Club. As John Richardson tells it, "I started saying that all the staff at Holly Hill had been fired. Then I looked up, and to my absolute horror, I saw Tony coming in. I realized, there's nobody next to me, and he's going to sit down." Trapped, Richardson asked directly for an update on Brooke and Holly Hill. As he recalls, "Tony went into this nauseating spiel — 'Oh, poor darling Brooke, it was such a strain for her going every weekend, she is so old. We said to her, "Brooke, it's much better if we close down the house and keep you comfortable in New York, you'll be closer to your doctor and hospitals and your friends."'"

Viscount Astor had been troubled by a disconcerting recent visit to Brooke but had chosen not to confront Tony Marshall. "She didn't recognize me to start with," he recalls, "but halfway through, she squeezed my hand and said, 'I'm having a miserable time — please take me away.'"

All these tales eventually flowed back to Annette, in her role as Brooke's best friend and ultimate protector. Although she, David Rockefeller, and Tony Marshall lived within a few blocks of each other, she suggested that the meeting be held at Rockefeller's office, for its aura of power and authority. The two white-haired men, only nine years apart in age, had always gotten along reasonably well. "We had a perfectly cordial relationship, not a close one," says Rockefeller, the elder of the two, who hoped there was enough of a bond for him to be persuasive.

At the appointed hour, Tony showed up at Rockefeller's office with the uninvited Charlene in tow. Everyone was extremely polite, almost exaggeratedly so, and yet tension radiated as the four of them sat at the small white marble table. Rockefeller urged the Marshalls to reopen Holly Hill, stressing that he thought Brooke would appreciate the fresh air and countryside. "She always loved it out there in the spring — she loved to see the daffodils, she had a whole field of daffodils," says Rockefeller. "It seemed cruel that she was unable to go."

Tony, straightforward and calm as always, stressed that his mother had a variety of medical problems and needed to be close to her Manhattan doctors. But Charlene could not camouflage her anger. A woman whose emotions often run close to the surface, she argued in an irked tone that Brooke disliked Holly Hill and Chris Ely but felt comfortable and safe on Park Avenue. Even though Charlene did not know Brooke nearly as intimately as the others in the room, her pseudo-certainty was not challenged. "We were upset," Annette recalls. "David and I were just sitting there looking at each other." Rockefeller, already perturbed by the sale of Brooke's Childe Hassam and Ely's dismissal, says, "By then I was concerned about the way Brooke was being treated."

As the meeting ended, when Tony and Charlene were halfway out the door, Rockefeller mentioned that he was heading up to Seal Harbor soon and offered to take Brooke and her nurses on his private plane to Maine so she could go to Cove End instead. "They said no, that would be even worse — she'd be farther away from her doctors," says Annette. "So we said goodbye. We didn't know they were already living in Cove End." Charlene, the new owner of the Maine property, had begun renovations, but her status as the owner was not widely known and certainly had not been shared with Brooke's friends. So even though David Rockefeller had made his offer as an impulsive gesture, Tony and Charlene may have perceived it as a threat. The next day, after consulting with Dr. Pritchett, Tony called Rockefeller to say that Brooke would be moved to Holly Hill after all. David Rockefeller was pleased: "What I said had an impact."

It certainly had an impact on Tony Marshall, although not entirely in the way that Rockefeller had envisioned. Tony was sufficiently annoyed by this interference that he mentioned it to Philip, who called to wish his father a happy eighty-first birthday, on May 30. Father and son had not seen each other for a year, but this ritual call remained an acknowledgment of their tie. At the time, Tony said, "Some of your grandmother's friends are trying to get me to open Holly Hill." Although he was not specific about the identity of these friends, Philip guessed that the instigators were Annette de la Renta and David Rockefeller, whom he knew slightly from an earlier visit to his grandmother at Cove End. "If I had not heard about that meeting, I wouldn't have known that David was concerned," Philip says. "My father was pissed off."

In hindsight, Philip believes he should have seized the opportunity to tell his father bluntly that he agreed with Annette and David that his grandmother would be happier in the country. "People always wonder, why didn't I talk to my father about this stuff? Give me another twenty years and I'll figure it out," Philip concedes. "I could have said, 'Why didn't you open Holly Hill? My grandmother can afford it.' But such is our relationship that we couldn't have that conversation. By then, I knew that Charlene was running things."

Brooke spent the summer at Holly Hill, but she was forlorn without Ely to keep her company and attend to her needs. Boysie and Girlsie, her beloved but boisterous dogs, were now kept away from her for fear that they would scratch her delicate skin. In prior years Ely had draped Brooke in blankets and towels for protection and allowed the dogs into the room under his supervision. "We were told she shouldn't have the dogs," says Beverly Thomson, the nurse. "The dogs would sit on her and rest on her and she'd have a bruise, so we would try to avoid that." Gone too were the long country drives. "She did not leave the property," recalls Pearline Noble, who pushed Brooke in a wheelchair to the boundaries of Holly Hill. Her patient became agitated when she saw that one of the gates was padlocked.

Mortality was constantly on Mrs. Astor's mind now. One evening, as Minnette Christie gave her employer a facial, Mrs. Astor, gazing at her own unadorned face in the mirror, announced, "When I die, don't let anyone see me like this." Pointing to her eye shadow and rouge, she added, "You put on the blue, and the red."

Brooke Astor's mortality was also on the minds of Francis Morrissey and G. Warren Whitaker that summer. They wrote a memo on August 23, 2005, noting that Anthony Marshall would be handling his mother's funeral arrangements. The lawyers wrote that "it is unlikely that the Attorney General or the charities will contest the will . . . It is also unlikely that Terry Christensen will contest the will, or that he would be permitted to do so if he wanted to, since the will and codicils show a consistent pattern of giving greater control and authority to Anthony Marshall."

When Brooke returned to Park Avenue that fall, there were fewer familiar faces to greet her. Tony and Charlene had decided to purge more longtime retainers from the staff to reduce the payroll. Marciano Amaral, Mrs. Astor's chauffeur for the past ten years, was given a month's pay and thirty days to vacate a small apartment on East Seventy-second Street owned by Mrs. Astor. "I was a driver and a companion," Amaral says, recalling how he took her to Central Park frequently and walked her dogs several times a day. "She made me promise that I will stay with her until the last day of her life."

The next staffer to be shown the door was the bookkeeper Alice Perdue. "Tony said that he was terribly sorry he had to let me go, but he had so much work that he needed someone who could take shorthand and was more savvy with the computer," says Perdue. "These two things are diametrically opposite." The bookkeeper had been so worried for two years about Tony's unorthodox spending that she had started keeping a file at home listing questionable transactions. Perdue, who needed the job, had never directly challenged Tony's orders. But she wondered whether her facial expression or tone of voice might have signaled her growing disquiet to Tony or, more likely, to Charlene. "Mrs. Marshall had stopped talking to me a year or so before," Perdue says. "I think she felt I was too loyal to Mrs. Astor. They assumed Mrs. Astor was dying soon and wanted people loyal to them."

Brooke Astor, whose values came from an era when lifelong retainers were the norm in wealthy families, prized loyalty. As a sign of enduring gratitude, she had left Amaral $25,000 and Perdue $10,000 in her 2001 will. But both these bequests had been dropped without explanation from her 2002 will.

The Marshalls had previously installed one employee who was presumably loyal to them, the social secretary, Erica Meyer. But Meyer too received her walking papers that September, just after returning from her honeymoon.

In the wake of the departures, there was a new and unlikely arrival at 778 Park Avenue, Daniel Billy, Jr., a middle-aged man with a background in marketing and fundraising who was hired to supervise the staff. "Ambassador Marshall wanted someone to answer the phone who wasn't a servant," explains Billy, who had come into the picture through Charlene and a friendship forged at St. James' Church. To Mrs. Astor's oft-belittled son, Billy's admiration for "Ambassador Marshall" must have felt like a burst of sunlight after decades of chill. "If I didn't already have a terrific father, I would have wanted Tony for my father," says Billy, the son of a professional golfer. "Listening him talk about Richard Bissell and the U-2 plane was a wonderful tutorial. It's a pleasure to hear his stories. I've told Charlene that it breaks my heart that his sons have not had the experience with him that I've had."

The new major-domo, inexperienced in running a household staff, quickly discovered that he had entered a combat zone. "It was warring factions," Billy says. Mrs. Astor's all-woman staff, of various ethnicities and with different perceptions of their own social status, were at each other's throats. "The nurses treated the servants like servants," he says. "The household staff felt their job was to make Mrs. Astor comfortable. I do believe that everyone saw Mrs. Astor's comfort as a priority. But the execution was problematic."

Loyal to the Marshalls, Billy took on the role of gatekeeper. Tony now required almost everyone to call him in advance for permission to visit his mother, making only a few exceptions, for the likes of Annette de la Renta and David Rockefeller. "You'd make an appointment to go see her, and then Tony would cancel, several times," says Robert Pirie. "One time I was at the door of the apartment building and my secretary called to say he'd canceled. He wanted to control who saw her." Pirie finally gave up, but his last visit was poignant. "It was so sad to see her," he says. "She wasn't properly dressed, the flowers were dead, the place looked like hell. Yuck." Equally sad for Pirie was that it took Brooke four or five minutes to recognize him, at which point she said, "We had a lot of fun together, didn't we?" Pirie, who had always teasingly called her "kid," replied, "Yeah, kid, we had a good time.'"

The elevator was broken on September 16, 2005, when I went to see Tony and Charlene Marshall at their apartment at Seventy-ninth Street and Lexington Avenue, so I walked past the garbage bins and up the back stairs to the second floor and entered through the kitchen. An elaborate silver service that appeared to have been just polished was on the table. Tony escorted me past the dining room to the front of the apartment and the sunny corner living room, decorated with comfortable chintz furniture and a spinet piano, where Charlene was waiting.

I had been asked by *New York* magazine, where I was a contributing editor, to write an article about Brooke Astor, who had disappeared from public view. When I telephoned Tony right after Labor Day to request an interview about his mother — having no idea that this was a potentially explosive topic — he was friendly and obligingly invited me over, saying that he would be "delighted" to talk. I learned only much later that this was right around the time that the Marshalls fired both Alice Perdue and Erica Meyer and installed Daniel Billy. There may be no connection, but Tony's warmth had inexplicably vanished by the time I arrived to talk about Mrs. Astor.

After iced tea was served, Tony abruptly announced that he had changed his mind about the interview. "I really don't want to talk about my mother," he said. "She's going to be one hundred and four next March, and I feel uncomfortable. She can't talk for herself, so I don't think I should talk for her. She has said what she wanted to say during an active life, and now is a moment of peace for her. Maybe you should have your drink and go." Perhaps to temper his brusque dismissal, he suggested an alternative. "I thought that maybe you wanted to talk to me about my life, which I would be delighted to do."

Curious about where the conversation might lead, I began plying him with questions while looking at all the framed photographs perched on the piano and bookshelves showing Tony with his mother during various stages of their lives. During the next forty minutes, Tony ended up talking volubly about his mother, or at least around her, with a mixture of pride and pique. The Marshalls' dachshund, Pichou, lay at his feet, barking whenever his master tensed. Charlene, her arms folded across her chest in disapproval, kept vigilant watch, often interrupting with a hostile word whenever I displayed too much interest in Mrs. Astor rather than Tony. She seemed to view Brooke Astor as She-Who-Must-Not-Be-Named.

"I've had a very independent life," Tony began. Yet even as he listed his accomplishments (the Marine Corps and storming the beaches at Iwo Jima, the intrigues of the 1950s CIA, his exotic ambassadorial service under Nixon, his self-published novel *Dash,* and his prestigious boards), all roads led back to his mother. He mentioned that he had put aside his own career to manage the Astor money, insisting, "I was happy to do it." Even though he portrayed himself as a dutiful son, he could not resist a bit of one-upmanship, saying, "I'm on the board of Lincoln Center for the Performing Arts. My mother was never on that."

In an effort to prolong the odd conversation, I mentioned that the Marshalls did not seem to be involved in the Upper East Side social circuit, unlike Mrs. Astor; was I right? "Yes, you are," Tony replied. "My mother loved people. I love people but on a different basis. My mother had" — he corrected himself — "has lots of friends, although a lot of them are dying off." When I followed up by remarking that he and his wife were not regularly featured in the *New York Times* Sunday society pictures by Bill Cunningham, Charlene interjected, "No. We're not by choice."

Then Tony turned the conversation to his life with Charlene, talking with palpable enthusiasm about their experience together as theatrical producers and her involvement at Juilliard and St. James' Church. Smiling at his wife with affection, he said, "We support each other's interests." With the dachshund at his master's feet, I asked whether Pichou was a relative of the famous Boysie and Girlsie. "No," he replied.

"Pichou means 'darling' in Genoese," he explained. "My mother had a house in Portofino that we went to for many summers, from 1932 until the war broke out in '39. She had a dachshund, and the staff called the dog Pichou."

Most of what I knew about Tony Marshall before this interview was derived from his mother's autobiography *Footprints*. Using my memory as a guide, I asked about parts of his life described in the book. The conversation remained pleasant until I brought up Brooke's admission that Vincent Astor had been jealous of the time she spent with her son. Tony became silent, and Pichou, sensing his discomfort, howled. "It must have been complicated," I ventured, puzzled by what I had blundered into. Tony started to say something, and Charlene cut him off, saying, "No comment."

Then, unprompted, Tony began to reminisce about the one family member who had given him unconditional love: Brooke's father, Major General John Henry Russell. "My grandfather was the compass of my life. Still is, although he died in 1947. He was a wonderful person — good judgment. I spent a lot of time with him," Tony said, the words pouring out in a torrent. "He wrote me a great deal, gave me very good advice on life. I was the only grandchild. He never dictated to me. He never said, 'You must do this, must do that.'"

Tony looked so animated in expressing his love that I dared to ask, "Did you feel that your family, your mother and stepfathers, were supportive of you too?" Charlene interrupted, saying, "You don't want to get into that." Tony echoed her, saying, "No, that's too close." Pichou howled again.

Eager to terminate the interview, Tony decided to wrap things up by moving to a safer family topic — his son Alec. "I love photography. One of my sons, Alec, got the bug," he said. "I gave him a camera when he was eight. He's a professional photographer, done eighty or ninety assignments for *Architectural Digest*. He's very good, very attentive to details." After hearing this recital of paternal pride, I asked about his other son, Philip. Tony was dismissive, saying vaguely, "He's in historic preservation. He writes, does consulting work, he teaches." There was so little affection in his voice that it was evident there was some kind of strain between the two. "Your family has worked out their own worlds?" I asked. "Very much," Tony replied. "Very much indeed."

On October 25, Tony Marshall was in his element, receiving an honor named after his grandfather, the Major John H. Russell Leadership Award, from the Marine Corps University Foundation, a group that had been launched with the aid of a $100,000 grant from the Vincent Astor Foundation in 1980. Tony had been its founding chairman, and now he was receiving its highest honor in a roomful of generals and other successful Marines. Tony gave a sentimental and self-indulgent speech, offering glimpses of himself as a ten-year-old visiting his grandfather and firing his first shot at a Marine Corps shooting range. He invoked General Russell's heroism in Guam, Mexico, and Haiti and spoke earnestly about what a powerful influence the general had been on his life. "I think of my grandfather every day and have shared stories time and again with my mother about Bulba," Tony said, using his childhood nickname for the general. Reiterating the words he had used with me, he added, "He was the compass of my life, and he set me on the right course."

It was a heartfelt and triumphant address, but in hindsight it had a note of the-right-course-not-taken sadness. This would be Tony Marshall's last unchallenged moment of glory in his brief, late-in-life season basking in public acclaim. Little did this distinguished-looking eighty-one-year-old man with a hint of military bearing in his posture know how far and how fast he would fall.

Daniel Billy wrote a memo to Mrs. Astor's staff on December 9, 2005, detailing who was allowed to visit: two Episcopal ministers, Mrs. de la Renta and Mr. David Rockefeller, Mr. Melhado, Ms. Barbara Walters, Emily Harding, Randy Bourscheidt, Mr. Alexander Marshall, and Mr. and Mrs. Philip Marshall. The memo stated that several former staff members were not permitted unless specifically invited: Chris Ely, Erica Meyer, Marciano Amaral, a housekeeper named Natalia Patornal, and the former chef, Daniel Sucur, and his wife, Liliane. The memo warned, "*NO ONE* is to be allowed on the premises without prior approval."

Tony Marshall, like any employer, might have legitimate concerns about aggrieved former employees. But for the voraciously sociable Mrs. Astor, who had spent months in her apartment with no distractions, deprived of familiar faces, this was a lonely existence. Now being treated for skin cancer with radiation and sporting unsightly bandages on her nose, she had also lost her frequent outings to Central Park. As Marciano Amaral angrily says, "If you put me inside an apartment and I don't go out, I don't see friends, I'm not entitled to do anything, it's like being in a prison. This was murder in slow motion."

Christmas at 778 Park Avenue that year was short of good cheer for Brooke Astor's staff and caregivers. Pearline Noble, who earned $20 an hour as a nurse's aide, had recently requested her first raise after two years: she was granted a mere eighty cents an hour, a 2 percent raise per year. Rounding that number up to a dollar an hour would have cost Mrs. Astor an extra $8 a week. "They said there's no way they could go over this because things are hard," Pearline says. "They didn't expect nurses would take up so much money." With her perfect (presumably inadvertent) knack for making remarks that rub salt into wounds, Charlene announced to Pearline that her own children had worked for less money at minimum-wage jobs and they had survived just fine.

The Christmas bonuses were similarly meager. Private-duty nurses on the Upper East Side, who command $50 to $70 an hour, typically receive a week's pay at the holidays, perhaps as much as $2,000. Tony Marshall showed his appreciation by giving his mother's nurses $100 each. As even one of Tony's defenders later acknowledged, "He was really, really cheap."

But Mrs. Astor's generosity knew no bounds when it came to her daughter-in-law. On December 20, Charlene wrote her a note of "heartfelt thanks" for contributing $100,000 — the entire endowment — to a fledgling charitable entity, the Shepherd Community Foundation, which had the third Mrs. Marshall as its president. The lawyer Peter J. Kelley explained that Francis Morrissey had asked him to draw up the paperwork to create the foundation, in 2002, in anticipation of Brooke Astor's demise. "They could see that she was declining," Kelley says. "The will provided for a goodly part of her fortune to be put into a foundation to be set up later. So he [Morrissey] figured it would be good to set it up in advance."

Francis Morrissey appeared to have discovered a legal loophole that would allow the Marshalls to circumvent the conditions established by Terry Christensen in the first codicil to Brooke Astor's will. That codicil, which would transfer some $30 million from Vincent Astor's trust to the Anthony Marshall Fund upon Mrs. Astor's death, pointedly excluded Charlene. She could not be a trustee, and the fund would cease to exist when Tony died. However, if Tony's foundation wanted to give millions to a charitable foundation run by Charlene, there was no legal stricture preventing him from doing so. Now, thanks to that $100,000 infusion, Mrs. Marshall, the president of the Shepherd Community Foundation, could write her own charitable checks: the Juilliard School received $12,500, and St. James' Church benefited too. Just as Brooke had burnished the Astor name with her philanthropic gifts, Charlene was on her way to enhancing the Marshall name as well as her own social standing.

While Roger Williams University was on winter break in early January 2006, Philip Marshall used his precious free time to head into Manhattan to visit friends and his grandmother. When he was in New York, he usually stayed either with his brother in Ossining or in the basement of his friend Tenzing Chadotsang's home in Queens. Despite his pedigree, he had never felt comfortable on the Upper East Side. The Chadotsangs, devout Buddhists, had a prayer corner in their brick home where Philip would perform his devotions along with the Tibetan family. His hosts were mystified by the formality of his relationship with his father, since they could not believe that he had to make an appointment to see Tony. As Tenzing Chadotsang put it, "If I want to see my father, I show up."

When Philip went to see his grandmother on Park Avenue, he arrived late in the day, when he assumed that his father and Daniel Billy, Jr., would not be on the premises. "I did not want my father to be chaperoning," he said. He usually did not linger. "My grandmother was a twenty-minute visit, because she'd fall asleep," he said. "Sometimes I'd just sit there. What do you do with someone who is a hundred and four years old? You hold their hand, you give them a very gentle foot massage. You say 'I love you' a lot and make kissing sounds. My grandmother liked that."

Brooke no longer greeted her visitors in the red-lacquered library. Now her days were spent in the blue room, a sitting room adjoining her bedroom. Decorated with a floral tapestry rug, a pink-and-blue chintz couch, blue drapes, an antique mirror, and a framed dog painting, it had become a bit of a jumble, with books piled every which way and wear and tear evident on the furnishings. Brooke ate her meals there, watched *Animal Planet* on the ancient 13-inch TV, and dozed on the couch. On this visit, Philip sang children's songs to her; she smiled sweetly in response, closed her eyes like a child who has heard a comforting lullaby, and drifted off.

As Philip was leaving, he chatted with Pearline Noble and greeted Minnette Christie when she arrived for her shift. There was no overt agenda, just a chance to show his concern and appreciation by asking a few questions about his grandmother's life. Rarely have such pleasantries provoked such an outpouring. Emboldened by Philip's interest and fortified by each other, the nurses seized the moment and expressed all their frustrations and fears.

"Minnette said my grandmother was only going to the doctor once a month, and she wasn't going outside at all," Philip explains. The nurses complained that Tony had turned down their requests for equipment, from a hospital bed to an air purifier. They mentioned an unusual year-old memo from Erica Meyer instructing them not to call 911 immediately if Mrs. Astor had a medical emergency but to contact people on an attached list instead. The women claimed that the household was a shambles because no one was in charge and Daniel Billy was too polite to enforce a semblance of discipline. As a result, Boysie and Girlsie were not being walked regularly, with predictable results. Minnette said that she had complained to Dr. Pritchett that Mrs. Astor was being fed the same meal of leftovers four days a week. Tony and Daniel Billy had been told and had demanded that the cook make fresh meals daily, but those instructions had promptly been ignored.

There was more, much more. Minnette and Pearline also mentioned the curious ubiquity of Francis Morrissey. On the one hand, the lawyer had always gone out of his way to be kind to the staff, even handing Pearline $100 when she complained about how poorly she was being paid. At the same time, the nurses could not forget Mrs. Astor's distress before and after every meeting with Morrissey and the other lawyers.

The two women believed that they were blowing off steam and did not expect to be taken seriously. "We weren't saying anything bad about anyone in the family," Pearline later insisted. "Things were not getting done. We weren't trying to set the son against the father, never."

Philip walked out of Brooke's apartment in a daze. His father and Charlene either were not paying attention or were callously ignoring obvious problems. The nurses, who knew they were risking their jobs if their words were seen as disloyal, seemed motivated by genuine concern for his grandmother. Baffled as to what to do next, Philip needed a confidant who could put the nurses' words in a larger context. The obvious candidate was Chris Ely, who eagerly met Philip in Manhattan the next day at the Pershing Square Café, across from Grand Central Station. Unlike their conversation a year earlier, after Ely had been fired, this time the former butler spoke bluntly about Tony and Charlene and their "meanness" to Mrs. Astor. As Philip remembers, "Chris egged me on. He was really angry."

At the Chadotsang home, Philip telephoned other members of the Astor staff who had been fired by his father. He hit pay dirt with a call to Alice Perdue, who was relieved that someone was interested in hearing her tale about financial irregularities and odd disbursements from Mrs. Astor's accounts to Tony and Charlene. "I thought, 'Oh, good, I can tell someone,'" Perdue says. Philip also reached Lourdes Hilario, the remaining bookkeeper who handled Mrs. Astor's accounts, and she was also willing to talk. "By the time I left Manhattan," Philip says, "I knew that things were much worse than I could ever have imagined."

At home in South Dartmouth, Philip ran a Google search on Morrissey and immediately found the 1993 *New York Times* article detailing the attorney's ethics problems surrounding his fee dispute with Mar Oil. Why would Tony hire a lawyer with such a history? "It was really tearing Philip up," says Toby Hilliard, Philip's prep school friend, who lives in New Mexico. "I spent hours on the phone with him. I was a good sounding board, since I was far away from the scene."

As a professor of historic preservation, Philip's specialty is paint-chip analysis, in which decades of grime and multiple coats of paint are scraped away to determine the original color and chemical formula. State agencies wishing to know the original color of bridges, railroad stations, and historic landmarks seek Philip out. Applying his skills at historical documentation to his grandmother's life, he tried to learn as much as he could about her medical and financial history. Although Tony's main office was at 405 Park Avenue, he kept a computer and some files in Daniel Billy's office in Brooke's apartment. On a return trip to New York, Philip, feeling a trifle ridiculous in this cloak-and-dagger role, went sleuthing. He snapped photographs of the peeling paint on the window frames and the stained carpets — signs of neglect — and poked around the fifteenth-floor office.

The more he learned, the angrier he became. The paper trail appeared to show that his father and Charlene had excised virtually everyone and everything that gave Brooke Astor pleasure. Their actions were more than aggressive cost-cutting; it felt to Philip like a vendetta. The Marshalls were using Brooke's money to buy everything they had ever wanted. The juxtaposition of their actions and his grandmother's straitened circumstances fueled Philip's rage. Unwilling to face his father's culpability, he blamed Charlene.

As Philip pondered his options, he conferred with Boston lawyers recommended by Nan's family and then was handed off gracefully to the venerable New York law firm of Milbank Tweed, which, not coincidentally, represented David Rockefeller. The Milbank lawyers told Philip that he might indeed have a case in challenging Tony Marshall's care of Brooke Astor. But they cautioned that the cost would be astronomical, far out of the reach of a college professor. As a last resort, Philip contacted David Rockefeller, since the retired banker had been the one who had convinced Tony to open Holly Hill for Brooke the previous summer. On March 6, 2006, Philip wrote:

> Dear Mr. Rockefeller,
>   I am sending you the enclosed material in light of our shared concern for Brooke and given what I have found out about her circumstances. I am extremely concerned about

and frustrated about Brooke's situation. I am looking for your advice.

My father does not seem in control of his fiduciary obligations to Brooke — or his own affairs. Control of Tony's affairs, and those of Brooke, appear to be in large part decided by Charlene. These circumstances, with their profound, negative effect on Brooke, are the major factors in my decision to pursue options . . .

In short, while I would like to be able to have someone (other than Tony) appointed as Brooke's guardian, and to take measures to begin to right these wrongs, there are no ready options that would not find us bogged down in costly litigation, a process that might further compromise Brooke and her health — our immediate concern.

The letter was sent overnight by FedEx but prompted no immediate reply. The ninety-year-old Rockefeller was in Paris, promoting the French edition of his autobiography. While Philip waited for a response, he kept waking up in the middle of the night, going to his computer, and writing letters to his father — letters he never sent.

Finally a Rockefeller staffer contacted Philip and arranged a meeting for May 19 — two long months later. Rockefeller insists that he was pleased to hear from Philip, "delighted" to try to help, and that he asked Annette de la Renta to join in the cause. "I talked to Annette about it," Rockefeller says. "We were the people who had the best chance of being able to do something."

Philip Marshall was so eager to be punctual for the May 19 meeting in Rockefeller's office that he arrived in midtown Manhattan way too early, so the Episcopalian-turned-Buddhist stepped inside St. Patrick's Cathedral and meditated in the hushed church with its vaulted ceiling and stained glass windows. Then, walking the two blocks to 30 Rockefeller Plaza, he passed the 1930s sculptures of Atlas and Prometheus and melodramatically wondered for just a moment whether he was overreaching, like Icarus.

Seated at the same white marble table where his father had defended his care of Brooke, Philip painted a grim picture of her life and finances.

"I was amazed at how much information Philip had," recalls Annette. Fifteen minutes into the discussion, Rockefeller summoned James Sligar of Milbank Tweed, and the lawyer arrived so quickly that it seemed he had been standing, briefcase in hand, by the elevator. After ninety minutes, a plan of sorts evolved for the rescue of Brooke Astor. Sligar recommended that Philip and Annette speak to Ira Salzman, an attorney with expertise in elder law. Rockefeller volunteered to fly to Northeast Harbor to meet face-to-face with Tony and Charlene, but the others insisted on gathering more information before confronting the couple.

Tony Marshall's eighty-second birthday was just eleven days later, on May 30. But this year the family tradition was broken: Philip did not call his father. "I wasn't going to fake it at that point," he says. Puzzled by the omission, Tony later mentioned it to his lawyers as a warning sign that he had missed.

About this time, the Marshalls were extricating themselves from their theatrical production company. The late 2005 London production of *I Am My Own Wife* had been a money-losing disaster, and Delphi investors were restive. "I never made any money," says one Broadway angel who wrote a check to the company. Richenthal (who would later be a vocal public defender of the Marshalls) moved his belongings out of the fifteenth-floor office in Brooke's apartment, but the parting was amicable. As the producer later said, "I have known Tony and Charlene socially for many years. They have very fine cultural and aesthetic tastes."

While Philip moved inexorably toward challenging his father in court, he was meeting resistance at home. Nan, now pursuing a master's degree in mediation, believed that Philip should try to resolve this problem without resorting to lawyers. "I guess it was a fantasy of mine that this could be mediated in some way," she said later. "Tony was not approachable. I had to question myself about the old WASP thing — at all costs don't hang your laundry out. I didn't want to believe what I kept hearing, how bad it was." Philip told his mother about his plans, and she too tried to talk him out of it. "She's a mom — she didn't want me to be beat up," he says. His brother, Alec, wanted no part of this fight either.

While Alec agreed that Brooke would be happier at Holly Hill, he was not convinced that a lawsuit was the way to resolve any problems surrounding his grandmother's care.

Without family support, Philip turned to his friends. "No one wanted him to do it," says Tenzing Chadotsang. Philip agonized over lunch at the aptly named Feast or Famine restaurant in Rhode Island with his friend Sam Adams. "Philip is mild-mannered," says Adams. "I've never seen him express animosity towards his father. But he saw something wrong. He felt he couldn't shirk from it." As Philip explained later, "People ask me, 'How could you do this to your father?' I just kept thinking, 'How could he do this to his own mother?'"

During this period, Philip's visits to his grandmother created an uneasiness in the household. Marta Grabowska, the weekend cook, ran into Philip at 778 Park Avenue. "He spent a long time with his grandmother, and when he was leaving, he said to me, 'Please don't tell my father I was here,'" she says. Grabowska, a Polish immigrant who had been working for Mrs. Astor for only one year, felt uneasy: "That was complicated for me."

Stopping by to see Brooke in early June, Philip was alarmed to discover stacks of boxes of paperwork, photographs, and records piled up in preparation for shredding. Invoices from CodeShred of Island Park, Long Island, later documented that fifteen boxes were picked up at 778 Park Avenue on June 8, 2006, for a charge of $276, and on June 28, 2006, the company carried away eighty boxes from Holly Hill, at a cost of $1,449. Unable to understand why his father was suddenly clearing out documents and memorabilia, Philip rummaged through some of the boxes in Brooke's apartment and plucked out a few papers that looked intriguing.

"If you consider a scrap of paper with the name of a physiotherapist in Baden-Baden from 1954 to be memorabilia, then yes, we got rid of memorabilia," says Daniel Billy, who spent months going through the papers with Tony. "There were a hundred and fifty train schedules to Ossining, there were birthday cards from people she didn't know, there were boxes that had been in the closets for decades." Billy stressed later that there had been nothing sinister in the decision to send this material to the scrap heap. "'Shredding' had an ominous sound," he says, "but we didn't want these scraps of paper floating around when they came to pick up the garbage on Park Avenue."

Annette and Philip, joined by several lawyers, met with David Rockefeller for the second time at the fifty-sixth-floor office on the afternoon of June 19. In recent weeks, Rockefeller's protective staff had repeatedly tried to talk him out of getting involved in this family donnybrook, but he was adamant — he had to act. Philip and Annette were relying on him; they would not have gone ahead without his blessing. And he could not, in good conscience, ignore his mounting concerns about Brooke's well-being. Their legal plans were to file a petition for guardianship, but they had not decided whom to recommend. Since Philip lived in Massachusetts and David Rockefeller was ninety-one, by the process of elimination Annette seemed to be the obvious choice.

But Annette had her own burdens, though no one else in the room knew about them. Just before Memorial Day, her seventy-two-year-old husband had visited his doctor for a routine checkup and had been diagnosed with lymphoma. Oscar's days were now defined by a grueling treatment regimen of radiation and chemotherapy. "It was very traumatic," says Oscar, whose cancer eighteen months later was in remission. "My wife was helping me and helping Mrs. Astor. Annette wouldn't even let me go to the hospital to get a blood test alone. But at the same time, she loved Brooke and felt she was not having the life in her old age that she deserved." In the meeting with David and Philip, Annette acknowledged her situation in a backhanded way, mentioning that she would be in Manhattan this summer anyhow because of Oscar's cancer treatments and so would be available to take on the responsibility of being Brooke's guardian. Her friends believe that the timing of the lawsuit was fortuitous. "In a way it was a good thing that the two things happened together, because it took Annette's mind a bit off Oscar's cancer," says John Richardson. "Otherwise, Annette would have been consumed."

In retrospect, Annette admits that she did not realize just how much she was taking on by agreeing to become her friend's guardian. "I thought I was doing the right thing by her. I didn't know it was going to be Armageddon," she says. "I thought I was defending her, with David and Philip. Get her back to Holly Hill, get her with Chris and the dogs, be warm and cozy."

David Rockefeller kept clinging to the hope that Brooke's final months could be spent in peace and comfort without the need for a divisive and debilitating court fight. Once again he offered to fly up to Maine and sit down with Tony and Charlene. He had negotiated with presidents and princes; surely he could work things out with the Marshalls. But he bowed to the others' fears that they could not risk alerting the Marshalls of their plans. "We knew the trickiest part was that if my father got wind of this, he would fire the nurses," Philip says. "My grandmother trusted the nurses. So many people had been fired." Boxes of paperwork had been shredded, creating a concern that potential legal evidence might be destroyed. At the end of the meeting, as a sign of his resolution, David Rockefeller announced that he was heading immediately to 778 Park Avenue, saying, "I want to visit Brooke now."

Once everyone had agreed to proceed, Nan Starr says, her husband stopped agonizing. "Philip was the most stressed out in the year beforehand, because he didn't know what he could do, if anything," she recalls. "The minute the ball got rolling, he never looked back."

Although Henry Kissinger did not attend these sessions, he served as a behind-the-scenes adviser. A friend to both Annette de la Renta and David Rockefeller, the former secretary of state admits he was startled to hear that they were convinced that Tony Marshall was treating his mother callously. "I had to believe what I was told," he says. "But would I have predicted it five years earlier? I would have said no."

With the clock ticking toward filing the lawsuit, Philip panicked when Alec announced that he and his fiancée, Sue Ritchie, were about to visit Tony and Charlene in Maine. "I was freaking," Philip recalls. "I told him if you go, you may be up there when the petition arrives." But Alec was adamant: he wanted to see his father, and he had nothing to do with the lawsuit. Alec and Sue arrived at Cove End on July 7 and spent four sun-dappled days sailing on the *General Russell*, hiking in the mountains nearby and enjoying the large guest cottage right by the water. Loyal to Philip and praying that a lawsuit might be averted at the last minute,

Alec did not offer a syllable of warning to his father. Tony would find this omission unforgivable.

And what of Brooke Astor, who was unaware of her role at the center of what would soon become a searing family drama? Conditions at 778 Park Avenue that summer had further deteriorated, with tasks left undone as the staff sulked. The nurses and housekeepers were arguing over who did this and who should have done that, defending themselves and blaming others. "I said, 'Let's call a meeting with Mr. Marshall to tell him all the things we thought his mother should have,' but I couldn't get anywhere," insists Beverly Thomson. Marta Grabowska says that she tried to tempt her employer with freshly prepared mashed potatoes, flan, stewed prunes, vegetables, and meats, all pureed in deference to the weakness of Mrs. Astor's teeth. But she complained that the weekday cook was barely making an effort. "I saw two big plastic containers, red and green, in the refrigerator," she continues. "They were constantly giving her a bowl from one or the other. It upset me — I thought she should have more variety."

Sandra Foschi, the physical therapist who had been treating Mrs. Astor for two years, noticed with concern that her normally motivated client was emotionally retreating from life. "It was hot and stuffy in the apartment. She slept a lot more," Foschi recalls. "She was having a hard time."

The legal papers that Ira Salzman would draw up, with the active assistance of Philip Marshall, needed to build a strong case that Tony was mismanaging his mother's care and her household. The best witnesses to persuade a judge to rescind Tony's power of attorney were members of Mrs. Astor's staff. Chris Ely gave Salzman an affidavit on July 3, and a few days later the lawyer took statements from Pearline Noble, Minnette Christie, and Beverly Thomson. "Make no mistake, this was a staff revolt," says Salzman, a partner in the firm Goldfarb, Abrandt, Salzman & Kutzin. Based on these statements, the lawsuit would charge, for instance, that Mrs. Astor's nursing staff had been reduced from two aides at all times to one, that a $1,000-a-month prescription for Procrit to treat anemia had been halted for no medical reason, and that Charlene had ordered the nurses to stop using a $60 enzyme supplement and replaced it with a less expensive diluted version that she had found on the Internet. The everything-but-the-kitchen-sink legal petition even threw in the couch. Since the staff had complained in passing that the sofa in the blue room had become fetid, the offputting image of a dog-urine-stained couch went into the lawsuit too.

Unable to visit Park Avenue or to interview Dr. Pritchett for fear that the physician would alert Tony, Salzman relied on the statements provided by Mrs. Astor's staff and Philip, Annette, and David. Ultimately, some of the concerns turned out to be justified (inadequate housekeeping, poor meals, staff cutbacks), but others would be prove to be based on misunderstandings. Dr. Pritchett later stated that he alone had discontinued the Procrit prescription. In the nurses' eyes, the memo from Tony Marshall's secretary telling them not to call 911 — a piece of paper they had not saved — implied that the Marshalls wanted to let Mrs. Astor die. But Pritchett later insisted that he had independently told the nurses to call 911 only if there were treatable medical problems, in keeping with Mrs. Astor's living will.

In presenting his case, Salzman included not just the gravest charges but myriad small details. An aide said that Tony had complained upon seeing Brooke wearing a scarf: "Mr. Marshall was concerned about the $16.00 dry cleaning bill." The petition quoted Philip chiding his father for reducing Brooke's usual elaborate flower arrangements and substituting bouquets from Korean greengrocers. But that charge wilted on closer scrutiny. At 104, Mrs. Astor was no longer entertaining and did not require an apartment full of blooms. Sam Karalis, the owner of Windsor Florist, which had supplied Mrs. Astor with flowers for two decades, later told me, "When she was feeling well, she had the whole house filled with flowers. Toward the end, she was in bed all the time — she didn't use so many flowers. One bouquet a week for the bedroom, roses and lilies."

The guardianship lawsuit was never meant to be about money or property, but the entangling of Brooke's and Tony's finances was thrown in like a garnish on a Wedgwood plate. Philip had provided Salzman with financial documents including details about the sale of Brooke's Childe Hassam painting and his father's 2005 tax return. Tony later admitted that he had given himself a huge raise and a bonus — the W-2 showed that he had received $2.38 million that year for managing Brooke's money, five times his usual annual salary, $450,000. "All the money stuff was thrown into the lawsuit for leverage," Salzman recalls. "We didn't care about the money."

Caught up in the Oedipal implications of what he was about to do, Philip unburdened himself to Salzman, describing his pent-up frustrations and suspicions over the behavior of his father and Charlene. In constructing Philip's affidavit and his own cover letter, Salzman reflected that intensity of feeling. But these legal arguments were never designed for public consumption (let alone tabloid headlines) but were crafted to convince a judge in private of the dire nature of Brooke Astor's problems.

"Her diet is inadequate, endangering the life and safety of this slight and sickly 104-year-old woman," read Philip's affidavit. "Her Park Avenue duplex is in such a dirty and dilapidated state that she's been forced to live among peeling and falling paint and dusty and crumbling carpets. Her bedroom is so cold in the winter that my grandmother is forced to sleep in the TV room in torn nightgowns on a filthy couch that smells, probably from dog urine . . . Why should my grandmother, who was accustomed to dining with world leaders and frequented 21 and the Knickerbocker Club, be forced to eat oatmeal and pureed carrots, pureed peas and pureed liver every day, Monday through Friday months on end?"

In hindsight, Philip concedes that the language in the affidavit was harsh but argues, "If we weren't effective, things were going to be really bad for my grandmother." In reality, there were two elements to Philip Marshall's guardianship lawsuit. The Marshalls were indeed inexcusably tightfisted and the household was poorly run; basic hygienic tasks such as walking the dachshunds were ignored, and maintenance of the apartment was neglected. But Salzman's petition went further by giving the impression that Brooke Astor was living in squalor that endangered her health. Philip's hurried financial investigation was designed merely as an ironic contrast, demonstrating that his father and Charlene were skimping on Brooke's care while living off her money. But the

Watergate-era dictum — Follow the money — would prove irresistible to the district attorney's office. What began as a sideshow — Tony's fiscal stewardship — would prove to be the main event.

The guardianship petition would have provoked an ugly fight whether conducted in the hushed offices of $700-an-hour lawyers or in a judge's chambers. But once the family feud hit the newspapers, what gave it such a long-lasting and lurid quality was the colorful language of the petition. The frame for the story became "elder abuse," a phrase that Philip, as the petitioner, never used but that Salzman included on the first page of his own cover letter.

At 4 P.M. on July 21, 2006, the phone rang in the Times Square law office of Susan Robbins. The forty-nine-year-old Robbins, an outspoken former social worker, was well known in the city's courthouses for her impassioned advocacy on behalf of nonprofit social service agencies that served as guardians for elderly and incapacitated clients. On that sleepy Friday afternoon, the lawyer was intrigued by the request from Ann Gardner, the law clerk for Judge John Stackhouse: would she agree to be the court evaluator for a new client without knowing in advance who that client was? "I knew it was something weird or out of the ordinary," Robbins recalls. "I said, 'I'll do it.'" And that was how Brooke Astor acquired a lawyer far different in background and style from, say, the Harvard-Yale norm at Sullivan & Cromwell.

Robbins, who is single, lives by chance in Astor Court, an Upper West Side building with a courtyard that Vincent Astor constructed in 1916. Even though she did not follow the society pages, she remembered reading about Brooke Astor's remarkable one hundredth birthday party. A graduate of Cardozo Law School, Robbins, the daughter of a music publisher, already had a full caseload. There was a sexual harassment case, a quadriplegic with housing problems, a mentally ill young woman whose caretaker grandmother had died, and a schizophrenic man afflicted with a brain tumor and warring doctors. "You can take the girl out of social work," her father constantly teased, "but you can't take the social work out of the girl."

Against the backdrop of her normally earnest but unglamorous battles, these new court papers were riveting. The words "elder abuse" and

"Brooke Astor" in a guardianship lawsuit gave Robbins a jolt. A curvaceous woman who wears her hair in an old-fashioned bun and pairs serious suits with sexy scoop-necked tops, Robbins is a smoker. This news required a calming Marlboro.

Over the next few days, her role changed from neutral evaluator to Mrs. Astor's court-appointed lawyer, with the daunting task of attempting to find out what Mrs. Astor herself wanted. The 104-year-old could scarcely communicate, uttering mostly incoherent words, and suffered from tremors. She had a painful tumor on her leg and had been diagnosed with a chronic form of leukemia. Indeed, with all that was afflicting her, it was a tribute to her iron will that Mrs. Astor did not just let go.

Three days earlier, the conspirators had held a final meeting at Ira Salzman's Empire State Building office. Philip Marshall participated by speakerphone, Annette de la Renta was there in person, and David Rockefeller sent as his emissary Fraser Seitel, the veteran communications consultant who had handled the press at Chase Manhattan Bank and now had his own firm. Salzman outlined the steps he planned to take to file the lawsuit while keeping it confidential. "I thought it would be taken care of privately," Annette recalls. But Seitel warned that a lawsuit involving a woman as famous as Brooke Astor would be virtually impossible to keep under wraps, regardless of what legal precautions were taken. Philip was heard to say, "I'm worried that this will be on Page Six if it's not sealed," referring to the *New York Post*'s fearsome gossip column. Salzman replied in words that would prove prophetic: "No, Philip, you don't understand. It will be on page one."

11

Blue-Blood Battle

UNAWARE OF WHAT was happening in New York, Tony and Charlene Marshall were enjoying a late July weekend at Cove End and the last peace of mind they would have for years to come. Annette de la Renta relaxed with her husband and her many dogs at her country retreat in Kent, Connecticut. The situation was about to go thermonuclear, but even the instigators of the guardianship lawsuit were still expecting a closed-door battle. If the protagonists had caught a whiff of where they were all heading, they might have taken a breath, a nap, or a tranquilizer, since "the Astor affair" was about to fulfill every aspect of New York's obsession with the foibles of the upper class.

The elements were irresistible, from the iconic 104-year-old victim to the roster of Social Register names to the easy-to-grasp presumed motive — greed. It was not a trip to rehab or a political sex scandal, but the continuing story featured that time-honored puller of heartstrings, an old woman in distress, as well as an unlikely trio of heroes trying to rescue her from the clutches of briefcase-wielding men in suits. An avaricious son and a scheming daughter-in-law provided classic stock-company villains. It was the kind of story that could only be missed if you were touring the Amazon rain forest in a dugout canoe and your satellite phone was on the blink. From Shanghai to Sydney to the banks of the Seine, the Astor docudrama was destined to be a global event.

On Sunday night, June 23, 2006, at Brooke Astor's apartment, when Marta Grabowska left and the nurses changed shifts at seven o'clock, the departing staffers believed that all was well with the lady of the house. "She was perfectly fine," insists Grabowska. The day nurse, Beverly Thomson, seconds that view. "I worked with Mrs. Astor that Sunday. She didn't talk much — she'd nod her head to say 'Thank you,'" recalls Thomson. "When I left, she was okay. But when I got home, I got a call from Minnette, who said, 'Beverly, we're losing her.'"

Either Brooke Astor had suddenly taken a turn for the worse or the two staffers had missed the warning signs. Minnette Christie, the night nurse, says that she became concerned as soon as she checked on Mrs. Astor. "I thought she had fluid in her lungs," says Christie. "I thought she had pneumonia. But I'm not a doctor — I'm not supposed to diagnose." Alone with her patient, Christie called Dr. Pritchett and reached his answering service. When the physician covering for him called back, he asked about Mrs. Astor's vital signs and then advised the nurse to monitor her patient closely. Christie phoned several nurses for backup help before reaching Pearline Noble, who raced over. Late that night the two caregivers became so worried that they called an ambulance to take Mrs. Astor to the nearest medical facility, Lenox Hill Hospital. In the emergency room, she was diagnosed with pneumonia. "For a person of one hundred and four, pneumonia can easily be fatal," explains Dr. Sandra Gelbard, her doctor at Lenox Hill, who signed a do-not-resuscitate order. "I was not going to put in a breathing machine or shock her heart or use aggressive measures. But I was going to treat her."

Christie and Noble had accompanied Mrs. Astor to the hospital, and Christie used her own credit card to guarantee that Mrs. Astor got a private room on the VIP floor. In normal circumstances, Mrs. Astor's nurses would immediately have contacted Tony Marshall, but since they, unlike Tony, knew that the guardianship lawsuit had been filed forty-eight hours earlier, they telephoned Philip instead. (Tony got the news several hours later from Dr. Pritchett.) As soon as Annette heard, she drove into the city and went straight to Lenox Hill to keep an all-night vigil. On Monday morning, when Susan Robbins learned the whereabouts of her new client, the lawyer decided to delay making contact, reasoning that "very elderly people who go into the hospital do not usually come out." But once again, contrary to expectations, Brooke Astor gradually responded to antibiotics and rallied.

Tony and Charlene arrived at Lenox Hill after 10 P.M. on Monday, having been told earlier in the day by Philip about the guardianship lawsuit. In Mrs. Astor's hushed room, they immediately ran into two of their accusers, Pearline Noble and Beverly Thomson, who had given signed affidavits to Ira Salzman. "Mrs. Marshall burst in and he followed behind," says Noble. She added that Charlene angrily asked, "What have I done to you? Why did you do this to me?" While Charlene glared, Tony worriedly focused on his mother's health, inquiring with concern about what the doctor had said and whether she would be all right.

For two days the outside world did not know that Mrs. Astor was in the hospital, although she was registered under her own name. But once the *Daily News* broke the page-one story on Wednesday, July 26, about the lawsuit — dubbed the "Battle of N.Y. Blue Bloods!" — the hospital was besieged. "This was like nothing I've ever experienced," says Dr. Gelbard, a thirty-five-year-old New York native. "I'm unlisted, but the press got my beeper number. You have to answer your beeper, because it could be an emergency." Gelbard had been consulting on all medical decisions with Annette de la Renta, since Judge Stackhouse had named her Brooke's temporary guardian. The doctor, however, never spoke with Tony Marshall. "He was at the hospital," she says, "but I wasn't there when he was there."

Security guards stood watch over Mrs. Astor's hospital room — which had mahogany walls and hotel-style amenities — as if it were a branch of Harry Winston. "The whole floor was blocked off," Dr. Gelbard recalls, "but the press was still trying to break into the room." With rumors that the newspapers were offering $75,000 for a picture of Mrs. Astor, the nurses covered the windows for privacy, blocking out the sunlight. One reporter managed to get onto the floor by claiming to be the son of another patient, but he was escorted out once he neared Mrs. Astor's room. The *Daily News* ran a follow-up story quoting an unnamed hospital staffer as claiming, "She weighs seventy-three pounds and she's completely emaciated and bony." Among the authorized visitors granted safe passage to the suite was Chris Ely, who had not been allowed to see her for a year.

Philip Marshall, who had driven to New York after the nurses called him, visited daily, often at the same time as Annette. But reporters initially raced to his home in Massachusetts after the *Daily News* story broke. His wife's trepidation over the lawsuit was fully justified by the family's first exposure to the paparazzi. "Winslow went out to mow the lawn, and someone jumped out of a car and started snapping pictures," Nan Starr says. "He ran back in the house, white-faced." Soon the reporters knocked on her door. From the other side of the screen, Nan icily informed them that her husband was not home. But an hour later, after she calmed down, she took freshly baked banana bread and bottled water to the photographers and reporters camped outside on this sweltering day. "The mediator side of me kicked in, and I realized they were just doing their job," she says, adding shrewdly that she hoped her gesture would convey "that we are regular folks." When the press corps decamped several days later, they left a fruit basket and a note of apology. It was a small but telling predictor that Philip and Nan would hold the upper hand in the bitter public relations war.

But for Tony and Charlene — blindsided by the charges, shocked by the betrayal of Philip and erstwhile friends such as David Rockefeller — every day brought a new indignity. Overnight the Marshalls had gone from being proper Upper East Siders, welcome in any exclusive club in town, to Public Enemies. They had to endure headlines like this July 29 gem from the *New York Post:* "'EVIL' SON SEES ASTOR IN THE HOSPITAL." Everyone close to the Marshalls was hounded for comment by the press. The homebound Marshalls, who often held hands and cried during this ordeal, complained to friends about being stalked by reporters, receiving malicious late-night phone calls and about Justice Stackhouse's highhanded action in cutting off Tony's salary (for managing Brooke's money) without even holding a hearing over the allegations. Loyal friends expressed incredulity. "I thought, oh my God, how could anyone say this?" says Moises Kaufman, the director of *I Am My Own Wife.*

Clinging to his honorific, Ambassador Anthony D. Marshall issued a statement saying that he was "shocked and deeply hurt" by the "completely untrue" allegations and insisting that he authorized $2.5 million a year to pay for Mrs. Astor's care. "My mother has a staff of eight with instructions to provide her with whatever she needs and whatever they think she should have," he wrote. Tony portrayed himself as a victim, and as outraged that Philip and his conspirators had not spoken to him before racing into court: "I am very troubled that allegations like these would first be made in a court petition, instead of discussing any concerns with me directly." Stressing that he was more invested in his mother's health than these interlopers were, he added, "I love my mother and no one cares more about her than I do. Her well-being, her comfort, and her dignity mean everything to me." But public opinion was at flood tide against him. When the *Daily News* reported on Tony's statement, the newspaper punctuated it with the sarcastic headline "I AM SON KIND OF WONDERFUL."

Locked out of his office at 405 Park Avenue by Judge Stackhouse and unable to retrieve receipts and paperwork attesting to bills paid on his mother's behalf, Tony was at a disadvantage in defending himself. This was war, and the Marshalls needed legal gladiators. Initially they hired Harvey Corn, of Greenfield, Stein & Senior, a respected former clerk to a surrogate court judge with an estate law practice. To supplement Corn's avuncular approach, the Marshalls brought in Kenneth Warner, an aggressive litigator whom they had met through Richenthal. Warner threw himself into the case as Tony's legal spokesman by lashing out at every perceived foe, from reporters covering the case to Susan Robbins, with no-holds-barred ferocity. A crisis management firm run by Warner's brother-in-law, George Sard, was hired to do damage control. It was a Sisyphean task, and as a result the Marshalls ended up working with four different PR firms during the next sixteen months.

While the Marshalls were losing every spin cycle in the newspapers, the lawyers quietly tried to work out a settlement offstage. Harvey Corn went to see Ira Salzman to assess the likelihood of a quick resolution. "In these family fights, everyone gets dirty, legal expenses get run up," Corn explains. "I tried to see if we could resolve it right away." The negotiations fell apart, however, after Corn and Salzman mutually broached the possibility of making Annette and Tony coguardians.

Upon being told of the tentative plan, Annette flatly refused. Annoyed that Salzman would even float such an idea, she hired her own lawyer, Paul Saunders, a partner at Cravath, Swaine & Moore, who had been recommended by Henry Kissinger. An urbane Harvard-trained lawyer whose expertise was international litigation, Saunders was more at home negotiating border disputes than refereeing a family squabble. "He was the class of the field," says a staffer for Justice Stackhouse. Susan Robbins joined with Annette in turning down the coguardianship proposal, based on her growing concerns about Tony Marshall's conduct. As she told Salzman in an incredulous tone, "Are you kidding? Tony can never be a guardian."

At Holly Hill on Friday, July 28, Chris Ely was eagerly readying the house for Mrs. Astor's return, patrolling the stone mansion to make sure that everything was in perfect order. The butler, who had been rehired by Annette, had also started taking inventory of missing property, from a chinchilla blanket to a set of breakfast china to a large painting of a dog that had been the centerpiece of a grouping of similar art in the hallway stairwell. Mrs. Astor's guardian had also rehired Brooke's French chef, Daniel Sucur, and his wife, Liliane. The pillows were fluffed, the kitchen was restocked, and the house was about to become a home again.

That rainy evening Susan Robbins finally felt it was time to go to Lenox Hill Hospital to meet her new client. She discovered that the place resembled an armed camp. "There was a guard in the hallway and a guard at her room," recalls Robbins. "Mrs. Astor was sleeping. She had been really sick. If she hadn't come to the hospital, she probably wouldn't be with us. She was very, very thin." Robbins stayed for three hours, talking to Dr. Gelbard and the nurses until her client woke up for dinner. "The cases that I've been on before when people are out of it, you can't talk to them," Robbins says. "But she was sitting up. She has beautiful blue eyes. She did try and talk a little bit. I thought there was recognition."

Robbins also got an earful from Mrs. Astor's private-duty nurses. "The staff really hated Charlene," said Robbins. "Charlene had come into the hospital, and she was really pissed off that the nurses had given these affidavits." For their part, the nurses complained that Mrs. Marshall had been disruptive and intimidating.

The next morning, at the start of an elaborately choreographed getaway, the nurses dressed Mrs. Astor up in a wig, makeup, sunglasses, and a large hat, as if she were a publicity-shy Greta Garbo in need of a dignified disguise. Then they helped her into a wheelchair, spirited her out the back entrance of Lenox Hill, and put her in a waiting ambulance. Destination: Holly Hill. "She was stable to go," says Dr. Gelbard. "I didn't know whether she would live for three weeks, three months, or a year."

No one had the courtesy to tell Tony Marshall that his mother had been discharged from the hospital. When he and Charlene showed up at Lenox Hill later in the day, they discovered that Brooke's room was empty, and no one would tell them her whereabouts. Tony repeatedly asked, "What do you mean, she's not here?" He was stung to see that the only flowers left in the room were a vase of pink roses that he had brought to his mother.

Trailed by the press corps, Tony and Charlene went in search of the missing Mrs. Astor, their every word and movement chronicled for the curious masses. After entering her apartment building and speaking to the doorman, Charlene informed their entourage from the fourth estate, "She's gone to the country, up to Westchester." She then complained that she had been hoping to get some rest. The next stop for the Marshalls, after lunch at home, was Holly Hill. As the *New York Times* reported, Tony introduced himself to a security guard at the Briarcliff Manor estate, saying, "I'm here to see my mother." The gates were opened, and Tony and Charlene drove up the winding driveway to the imposing stone mansion.

Brooke was seated in the sunroom, a pale green ground-floor room with framed bird prints, rattan chairs, overstuffed white couches, and a glass-walled view of her gardens with the Hudson River in the distance. Philip was sitting right beside her, holding his grandmother's hand. It was everything that Tony had ever feared: he had been replaced in his mother's affections by his own son. Philip stood so that his father could take his seat. He even made a filial gesture toward Tony, as if in denial about the blows he had inflicted to his father's reputation. "I touched him on the knee, and that did not come off right," Philip says. "It was probably not appropriate." Tony was infuriated, later telling *Vanity Fair,* "Ordinarily, it would have been a gesture of sympathy, courage. It made me want to . . ." According to the magazine, Tony's voice trailed off then, "his eyes blazing in fury."

Tony Marshall, with a worldview that equates repression with good breeding, is not a man who raises his voice or loses his temper in public. Not so with Charlene. The humiliations had piled up to the point where she could not take the strain anymore. Her explosive rages were stunning to behold when witnessed by anyone — nurses, employees, family members, or prying reporters — in the vicinity. Those "cheeks like apple blossoms" in her Ashley Hall yearbook turned scarlet, and with her blue eyes flashing and her white hair bobbing, the third Mrs. Marshall resembled a wounded animal flailing at her enemies. A protective wife and mother of three, a respected lay minister who administered healing prayer to troubled parishioners at St. James' Church, she had seemingly lost all emotional governors.

On that July day at Holly Hill, Philip recalls, "Charlene was seething." Railing at the nurses, she became teary-eyed in recounting how the press frenzy at Cove End had sent her pregnant daughter, Inness, to the hospital. "Mrs. Marshall was trying to make us feel guilty," says Pearline Noble, who was tending Mrs. Astor that day. "Her face became red — she was carrying on." Even defenders like Daniel Billy, Jr., would later acknowledge, "Charlene is a Leo, a lioness. If anything comes up that jeopardizes her husband or her children, watch out."

Charlene's public trials were just beginning, as her image was transformed by the press into that of a man-stealing, child-neglecting, money-hungry adulteress who had become Brooke Astor's daughter-in-law from hell. The tabloids dispatched reporters to Northeast Harbor and gleefully recounted the tawdry details of her affair with Tony Marshall and her divorce from Paul Gilbert. The *New York Post* headlined a story by Stefanie Cohen: "ASTOR'S HAYSEED DAUGHTER-IN-LAW LEFT HER FIRST HUBBY WITH JUST . . . $578" and then, the next day, ran a follow-up depicting Charlene as a bad mother who had abandoned her own children to be with Tony: "ASTOR IN-LAW DUMPED KIDS." Adding insult to injury, tabloid articles about Charlene's Charleston roots made it sound as if her family had a rusted pickup on cement blocks in their front yard, depicting them as lowbrow trash rather than shabby gentility.

The next day, when the Marshalls again visited Holly Hill, they took along a living symbol to convey their moral authority. This was Reverend John Andrew, the Episcopal priest from St. Thomas Church who was close to Brooke Astor and had married the Marshalls. Tony read another statement to the press corps camped by the side of the country road. "I know that I am right and they are wrong," he said. "I am devastated and regret only that we will never be able to erase the damage that has done by these people to us, our family and my mother." Asked why his son had issued such a damning public petition against him, Tony replied, "Oh, I couldn't possibly answer that question." The Marshalls' efforts to win the headline handicap were ham-handed. A spokeswoman for Tony, Brooke Morgenstein, later e-mailed a statement attacking Annette de la Renta to the *New York Sun:* "No protégée of Brooke Astor would conduct herself in this manner. Mrs. de la Renta is taking Mrs. Astor's name in vain and is acting contrary to everything Mrs. Astor has always stood for."

Charlene's tirades, which sometimes occurred in the presence of her fragile mother-in-law, had handed the opposition a useful weapon. At the next closed-to-the-press courthouse meeting, when Justice Stackhouse suggested making a list of those who would be permitted to visit Mrs. Astor, Paul Saunders, Annette's lawyer, requested that Charlene be banned from Holly Hill. "I understood that Charlene had been disruptive with the staff," Saunders recalls. "I was concerned that this would spill over and have an effect on Mrs. Astor's well-being." Susan Robbins also voiced her concerns about Charlene's behavior. Taking these complaints to heart, the judge barred Tony's wife from visiting her mother-in-law. From that day forward, if Charlene accompanied Tony to Holly Hill, she had to wait in the car or walk in the gardens, since she could not legally enter the house. Charlene would never see Brooke Astor alive again.

In this game of legal tit for tat, Ken Warner informed the judge that there was bad blood between his client, Tony Marshall, and Chris Ely.

The judge ordered Ely to stay out of Tony's way and let the nurses chaperone Mrs. Astor's son. It may have seemed like a small legal victory to Warner, but in truth it was a huge relief to Chris Ely. The butler had already received the reward he craved, a gesture of affection from his 104-year-old employer. Although Mrs. Astor mostly spoke in fragments, a few days after returning to Holly Hill, she put her head on the butler's shoulder and croaked a plaintive four-word inquiry: "Where have you been?" Ely finessed the answer, simply replying, "I've been around." Everyone at Holly Hill had agreed to sensible rules: there would be no mention of the lawsuit in front of Mrs. Astor, nor any criticism of her son. She would be carried through this time with loving arms.

Astorgate was quickly becoming God's gift to the legal profession. Fortunes in billable hours were being created from exhaustive simultaneous investigations into all elements of Brooke Astor's life. JPMorgan Chase, the bank that assumed control of Mrs. Astor's finances, hired its own team, led by Leslie Fagen, from the law firm Paul, Weiss, Rifkind, Wharton & Garrison to examine Tony's handling of his mother's books. Paul Saunders began rounding up Mrs. Astor's voluminous medical records on behalf of her guardian, Annette de la Renta. Susan Robbins knew that she would have to be a virtual mind reader, since her client was incapable of answering questions, but this was a common circumstance in her practice. Although the 104-year-old was obviously mentally incapacitated, Mrs. Astor's staff had mentioned her numerous meetings with lawyers in recent years. Wondering when Mrs. Astor had ceased to understand what she was signing, Robbins won permission from Justice Stackhouse to examine her client's recent wills.

Justice Stackhouse chose another lawyer, Sam Liebowitz, as the court evaluator, the judge's eyes and ears in researching the facts surrounding Brooke Astor. Already alerted that Mrs. Astor feared men in suits, Stackhouse gave Liebowitz sartorial advice: "When you go to see her, Sam, no suits — sneakers, T-shirt, jeans." Liebowitz replied, "Not a problem, your honor." This was a moment richly symbolic of how the world of the grande dame of New York society had tilted off its axis — sneakers and jeans to meet Mrs. Astor, a woman who had been thrilled when her nine-year-old great-grandson had worn a jacket to dinner. But the fashion advice proved irrelevant; when Liebowitz and Robbins went to Holly Hill on August 6, Mrs. Astor slept through their visit. Instead of speaking with her, the casually dressed lawyers spoke to the staff and admired the "memory room," a study where every inch of wall space was covered by photographs of Brooke with celebrities from Jimmy Stewart and Lady Bird Johnson to Princess Diana. Amid the plentitude of lawyers, strategic alliances evolved. Although Susan Robbins, Paul Saunders, Ira Salzman, and Les Fagen all worked independently for different clients, they began to share documents and discuss strategy.

When lawyers from both sides descended on 778 Park to view Brooke Astor's living situation, Louise Milligan, a Chase managing director who had sealed the apartment earlier, pointed out that a table had mysteriously appeared in the dining room. There were other inexplicable changes. "Someone got in there," recalls Robbins. "There were no clothes. Where were all her clothes?" The Chanel suits, the thousands of dollars' worth of designer ball gowns — treasures that might well have been auctioned off at Sotheby's or donated to the Metropolitan Museum's Costume Institute — had gone missing. To this day, the disappearances have never been explained.

Like perfume testers, the lawyers lined up in a procession to sniff the infamous couch in quest of the elusive scent of dog urine. The consensus was that the sofa was odorless — a point in favor of Tony. His lawyer Harvey Corn wrote in court papers: "The couch referred to in the petition is richly upholstered and without any bad smell, urine or otherwise." But the argument from the other side was that the couch had been surreptitiously cleaned. The public relations consultant Fraser Seitel insisted, "We don't know who did it and we don't know when." With black humor, Philip Marshall joked with Annette and Chris Ely that he hoped to bring Boysie into court as a witness.

During this summer when New Yorkers were bewitched, bothered, and bewildered over Brooke, prosecutors in the Manhattan district attorney's office were reading the headlines too. Susan Robbins received a voicemail message from Elizabeth Loewy, the prosecutor who ran the elder abuse unit in District Attorney Robert Morgenthau's office. Robbins decided not to respond to Loewy's offer of help. She saw her responsibility as trying to determine Mrs. Astor's wishes, and she could not believe that any mother would want her son investigated by criminal authorities.

At home in South Dartmouth, Philip spent hours on the phone with the lawyers and the press while sitting in his small second-floor office, with a window overlooking the backyard trees. The room, decorated with American Indian pottery from his stepfather and a landscape painted by Nan, was just a few steps away from the Buddhist prayer corner tucked into a stairwell, featuring a small bronze Buddha, incense, a rug, and beads. The rest of the house was filled with mementos of happier times: an oil portrait of Brooke Astor in her heyday, framed photos of Philip's father and mother during their marriage, snapshots of Winslow and Sophie with their doting great-grandmother. One evening Philip drove to Providence for a drink at a riverfront hotel with his vacationing aunt, Sukie Kuser, Tony's half-sister. "I was on Philip's side from the beginning," explains Kuser. Commiserating over their fractured family, they both blamed the same person for all that had gone wrong. As Philip says, "We kept talking about 'What did Charlene think she was doing?'"

What Tony and Charlene were actually doing at this moment was taking a hard look at their finances. Without access to Brooke's money to pay for the Maine expenses and with their legal bills piling up, the couple decided they needed to cut back. Steve Hamor, aged sixty-three and Mrs. Astor's Maine gardener for forty-one years, learned during a phone call that he and his two sons were about to be unemployed. "Mr. Marshall told me, 'I have bad news — we're going to have to let you go,'" Hamor recalls. He offered to take a pay cut, but the couple was adamant, granting three months' severance pay to Hamor and his sons, Steve Jr. and Scott. It was not until a year later that Hamor discovered that Brooke Astor had left him $50,000 in her will, but with the condition that he had to be working at Cove End at the time of her death. Tony knew, just as he had when he had fired Chris Ely, that he was depriving the loyal employee of Mrs. Astor's bequest.

During Act One of the Astor affair, the playbill kept producing characters on the periphery of Brooke Astor's life, who emerged for a moment into the spotlight, some by choice and others unwittingly. Paul Gilbert, now living quietly in Charleston with his third wife, was startled when a *New York Post* photographer turned up at his front door — he was now immortalized as Charlene's wronged first husband. Alice Perdue voluntarily went to the *New York Times* as the scandal's whistle-blower ("A Former Astor Aide Tells How Spending Habits Changed"). But no character made more of a grand entrance, or an impression on the critics, than Francis X. Morrissey, Jr. For a graying middle-aged man who usually blends into the background, he initially appeared in the press with such an ominous drum roll that he might just as well have been wearing a black hat and a sandwich board emblazoned with the identifier VILLAIN. Morrissey's tangled legal history caught up with him as reporters searched happily through the boxes of documents on public file: "Lawyer Advising Astor Affairs Was Suspended for Two Years" (*New York Times*); "ASTOR LAWYER'S WILLFUL DECEIT? HE INHERITED MILLIONS FROM ESTATES OF OLD FRIENDS" (*Daily News*); "'THERE IS EVIL IN ME' — ASTOR LAWYER $HAME" (*New York Post*).

For Tony and Charlene, this was death by a thousand cuts. Their lawyers insisted to the press that Morrissey was a trusted family friend and that they were unaware that he had ever been suspended from practicing law. After the *Times* ran an editorial about elder abuse ("The Brooke Astor Effect"), noting that the "philanthropist now appears to be getting the attention she needs," Ken Warner and Harvey Corn jointly wrote a published letter to the editor: "Mr. Marshall has been lovingly devoted to his mother and her care. He does not deserve the one-sided, unremitting media attack that he and his wife have been subjected to."

Yet even as Tony continued to claim that his conduct was blameless, new documents emerged to suggest otherwise. While at Holly Hill in mid-August, Philip found the nurses' notebooks in a second-floor bedroom. Skimming through a few pages, he became transfixed by the details, including his grandmother's worry that "they" were considering "putting her away" and her nightmares of a man trying to kill her. Just then he heard the sound of a car; it was his father and Charlene. Philip hid upstairs and kept paging through the heartbreaking notebooks, a litany of his grandmother's sorrows.

Under normal circumstances, Brooke Astor's final 2002 will and its three codicils would have become public only upon her death, when submitted for probate in Westchester County Surrogate's Court. Earlier wills and all correspondence involving the lawyers (including Terry Christensen, Francis Morrissey, and Warren Whitaker) would have remained private documents forever. But instead, Susan Robbins was reading her way through voluminous paperwork with a mixture of disbelief and gusto. Who could have imagined that an intricately plotted legal thriller worthy of Scott Turow could be found by reading between the lines of Brooke Astor's ever-changing final wishes? Robbins kept getting up and going into the office of Geoffrey Chinn, a colleague in her firm, to announce: "Oh my God, this doesn't make any sense."

Robbins knew that Brooke Astor had closed the Vincent Astor Foundation rather than let Tony run it. She could see that earlier wills bequeathed the Childe Hassam to the Metropolitan Museum, and even the most recent 2002 will gave an interest in Cove End to Philip Marshall and the bulk of her estate to charity. So it appeared implausible that after reaching age one hundred, the elderly philanthropist had suddenly decided to tear up her entire estate plan and make every subsequent change benefit her son.

Most out of character was the firing of Sullivan & Cromwell, the firm that Brooke Astor had trusted for four decades. But given Mrs. Astor's age and apparently limited mental acuity, Robbins was also skeptical about the first codicil, prepared under Sullivan & Cromwell's watch by Terry Christensen. Typically, Brooke exchanged letters with Christensen when she wanted to change her will, but Robbins did not see any correspondence indicating that Brooke had sought this codicil. As Robbins says, "I had a clear vision that all the lawyers were doing bad things to her. It was just so obvious."

When Terry Christensen met with Robbins and Chinn at his impressive Sullivan & Cromwell office on the waterfront at the tip of Manhattan, he declined to offer enlightenment as to why he had used the unusual phrase "first and last codicil." To Robbins, those magic words signified that "something wasn't right and he knew it. No lawyer ever says that." Christensen spoke with anger about Tony Marshall's decision to cut his mother's ties to Sullivan & Cromwell. As Robbins recalls, "Terry told us it was a balancing act for him, dealing with Tony and Mrs. Astor and trying to please them both."

Another mystery that perplexed Robbins was Brooke Astor's signature on the third codicil. "It was too perfect," Robbins says. "If you look at the two codicils before, she could barely sign her name. How did her signature get so good on this one?" The lawyer initially thought an old-fashioned ink stamp must have been used. When Robbins and the other lawyers took a field trip to Tony's office at 405 Park Avenue to examine his files, she sat at Tony's desk and searched in vain for the stamp.

Francis Morrissey was actually eager to talk to Robbins when she requested a meeting, since he welcomed the opportunity to defend Tony and Charlene on the charges of elder abuse. As someone who had seen Brooke constantly in recent years, he viewed himself as a character witness for the embattled Marshalls. He was cautious enough, however, to bring his own lawyer, Michael Ross, who had helped him regain his law license, to the late August meeting at Robbins's office. Morrissey kept insisting that he and Tony had done nothing wrong. His voice at times rose in passion and conviction as he repeatedly spoke of Mrs. Astor's late-in-life desire to shower her son with love.

The two-hour meeting was an exercise in mutual frustration. Morrissey later told a friend that Robbins was "crude and unsophisticated" in her questioning and that he found it difficult "to control my big Irish temper and keep my mouth shut." Robbins was so irritated by his unyielding tale of maternal love that at the end of the session she lectured him: "You should be ashamed of yourself. You're the reason that Brooke Astor is afraid of men in suits."

12

The Art of Shunning

THE BOARD OF TRUSTEES of the Metropolitan Museum of Art meets twice a year in the serene C. Douglas Dillon boardroom, with members taking their places around a richly stained dark brown oak table crafted by Viscount David Linley, the son of Princess Margaret. Those chosen for Manhattan's most sought-after board memberships represent a mixture of New York aristocracy, both old money and new money, culled from society and Wall Street.

Annette de la Renta, a board member since 1981, is vice chairman of the museum and heads the acquisitions committee, two powerful positions. On the afternoon of September 12, 2006, when the first board meeting since the Astor scandal hit the newspapers was scheduled, the museum staff believed that Tony Marshall would not be attending, since he had not RSVPed. Many gathered at the handsome table had been angry to learn that Tony had not only sold his mother's Childe Hassam, repeatedly promised to the museum, but made off with a $2 million commission. The assumption was that Tony would be too embarrassed to show his face. So there was a collective gasp when, just as the meeting was beginning, he strode in. "We thought he did it for shock value," says one staffer. Heads swiveled to Annette de la Renta, who conveyed her fury with a what-the-hell-is-he-doing-here grimace.

"I debated, should I go or not?" Tony told me several months later. Elected to the board in 1986, he had graduated to nonvoting emeritus status in 2000 when he turned seventy-six, so his appearance at this meeting was primarily symbolic. "I thought, Look, I know I'm right. I know the truth, we know the truth. I'm not going to shy away from there. I want to see how people react to my being there."

The answer was immediately apparent: he was persona non grata. The museum's director, Philippe de Montebello, recalls, "I averted my eyes — my gaze never met his. Everyone did. We were rather surprised that he showed up." For Tony, walking to his seat was the equivalent of a long day's journey into social death. It was a shunning worthy of Edith Wharton, although Tony lacked the rebelliousness of Lily Bart in *The House of Mirth*. Out of compassion, two men broke ranks. Carl Spielvogel, the retired advertising CEO and Clinton ambassador, turned to Tony and simply asked, "How are you?" Malcolm Wiener, a wealthy commodities trader, made a point of walking all the way around the table to be gracious, saying, "I'm sorry to hear about all this. Did you know about it beforehand?" Tony replied, "Absolutely not." Wiener replied, "That's appalling." Tony was so grateful for the gesture of support that he later wrote Wiener a thank-you note.

As de Montebello launched into his description of upcoming exhibitions, the other board members kept glancing at the adversaries. "It was an unpleasant situation," Annette de la Renta says. "I just did not look at him." Tony, who had seated himself across from Annette, carefully watched her reaction, happily remarking later, "By my being there, for the next hour and forty-five minutes, she was visibly upset." Spouses had been invited to join the members after the meeting for a private tour of the new exhibit, "Cézanne to Picasso," but Charlene stayed away, maintaining an anxious vigil at home with Daniel Billy. When the meeting ended, Tony headed for the exit. "One female — I won't say who it is — went down in the elevator with me," Tony says. "She gave me the worst look you can possibly imagine, this stare." But he had shown up, and he was rather proud of having faced everyone down. He vowed to me that he would not be forced out by social stigma, but this would turn out to be his last board meeting.

• • •

In public, Tony Marshall was sticking with his Marine Corps attitude, holding his head high and being tough under fire. But in private, his life was a shambles. Ten days before the Metropolitan board meeting he had sent Alec a two-page typed letter that was a howl of pure pain, describing the sleepless nights, death threats, and damage to his reputation. Tony painted a bleak picture of himself and Charlene cowering at home, weeping. With skyrocketing legal bills and no salary, Tony wrote, he was worried about running out of money.

The other melody in this chorus of woe was an unsubtle effort to convince Alec to pressure Philip to back off. Tony stressed that the lawsuit was a huge drain on Brooke Astor's resources and might diminish Alec's and Philip's inheritance. To Alec, parts of the letter read as if they had been vetted by a lawyer; Alec thought that the words did not entirely sound like his father's voice. Tony closed with the accusatory sentence "Is this what Philip wanted?"

Although Alec was still trying to play Switzerland in his family's war, this neutral stance was becoming increasingly hard to maintain. Philip had become his frequent overnight guest, taking advantage of Alec's proximity to Holly Hill, only a five-minute drive away. Of course Alec showed Philip the letter from their father. Philip became angry at Tony's divisive effort to set brother against brother. As he puts it, "That letter was so manipulative."

Charlene's safest refuge was St. James' Church, where she sought comfort from the rector, Brenda Husson. "She certainly came to me to talk and pray," says Husson. "To have your picture splashed in the paper and people stopping you on the street, that can't help." At Sunday church services, Charlene appeared anxious about the reactions of her fellow parishioners. "She'd sit in the back of the church, try to be like a little mouse not to be seen, and people would swarm around her," says Sam Peabody. "When all this hell broke loose, she was very needy. She was teary-eyed — she never thought she could get through something like this. She was called a gold digger, which was really disgusting."

New York scandals usually fade fast, but the Astor saga was becoming as hardy a tabloid perennial as outbursts from George Steinbrenner and his sons. Christopher Meigher, the CEO of Quest Media, publisher of the on-line magazine *New York Social Diary*, marveled at the public's seemingly endless appetite for the latest Astor news and gossip. "You would think that people would get tired of it, but they did not want to let it go," Meigher says. "Just like Diana, she was of interest to several generations. Any story having to do with Mrs. Astor, our traffic jumped fifty to sixty percent."

The plot had shifted from a family feud to a fight over Brooke Astor's money. Les Fagen, representing Chase, alerted Justice Stackhouse that the bank was looking into whether Tony had improperly obtained $14 million, including cash and Cove End, from his mother. Fagen's legal document was filled with moral outrage: "Was Mrs. Astor competent to understand and then authorize or intend these transactions at the relevant times? . . . Who are the witnesses to these transactions who can support or contradict Mr. Marshall? . . . And above all, is Mr. Marshall telling the truth?" Chase's lawyer asked for expanded powers to investigate. The judge denied the request as being "overly zealous and premature at this time, however well-intentioned."

As part of the ongoing blizzard of legal paperwork, Tony Marshall had submitted a thirty-page affidavit denying all charges and insisting, in a wounded tone, that he loved his mother. He blamed Chris Ely for instigating the lawsuit out of spite over losing his job. He said he had deferred to Dr. Pritchett on Mrs. Astor's medical care, and submitted a purveyors-to-the-queen list of the Upper East Side gourmet shops (Marche Madison, Butterfield Market, Ottomanelli's) where he maintained charge accounts for his mother's food. In an effort to demonstrate his mother's affection, Tony even included poems and notes from Brooke, some dating as far back as twenty-one years, such as this birthday note from May 30, 1985:

> Darling Tony — On this very special day, your birthday, I feel so proud, so grateful and so happy that you are my son. Of all the creations *you* are the Best! But I want to tell you what a difference it has made in my life having you here after all those years abroad. I no longer feel alone because I know that you are there with your wisdom and common sense and affection to help me. It has meant more to me than I can possibly tell you — But I hope that you know.
> With much love and Very Happy Birthday, Mother

There was another, undated birthday poem from Brooke, with the lines "How much you mean — how much you better my life, being my son and with your own dear wife, Who brings such joy to you and me too, so thank you both and without much ado." Tony also included a limerick that his mother wrote on May 29, 1989:

> There is a young man named Tony
> Who can't stand anything phony
> He likes things to be clear as a bell
> and will go through hell
> in order to avoid cacophony.

Scholars of Astor history drily noted that at least two of these missives were written before Tony became involved with Charlene and the third was undated. But the image of Tony Marshall desperately searching through memorabilia to prove his mother's love to the world was ineffably sad.

In the New York social strata where the latest news about Brooke had become ubiquitous, the most surprising development was the revelation that Tony had won the support of Freddy Melhado, Brooke's dancing partner of forty years. Tony had invested millions of dollars of Brooke's money with Melhado, and he had done well for her via hedge funds (the most impressive was a $3 million investment that climbed to $20 million). Melhado filed an affidavit stating that Brooke was "impeccably dressed," that her apartment was "clean and well-maintained," that Tony was astute in managing her money, and that "Brooke loved Tony very much and it was obvious to me that Tony felt exactly the same way."

Melhado knew that he was backing the unpopular side and says that his friends "were furious at me." Sitting in his Park Avenue apartment, with sadness in his voice, he asks, "What else can I do? I wasn't going to lie about Tony and lie about what I saw. I never saw in the apartment any neglect or abuse, or think, 'Oh, God, she's got to get out of here.'" Melhado called Annette at her country home to smooth things over and was relieved when she came in from the garden to take his call. "I've known you all my adult life, and I love your children," Melhado says he told Annette, "and I just want you to know that this has nothing to do with the way I feel about you." He adds, "She said she understood. But I'm sure she's not happy with me."

Indeed, he soon received an ominous legal letter from Annette's lawyer, Paul Saunders, demanding the return of the dog painting that had vanished from Brooke's stairwell at Holly Hill. Melhado explains that he had lent Brooke the painting twenty-five years ago; Tony agreed to return the art, but Melhado claimed the staff sent him the wrong painting. "I would never take advantage of Brooke," Melhado insists. "That's what burned me up so much, when they implied that I did." Word of the purportedly purloined painting made it across the Atlantic Ocean to Viscount Astor. "If anyone deserved a painting, it would be Freddy — he was incredibly kind to Brooke," Astor says. "But Freddy behaved in a stupid manner. The painting he said he lent Brooke was six inches by six inches, and the picture he collected was six feet by four feet. Freddy is a nice man who got on the wrong side. He got sucked into Tony Marshall's web, Charlene's web."

The painting that provoked intense interest, however, was *Flags, Fifth Avenue*, long gone but hardly forgotten. Tony abruptly admitted to his lawyers that he had made a major error on his mother's 2002 tax return in reporting the sale of the painting. Tony had claimed to the IRS that Brooke originally paid $7.42 million for the artwork, although the actual purchase price was $172,000. Tony Marshall's inaccurate number dramatically reduced the capital gains tax due after the painting was sold for $10 million. Tony never explained or provided documentation for the figure of $7.42 million.

This admission of potential tax fraud was a major blow to Tony's credibility and virtually guaranteed that Justice Stackhouse would never allow him to resume control of his mother's finances. Tony blamed the error on Brooke Astor's accountant, Samuel M. Cohen. Of course the accountant, who had kept copies of the paperwork that Tony had provided, did not let this accusation go uncontested. Alan Pollack, Cohen's attorney, says, "My client was outraged that Tony was looking to make him the scapegoat. The WASP is trying to hang the Jewish accountant out to dry?"

Despite the anticipated high drama of a courtroom confrontation over Brooke Astor's care, the action was taking place either offstage or on the written page, with histrionic claims and counterclaims punctuating the deluge of documents filed with the court clerk at 60 Centre Street. Out at Holly Hill, an unlikely trio had forged a close bond that transcended class boundaries: Annette de la Renta, the intimidating and super-wealthy philanthropist; Chris Ely, the ever-proper butler; and the free-wheeling college professor Philip Marshall were now in this together, joking and talking and confiding in one another with abandon. Annette later said, "I consider Chris and Philip to be among my closest friends."

Susan Robbins had also won their trust and they hers. She hitched a lift with Annette one afternoon to Holly Hill. "I liked her immediately," says Annette; a year later she recommended Robbins to a friend for another guardianship case involving a wealthy family. Robbins, in turn, had been skeptical about Philip Marshall and his motivations for filing the lawsuit, so she was surprised by her own reaction when they met at Holly Hill in September. "I loved him," she says. "Maybe it's the Buddhist part, that inner peace and genuineness. At first I thought, This guy is too good to be true. I thought I was being taken. That was what I was really afraid of. But I never saw any evidence of it." Philip watched Robbins gently speaking to Brooke and trying to make eye contact. "She was so great with my grandmother," he says. Philip drove the lawyer to the station afterward; she lit a Marlboro and he bummed one; she mentioned that she had a twin brother too; and so it went. From then on, Philip took to calling her more often than his own lawyer to chat about the case.

As a son protective of his mother's image, Tony Marshall had stalwartly kept her secret for nearly six years, confiding in just a handful of people he trusted. Now, out of the blue, that secret surfaced, at exactly the worst moment for Mrs. Astor's son, and became a weapon to be used against him.

Although Tony had told his sons and Chris Ely that Brooke had Alzheimer's disease, the name of her doctor and the actual date of the diagnosis had been shrouded in mystery. Even when nurses were hired to care for Mrs. Astor around the clock and were briefed on her physical ailments, in mid-2003, they were apparently never directly informed that she suffered from dementia. Tony had given Chris Ely a handwritten list of symptoms that seemed to have been copied from an Internet site. For all anyone knew, Tony could have come up with the Alzheimer's diagnosis himself by watching his mother's behavior and putting two and two together.

But while paging through Brooke Astor's medical records, Ira Salzman noticed the name of Dr. Howard Fillit, a geriatric specialist, in the file of another one of her doctors. Paul Saunders contacted Dr. Fillit, asking for any records relating to Mrs. Astor. An astonishing document materialized, a letter more damaging to Tony Marshall than any allegation in the original guardianship petition. As Paul Saunders circulated this letter to the other lawyers, he announced that he had found the smoking gun. After a quick read, Susan Robbins promptly e-mailed him back to say that this "was a smoking cannon." Ira Salzman recalls being equally amazed, saying, "It was an oh-my-God moment."

It was a deep, self-inflicted wound for Tony Marshall. What he had done, after taking his mother to be examined by Dr. Fillit, was to write the physician a remarkably revealing seven-page follow-up letter, dated December 26, 2000, describing his mother's mental decline. Tony's tormented outpouring covered everything from Brooke Astor's inability to understand and remember simple things, such as basic arithmetic, to her hostile mood swings and delusional behavior. The letter read as if it had been cathartic to write, a way for Tony to put down on paper how wrenching it was to watch his mother deteriorate and to deal with her constant hurtful remarks to him, her loving son.

For the lawyers, however, it was the date on the letter that had overwhelming significance, because that proved that Tony, fully aware that his mother had Alzheimer's, had nonetheless allowed and encouraged her to make monumental changes in her estate plan and revise her bequests, from selling the Childe Hassam to signing a new will in 2002 and the three codicils in 2003–2004.

Tony wrote the letter on the day after Christmas, just hours after he and Charlene returned to Manhattan after spending the holiday with Brooke at Holly Hill. "I don't know what's the matter with me. I feel awful. I feel like I'm losing my mind," Brooke told her son that day as he was leaving. Tony described how his mother had resisted seeing Dr. Fillit, even trying to discourage Tony from accompanying her to the doctor's office. "When I arrived, Mother, who was half-an-hour late to leave for her appointment with you, said to me: 'You only want to come to see how soon I will die. Why are you coming?'"

Brooke, then ninety-eight, was constantly misplacing things, Tony wrote, adding that "writing/spelling are increasing problems" and that numbers had become "incomprehensible." "Mother asked me, 'What is my income?'" Tony informed the doctor. "I told her, giving the annual figure. 'Is that for the month or the year?'" Given that Tony's entire income came from his mother, that remark made it sound as if she had no idea what she was paying him.

Yet she was determined to carry on, and Tony sounded baffled about how to protect his mother, given her iron-willed insistence of keeping up a schedule that would wear down a person half her age. "Mother has an overpowering drive to 'keep going' and her resource of adrenaline keeps her on the move," he wrote, but he conveyed that her outings were tinged with the constant potential for disaster. She did not recognize people, her hearing was poor, and there had been embarrassing incidents when his mother had become incontinent.

So much acuity had been lost. "She is delusional at times having asked me, 'Are you my only child?'" Tony wrote. He closed by telling the doctor that "now that you have provided me with a diagnosis of my mother's illness," he had passed along the news to her lawyer, Terry Christensen, her social secretary (then Jolee Hirsch), and Chris Ely. "While I'm deeply saddened by the news you've given me it is, at the same time, a relief for me (and an enormous help to the three in whom I have confided) to know what the problem is and not that she is just an elderly person being difficult."

The letter raised many questions, but one dominated everything: how could Brooke's trusted lawyer, Terry Christensen, knowing of her diminished condition, let her make changes in her will? The timing of Tony's decision to take his mother to the doctor was intriguing too. He sought the diagnosis of dementia just a few months after his mother had expressed her desire to give her Maine cottage to Philip. It appeared as if Tony initially wanted a legal rationale to stop Brooke from giving away possessions but then ignored her mental state when the diagnosis was inconvenient for him.

Paul Saunders wondered whether Tony had simply forgotten about the letter or had not informed his lawyers about it. "We knew it was a significant piece of evidence," Saunders says. "It was not consistent with a lot of things Tony said in his petition." Tony, in his affidavit, had portrayed his mother as dancing the night away at parties and being fully cognizant of events.

For Susan Robbins, this letter was an ace to be played to complete a winning hand. Arguing that the document proved that Brooke Astor had been incompetent since 2000, she asked Justice Stackhouse to give her access to Mrs. Astor's original wills and codicils, not mere copies, and to permit her to hire a handwriting expert. The opposition was caught off-guard: Tony's lawyers responded by personally attacking Robbins's reputation. Ken Warner charged that she was "on a witch hunt of her own creation, having long ago abandoned the role of Mrs. Astor's advocate." In thunderous language, Corn insisted that "Mrs. Astor was obviously competent when she executed the first and second codicils. Is Mrs. [Ms.] Robbins alleging that Mr. Christensen, whose firm had represented Mrs. Astor for decades, performed a will signing ceremony with an incompetent Mrs. Astor?"

That was exactly what Robbins was suggesting. Ignoring the complaints of Tony's lawyers, the judge gave Robbins the go-ahead. To protect Brooke Astor's privacy, Robbins had filed the Fillit document under seal from the press, the status that Mrs. Astor's medical records had. Tony Marshall's letter to Dr. Fillit would not become public for another year.

With the guardianship hearing scheduled for mid-October, Tony put his money into public relations. Unhappy with the firm of Citigate Sard Verbinnen, which billed them $42,375, the Marshalls hired Sean Healy and Christopher Tennyson of Fleishman-Hillard. For the first major interview with Tony and Charlene — a classic journalistic "get" — the new PR men chose an unlikely venue: *Forbes* magazine, for its annual "400 Richest People in America" issue. During the three emotional hours that the financial writer Neil Weinberg spent with the Marshalls, at the PR firm's offices in the former *Daily News* building on Forty-second Street, the couple portrayed themselves as victims of a society conspiracy. "What I'd really like to know is, who is giving orders," Tony said. "It isn't Henry [Kissinger]. Is it Annette? Is it David? It certainly isn't Philip. It's out of his ballpark." After minimizing his son, Tony sought to elevate himself by comparing the current ordeal to being wounded during World War II: "This is worse than Iwo Jima because my wounds there healed." Published on October 9, 2006, Weinberg's short piece stated that some of the allegations "are clearly overblown, if not wrong." Weinberg gave Tony the last word. "The opposition's prime interest is not in my mother's care," Tony says, "but her estate and control over her life. This could happen to anybody."

In the full transcript of the interview, which Weinberg generously provided to me, the Marshalls alternate between rage, paranoia, and despair. They rip into the "cabal" that has ruined their lives, claiming that "Annette de la Renta wants to be the next Brooke Astor" and that "Philip wants more assets." Charlene criticizes Philip as a bad son, saying, "Not only was he not close to his grandmother, he wasn't particularly close to his father either. We saw Philip once a year." When Weinberg asked why Morrissey had become involved, Tony replied, "Francis Morrissey was a long-time friend whom my mother confided in."

The couple acknowledged that the press scrutiny had been brutal. Tony defended his wife, saying, "They're trying to make Charlene out as just after the money. We're not only in love, what's really nice about this is that we've gone through this together and not had one argument between us. Lots of people would have scratched each other to death, either mentally or physically."

On Park Avenue and in other wealthy enclaves the article was perused and deconstructed with the kind of minute attention usually given to changes in the capital gains tax. Tony and Charlene's claim that Annette was motivated by a desire to be "the next Brooke Astor," revealed a misunderstanding of twenty-first-century society. It was as if the couple envisioned a diamond tiara waiting to crown Brooke's heir, which Annette had rudely grabbed for. But Jane Engelhard's daughter had never had to grab for anything; now in her mid-sixties, she had a position that had long been secure. Old society was vanishing into the obituary columns: C. Z. Guest, Nan Kempner, Pat Buckley. New society, epitomized by Tinsley Mortimer and Tory Burch, was preoccupied with marketing the term *socialite* as a brand name. Brooke Astor, born in 1902, had been a legend, a self-created phenomenon, and was an irreplaceable creature of her white-gloved era. There would be no "next."

If you ask David Rockefeller whether Annette's motive in the guardianship fight was to elevate her social status and become the new Brooke, his face creases with merriment. When he stops laughing, he searches for the right word to convey his reaction. He's too polite to swear, so instead he replies, "The term I would use is not repeatable. It's completely absurd."

Yet if Tony's wounding remarks were aimed at an audience of one, he likely hit his mark. Annette de la Renta, who had spent her life avoiding the limelight, was now facing a daily diet of publicity and found all the stories mortifying. As Barbara Walters says, "Every time there was something in the paper, she died. If it was something critical, she wanted to hide under the covers."

For all the Marshalls' bravado in the *Forbes* interview, by the time the magazine hit the newsstands, the couple had already reached the reluctant conclusion that they could not win and it was time to find a graceful exit. The court evaluator, Sam Liebowitz, had been trying to broker a deal, and the couple leaped at the chance to retire from the headlines, as did their adversaries.

In the hope of heading off a potentially devastating inquiry into the Marshalls' finances, Tony grudgingly agreed to give up guardianship of his mother and his lucrative yearly salary. As Paul Saunders recalls, "They were deathly afraid the bank was going to sue them." In return, Tony and Charlene insisted the agreement had to include the phrase that they admitted to no wrongdoing; legal claims against the couple would be frozen until after Brooke Astor's death. "I wanted a standstill," says Harvey Corn, Tony's lawyer, explaining that the ordeal had become unbearable for the Marshalls. "My guy is eighty-two years old. He couldn't go outside his house." Tony and Charlene, along with Francis Morrissey and Terry Christensen, gave up any claim to serve as executors of Brooke Astor's will, which left the question of who would handle that task in limbo.

Susan Robbins was the lone dissenter during a settlement conference held at the offices of Chase's lawyers. "What would Mrs. Astor want?" she argued. Robbins was frustrated because she thought that the other lawyers were giving way to battle fatigue. Tony was on the ropes; he should be forced to give it all back. The three new codicils should be judged invalid; Cove End, along with the $5 million granted to Charlene and Tony's $2 million self-dealt bonus, should be returned. Robbins wanted to ensure that Mrs. Astor regained her financial position before the "men in suits" took advantage. "That's when I said I'm not signing it, and they were ready to kill me," Robbins explains. But as far as Saunders was concerned, this was just a lull in the proceedings; the real bombardment would begin in surrogate's court after Mrs. Astor's death. "Susan didn't want to let Tony off the hook," Saunders says. "But I knew that because of the structure of the settlement, he wasn't off the hook."

Even though Robbins refused to sign, she won a concession. She had noticed that Mrs. Astor, who had provided only $100,000 each for the education of her three great-grandchildren, had inquired in a note to Terry Christensen whether she ought to do more for them. Robbins negotiated an increase to $400,000 each for Philip's son, Winslow, and daughter, Sophie, and Alec's daughter, Hilary Brooke, included in the stipulation settling the guardianship. These college funds represented, of course, an indirect way to funnel money to Brooke Astor's two grandsons, who would otherwise have paid this tuition themselves.

The denouement arrived, fittingly, on the morning of Friday, the thirteenth of October, 2006, a mere six days before the case was to go to trial. Annette de la Renta, in a simple black sheath, white coat, pearl earrings, and stilettos, appeared before Justice Stackhouse. In a dingy courtroom with fluorescent lights, she spoke to the judge in a quiet voice. "I have known Mrs. Astor for approximately forty years," she said. "She was a friend of my parents before, when I was young." Stackhouse asked if she had been responsible for taking Brooke Astor back to Holly Hill. Annette replied, "Yes, that's what I considered to be her home." The judge concurred approvingly, saying, "That's what I believe she considered her home as well." There were no courtroom theatrics; it was all merely a formality.

Yet the actual legal agreement, available to the press, contained titillating details. It read as if Tony and Charlene had admitted to pulling off a daring daylight robbery from Brooke's apartment and bank account but had now agreed to load up a Brink's truck and take it all back, $11 million worth in cash, jewelry, and art. That included $1.35 million to Chase Bank to cover the tax penalties on the Childe Hassam sale. Tony had even agreed to put up his beloved boat, the *General Russell,* as collateral.

As for the possessions, the Marshalls had apparently prematurely taken home two gifts intended for them in Brooke Astor's 2002 will, the diamond snowflake necklace and a Giovanni Tiepolo drawing worth $500,000, plus valuables that had been designated for others. The couple returned a 10-carat diamond ring and three brooches; Brooke had requested that any pieces of her jewelry worth more than $1,000, with a few specific exceptions, be sold, with the proceeds going to charity. A John Frederick Lewis drawing (worth $500,000) and a collection of five gouaches by the eighteenth-century Venetian painter Francesco Guardi made a return trip to 778 Park Avenue; Brooke had left her drawings, in her will, to the Metropolitan Museum and the Morgan Library. Tony and Charlene were ordered to return the Astor flat silverware, which had been bequeathed to Viscount Astor. The couple also returned twenty-four volumes by Rudyard Kipling and two Chinese porcelain figures.

This turn of events was humiliating for Tony and Charlene, and they decided to go public yet again to defend themselves, this time to Vicky Ward of *Vanity Fair.* Raising a cudgel as if she were Margaret Thatcher waging war in the Falklands, Charlene announced, "There will be a battle royal when Brooke Astor dies." This was a threat and a promise. "The important point is that the money we are returning is not 'taken' money or 'stolen' money, but money for collateral, in case of future disputes," Charlene continued. "The things are presents given to us since 1992. They are in the will, and we expect to get it all back." Since Mrs. Astor's will was not yet public, Vicky Ward was unable to challenge Charlene's claims. Tony made similar remarks to Grace Richardson, a Juilliard Council member and friend, when she went by for tea. "Tony said those had been gifts from his mother at Christmas," Richardson recalls. "I said, 'Didn't she write you a note? "Dear Tony, I'm giving you these books, love Mom"?'" According to Richardson, Tony replied, "I gave them back, and I'll get them back later."

It was over, but it wasn't over. One week later, the nationally known forensic handwriting expert Gus Lesnevich submitted his report on the variations in Brooke Astor's signatures, and his findings were unambiguous. Mrs. Astor could not have produced the Brooke Russell Astor signature on the codicil dated March 3, 2004, he wrote, "due to the deterioration of her ability to write her name."

Woe to Francis Morrissey, who claimed that he had supervised while Brooke Astor signed the third codicil in the presence of two witnesses. This new and well-publicized development created a dilemma for Susan Robbins. Lawyers, as officers of the court, are required to report to the authorities when a crime has been committed. Robbins had brushed off the expression of interest in the case by the prosecutor Elizabeth Loewy. Now she had no choice but to offer to hand over her files. She met with Loewy, joined by Paul Saunders. Robbins had hoped that the prosecutor would focus on Morrissey. "I thought he was brilliant," she says. "I thought he had orchestrated the whole thing."

But Robbins, for all her legal zeal, was subject to the law of unintended consequences. "I never wanted this to be a criminal investigation against Tony," she says, sensitive that her client was Mrs. Astor. "Who would want their son to go to jail?" But the latticework of ties between Morrissey and Marshall made it nearly impossible to separate the two men in a criminal investigation.

The door was now open for the prosecutors to satisfy their curiosity about Mrs. Astor's will. Almost no one involved in the guardianship case had anticipated the legal ramifications for Tony. Philip had never imagined that he would be placing his father in criminal jeopardy. Annette de la Renta and David Rockefeller just wanted a way to restore Brooke to a more comfortable life at Holly Hill. So many things had to go wrong with this family to bring in the DA's office — such a confluence of misunderstandings, relationships torn asunder, words left unsaid, and, the most dangerous ingredient of all, money substituting for love. Yet now the fate of Brooke Astor's only son, Tony Marshall, was in the hands of the prosecutors. The investigation would last for a full year, holding the Marshalls and Morrissey in limbo.

Had all of this angst been worth it? If the yardstick was the well-being of the 104-year-old Brooke Astor, she was doing everything within her limited power to convey her appreciation. After her near-death experience at the hospital in July, she had chosen a tangible way to convey her renewed interest in life — she was eating again. At home at Holly Hill with meals cooked by her French chef, Mrs. Astor eventually added nearly fifteen pounds to her slender frame.

For her newly hired staffers, she was a daily source of inspiration and astonishment. "When I spoke to the doctor at Lenox Hill, the prognosis was not good. I didn't think she'd last six months," says Lois Orlin, the social worker hired to coordinate Mrs. Astor's care. "But it was amazing how well she did. Going back to Holly Hill was very positive for her mentally — she blossomed. Even when people are not aware of everything that's going on, certain things still filter through." For the nurses who had been with Mrs. Astor for several years, her revival was pure validation. As Minnette Christie recalls, "I kept telling everyone, 'Just you wait, she's going to surprise you.'"

Surrounded by an army of cheerful people united in the mission of keeping up her spirits, Brooke Astor spent her days in a carefully choreographed way. Opening the curtains in Mrs. Astor's bedroom in the morning, Pearline Noble would point out the birds pecking at the feeder perched in a tree outside the window. "Come on, Mrs. A., wake up. The birds are waiting — it's time to get out of bed," recalls Noble, explaining that if the feeder was empty, the blackbirds would knock on the window. "Mrs. A., the birds are knocking, they want breakfast. We have to hurry." The nurse says, "She would smile and say okay."

Mrs. Astor liked looking at pictures of her younger self (the house was certainly full of them) and hearing her own words. Sandra Foschi discovered that the best way to motivate her client to exercise was to read aloud Brooke's poem "Discipline," a paean to the importance of keeping going:

I am old and I have had
more than my share of good and bad
I've had love and sorrow, seen sudden death
and been left alone and of love bereft.
I thought I would never love again
and I thought my life was grief and pain.
The edge between life and death was thin,
but then I discovered discipline.
I learned to smile when I felt sad,
I learned to take the good and the bad.
I learned to care a great deal more
for the world about me than before.
I began to forget the "Me" and "I"
and joined in life as it rolled by:
this may not mean sheer ecstasy
but it is better by far than "I" and "Me."

"I recited it every time I treated her, three times a week, and she did respond," Foschi recalls. On sunny days Mrs. Astor was taken outdoors in a wheelchair to see the grounds, with Boysie and Girlsie frolicking along. Alec Marshall recalls that his grandmother enjoyed the change of scenery. "They'd wheel her all the way past the greenhouse, on a loop around the property to the gate," he says. "She'd wake up. She loved looking at the dogs running around."

Reunions with former staffers who had been fired by Tony Marshall were arranged. Naomi Packard-Koot, Mrs. Astor's former social secretary, and Marciano Amaral, her chauffeur, came out on separate occasions for tea. "You could see her eyes light up a bit and focus," says Packard-Koot. "It was wonderful to be there. I thought I'd never see her again after Tony and Charlene fired me — that was the most crushing thing." She brought along her husband, Michael Koot, a six-foot-six blond Dutch airline pilot. "Philip and I were laughing because Mrs. Astor was still doing her own version of flirting," Packard-Koot recalls. "She was making eye contact with Michael — she sat up straighter when he spoke."

Whether Mrs. Astor truly recognized people, or was even peripherally aware of the fight that had swirled around her, remained a source of debate in the household and among her friends. "Fortunately, I really don't think she ever knew any of these terrible things had happened," says David Rockefeller. "I don't think her life was made unhappy by them [the Marshalls], except to the degree they caused her to be less comfortable. She appreciated being at Holly Hill. She appreciated it when I came, and we had a good time." Noreen Nee, a new weekend nurse, said it was touching to see them together. "Mr. Rockefeller would hold her hand and say 'I love you, I'm here.' When he would get a response, he would be so happy, like he'd won a million dollars."

Reverend Charles Pridemore, of Trinity Church in nearby Ossining, visited every week and noticed that the rituals of religion still mattered to Mrs. Astor. "When I would give her communion, she made the sign of the cross. She knew it was me," he said, adding that she appeared to pay attention to the conversations in the room. "One day Philip and I were sitting around together, and he was talking. She raised her head and looked right over at him. I think she recognized him too."

But the relaxed environment vanished during visits by Mrs. Astor's son. Suddenly the household went to Code Red, aware that Tony Marshall was eager to spot any fault; he even brought a camera once and snapped pictures. When he gave his mother a plant and it wilted overnight, Chris Ely, fearful of being accused of being a plant murderer, tried to revive it by giving it the attention normally reserved for someone needing mouth-to-mouth resuscitation. "It was tense when her son came," says Noreen Nee. Most visitors sat next to Brooke, held her hand, and talked to her, but Nee recalls, "He would sit across the room and just look at her." Either unable or unwilling to express himself under the watchful eye of the staff, Tony communed with his mother in silence.

On Thanksgiving Day 2006, Tony and Charlene were guests at the annual party given by Sam Peabody and his wife, Judy, at the New York Racquet Club. Although he was a member, Tony had not been to the private club in months. As Peabody recalls, "All the staff came to him and said, 'Please come back — we miss you.'"

Philip, Nan, and their children spent the holiday with Brooke at

Holly Hill. The family shared turkey with the staff and then serenaded Brooke in the sunroom. "They sang for her like a band," recalls Pearline Noble. "They had different songs that they made up. Mrs. A. was awake, and blew kisses and smiled." Winslow played his guitar; Nan and Sophie harmonized on "Amazing Grace" and "Time of Your Life" and one of Winslow's original compositions, "Opportunities." Philip massaged his grandmother's feet. Sophie, then eleven, came away with another good memory of her great-grandmother. "We didn't have to be so formal," she says. "Every so often her eyes would just stare at us — that was really nice. I feel like at that point we had a different connection with her."

The next day the family drove to Manhattan, and while Nan took the children to join the crowds of Black Friday shoppers, Philip traveled downtown to meet with the two district attorneys, Elizabeth Loewy and Peirce Moser. As he began to answer the lawyers' questions, he broke down and wept. He was emotionally ragged, recalling Brooke's fear and despair from the nurses' notes, yet also facing the reality that he was providing damaging information about his father.

Pearline Noble and Minnette Christie, whose complaints to Philip had set off the lawsuit, were also summoned to meet with the prosecutors. Annette de la Renta sent a town car to take them to the DA's office. Both women, whom I later interviewed together, say that they were flabbergasted by the turn of events. "If I knew that things were going to get to this point, I would not have opened my mouth," says Minnette Christie. "I didn't want him to get into trouble. Believe you me, I was just doing this for Mrs. Astor." She continued, "After Mrs. Astor got out of that apartment, I thought it was over, kaput. When I got the call to go down to the DA, I didn't know what the hell I was going for." Pearline Noble insists, "I had no clue there was anything criminal. We didn't go after them, never."

For Brooke Astor, the financial cost of her move to Holly Hill turned out to be exorbitant, more expensive than spending a year in Palm Beach, chartering a fleet of yachts in the Caribbean, or taking up residency at the Connaught in London. The problem was not the bills for the ambulance from Lenox Hill or for sprucing up her country house, but rather the millions of dollars in legal fees arising out of the guardianship lawsuit, all paid out of her account, in keeping with legal precedent.

On December 4, 2006, Justice Stackhouse, ruling on the legal bills, began by noting that he had fee applications from fifty-six lawyers, sixty-five legal assistants, six accountants, five bankers, six doctors, a law school professor, and two public relations firms. (The number would have been higher, but Annette la Renta paid her own legal bills.) Asked to approve $3,044,055.71, the judge knocked the sum down to $2,223,284.42. The exactitude was comic, but the lawyers wanted every penny.

The warring legal strategies were on display by virtue of their final accounting. Tony's lawyers bore such animosity toward Susan Robbins that they had launched an effort to disqualify her as Mrs. Astor's lawyer, hiring another lawyer, David A. Smith, who billed $18,512.50 for research on Robbins. Stackhouse denied that request. The judge also refused to cover the public relations firms or lawyers' conversations with the press. Ken Warner, Tony's attorney, was the big loser: he had billed $35,000 for talking to journalists, which the judge noted primarily constituted of speaking to Serge Kovaleski of the *Times*.

The most newsworthy nugget was buried on page eight of this thirteen-page document — a simple sentence that dramatically changed the press coverage and public perception of the Astor case. Ruling that Tony was entitled to be reimbursed for $409,451.65 worth of legal bills, the judge announced: "I make this ruling based on the conclusion of the court evaluator that the allegations in the petition regarding Mrs. Astor's medical and dental care, and other allegations of intentional elder abuse by the Marshalls, were not substantiated."

That phrase, "not substantiated" would be repeated ad infinitum every time Tony and Charlene Marshall were mentioned in news stories. "ASTOR SON IS CLEARED," trumpeted the *New York Post*. This phrase allowed the couple to tell the world that they had been falsely accused. The *New York Times* initially tucked the story away on page B3, with a misleading headline: "In Aftermath of the Astor Case, How the Final Fees Piled Up." The next day the *Times* offered a follow-up on page one of the metro section: "Astor Son Claims Vindication Over Words in Judge's Ruling."

Justice Stackhouse had not intended his ruling to be an exoneration of Tony, according to a courthouse source, and expressed surprise at the "repercussions" from his statement. "Sure, there were things that concerned us — of course there were," says the person who spoke with the judge. "But if you're going to prove x and y in the apartment in New York, you have to have a trial. Don't forget, the house was opened, the staff was rehired."

Henry Kissinger, who carefully parsed the judge's phrasing and use of the words "not substantiated," made a similar point. "My understanding is that the judge didn't say it didn't take place," he says. Gallantly eager to defend Mrs. de la Renta, he added, "Annette did not go into this to prove anything against Tony. She went in there on the basis of facts presented to her by staff members and Brooke's grandson. She didn't throw around charges of elder abuse."

Court evaluator Sam Liebowitz's report on the Astor affair, according to those who have seen it, is a mixed bag, validating some of Philip's charges but not all of them. Liebowitz, who conducted interviews with Brooke's doctors, staff, and friends, acknowledged that her apartment was not in top-notch condition and that her dogs were not being regularly walked, with the dining room used as a dog run.

Tony Marshall was blamed for poorly supervising the household. Brooke Astor's mental decline was detailed with a series of examples depicting her as confused and unable to sustain a conversation. Tony had included in his legal papers the speech that his mother gave at the Knickerbocker Club in February 10, 2004, as proof of her acuity. But Liebowitz challenged this claim, noting that Dr. Pritchett stated that Mrs. Astor would not have had the ability to write or dictate the thoughts contained in the speech. The report concluded that Mrs. Astor was not the victim of elder abuse as far as her medical and physical care was concerned, but did not deal with the question of financial abuse.

For Tony and Charlene Marshall, the judge's ruling represented vindication, but not everyone in their social world agreed. Several days later there was a funeral for Eleanor Elliott, a former magazine editor who had attended Brooke's one hundredth birthday party and whose husband, Jock, had been the best man at Tony's first wedding. At the service, at the Frank E. Campbell Funeral Chapel on Madison Avenue, Charlene went over to commiserate with Louis Auchincloss. "She threw herself into my arms," he recalls with distaste. "It was disgusting."

At year's end, two players in the Astor drama wrote about their experiences. Fraser Seitel, the Rockefeller spokesman, had schmoozed the press corps and become a favorite. Objectivity is a journalistic ideal, but charm usually trumps. Seitel's essay ("Crisis Management Lessons from the Astor Disaster") in the December 2006 issue of *O'Dwyer's PR Report*, offered such helpful hints as "strike first," "anticipate leaking, loose-lipped lawyers," and "stick to the script."

Seeking normality, Charlene had returned to teaching a healing prayer workshop at St. James', although as Rector Husson says, "She came to it from a place that was pretty tired and weary." In the December 2006 issue of the *St. James' Epistle*, she wrote about her ordeal as a test of faith and humanity:

> As you may know, Tony and I have been going through a rather rough patch. But we've not had to endure this time of trial alone. You've all been there for us and our family Sunday after Sunday, week after week, with hugs, kisses and words of encouragement; praying for us when we couldn't stand, speaking for us when we had no words.
>
> There were some days that were so very dark and worrisome. On one of those days during my morning reading I came across a story about a prisoner in a concentration camp who had scratched on the wall these words: "I believe in the sun even when it doesn't shine, I believe in love when it isn't shown, and I believe in God even when He doesn't speak."
>
> I wept as I shared these words with Brenda [Rector Husson] that day because not hearing God speak in the midst of our troubles was very difficult for me. Tony and I arrived home later that evening after spending hours at our attorney's office and as I opened the day's mail, out of one envelope poured a whole array of words of love, affection and encouragement sent by all the Stephen Ministers at St. James' Church. And that was only the beginning. God has been speaking to us with a whole sym-

phony of voices — yours. Here, truly, at St. James', is the body of Christ. Jesus can only be so happy that you are his and love you more than ever. Thank you.

By publishing this heartfelt letter, Charlene was conveying her hope that the Marshalls' bad times were safely behind them.

But the periodic rumblings from One Hogan Place, the headquarters of the New York County district attorney's office, were disquieting. In February, Charlene and Tony Marshall celebrated the christening of a new grandchild, Inness's baby boy. The reception at their home afterward lacked the gaiety typical of such occasions. "We went, we made our excuses, and then we left," says Paul Gilbert. "Under the circumstances, it was not very joyous. I was there for Inness." Francis Morrissey, godfather to Inness's older child, chatted amiably with the other guests, who included Daniel Billy and Sam Peabody. The threat of indictment had not eroded Morrissey's close relationship with the Marshalls. They were all in this together, their legal futures entwined.

Morrissey had been heartily telling friends that he was convinced justice would prevail and his name would be cleared of the forgery allegations, but in truth he was deeply depressed. "It has nearly destroyed him," says Catia Chapin. "I said, 'Frank, this is very hard, but you have to stay in there, you cannot let this get you down. A lot of us have crosses to bear — you can do it.'" She adds, "This has gutted his soul." News accounts suggesting that Morrissey had been the criminal mastermind did not sit well with his friends. The retired high school teacher Chuck Merten, Morrissey's former neighbor in South Salem, New York, says, "I don't know Tony Marshall from Adam, but he doesn't sound like anybody's fool. He's misled by someone like Frank?"

To sustain a legal practice was difficult, given Morrissey's notoriety. He lost at least one client, a friend of twenty years' standing, the photorealist painter Richard Estes, who sounds mournful about the parting of ways. "I've never had a lot of legal things to deal with, but if I did, I'd call Francis," says Estes. "I took him out to dinner and said I didn't believe any of it. Then a month later, I sort of fired him." The painter adds, "I used to give him little pictures for my fee — he had a whole wall of things by me. For all I know, he's sold them, or doesn't want to look at them anymore." An Estes painting is not a trivial gift; his work commands hundreds of thousands of dollars. For Morrissey, it was distressing to look around his office and be constantly reminded of Estes's abandonment. He railed angrily to friends, What happened to loyalty and the presumption of innocence?

Morrissey was also weighed down by family tragedies: his sister Catherine was battling breast cancer; a niece had been injured in a cab accident; and he was underwriting the care of his elderly father, then ninety-six, living in Boston. The spry retired municipal judge Francis X. Morrissey, no stranger to scandal himself, offered a sympathetic ear.

Here they were, like actors taking a break between the matinee and evening performances, with time to contemplate the reviews and their relationships with their fellow cast members. Destiny and DNA plus Brooke Astor's unseen hand had led inexorably to this moment. What a troubled thread had passed down through the male line of the Astor family: Tony had been estranged from his own father, and now he was estranged from his son. Brooke Astor, charming and crafty, had contributed to family disintegration by heaping insults on her son and his wife while making loving gestures toward her grandson late in life. One look at her luminous, pleading eyes and Philip had leapt into action.

During this lull, I asked Philip, "Were you and your father ever close?" and a few weeks later he found and forwarded a copy of a letter that he had written to Tony on March 18, 1993, shortly after Tony had married Charlene and Philip's second child had been born. The letter brims with longing for a better relationship. As Philip wrote:

> So much has changed during the past few years. But during this time I feel that we have gotten closer to each other. Perhaps from your end it might be ascribed to leaving Tee or perhaps it may be the constructive influence and effect of your developing relationship with Charlene. But ultimately it is because of a changing dynamic between the two of us — when we are talking on the phone or seeing each other or even thinking of each other when apart. As for myself, many questions may remain unanswered and there is much in the past which could have been said and done, but wasn't. But

now I take a new look upon being a father and son, as I am both . . . it couldn't be a better time to talk — or write — as father, and friend.

Many years had passed since Philip had sent out this nakedly emotional note to his father. Maybe Tony had wanted things to be better too; maybe he had tried. But oh how things had gone badly awry. Philip admitted that he was taken aback when he found this letter, and said to me, "It's kind of a killer, don't you think?"

Tony was also reflecting on his life, and he too dug up an item of emotional import. In March 2007, he and Charlene went to the Marine Corps base in Quantico, Virginia, where Tony donated the pistol that had belonged to his grandfather to the National Museum of the Marine Corps. The gun had been used by the general in 1914 in Veracruz, Mexico, and given to his grandson for luck. Tony took the pistol to Iwo Jima and then carried it with him through many moves and marriages. "I always kept it in a drawer and would take it out once in a while and ask myself, 'What good is it doing here?'" Tony told the *Quantico Sentry,* an on-line newsletter. Maybe he had once considered giving it to his sons, but he was no longer speaking to them. Whatever his reasoning, he did not want to have a gun so close by anymore.

No save-the-date cards were sent out in the weeks preceding March 30, 2007. This year Brooke Astor's birthday would be celebrated in a very private fashion. But it was nonetheless an extraordinary occasion. She was 105 years old, an age when simply waking up each morning is an achievement. She was not in apparent pain. Mrs. Astor had lived to see one more spring with its glorious fields of daffodils and crocuses.

The lawyers actually negotiated over her birthday celebration. Ken Warner got in touch with Paul Saunders to inquire whether Charlene Marshall could visit Brooke. Saunders denied the request, recalling, "I said no, let things remain as they are. I had a court order to obey. They could easily have gone back to Justice Stackhouse. They never even went back during the settlement talks."

Warner disagreed with that premise. He was convinced that as a matter of law, the temporary restraining order had expired once Annette de la Renta became Mrs. Astor's permanent guardian, and thus Annette could have granted permission for the visit. But Warner decided for future strategic reasons not to force the issue with the judge. As a result, the two sides then had to coordinate the birthday visits so that Tony would not overlap with Annette, Philip, and the others. Of course the press would be writing about Mrs. Astor's birthday — yet another public relations opportunity for both sides.

Tony went to see his mother early in the day, taking pink azaleas. She slept through her son's visit. She often dozed in her chair when Tony came and then opened her eyes the minute he left, to the point where the staff wondered whether her actions were deliberate. "She does spend a lot of time sleeping," Warner was forced to explain to the Associated Press. "It can be difficult to catch the lucid moments. But he did see her." Fraser Seitel had the pleasure of telling the press that Mrs. Astor was awake for her party later in the day.

The nurses dressed her up in a white shirt, bright pink slacks, an orange and pink scarf, pearl earrings, and gold bracelets and rings, which she fingered with pleasure. Annette took a three-inch lemon cake with white frosting; David Rockefeller carried a bouquet of sweet peas from his greenhouse. Philip's daughter, Sophie, and Alec's daughter, Hilary Brooke, sang "Happy Birthday" several times, giggling and laughing, while their fathers looked on proudly. As Annette recalls, "She knew that everyone was there for her. It was really sweet. Everyone had a glass of champagne." The celebrants included Alec, Nan, Chris Ely, Naomi Packard-Koot, and the philanthropist Florence Irving. "My grandmother was taking it all in, smiling," recalls Philip. "David and Annette and I hadn't been together since our meeting in June. We had come a long way." The family was all there — but minus two key members.

13

A Wonderful Life

ALEC MARSHALL HAD never supported the guardianship lawsuit and had rightly feared the family chasm that the litigation would create. But now, a year later, he was nearly as estranged from his father as Philip was. But unlike his brother, Alec nurtured the hope of a partial reconciliation. On a July 2007 afternoon, Alec was about to leave his apartment for a 4 P.M. visit to his grandmother at Holly Hill when Chris Ely called to say that Tony and Charlene had turned up unexpectedly.

Alec had not spoken to his father since the legal fireworks went off. Tony had sent back Alec's Christmas gifts and in May had written a letter excoriating Alec for not speaking up in his defense on the elder abuse charges. Blaming Alec for ruining his and Charlene's lives, Tony insisted that by remaining silent, Alec had chosen to take his brother's side. The scorching letter concluded with Tony's statement that he was "ashamed" to call Alec and Philip his sons. Hurt by these words but determined to take the high road, Alec replied in a note: "I am very distressed about your letter. I am sorry that this is the way you feel about me. If your viewpoint changes, my door is always open to you. Much love, Alec."

Alec says he still thought their relationship could be salvaged. He loved his father, despite everything that had happened. So when he heard that Tony was at Holly Hill, Alec hopped into his Subaru station wagon and headed over. He could take advantage of the fact that Charlene was not allowed in the house. "I thought this was the only chance I had to talk to my father in a private conversation," Alec said. "I knew that once my grandmother died, that would be it. I arrived. I saw Charlene out in the car."

Alec waited downstairs. He was looking out the window at the lush summer scenery when his father walked quietly into the room. "I gave him a hug," Alec recalled. But Tony quickly backed off from the embrace. He had no interest in a heart-to-heart. No small talk, no hello, how have you been. Clearly he had already built to the crescendo, as he announced bitterly, "I never want to speak to you again." Then he walked out.

The next day Alec was driving north on the Taconic State Parkway en route to Vermont when his cell phone rang. Tony did not apologize, but he did ask whether Alec could come into the city to talk. Alec explained that he was heading out of state to see his fiancée. Tony asked him to call when he got back home. But the moment for reconciliation had passed. Alec was wary of his father's apparent change of heart. "I think that he and Charlene talked it over," Alec says. "I think they wanted to see what information they could get out of me. So I didn't call back."

Tony and Charlene had escaped to Northeast Harbor earlier in the summer, but while Maine was usually a refuge, on this trip they received a chilly reception. "Trust me, they're shunned up here," says Clare Stone, a photographer who is the widow of the renowned Manhattan art dealer Allan Stone. "I had a funny feeling about how things were going to play out when Brooke began to fail. I thought that he might make her life miserable. It's called payback. He's mean-spirited — he feels a slight and doesn't forget it."

The Marshalls' decision to fire Steve Hamor and his two sons upset the close-knit local community. "It was almost like we were all in mourning when they released the gardeners, because they had been with Mrs. Astor for so long," says Betty Halpern, from the Kimball Shop. Several doors down on Main Street, Dot Renaud, the proprietor of McGrath's newsstand, is positively vitriolic about the Marshalls. "They have a lot of nerve coming back here knowing that everyone in town dislikes them," she says. "They come in here to get the newspapers, she gives me this fake smile. She got what she wanted, she got the house."

Nonetheless, when I reached Tony in Maine, he sounded in reasonably good spirits and chatted pleasantly for a half-hour. "We came up the day before yesterday," he said. "It's the first time we've been able to give ourselves some time off in the last eleven months. It's a beautiful state." He and Charlene hoped to stay at Cove End for several weeks, but they ended up cutting their trip short. Reverend Mac Bigelow, of Union Church in Northeast Harbor, explains, "When the Marshalls came up to Maine, they were very tired and hoping to relax and refresh themselves. But the Marshalls were dealing every day on the phone with Tony's mother's care and medical issues. Tony finally said, 'I have to go back.'"

Even during last few weeks of her life, Brooke Astor valiantly tried to keep going. Breathe in, breathe out. At times the breathing was labored. Yet her extraordinary will to live was in evidence. The nurses reported that she was talking more, even if the words were unintelligible, as if she were trying to convey "I'm still here." After a difficult evening in which she had been truly gasping, the nurses put her in the wheelchair to take her downstairs to the sunroom. Chris Ely, looking up to the landing, called out that Mrs. Astor might prefer to stay in bed that morning. Noreen Nee recalls, "She grabbed my hand and shook her head as if to say, 'No, I'm fine.'" Brooke could still understand what was being said and make her wishes known. But she drifted peacefully off to sleep for most of the day.

August was quiet at Holly Hill, with few visitors. Before heading off to Seal Harbor, David Rockefeller stopped by to see Brooke one more time. "When I first went in the room, I think she knew it was someone she knew, but wasn't sure what my name was," Rockefeller says. "But then when I said goodbye, she looked me in the eye, I could feel that she did. Even at the end, I think she felt very close to me." Rockefeller, an old man himself, had no illusions about what was to come. As he recalls, "I thought that might be the last time that I would see her."

On Saturday night, August 11, Brooke began to say her goodbyes. She was having trouble breathing. After urgent phone calls, her local physician, Dr. Richard Strongwater, rushed to the house, Annette arrived, and Reverend Pridemore was summoned. "I was there from nine P.M. almost until midnight. It appeared it would be the end," Pridemore recalls. "We said all the prayers right up until last rites, and then she rallied. Her heartbeat and vital signs stabilized."

Tony and Charlene sped up from New York; they were the last to arrive. Charlene wanted to be there at the end. She had known Brooke Astor for twenty-five years, and so much history had passed between the two women. Tony wanted his wife beside him at his mother's bedside, to console him. At the front door, when the Marshalls arrived, Charlene started to walk in first, but Chris Ely blocked her way. "I'm sorry, but you can't come in," he said. The butler was nervous, but the judge had ruled that Charlene was not permitted to see Brooke. It was not Ely's place to disobey a legal order. "Even now that she's dying?" Charlene protested in disbelief. The butler replied, "She's feeling better now."

Inside the house, Tony found Annette talking to Pridemore and asked her permission to bring in Charlene. It was mortifying for him to be so powerless. He was rebuffed yet again. Tony later wrote that Annette was "heartless and hostile," adding that "when I asked her personally that night to allow Charlene and me to spend some final moments with my mother — after so many years of being together with her as a couple — she emphatically refused." But with Brooke near death, Annette felt strongly that she should prevent any encounter that might be stressful for her fragile friend. "I told Tony that was against the rules," she recalls. "I told him that he would have to discuss it with Mr. Saunders, my lawyer." Tony protested, saying, "My lawyer says it's fine." Annette says that she replied, "Tony, let it be. Go see your mother."

Tony sat on his mother's bed and held her hand and spoke to her. Pearline Noble and Minnette Christie, the two nurses who had caused him such trouble, were watching over their patient. "He glared at us, one to the other, like 'Get out of the room so I can be with my mother,'" says Minnette, adding that they felt uncomfortable, but it would have been irresponsible to leave. "She was on oxygen, and a nurse needed to be there in case there was a crisis."

Exacerbating the combative atmosphere, extra security sentries arrived at Holly Hill. Tony accused Chris Ely of bringing in guards to physically block Charlene from entering. The butler later explained that he feared reporters would descend on the house if Mrs. Astor died that night. The animosity on all sides precluded compassion and made every action seem suspicious.

Philip was in Vermont visiting his mother when the crisis occurred and drove the 180 miles to Holly Hill, arriving at 12:30 A.M. By then the medical emergency had passed and the visitors had left. On Sunday afternoon he headed back to Massachusetts. "There was a bit of a scare, but my grandmother is fine," he reported by cell phone, driving east on the turnpike. "She's amazing — she just keeps going. She still takes less meds than we all do." He wanted to believe that his grandmother, at 105, was immortal; he was not yet ready to let her go.

But on Monday morning the nurses saw signs of serious decline. "She was sweating, so we gave her a quick sponge bath," Minnette Christie recalls. "We got her back in bed, in a sitting position. Her pulse was dropping; her breathing pattern had changed." They dressed Mrs. Astor in a white chiffon nightgown embroidered with flowers, a matching robe, and white socks and white gloves. Chris Ely came into the room, to stay with her until the end, as he had promised.

Minnette sat on Brooke's bed and said, "Let's pray. Let's hold hands like old times." Brooke's eyes had been closed, but she opened them at the word *pray,* and her breathing became calmer, less ragged. Minnette, Pearline and Chris recited the Lord's Prayer, Brooke's favorite. Then, in unison, they added, "In my little bed I lie, heavenly father hear my cry, if I die before I wake, I pray the Lord my soul to take." Brooke Astor squeezed the nurses' hands. Minnette finished with a benediction: "May the Lord bless you and keep you. Let his face shine upon you and be gracious unto you and give you peace. Amen." Brooke let out a deep sigh. As Pearline recalls, "I will never forget that sound."

Annette's footsteps broke the reverie. Minette rushed out of the room to meet her and to report of Brooke, "She's traveling." Annette ran into the room and kissed her friend's face, saying, "Brooke, I'm here. Brooke, I love you." Brooke died a few minutes later, at 1:50 P.M.

For the next few hours, until Tony Marshall issued a statement, Brooke Astor's death remained a secret to the world at large. Philip, calling me a half-hour after his grandmother passed away, was so choked up that he could scarcely speak. Tony was at home in Manhattan when his mother died and wanted to see her one more time. Even though he had been expecting this call for years — for decades — the news was still wrenching. He and Charlene drove to Holly Hill. Annette had left by then, but Reverend Pridemore was waiting for them.

The staff finally allowed Charlene inside, enabling her to see Brooke literally over her dead body. The couple waited for the undertakers from Frank E. Campbell to arrive. Tony held on to Charlene's hand. As the Marshalls were leaving, Charlene made a point of graciously shaking Chris Ely's hand. The butler later admitted that he was startled by the gesture, but this was a day when all squabbling was temporarily put aside.

At 4:43 P.M. the Associated Press ran a news alert saying that Mrs. Astor had died. "I have lost my beloved mother," Tony said in his statement, "and New York and the world have lost a great lady . . . I will miss her deeply and always." Annette released her own statement, alluding to the guardianship fight: "Brooke left the world peacefully, in a dignified manner, in her own home. We could not have asked for more."

Reporters were staking out the Marshalls' apartment at Seventy-ninth Street and Lexington Avenue by the time the couple returned from Holly Hill. Asked if they had had the chance to bid Brooke farewell, Tony and Charlene gave answers that implied they had been at the bedside when she died. "He was able to cradle her in his arms," Charlene told the *Daily News*. "She looked at him. She knew he was there. He told her he loved her. We said a prayer over her." Reporters called around for confirmation; the *News* printed comments from an unnamed party stating that the Marshalls had not been with Brooke at the end. The public bickering had already begun. "The Marshalls got there after I did," Reverend Pridemore says. "But Tony did cradle her in his arms on Saturday night — perhaps that's what he was thinking of, since for all purposes, that was the end for him."

Newspapers around the globe donned black crepe with obituaries and reminiscences of Mrs. Astor. The *New York Times* immortalized her with the apt headline "Brooke Astor, Wry Aristocrat of the People, Is Dead at 105." Alec Marshall's teenage daughter, Hilary Brooke, wrote a note to her great-grandmother on the *New York Times* Web site, saying, "YOU PUT UP A GOOD FIGHT! I MISS YOU SO MUCH GAGI! RIP. LOVE ALWAYS." Yet the affectionate stories saluting Brooke Astor's philanthropy inevitably turned to the news, the scandal, the salable. The tributes to Mrs. Astor became coming attractions for the spectacle that lay ahead: the fight for her fortune.

Whenever Tony and Charlene stepped out the front door, a gaggle of reporters and photographers awaited them. At this time of mourning, they were forced to defend themselves. "The accusation of my having pocketed millions is untrue," Tony told reporters on the day after his mother's death. "I see no valid reason to contest this will. For twenty-seven years, I managed my mother's investments. I did extremely well for her. I made it very comfortable for her to live the life she led." Charlene fiercely jumped in to defend her husband and insisted that Brooke "adored" her only son. Then she added a grandiose sentence that infuriated Brooke's close friends, saying, "She was Brooke Astor because of him."

The legal war erupted within twenty-four hours of Brooke Astor's death, before the funeral arrangements had even been finalized. Aiming for a preemptive strike, lawyers representing Brooke's guardians, Annette de la Renta and Chase Bank, hastened to the Westchester County Surrogate's Court and filed papers on Tuesday, August 14, 2007. They charged that Mrs. Astor "was not competent to execute" any of her most recent wills and had been "under undue influence and duress" to do so. In a startling tactic, the lawyers urged the court to reject her final 2002 will completely and instead roll back the clock by five years and admit her 1997 will for probate, a document that gave significantly more money to charity and much less to Tony Marshall.

The implicit message was that the guardians planned to produce proof that Mrs. Astor had been mentally unsound for the last decade of her life. Her medical records had been sealed during her lifetime, but now, in death, every sad detail and diagnosis would be open to scrutiny.

Brooke Astor had valiantly tried to mask her decline in her last years, to dress beautifully and continue to grace social occasions. Even if she was not always contributing to or instigating conversation, she tried to give the impression that she was at least taking it all in. She had developed her skills as a performer, cherishing her role as Mrs. Astor, playing it with dignity until the end. Now her facade would be ruthlessly stripped away.

Her estate had been left in legal limbo with the settlement of the guardianship case a year earlier when Tony, Charlene, and the other executors all agreed to step aside. Annette de la Renta was determined to continue protecting her friend Brooke even after death. She and Chase Bank asked to become coadministrators of the estate. New York City's major cultural institutions, concerned about protecting their share of Mrs. Astor's nearly $200 million fortune, rushed to support Annette. Paul LeClerc, the president of the New York Public Library, filed an affidavit backing her and the bank. A few days later, the Metropolitan Museum, Rockefeller University, and the Morgan Library joined in the cause.

The Marshalls were stunned by the swiftness of the legal assault. They had known it was coming but hoped for a brief respite from the confrontational headlines. Charlene, drained, initially held her tongue, informing the reporters camped on her doorstep that she had no comment, but then, perhaps predictably, she erupted, telling the *Daily News* that Annette's maneuver was "disgusting." "For someone who is supposed to have cared about her so much," Charlene said, "it is very dishonorable. She isn't even buried yet." Tony later told me that he was enraged by the opposition's insensitivity and by the idea that Annette and the bank's lawyers were drafting paperwork within minutes of Brooke's death. As he put it to me, his manner grim and wounded, "I was at my mother's bedside holding her hands when they did it." Finally father and son had one thing in common. Philip was upset too by the rush into court. He did not return calls from the Chase lawyers, who were urging him to sign an affidavit. "I thought it was tacky," he says. "I didn't want to sign anything until after the funeral."

Paul Saunders, Annette's lawyer, defends the legal gambit. "It was unclear whether the bank's role as guardian of the assets continued," he says. "You have an estate with seventy-five acres, you have the apartment, you have assets and securities, you have bills to pay, you have staff — all these things someone needed to deal with." Saunders insists, "This had to be done, and done right away. It would have been malpractice for the bank as fiduciary to sit back and allow the property to sit there with no one in charge." Annette later added, "In a perfect world, we would have waited, but the bank felt they had to act."

A less incendiary step probably would have been equally effective. Lawyers for Chase and Annette later requested and received permission from Justice Stackhouse to continue as guardians until the Westchester Surrogate's Court chose administrators. If the lawyers had taken that simple action after Brooke Astor's death rather than immediately mounting a will challenge, there would have been fewer glaring headlines and less immediate family turmoil. Susan Robbins thought the legal haste was in bad taste, saying, "There was no need to do it this week."

Brooke Astor had been planning her own funeral for decades, specifying in writing the prayers, hymns, pallbearers, and guest list of dignitaries. Her parties had always been planned with meticulous detail, so how could she delegate the arrangements of such an important occasion? But she had left it to Tony to carry out her wishes with a service at St. Thomas Church, on Fifth Avenue at Fifty-third Street. Given the media Mardi Gras, it was a given that even the guest list would be news. Just as the *New York Times* had published the list of guests at Mrs. Astor's hundredth birthday party, the newspaper of record also featured "Funeral A-List: New Version of Mrs. Astor's 400." Included were Nancy Reagan, President and Mrs. George H. W. Bush, Caroline Kennedy Schlossberg, Walter Cronkite, Tom Brokaw, and Dan Rather. The list had not been updated for some time and included friends who had died, like Kitty Carlisle Hart. The *Times* article took a swipe at the Marshalls: "The list appears to not be an entirely direct reflection of Mrs. Astor's life. At least a couple of people on it — Whoopi Goldberg and [Martha] Stewart — are friends of Mr. Marshall but did not know Mrs. Astor well."

In Manhattan, where being on the right list is a constant source of status anxiety, an invitation to Mrs. Astor's funeral was perceived as an important validation. Liz Smith mentioned in her syndicated column that she had been among the anointed. "Our side didn't leak that list — it was convenient for the other side to create a misimpression," complained Daniel Billy, Jr. "This was always intended to be open to the public." He added that the publicity was painful for the Marshalls. "He's an eighty-three-year-old man and his mother just died. They are really stressed out."

Annette and Oscar de la Renta hosted a lunch at their Park Avenue apartment hours before the Friday, August 17, funeral. The guests represented a cross-section of those who had been Mrs. Astor's most vigilant defenders in final years: David Rockefeller and his executive assistant, Alice Victor; Henry and Nancy Kissinger; Philip, Nan, Winslow, and Sophie Marshall; Chris Ely; Minnette Christie and Pearline Noble; and Dr. Strongwater and Dr. Pritchett and their wives. (Alec, given his role as a neutral party, was not invited.) Annette told her guests, "Brooke would love to look around this table, because it represented her life." The menu was soup and a cheese soufflé, salad and peaches and cream, with Annette reassuring Sophie, a vegetarian, that she could eat everything. "It was a roomful of people who felt that they had done the right thing but didn't feel self-righteous about it," says Henry Kissinger. "It wasn't a combative lunch — it was not a discussion of the dispute or Tony. It was sort of a reflective lunch."

Their fight to help Brooke had imbued their lives with a sense of purpose. During the past year, this group had been in control of all arrangements involving Brooke Astor, but on this day they were powerless. The funeral, the guest list, the speakers — Tony was in charge of it all.

David Rockefeller had been worrying for months that he would not be allowed to say a few words at his dear friend's funeral. He feared that Tony would punish him by shutting him out. But several days earlier Tony had called him in Maine, inviting him to the funeral and then asking him to speak. "I was pretty much planning to do it," Rockefeller told me later, "and Tony called. I was glad that he did. It was a very nice for him to ask. Under the circumstances, it would have been wrong for me not to speak."

The two men had a cordial conversation, and Rockefeller felt relieved. But then Tony's lawyer, Ken Warner, had the temerity to call
Rockefeller's office to ask that he refrain from mentioning Annette in
his funeral remarks. Rockefeller planned to simply ignore the plea, as
"Annette was the person closest to Brooke."

Shortly after 2 P.M., the luncheon group filed downstairs, where town
cars were waiting to take them to the funeral. Crowds clogged the side-
walk in front of St. Thomas Church, although the ceremony wasn't
scheduled to start until 2:30. Police had erected metal barricades on
either side of the Fifth Avenue entrance to hold back photographers,
cameramen, reporters, and gawkers. As street vendors sold hot dogs,
crepes, and sodas, it was easy to forget there was a funeral.

The famous friends, the courtiers, the hangers-on, and the true-blue
pals were turning up and clustering together in front of the church. Sean
Driscoll, the owner of Glorious Food, who had catered many of Mrs.
Astor's dinners, and Albert Hadley, who had designed her red library,
were the first to arrive. Howard Rubenstein, the image-maker who has
handled decades of damage control for George Steinbrenner and Leona
Helmsley, was working the event. Hired the day before by the Marshalls, he had spent several hours with the embattled couple. (Three
days later he resigned from the account, citing a conflict with another
client, the New York Public Library. Even the battle-hardened Rubenstein probably concluded that no amount of cash would compensate
for alienating every major cultural institution in New York.) The *New
York Post* columnist Cindy Adams wrote that the Marshalls were shopping for a PR man and cattily commented, "I suggest maybe Osama bin
Laden's spokes-terrorist."

Tony and Charlene arrived inconspicuously at the church and entered through the side door on Fifty-third Street. Reverend John Andrew had married the Marshalls back in 1992, and although he was now
rector emeritus at the church, he was to conduct the service, at Mrs.
Astor's request. For the Marshalls, he was a familiar and consoling presence.

Alec arrived at St. Thomas along with his fiancée, his daughter, Hilary Brooke, and her mother, his first wife, Susie Secondo, and was directed upstairs to the family room, where he promptly encountered

Tony and Charlene. Alec thought they could at least grieve for Brooke together. "My father walked over to the other side of the room to get away from me," Alec recalls. He thought it best to leave the room.

When the large wooden doors of St. Thomas opened, all the guests rushed up the stairs to enter, stepping into the marble entry with its welcoming phrase, "Peace on Earth to Men of Good Will." Despite the predictions, many seats remained empty. Press reports later estimated that 900 people attended the service in this church, which seats 1,400. Many of the VIPs mentioned in the *Times* (Nancy Reagan, the Bushes) did not attend. It was a Friday in August, a time when New York is left to the tourists, and many of Brooke's close friends, such as Vartan Gregorian, were out of the country. In the more accessible Hamptons, several of Brooke's friends not so quietly let it be known that they were boycotting because Tony was in charge. But that may simply have been an excuse to avoid missing a day at the beach. Mrs. Astor no longer needed to be courted.

Philip and his family were escorted to their seats by Daniel Billy, Jr. He had seen the Marshalls in agony because of Philip's actions, but this was not the moment for confrontation. With a poker face, he politely introduced himself and walked Philip and his family to their seats. Philip got a warm welcome from those nearby, including the producer John Hart, who murmured, "I couldn't be more honored to be seated near you." Philip's expression changed as he caught sight of his father. "It was hard for Philip," recalls Hart. "He was looking at his father, but not wanting to."

The service began. Eight Marines carried the heavy wood coffin to the altar. After "Rock of Ages" — and the sight of Whoopi Goldberg running in ten minutes late to join Tony and Charlene — Mayor Michael Bloomberg rose to speak. He quoted a poem by Brooke that had been published in *The New Yorker* in March 1996: "Love is an apple, round and firm/without a blemish or a worm/Bite into it and you will find/you've found your heart and lost your mind." He added that the poem "was full of the tart insight that was Brooke's hallmark." He remarked on her love affair with the Big Apple. Then the mayor conveyed exactly where he stood in the family fight. "Thanks to Annette de la Renta," he began, "I had lunch once with Brooke in her apartment."

The mere mention of Annette enraged Tony's friends. The mayor closed his remarks by mentioning Brooke's well-known sartorial splendor: "There's a Yiddish saying that our mitzvahs, our good deeds, are the clothing of our soul. In more ways than one, Brooke Astor was always the best-dressed woman in the room."

David Rockefeller, the next eulogist, looked every bit his ninety-two years as he walked slowly to the podium. His speech was brief and heartfelt. He described Brooke as a "close and loving friend for five magical decades." "The most wonderful thing about Brooke, besides the fact she was great fun, was that she treated each and every person she met with warmth and respect," he said. "For those of us who were fortunate to know her well, it was always a warm kiss, especially for the men. How lucky we felt!" And then he added the sentence that Tony had dreaded: "Even in her final peaceful days, when I visited Holly Hill with her dear and loyal friend Annette, Brooke would still look at us with that amazing twinkle in her eye, which she always had and never gave up."

Next it was Tony Marshall's turn to speak, not only to face his critics but to claim his mother for himself. "My mother was an only child and so was I," he began. "This gave us a closer understanding of each other. We shared a love of nature. And we particularly loved the times when Charlene and I were alone with my mother, either in New York or on trips we took together here and abroad . . . We also shared a sense of humor," he continued. "Three years ago, on my eightieth birthday, Mother informed me with a twinkle in her eye, 'You are only halfway there.'" These words were greeted with warm laughter.

Then Tony read aloud a "declaration of faith" that Brooke had written many years before to be read at her funeral. Wonderfully narcissistic and poetic, this was vintage Brooke. "When I go from here, I want to leave behind me the world richer for the experience of me," she had written. For Brooke Astor, who loved to hike and hug trees, nature was much on her mind. "I want to leave the trees rustling with my thoughts," she wrote, adding that she hoped that the "tears that I shed for love" would return to the earth as dew. With the wisdom and joie de vivre of a woman who relished her 105 years, her farewell message was to tell her fellow man that "death is nothing and life is everything."

After he finished, Tony paused, a deliberately theatrical moment. "Yes, New York and her many friends have lost a wonderful person," he said. Then his voice choked up, as he added in a tone of almost childish disbelief, "But I've lost my mother." It was a cry of anguish, particularly moving because on some level he may have felt that all the world had gotten more of her than he had.

At the close of the service, Reverend Andrew Mead, the current rector of St. Thomas Church, made a point of announcing that Brooke Astor had chosen all the prayers. It seemed like an unnecessary comment, but his rationale for making it became clear once he read the next prayer.

"Lord, make us instruments of thy peace," he read. "Where there is hatred, let us so love. Where there is injury, pardon. Where there is discord, union. Where there is doubt, faith. Where there is despair, hope. Where there is sadness, joy. Grant that we may not so much seek to be consoled as to console. To be understood as to understand. To be loved as to love. For it is in giving that we receive. It is in pardoning that we are pardoned. And it is in dying that we are born to eternal life. Amen." People looked around with raised eyebrows. As one woman said later, "It was if Brooke were talking from the grave."

A bagpiper played "Amazing Grace" as the Marines carried the coffin down the aisle and the congregation followed them out. Tony and Charlene clutched each other's arms for support. Philip was fighting back tears; his wife reached into her purse and handed him a tissue. The doors to the church opened to reveal an astonishing scene: hundreds of people lining Fifth Avenue, waiting for a glimpse of Brooke Astor's coffin, while traffic was halted by the police. The scene of the crowd, just for a moment, resembled Brooke Astor's painting *Flags, Fifth Avenue*, with New Yorkers of all social strata stopping to bear witness. It began raining just as the pallbearers walked down the stairs and the church bells rang. People applauded, as an impromptu thank-you. As the men loaded the coffin into the hearse, the rain stopped.

A small card in the program left on the seats in the church invited all the guests to a reception given by Tony and Charlene at the Colony Club. But Philip and Alec and their familial entourages opted instead to go to Starbucks in Rockefeller Center, where they watched the CNN coverage of the funeral.

At the Colony Club, waiters served salmon rolls and chicken brochettes and passed around trays of white wine to 120 people who came to pay condolences. Alice Astor's two daughters, Emily Harding and her half-sister, Ramona McEwan, who had flown over from London for the funeral, stopped by to honor Mrs. Astor. "It was perfectly pleasant, but what was clear was that a great many people did not come," says Harding. "They were clearly making a statement, the Annette de la Renta camp. I didn't want to be in any camp. John Richardson and Kenneth Jay Lane, people whom I've known for years, did not go to the Colony Club."

The guests at the reception sponsored by Tony included the Metropolitan Museum trustee Carl Spielvogel and his wife, Barbaralee Diamonstein; the president of the Museum of National History, Ellen Futter; Barbara Goldsmith; Elihu Rose; Marshall Rose; Randy Bourscheidt; and Whoopi Goldberg. Out of earshot of the Marshalls, some quietly murmured about the feud. As one woman speculated, "It's as if Tony and Annette are fighting over whose mother Brooke was."

There was a fierce thunderstorm that afternoon, but the next day was sunny and clear. Tony and Charlene had decided to bury Brooke privately at Sleepy Hollow Cemetery, her chosen spot, without informing the rest of the family or Brooke's friends. The *New York Post* assigned a reporter and a photographer to stake out the cemetery, and the team caught a shot of the couple praying over the flower-strewn coffin, accompanied by Father Andrew. The Marshalls left before the grave was filled. An hour after they had gone, Alec arrived with Sue Ritchie and was startled to discover that the burial was still in progress. "We just stopped by to pay our last respects," he told the *Post*. "I didn't even know [the burial] was today." To his surprise, Alec recognized the worker tending the plot: Ramon Acosta, who had been the head gardener at Holly Hill for eight years, until Tony Marshall had cut back on staff. Acosta paused to reminisce about how much Mrs. Astor had loved her daffodils and her flower garden, saying, "I never thought I'd be burying your grandmother." Alec lingered on at the cemetery, to watch as the last shovels of dirt were placed on Brooke Astor's grave.

14

Family Plot

ON THE MORNING of September 5, 2007, Philip Marshall stood out-side the Westchester County Surrogate's Courthouse, fiddling with the Buddhist prayer beads wrapped around his left wrist, dreading the next few hours. He had driven from Massachusetts the night before to go out for sushi with Chris Ely. The butler was acting as caretaker at Holly Hill, but family members were no longer allowed on the premises in the af-termath of Brooke's death. Philip had spent the night at Alec's apart-ment in Ossining and had asked his twin to keep him company in court today, but the conflict-averse Alec had declined.

Today marked the first time that all the antagonists would be in the same room since Brooke Astor's funeral. Oral arguments were sched-uled before Supreme Court Judge Anthony Scarpino, Jr., over the ques-tion of choosing the temporary administrators for Brooke Astor's will. While Annette and Chase Bank had jointly proposed themselves, Philip had filed legal papers asking to be considered for the responsibility if Annette was not chosen. Tony's lawyer Ken Warner had instead sug-gested tapping the service of a neutral party, a retired seventy-five-year-old judge, Howard Levine, and a new bank, Fiduciary Trust.

A black large car pulled up in front of the courthouse, and Tony and Charlene stepped out. Philip hung back about 100 yards away; he was not ready to face them yet. Once the couple had headed into the building, Philip walked over to the car to greet his father's longtime driver, Luis Vasquez. They were joking and laughing together as Susan Robbins arrived.

For Robbins, this hearing marked her return to the Astor affair after nearly a year on the sidelines. She and Philip had developed a strong bond during the guardianship battle. "We connected straight up," Philip says, "and we've been in touch ever since." Her specialty was guardianship law, not trusts and estates. But facing a will battle, Philip hired an attorney whom he trusted — Robbins. She felt that this was her second chance to restore Mrs. Astor's wishes. "I feel a bit like I betrayed her, that I didn't fight hard enough for her," says Robbins. "So this would allow me to feel better."

In the sunny, wood-paneled, high-ceilinged eighteenth-floor courtroom, Annette de la Renta had already taken an unobtrusive seat in the fourth row on the left, flanked by her lawyer, Paul Saunders, and two associates. With her hair pulled severely back and wearing a black sheath dress with a flared hem, a black sweater, and stilettos, she looked as if she were attending a funeral. Charlene and Tony Marshall were at the front of the courtroom on the right side. Charlene, whose white hair was held back by a girlish headband, wore a black skirted suit and a white blouse and kept craning her neck to see who was coming in and then whispering to Tony.

At 9:30 A.M., Judge Scarpino, a middle-aged man with a mustache, wire-rim glasses, and a dry sense of humor, strode into the room. When the clerk called the Astor case, a phalanx of fifteen lawyers marched to the front, representing beneficiaries from the Metropolitan Museum and the New York Public Library to the Animal Medical Center. Like grownups caught in a polite game of musical chairs, the lawyers milled around, since there were not enough places to sit. Eager to make a good impression, Philip grabbed a chair from the back of the courtroom and carried it on his shoulders up front and then joined Annette as his father looked on impassively. "This is a nightmare of a case," the judge began, pausing for effect — everyone in the room nodded knowingly — and then he delivered the punch line: "for the court reporter."

Ken Warner, Tony's lawyer, led off with a forty-five-minute monologue in which he attempted to refight the guardianship lawsuit. He insisted that "Mrs. de la Renta and Chase bring enormous bias and hostility to the case." Annette closed her eyes, as if imagining she were somewhere else, letting the words roll over her. Warner complained that the bank was trying to hurt Tony by getting him into trouble with the IRS. Chase had filed 1099 forms with the federal authorities, claiming that Tony should pay additional taxes on the transfer of Cove End and the $5 million to Charlene, which he had claimed as gifts from his mother rather than taxable income.

The judge noted in a puzzled tone that Tony had agreed a year earlier to let Annette and Chase serve as Brooke's guardians, asking, "They were originally acceptable to your side at that time?" Warner testily replied, "We accepted them." The judge shot back, "Your clients have grown to be uncomfortable with them now?" The courtroom erupted into laughter. An annoyed Warner then raged over the allegations in the guardianship proceeding, insisting that in the past year "actions were taken, large and small, just to dig and to hurt Mr. Marshall."

Susan Robbins, who was next, was calm and measured in her brief seven-minute presentation. She avoided inflammatory language, insisting that Philip had pursued the guardianship "out of love and concern for his grandmother." She added that "Philip does not have hostility to his father. He understands that his role is to marshal the assets and distribute them, whichever will is chosen." She did not criticize Tony in her remarks.

But the next two lawyers, Leslie Fagen, representing Chase Bank, followed by Paul Saunders, attempted to eviscerate Tony verbally, accusing him of mismanaging his mother's financial affairs. Fagen began by calling Tony's lawyer's legal filings "vituperative" and full of "frantic accusations." He added that Annette had been called "every name under the sun."

Then Fagen claimed that after investigating Mrs. Astor's finances, Chase had discovered that $18 million of her money had been diverted to Tony Marshall in questionable transactions at a time when she was "ill and incapacitated." He went through a litany of alleged offenses, listing the items that Tony claimed had been gifts from his mother.

Next up was Paul Saunders, a confident man with a dry wit. He insisted that his client, Annette de la Renta, "is not doing this to get even with anybody . . . She's doing this solely out of love and respect for Mrs. Astor." He went into the history of Brooke Astor's wills, pointing out that the codicils added in 2003 and 2004, which benefited Tony, represented an unusual change in her behavior. The attorney suggested that he had evidence to prove that Mrs. Astor had been coerced. "The nurses took detailed notes," Saunders warned. "We know who visited, what she said, what they asked her to do." He said of Annette, "She wants the truth to come out."

The judge asked to speak to Annette, and the wraithlike sixty-seven-year-old gave a tremulous smile as she approached the bench. Speaking so softly that she could scarcely be heard, she reiterated that she would willingly take on the administrator's role without payment. Philip was then asked to come forward for two minutes — Tony physically flinched as Philip walked to the front of the courtroom — and in answer to the judge's question, Philip said, "I would accept a fee." Judge Scarpino nodded and said he understood that choice, since administration would involve an enormous amount of work. Howard Levine, the retired judge requested by Tony, indicated that he too would expect a fee if chosen.

By now it was 1 P.M., and the attorneys had been speaking for nearly three hours. Lawyers from the Metropolitan Museum and the New York Public Library briefly stood to back Annette's bid to be the temporary administrator. Warner then rose to talk about how Mrs. Astor had been in amazing physical shape in her later years — "She was dancing around" — and said that her doctors had advised her "to cut down on the late-night dancing and parties." He insisted that Brooke Astor had liked her daughter-in-law, noting that in 1997, when Brooke fell in the ladies' room at the Museum of Natural History and broke her hip, "she called out for one person to come to her aid. She said, 'Please get Charlene.'" Annette rolled her eyes at the implication that this anecdote indicated affection. Warner added, "When she got the highest civilian award from President Clinton, they [Tony and Charlene] were the ones that Brooke took."

Like many assertions confidently made in court, the story surrounding Mrs. Astor's 1998 Medal of Freedom was more complicated than it was made to appear. When Robert Pirie heard about Warner's courtroom comments, he chortled at the notion that the trip to Washington, D.C., had been a manifestation of Brooke's love. He had flown with Brooke to the ceremony, along with David and Laurance Rockefeller, on the Rockefeller family's plane. Tony and Charlene had been demoted to a separate aircraft, along with Brooke's French maid. "Brooke specifically didn't want them on the same plane," Pirie said. "The passenger manifest was not an accident. During the ceremony, Brooke hissed at me, 'Look at Charlene — isn't that disgusting? She's putting herself in every picture.'"

Tony's devotion to his mother was a constant theme in Warner's presentation to Judge Scarpino. "I think that Philip Marshall visited about twice a year," the lawyer said. "I heard that Mrs. de la Renta came twice a month, but there was one visitor who came all the time and that was Anthony Marshall. He was always there for her." The judge listened patiently, but his body language suggested that he was counting the minutes until Warner finished. Warner closed by urging the judge to appoint Howard Levine and Fiduciary Trust as temporary administrators, saying, "We ask you not to put in place declared adversaries."

After listening to hours of acrimonious exchanges, Judge Scarpino nonetheless urged all sides to settle. "There's very little doubt in my mind what the intentions of Mrs. Astor were. She loved her charities. She loved her family. She loved her son," the judge said. "I wouldn't say she would be happy to see what's going on now." The judge made it clear that he did not want to be in the middle of this mess. "It's our hope that you folks will be able to make a decision, and not require me to make a decision." Ending the session, he asked the lawyers to meet with the clerk to schedule settlement conferences.

Leaving the courtroom, Tony and Charlene walked over to a hallway window, where they stood by themselves. It had been two months since I had spoken to Tony by phone. I drifted over and said, "This must be surreal for you." "Torturous," replied Charlene. When I said that I was sorry they had not had more private time to mourn before the legal wrangling began, Charlene replied, "So are we." Tony seemed subdued and sad but controlled; she was angry and protective, her emotions flickering across her face. "The truth and our love, truth and love, that's how we're getting through this," Charlene said. She reached over and touched Tony affectionately on the cheek, then said, "We're going to take care of each other." He smiled a weary smile and said, "I'm eighty-three years old," as if in disbelief over his predicament. Excusing himself to go find a place to sit down, he suddenly thrust out his hand, a surprisingly courtly gesture, and I shook it.

In this small corridor on the eighteenth floor, there was only one long wooden bench. Annette huddled on the right side with Philip beside her. Tony and Charlene walked over and perched on the far left side. Father and son, so near and so far. In the past four hours, they had choreographed their movements to avert eye contact. Newspaper photographers were waiting outside the building, but this was the money shot — these two members of this feuding family trying desperately to avoid each other.

Driving down the Bronx River Parkway afterward in his silver Subaru with Robbins and me, Philip used speed as his catharsis, darting in and out of traffic like a New York cabbie, eager to distance himself from the emotionally fraught morning. At an outdoor table at the Village Cafe in Bronxville, Philip and his lawyer talked about all the might-have-beens, about how this family fight could have been avoided. If only Tony had hired a geriatric social worker to look after his mother's care and supervise the nurses and helpers. If only he had not fired Brooke's favorite staffers. And, the biggest if of all, if only he and Charlene had been content with the millions guaranteed under earlier wills. Philip sounded worried about his father's health. "I didn't think he looked well," he said. "I feel sorry for him." There was wistfulness in his voice as he added, "I just wish I could talk to him without Charlene around."

Five days later, while the judge was mulling over his decision on choosing the administrators, the publicity battle erupted again, via a strategic leak of documents to the *New York Times*. "Astor's Mental State Questioned Before She Signed Final Will" was the headline of the story written by Serge Kovaleski. A year earlier, the lawyers in the guardianship case had been astounded when they discovered the letter that Tony had written to Dr. Howard Fillit describing Brooke Astor's diminished mental capacity. Now the public could read this devastating document as well.

Even the most oblivious newspaper reader could not help reaching the obvious conclusion: Tony and Terry Christensen were aware that Brooke Astor suffered from Alzheimer's disease when they allowed her to revise her will. Tony's lawyer, Ken Warner, was reduced to telling the *Times* that he had a "mountain of evidence" to prove that Mrs. Astor was competent for many years after that diagnostic letter was written. Trying desperately to put a positive spin on this news, Warner played the dutiful-son card, saying, "The real significance of this letter is to show that Mr. Marshall was unquestionably a wonderful, loving son who focused enormous attention on his mother's well-being."

Brooke Astor's funeral in August had been boycotted by many of her friends because Tony had organized the service. But on the evening of September 11, she was honored by her two favorite New York institutions in back-to-back events, providing her confidants with an opportunity to pay homage. At 4 P.M. the Metropolitan Museum held its semiannual board meeting, followed by a reception to celebrate its beloved trustee. Tony Marshall sent word that he would miss the meeting but would attend the cocktail party at Astor Court, the tucked-away sanctuary on the museum's second floor. The trustees kept looking around for him, but he did not appear. Finally Philippe de Montebello went ahead with the tributes and the toasts.

At 5 P.M., the New York Public Library held an invitation-only memorial service to honor Brooke Astor. Annette raced down Fifth Avenue from the Metropolitan Museum event to the library, arriving with Oscar in tow. Nearly four hundred people appeared at the grand Cecile Bartos Forum to hear speakers, including Vartan Gregorian, Charlie Rose, Liz Smith, and Robert Silvers, tell their favorite stories about the beloved philanthropist. The writer Toni Morrison and the actress Marian Seldes read selections of Brooke Astor's poetry and prose. For those who had missed or skipped the funeral, this was a personal goodbye. Vartan Gregorian embraced Philip Marshall in a bear hug.

Tony and Charlene did not attend this event either. "We were not invited," Tony told me later, adding with bitter irony in his voice, "It was a small party — three hundred people." This was the ultimate insult, to be ostracized at an occasion where his mother was being lionized. Society was striking back, closing ranks against the couple. None of the speakers even mentioned that Mrs. Astor had a son. The program included a photograph of Brooke with Annette, but none of Tony. He was being erased from his mother's life. Liz Smith got up and told a funny but pointed story about visiting Brooke Astor in Maine. Standing with her hostess in a hallway trying to choose among stacks of new books arranged on a chest, Smith had picked up a biography of Violet Trefusis, Vita Sackville-West's lover. "Brooke said, 'Oh, I can't stand that woman, I despise her.' I said, 'Why, because she was a famous lesbian?' Brooke said, 'I don't care about that. She was horrible to her mother.'" Amid the gales of laughter, no one laughed harder than Annette and Philip.

When it came to tributes to Brooke Astor, more was more. On Friday night, September 28, the Metropolitan Museum of Art celebrated her life again, this time with a large gathering in an auditorium open to the public. Everyone entering the museum that evening, from socialite to schoolchild, was given a commemorative blue Brooke Astor metal button. The front rows on the right side of the auditorium were reserved for the "Astor Family." Tony and Charlene stood alone in that section, and until the auditorium had filled to capacity, no one went to sit with them.

Charlene had dressed up for the occasion in an elegant white silk blouse and dark skirt. She told me that this was a rare night out but that she had been looking forward to this evening. "All we do is spend our time with lawyers and take naps in between," she said. "But we wouldn't miss this." A grand jury was convening in three days to investigate the Marshalls and Francis Morrissey. Many in the auditorium had received subpoenas to testify, including Philip, Alice Perdue, and Naomi Packard-Koot, seated in the center of the room, and Chris Ely, Minnette Christie, and Pearline Noble in the back row.

The first speaker was Viscount William Astor. Walking onstage to the lectern, he found himself standing directly in front of Tony and Charlene. "It was the most extraordinary thing — he was in the front row," Astor told me later. "I thought, If I catch his eye, I don't know what

I'll do." In his remarks, Astor pointedly thanked David Rockefeller and Annette de la Renta for making Brooke Astor's final year comfortable, a public putdown of Tony and Charlene.

Maxwell Hearn, the curator of Chinese paintings, then gave a lengthy description of Brooke Astor's role in building Astor Court, the museum's imported Chinese garden, and showed slides of her posing with the Chinese workmen. Then he pointedly echoed Lord Astor's comments, also thanking Annette and David Rockefeller for what they had done for Mrs. Astor. There was an intake of breath as Hearn opened a second front against Tony. The Marshalls looked shaken. Afterward, Hilary Marshall, who had been sitting with her uncle Philip, innocently bounded up to her grandfather and gave him a hug. But Tony seemed inconsolable and walked slowly out of the auditorium holding Charlene's hand, as if having trouble understanding why people felt such enmity toward him.

At a private reception upstairs given by Annette, the mood was festive. This was a gathering of Brooke's friends and also a reunion of those who launched the lawsuit. Susan Robbins chatted with Alice Perdue, Minnette Christie, and Pauline Noble. Philip and Chris Ely hugged each other. Annette played hostess, making introductions and posing for pictures with the staff. Summing up the efforts of the past year, Alice Perdue said, "All the help, helped."

In wandering around the party, I had mentioned in passing to two of Mrs. Astor's friends that I felt sorry for Tony Marshall. It was as if I had announced that Pol Pot was actually a misunderstood guy. The words ricocheted around the room. Earlier in the evening, Chris Ely had spurned my request for an interview, politely saying, "I'd rather say things under oath in a court of law." But as security guards were ushering us out of the museum, I fell in step with Ely. Informed by others of my comment, he wanted to respond, asking, "Are you getting the level of meanness? The Marshalls start out so nice, then they teach everyone to dislike them." He continued, "I was employed by Brooke Astor — my loyalty was to her. I promised I would be there always for her. Everyone here did what they did for the love of Mrs. Astor."

• • •

Back in the tabloid bull's-eye, Tony and Charlene Marshall tried to carry on, but every encounter was fraught with potential humiliation. The Marshalls were celebrities now, for their notoriety, and their routine movements were breathlessly tracked in the gossip pages. The *New York Post* noted in its sightings column that the couple had attended the dress rehearsal of *La Traviata* at the Metropolitan Opera. They were subject to whispered asides and outright snubs. Marilyn Berger, who had written Brooke Astor's obituary for the *New York Times,* chatted with the Marshalls at an October gala honoring Mike Wallace at the Waldorf-Astoria Hotel. "If one didn't know, they didn't seem like they were having any troubles," Berger said. "But everyone knew. Some people did not want to shake their hands. People circled around the other way to avoid them."

On October 18, 2007, the Marshalls, accompanied by Ken Warner, traveled to Westchester Surrogate's Court for yet another session. This time Philip and Annette did not attend. Judge Scarpino, ending the public session after less than ten minutes, sent the fifteen lawyers to a private conference room for an hour to schedule depositions. I sat with Tony and Charlene on the hard wooden bench in the hallway waiting for the lawyers, and we started to chat. Eventually I pulled out a notebook.

Charlene's cell phone kept going off every few minutes, and Tony responded by cocking his eyebrows and murmuring that the world would be a better place without cell phones. "They are the death of civilization, but they are convenient," he said. Well-mannered and polite, he was wearing his Marine Corps tie and tie clip but was fiddling with his hearing aids, totems of his youth and old age. He wanted to stress to me his continued happiness with Charlene. "Two things have taken us through all this from day one, from the minute it happened," he said. "We know the truth no matter what was printed and published. And the other thing is our love for each other. While some people who did not like us hoped it would do damage to us, it has made us closer together."

I mentioned that several people had told me that Charlene had brought him the only real love in his life. "That would suggest that I didn't love my mother, or didn't love my wives when I married them," he said, adding, "Things happen in marriages that set people apart." Charlene, who had just gotten off the phone, picked up the thread of conversation and interjected, "I adore him. And I will protect him with the last breath of my life." She said it in a passionate and vehement tone of voice, for her husband's ears as well as mine.

The Marshalls had given their friends permission to speak with me, and so I passed along a few compliments, mentioning that a theatrical producer had raved about Charlene's charm and a book editor had called her sexy. Today she was wearing a black skirt, black flats, a white blouse, a blue silk scarf, and a pale blue sweater tied around her shoulders, soccer-mom style. Charlene laughed, saying, "One of the newspapers called me a little hottie. I thought, I'll take that." She turned to Tony and said affectionately, "You wouldn't understand that, dear."

After the previous court hearing, I had left with Philip Marshall. Now Charlene wanted me to pass along a message to her stepson. Her voice turned raw and anguished as she said, "You talk to Philip all the time. Why doesn't Philip talk to his father? Why doesn't he just call him? I don't care if he hates me, but he should talk to his father."

It seemed as if Charlene hoped to spark a reconciliation. But a few minutes later she took the conversation in a direction that was not meant to promote father-son harmony, urging me to try to find out how Philip had dug up the financial details contained in the lawsuit. Hinting at legal repercussions, Charlene suggested there might be "something criminal" in how he got the information. She ended the conversation by saying, "What does it matter what you print? Our friends know us and we know what happened." She urged Tony to get to his feet, saying that he had been sitting too long; it was not good for him. The two of them went off to pace the corridor, back and forth, back and forth.

When Judge Scarpino issued his legal decision on October 26, he gave aid and comfort to both sides in this battle. He turned down Annette's and Philip's requests to be temporary administrators of Brooke Astor's estate and chose retired judge Howard Levine, as the Marshalls had requested. But Scarpino retained Chase Bank as an administrator. "That was perfectly acceptable to us," says Paul Saunders, Annette's lawyer.

"Mrs. de la Renta's priority was to keep the bank in the picture, since the bank had a year's worth of knowledge that no one else had." Chase had indicated that it planned to pursue the charges of financial mismanagement by Tony vigorously. Philip was disappointed, since he wanted to oversee his grandmother's wishes. Ken Warner, representing the Marshalls, viewed this decision as a victory, since he had been successful in removing Annette de la Renta as an administrator of Mrs. Astor's will.

But the jousting over Brooke Astor's fortune was about to be reduced to a minor plot line in an infinitely more dramatic story. On October 30, Dan Castleman, chief of the district attorney's investigative division, and the prosecutors Leroy Frazer, Peirce Moser, and Elizabeth Loewy held a meeting with Tony's new criminal lawyers, former prosecutors Gary Naftalis and David Frankel. This was show-and-tell time, a chance for the prosecutors to sketch out their criminal case in advance before indicting Tony. Castleman, who had played a recurring bit part on *The Sopranos* as a lawman, told them that Charlene ought to get her own criminal lawyer. The prosecutors were considering charges against her too.

On November 5 the group reconvened at Castleman's eighth-floor corner office, and Tony's lawyers presented their version of events, offering facts that caused the prosecutors to remove a few potential charges. The DA's office did not pursue tax fraud charges against Tony Marshall for his error over the Childe Hassam painting. Prosecutors also did not challenge the first codicil of Brooke Astor's will, giving weight to the fact that it has been prepared by her longtime lawyer Terry Christensen. However, that codicil was still expected to be disputed in the battle in surrogate's court over Mrs. Astor's will.

Even the jaded prosecutors had been fascinated by the father-son drama that led to this full-fledged investigation of Brooke Astor's final wishes. "If it wasn't for Philip, none of this would have come out," said Castleman. "It all would have sailed through. No one would be the wiser. No one ever thought these things would see the light of day."

With an indictment looming, Tony and Charlene unburdened themselves to Steve Fishman of *New York* magazine, for a story strategically timed to hit the newsstands on November 12. The Marshalls hoped for a sympathetic portrayal, but the *New York* cover story, "The Curse of Mrs. Astor," had an edgy tone. Fishman wrote that Tony Marshall was in the "pathetic" position of trying to prove his mother's love for him. Tony was reduced to reaching back into his childhood for anecdotes, saying, "When I had a terrible nosebleed, my mother put me next to her in bed. I stayed right in her bed till the next day." Charlene kept trying to bolster her husband's ego during the interview, referring to him as Mr. Marshall and exaggerating his investing skills, saying that he had made "all the money" for Mrs. Astor to give away. Tony had to correct her, saying that he had managed his mother's personal funds, not her foundation money.

Tony dug himself in deeper with his efforts to explain the $2.4 million bonus he had given himself in 2005 from his mother's funds. "If Mother was interested in financial details, I'm sure she would have agreed," Tony told the magazine, conceding, "In retrospect, I shouldn't have done it. It doesn't look good." He and Charlene insisted that Brooke had changed her will to make amends. "I think a certain amount of guilt came into her decisions, for not being the best mother," Charlene said, to which Tony added, "Atoning." They excoriated Annette de la Renta for challenging the wills. "The only word that comes to my mind is jealous," said Charlene. "That we were happy," added Tony. Charlene finished his sentence, saying, "That Brooke and I did get along so well."

Nothing inspires rumors so much as when the wheels of justice seemingly slow for a stop sign. The district attorney's office had been telling reporters that the indictments would probably be handed down in early November. But a sudden silence from Foley Square provoked a torrent of speculation. The most common theory — totally unsubstantiated, as it turned out — was that Tony Marshall was negotiating a plea bargain.

In truth, it was Charlene's fate that was being decided. The prosecutors held spirited debates among themselves over whether to indict her for conspiracy and larceny — to treat her akin to the woman who drove the getaway car. Charlene was believed to have been present when two of Brooke's valuable paintings were taken from her walls and rehung in the Marshalls' apartment. But the burden of proof is high, and the prosecutors were not convinced that they could make their case. Charlene was off the hook.

A few days before Thanksgiving, Dan Castleman alerted Tony's lawyers that the indictments would be coming right after the holiday weekend. Tony and Charlene turned down an offer to spend the holiday again with Sam Peabody at the Racquet Club, opting for a quieter time. Philip and his family drove to Vermont with Alec to spend Thanksgiving with their mother. A pall hung over the weekend. Philip had been pacing his house in the middle of the night, sending off e-mail at 3 A.M. He wanted . . . well, he did not know what he wanted. As Nan says, "Philip has not looked back and said, 'Whoa, did I just open a huge can of worms.' He does not want his father to go to jail, but the can of worms was much bigger than he knew."

On the Monday morning after Thanksgiving weekend, prosecutors called Tony Marshall's and Francis Morrissey's lawyers and quietly informed them that their clients had been indicted and were required to turn themselves in the following day. Bail negotiations began immediately. Morrissey was in Argentina, and his lawyer, Michael Ross, told the authorities that he would return as soon as possible. Charlene called her children to tell them the bad news; they promptly contacted their father, Paul Gilbert.

There was no press announcement, but Serge Kovaleski, the *New York Times* reporter who had repeatedly made news on the Astor beat, got this one first too. His story appeared on-line at 4:30 P.M. A half-hour earlier, Kovaleski called Philip, who was at home in South Dartmouth, to inform him that his father had been indicted. Although Philip had been expecting this call for months, it still choked him up, and he declined comment. Later in the day, Alec Marshall looked out the window of his second-floor apartment in Ossining and saw photographers below on the street. As Alec says, "I thought of going downstairs with my camera and taking pictures of them."

The next morning Tony Marshall faced the Social Register's version of the O. J. Simpson trial. When he showed up at One Hogan Place to turn himself in, he was met by a firing squad of photographers and TV crews. Tony and Charlene and Tony's lawyers stepped out of a black town car, and the entourage went through security and up to the ninth floor. Charlene and the lawyers were allowed to stay with Tony for a few minutes in the squad room, but then they had to leave; he belonged to law enforcement now.

At his Massachusetts home, Philip responded to a knock on the door and was greeted by a *Daily News* reporter, Melinda Grace, and a photographer, Anthony Delmundo. Philip did not let them inside but agreed to go for a walk on a nearby beach, where he posed for a photo and provided a quote, saying, "I sincerely hope there is a way that justice can be achieved without my father going to jail." Meanwhile, at Holly Hill, appraisers from Sotheby's arrived as scheduled to look over Brooke Astor's possessions for insurance purposes and perhaps eventual auction. Her worldly goods, her child, her entire life, was being appraised and deconstructed on so many different levels.

Down at One Hogan Place, Robert Morgenthau, flanked by eight staffers, walked into a small conference room on the eighth floor at 11:30 A.M. and sat down at a table behind a mound of microphones. The eighty-eight-year-old district attorney, the son of Franklin Roosevelt's treasury secretary and a man whose social circle overlapped with Brooke Astor's, came from his own line of Manhattan royalty. He read with relish from a press release, declaring that Anthony Marshall and Francis Morrissey had been indicted for "swindling Mrs. Astor out of millions of dollars and valuable property" and "took advantage of Mrs. Astor's diminished mental capacity." The fourteen-page, eighteen-count indictment charged that Tony "falsely informed his mother that she was running out of money in order to induce her to sell one of her favorite paintings" — the Childe Hassam. The indictment accused Tony of having stolen a $2 million commission for the sale.

Tony was also charged with spending $600,000 of his mother's money, without her knowledge, to pay for the upkeep of Cove End in Maine after ownership had been transferred to him and then Charlene. The indictment made it seem as if Tony had used a vacuum cleaner on his mother's finances, sucking up everything but the loose change under the cushions of her blue chintz couch. It alleged that he used Brooke's money to give himself an unauthorized salary increase (from $450,000 to $1.4 million in 2005), to underwrite the salary of his personal boat captain on the *General Russell* ($52,000), and to pay for a secretary (Erica Meyer) who was primarily working for his theatrical production company. He was also accused of walking off with two of his mother's major artworks, a drawing of donkeys by Giovanni Tiepolo, an eighteenth-century Italian Rococo painter, and a painting by John Frederick Lewis, a nineteenth-century British artist, each worth half a million dollars. His mother had left him the Tiepolo in her will, but the district attorney's office objected that he had taken the painting home while she was still alive.

If convicted of first-degree grand larceny, Tony could receive up to twenty-five years in jail, which theoretically would put him behind bars until he was 108 years old. It was an astonishing plunge for a man with such a polished pedigree and pretensions, this aged ex-diplomat who had served on the city's most prestigious cultural boards.

Francis X. Morrissey, Jr., was charged with conspiring with Anthony Marshall to induce Brooke Astor to sign two codicils to her will and with forging the second document.

The press conference was raucous as Robert Morgenthau and Dan Castleman took turns answering questions. Early on, Steve Fishman of *New York* lobbed a query that seemed like a softball, asking, "Is there any chance his mother meant him to have those things?" When the laughter died down, Castleman replied, "Not according to the grand jury." A British journalist called out, "What was the motive? Wasn't he rich already?" Castleman couldn't resist the easy answer: "You'd have to say the motive was greed." A tabloid reporter followed up with, "Was the motive Charlene?" People roared as Castleman added, "We'll let you make that decision."

The district attorney stressed his hope that this high-profile indictment would send a message. "It happens fairly frequently that a son or daughter or grandson will steal from their parent or grandparent," Morgenthau said. "That's why these cases are important, because we want the public to know that if you take advantage of an elderly person with diminished capacity, you're going to get prosecuted." If Tony Marshall had hoped to be treated leniently by this fellow octogenarian, these words did not bode well.

Tony Marshall was supposed to be arraigned before Justice A. Kirke Bartley, Jr., at 2:30 P.M. in a ninth-floor courtroom at 111 Centre Street, but he was delayed because of the fingerprint snafu. Charlene Marshall, wearing a fitted heather blue wool suit, a gold snake bracelet on her right wrist, and a matching ring, arrived on time. The attitude of the press corps toward her was contemptuous. The reporters whispered loudly: "I think she wears the pants," and "She's the brains of the outfit." Shirley Shepard, a sketch artist for TV networks, walked over to Charlene and stood in the aisle with a makeshift easel to capture her likeness. Shepard leaned over to inquire about the designer label on Charlene's suit, asking, "Whose suit is that?" Charlene looked dumbfounded and replied, "It's mine." Shepard, softening, replied, "You're much prettier than your photographs." Charlene burst out laughing, saying, "That was the kindest thing anyone has said to me today."

Tony's courtroom appearance was brief, although he appeared distraught when he arrived, barely able to take in the proceedings. His only audible words were "Not guilty." He signed a personal appearance bond for $100,000 and handed over an old passport, which was later discovered to have expired. (The mistake required a return trip to the courthouse the following week with his valid passport.) Then he and Charlene were free to leave, the day's ordeal over.

Charlene handed Tony his wooden cane, and he shuffled slowly out of the courtroom and rested on the bench in the hallway while she went off to call for their car. Gary Naftalis, trying to cheer up his client, turned to Tony and said supportively, "We've got a lot of work to do. It's our turn next." He asked Tony which was worse, this day in court or being shelled at Iwo Jima. Tony grimaced. Once they hit the street, Barbara Ross of the *Daily News* asked Naftalis how Tony was doing. The attorney smiled and waved her off, and as he walked away, she wisecracked, "There won't be any violins in my story unless you play them."

Late that afternoon Philip sat at his kitchen table at home with Nan. A funeral wreath made of branches still hung on the wall, a gift from a student in honor of his grandmother. He was exhausted beyond description. He had promised to give a quote to the enterprising Stefanie Cohen of the *New York Post,* but his mind had gone blank. He and Nan still had to tell Sophie and Winslow about the indictment, a task they were dreading. Sophie arrived home from school and swept into the room, a graceful, athletic girl with long brown hair and a radiant smile.

They told her that her grandfather had been indicted, the climax of this long, strange, sad year. Philip then mentioned his dilemma in finding the right words for the newspaper. Sophie thought for a few minutes. Then Brooke Astor's self-assured great-granddaughter came up with two sentences, which Philip promptly e-mailed to the *Post:* "My concern for my grandmother's health and well-being prompted me to help her. Little did I know the outcome would be so profound."

In London, Viscount Astor reacted to the news by saying to me in a telephone interview what many others close to Brooke were thinking: "They may have arrested the wrong person." He believed that Charlene was largely to blame. "The whole thing came down to the fact that the new wife realized that if Tony died before his mother, she didn't get any money," Lord Astor said. "I'm irritated that he was trying to take Astor money that was going to New York institutions and grabbing it for himself." He insisted that he took no pleasure in the indictment and hoped that there would be a financial resolution. "I don't want to see any person aged eighty-three go to jail. Just give the money back." But he was angry that Brooke's final years had been marred. "What rankles me is not only the unkindness, but that they figured it all out — it wasn't spur-of-the-moment or done in anger, it was cold-hearted planning," he said. "They're the ultimate cold-hearted couple out of an Agatha Christie plot."

On Friday afternoon, November 30, Francis Morrissey surrendered to the authorities. The night before, a neighbor in his building on East Fifty-first Street, had shared an elevator with Morrissey and noted, "He was ashen and agitated. He couldn't look people in the eye." At the courthouse Morrissey, wearing glasses and a dark blue suit, did not get as much press attention as his codefendant but had a worse time in custody. Unlike Tony, he was handcuffed when escorted across the street by the officers, and the cuffs were removed only when he was taken into court. Morrissey did not say a word in response to the charges of forgery, leaving it to one of his lawyers, Pery Krinsky, to utter the words "Not guilty." He tried to avoid eye contact with reporters as he left the courthouse. Five weeks later, Morrissey's father died, at age ninety-seven. Morrissey mournfully told friends that it was the great tragedy of his life that his indictment had been his father's last memory.

The weekend after the indictments were announced, Philip Marshall drove into New York to join his historic preservation students on a tour of New York landmarks. En route he spent forty-five minutes on the phone with me discussing the week's events. "I can argue that I brought this on him or that he brought it on himself," Philip said, as if having that argument with himself. "I hope I'm not delusional, but I hope there is an opportunity here. I hope that he can face the harsh reality. I'm afraid he's going to try to fight this. I'm totally sad."

Charlene and Tony did not go to services at St. James' Church that Sunday. The curious congregation kept looking at the couple's usual spot, but they did not appear. Charlene did, however, take the strange step of showing up a week or so later at a reading by the writer Frances Kiernan, the author of *The Last Mrs. Astor*, at a Barnes & Noble across from Lincoln Center and the Juilliard School. The widely praised biography of Brooke Astor does not devote much space to the controversy, but Kiernan's nine-page summary portrays the Marshalls in an unfavorable light. When the book had been published eight months earlier, Charlene and Tony had attended Kiernan's lecture at the Colony Club.

Charlene's return visit to hear Kiernan at this well-publicized event did not appear to be motivated by a fan's desire to see a favorite author. Charlene had alerted her ex-husband, Paul Gilbert, about her plan to attend the event, and he had tried unsuccessfully to talk her out of it. As Gilbert told me later, "I think that Tony and Charlene believe they did nothing wrong and are determined to prove that."

Charlene took notes as Kiernan, an elegant woman who wears her long white hair wrapped into a braid and pinned up to frame her face, read from the book and answered questions. At the very end, Charlene stood up and waved her hand, and Kiernan called on her. Charlene then angrily asked questions aimed at undermining the author, suggesting that Kiernan had met Mrs. Astor only once (they had six meetings) and complaining that Kiernan had downplayed how often Tony visited his mother. It was an astonishing performance before an uncomfortable but rapt audience of sixty people, including Alice Perdue. "Charlene was so hostile," recalls Kiernan. "I was very guarded. I kept thinking, 'This has to be so painful for you. Why are you here?'"

Twenty-four hours later, the Metropolitan Museum of Art's executive committee quietly took the unprecedented step of voting to suspend Tony Marshall as a trustee emeritus. The decision was never publicly announced. Annette de la Renta recused herself from that vote. In the legal system, Tony might be presumed innocent, but in the court of public opinion, the verdict was already in.

That weekend Paul Gilbert came to Manhattan to fulfill a longstanding date to be the Sunday guest preacher at St. John's in the Village Episcopal Church. The small modern brick church was busy for the eleven o'clock service, and the congregation included his oldest daughter, Arden Delacey, a pretty redhead who resembles her mother, Charlene. Wearing white clerical robes, Gilbert went to the pulpit toward the end of the service to give the homily. With a compelling speaking style, he gave a curious speech, in light of the indictment of his children's stepfather, a man who had stolen his wife away. He spoke of violence in the Bible, using as his very first example an adulterer who died for his sins. He described the common desire that people have for "revenge and justice." In an empathetic tone, he stressed the importance of "compassion" and of learning to "let things go." It was a traditional Christmas season sermon, with a theme of renewal and redemption. But given the events of recent weeks, it was also more than that.

Meanwhile, other important characters in Mrs. Astor's life were enveloped in affection. Her dogs, Boysie and Girlsie, had been relocated to the Dachshund Love Kennel in Vermont. Mrs. Astor's friend Iris Love, the archeologist who breeds and shows dogs, adopted the aging animals, both born on July 4, 1997. "Girlsie is a total princess," says Molly Flint, the kennel manager. "All the other dogs go in and out of the doggie door. She stands there, so you can open the door for her." In contrast, Flint says, "Boysie is a busybody, he wants to see what everyone else is doing." In Love's home, a photograph of Brooke Astor was hung in a place of honor on the living room wall. Commandeering an old leather chair nearby, Girlsie could be found on many afternoons snoozing underneath her mistress's benevolent gaze.

The Ossining train station is a short drive from Sleepy Hollow Cemetery, where Brooke Astor is buried. Alec Marshall picked me up at the station, and we drove a few blocks in his blue Subaru station wagon to the quaint downtown, dominated by several churches. "My grand-mother used to say there were more churches in Ossining than any town nearby," he says during lunch. A slender, careworn man, dressed that day in a pinstriped shirt, a green sweater, and black slacks, Alec looks like his twin — and yet he doesn't. Shorter and more convention-ally handsome, he suffers from the aftereffects of surgery for a nonma-lignant brain tumor fifteen years ago, including loss of hearing in one ear and partial paralysis of his forehead.

His father had been indicted just two weeks earlier. "For someone with my father's background and heritage to end up this way — how sad," Alec said over a grilled vegetable sandwich at Mauro's restaurant. "For your own father — you could never imagine it, it's impossible." Alec had not spoken to Tony or Charlene since Brooke's funeral in Au-gust and had no plans to call them. A few minutes later, an acquaintance stopped by the table to say a warm hello and then blurted out, "I've been reading about your family in the newspapers." Alec nodded po-litely, still adjusting to the etiquette of having a father facing jail time. After lunch he headed over to Sleepy Hollow Cemetery to see the gran-ite headstone that had just been placed on Brooke's grave.

Ten days earlier the *New York Post,* in typical intemperate fashion, had excoriated Tony Marshall as a "STONE-COLD HEIR" in a page-one story, "GRAVE INSULT," charging that Brooke's final resting place was "a shocking pit of neglect resembling a pauper's grave" covered with dead leaves. When called about the story, Philip, rather than saying "no comment," had fanned the flames with a quote: "We are dismayed that there is still no memorial stone." Ken Warner, Tony's lawyer, told the *Post* that the "lovely pink" headstone was on order. The stone has since been installed.

After turning through the cemetery's ornate gates, Alec drove up a road that twisted and turned, pointing out Leona Helmsley's grave (the "queen of mean" had died a week after Brooke Astor, leaving $12 million to her dog, a sum later reduced by the court). Vincent Astor had origi-nally been buried on his estate in Rhinebeck, but when Brooke sold that home, she had had him moved here. She chose this new resting place based on proximity to her home and the presence of friends who were interred nearby. David Rockefeller had told me, "My family's cemetery is abutting the one that Brooke is in. Years before she died, she picked the lot that was right next to our family, my parents, my brothers. That's where she wanted to be."

Vincent and Brooke Astor's graves, side by side, are tucked away inconspicuously near the top of a hill, facing the Hudson River and the cliffs beyond. It's a peaceful spot, with the kind of unspoiled scenic panorama that inspired nineteenth-century Hudson River School paintings. "My grandmother used to always say she got the last plot with a view," Alec said. The wind was brutal, whipping the remaining leaves around. The earth looked fresh and newly raked, and a Christmas wreath had been carefully placed just above Brooke's elegant faintly pink tombstone, which was engraved just as she had requested: "I had a wonderful life."

The next stop on this family tour was a drive by Holly Hill, just a half-mile or so away. Fenced in from all sides, the sprawling property with the stone mansion is just visible from the road. Driving by one of the two entrances, Alec described how Brooke used to walk to the edge of the property and touch and kiss the gates. He apologized that he could not go inside, but family members cannot visit now. The only people allowed on the premises are Chris Ely, the gardeners, a maid, and security guards.

Alec's apartment is nearby, a jolting return to reality after the grandeur of his grandmother's world. It is a spartan, meticulously neat one-bedroom apartment, roughly 800 square feet, decorated with old wooden Mexican furniture and posters on the walls. The living room doubles as Alec's office and Hilary's bedroom when she stays over on weekends. The sun was setting. Looking out the window, with the view similar to that from his grandmother's grave, of the Hudson River and the cliffs, Alec described how his grandmother used to tell him to watch for the last spot of sun hitting the cliffs before it disappeared below the ridge and say, "Let's make a wish." Brooke Astor was a sophisticated woman, yet she took an innocent pleasure in small things, and these memories are her real legacy to her grandsons.

Like his brother, Alec has family photographs displayed everywhere. His refrigerator door features pictures of his daughter, his mother, Philip and his family, and a shot of Brooke with Alec's fiancée, Sue. A metal cabinet in his office is plastered with photos, including a wintry shot of his father looking dashing in the snowy mountains of Switzerland with a walking stick. "You haven't banned your father?" I asked. "Of course not," he replied.

Alec pulled out random sheets of slides and placed them on a light board with a magnifying glass to view details, and suddenly Brooke's life could be seen in reverse, from the cemetery back: she is laughing on a boat with a youngish Nelson Rockefeller; she is playing croquet with Tony, with her dachshunds getting in the way of the ball; she is climbing a steep mountain in Maine; she is entertaining friends at lunch; her gardens are extraordinary, bursting with brilliant reds and yellows and purples. And then there was an inadvertently heartbreaking photo: Tony and Philip together on a boat bobbing across the sea in Maine in 1985, Tony beaming with relaxed pleasure at his son, Philip in animated conversation by his side, and Alec as the unseen witness, the photographer capturing the moment.

Back at the kitchen table, over tea, Alec wanted to stress one final thing — that despite everything, he still loves his father. "I don't take grudges," he said. "My relationship hasn't changed with Phil, nor has my relationship changed with my father. He changed it, I didn't change it." Driving me back to the train station, he gave a rueful smile and offered up a haiku-like summation of the situation, saying, "Small family, big problems."

The Astor chronicles went on hiatus during the eight months following the indictment, with no progress toward a resolution of either of Tony Marshall's legal battles. At the urging of the Manhattan district attorney's office, the Westchester County Surrogate's Court postponed consideration of the challenge to Brooke Astor's will until the criminal case against her son is resolved. Both Tony and Francis Morrissey cut their ties to the criminal attorneys who had handled their indictments and brought in new courthouse lawyers.

As part of a subplot that might have been lifted from a Viennese light opera, the well-connected Morrissey was scolded by prosecutors for dispatching none other than Prince Paul of Romania and his wife to track down a witness, Lia Opris, Mrs. Astor's former aide, now living in that country. As Liz Loewy explained at a February court hearing,

Opris "was upset" when the royal couple showed up unexpectedly at her door, and wanted to be left alone. In April, Tony experienced health problems, missing a court appearance because he was resting after a brief hospitalization for a stomach ailment. With neither side proposing a plea bargain, the judge set a tentative trial date for early 2009.

Marshall and Morrissey had become outcasts in society, unwelcome at their former haunts. The 137-year-old Knickerbocker Club, flourishing in Edith Wharton's era, made the shunning treatment official by suspending their memberships.

By the standards of both old and new money, Tony Marshall was still destined to become a wealthy man due to his mother's generosity. Even if he was convicted of grand larceny and conspiracy — even if he lost his effort to have his mother's 2002 will and the three codicils admitted to probate — Tony would not have to worry about providing for himself and Charlene. In any scenario, at minimum, he would inherit his mother's Park Avenue apartment and her Holly Hill estate and receive an annual stipend of several million dollars. But with the assets tied up in court and legal bills mounting, he and Charlene decided to reduce their expenses. After giving notice to their chauffeur, the couple switched to driving themselves around in a Toyota Prius.

The family Astor, torn asunder, showed no signs of mending. Contemplating the wreckage of his family, Philip Marshall remained bitter toward his stepmother. "I don't care about the money," he said over dinner in Manhattan in April 2008. "She stole my father." Tony Marshall's eighty-fourth birthday, on May 30, came and went without a visit, a phone call, or a note from either of his sons. The three Marshall men grasped the emotional significance of the date, and each, in his own stubborn way, lamented the anguished silence.

Epilogue

A Sunset in Maine

FIVE DAYS. How much difference can five days make in the life of a family? So many layers of experience mount up, and the cracks are re-plastered and new touch-up paint is applied, but the architecture of the relationships remains the same. Still, every now and then there is a moment, a glimpse of what might have been and what still could be. Forget the artifice of redecorating — what if the support beams were demolished and replaced by sturdy new construction? During five magical days in Maine, Brooke Astor, at ninety-eight, knew that something special was occurring. A beatific smile played constantly over her expressive features.

Family visits chez Astor usually occurred en masse, with four generations offering homage at the table. But in the summer of 2000, Tony and Charlene Marshall scheduled their visit to Brooke in mid-July, stayed for three weeks, and departed on August 6. So when Philip Marshall and Nan Starr drove up to Cove End on August 21 with Winslow, nine, and Sophie, seven, in the back seat, they anticipated a rare experience — they would have Brooke all to themselves.

When Tony and Charlene were with them, family tensions inevitably surfaced. "We were freer to be ourselves than when other family members were there," says Nan. "Being relaxed and happy came more naturally." Brooke, to be sure, was adept at stoking intergenerational rivalries in the family. She turned things into a competition about who loved her the most; it was as if she couldn't help herself. Years earlier at Holly Hill, Brooke had offered Philip an old side table from the attic; after he carried it downstairs, Tony spied it and promptly claimed the prize for himself. Brooke let it pass, although she must have noticed the struggle between father and son.

Cove End is full of nooks for children to explore. Once the Marshall family had unpacked — a major production, since Brooke required resort wear during the day and jackets and dresses for dinner — at the spacious two-story guest cottage by the water, they made their way along a wooded path to the main house, where Brooke waited. Winslow stopped by the Chinese gong and banged it with delight, an exuberant way of emphasizing "We're here!"

Brooke was eager to tell them about the plans she had made. It would be a busy few days, but there would still be time for lolling around. Her staff would take care of anything they needed. Chris Ely was there — he was always there — and Sophie and Winslow greeted him warmly. They associated him with fun, since Easter Sunday at Holly Hill was one of the butler's fortes, and he decorated the house with stuffed Peter Rabbit dolls and toys just for them.

That first night at Cove End, Brooke was in storytelling mode, happily regaling her grandson and great-grandchildren with stories of her globe-trotting girlhood. "She had all these trinkets in the house, and they'd end up being props for stories," recalls Philip. "She'd pick something up — 'Here's a box with a little splinter of bloodstained wood from Nelson's mortal wound at the Battle of Trafalgar.'" When it was time to move into the dining room for dinner, Winslow offered his arm to his great-grandmother. She could not believe it — such perfect manners for a nine-year-old boy. That was Nan's doing; she worked hard to raise well-behaved children. As Sophie recalls, "Every time we went to see Gagi, we had to be on our best behavior. We had to sit up straight and not start eating until she started and put our napkins in our lap." Winslow adds, "And not drink the water out of the finger bowls."

While having breakfast in bed the next morning, Brooke spoke fondly about Sophie and Winslow to her housekeeper, Alicia Johnson. "She loved the little girl," recalls Johnson. "Mrs. Astor said, 'She danced for me.' She thought Philip's son was such a little gentleman — he had a tie on at dinner. She was proud of Philip."

Brooke had chartered a boat that day to explore the waters off Mount Desert Island in search of seals. The family posed for a photograph on the waterfront. In a white straw hat, pearls, a green blouse, white pants, and a stylish white coat, Brooke is beaming in the center of the picture. On the left, Philip, balding and tall, wearing a windbreaker, a polo shirt, and shorts, is grinning, his arms around his shyly smiling daughter. On the right, Nan, short-haired and athletic, looks affectionately at the camera, resting her hands on Winslow's shoulders. On the boat, Philip sat close to Brooke, whispering in her ear as they bounded over the deep blue water with the mountains in the background.

At Cove End the next day, Annette de la Renta arrived by private plane from the Dominican Republic, just for lunch, in an extravagant gesture of affection. "I'd never met any of them," says Annette. "Brooke didn't talk so much about them." Here she was, Brooke's closest friend, and yet Brooke's grandson and his family were strangers. Brooke was the queen of New York, the world's most famous philanthropist, a best-dressed icon, and her family had never come first. But now she was Gagi, an affectionate matriarch trying on a new role extremely late in life. "I saw her having a great time. Her great-grandchildren were all dressed up and performing for her," Annette recalls. "It was nice to see Brooke that way."

Brooke wanted to share her family with yet another close friend, so David Rockefeller came over for lunch the next day. The group got into a lively discussion about the upcoming presidential election. As Nan recalls, "Brooke and I were trying to convince David to vote Democratic." Brooke, once a GOP stalwart, was annoyed that George and Barbara Bush, unlike previous presidents, had not included her at state dinners, although they were social acquaintances. "She was a little offended," says Rockefeller. "She felt that the Bushes had not paid a lot of attention to her."

Gagi was not lacking for attention during this visit. Sophie and Winslow tried to entertain her with their athletic talent. "She was impressed when I was doing back flips into the pool," Sophie recalls. "I did gymnastics in her yard, cartwheels — she liked that."

At the end of the five days, Brooke had an impulsive inspiration: she decided to give Philip and Nan the cottage by the water. She loved them; they loved Maine; it would make her happy to imagine Sophie and Winslow cavorting for decades to come. Of course, if she had given this gesture much thought, she would have known that Tony would be irked. But the property was hers, and she was already leaving Tony so much — Park Avenue and Holly Hill and the main house at Cove End. What could a single cottage matter?

What stayed with Nan was Philip's happiness. "It was really, really important to Philip for the kids to have a connection to their great-grandmother, and not for any reason but sentiment," she says. "He wanted some normalcy. He romanticizes those days, but it meant so much to him."

Brooke said her goodbyes and the family drove away. The blue sky and ocean water, Brooke's riotous garden of pinks and purples, Sophie in a blue dress at the swim club, Winslow in a yellow life jacket — all now photos for the scrapbook. Five days in the life of a family is so little time, but sometimes the memories, and their repercussions, can last forever.

ACKNOWLEDGMENTS

NOTES

BIBLIOGRAPHY

Acknowledgments

MANY PEOPLE helped make this book possible, but at the top of the list is my agent, Gail Hochman, who stirred up a bidding war in August, no less, and has been tremendously supportive and involved at every stage of this process.

To the more than 230 people who agreed to be interviewed for this book, I send all of you my sincere thanks for your time and your trust. A handful of people were very helpful on a background basis: you know who you are, and I am immensely grateful.

As I wandered around in Columbo fashion with just one more question, a number of people showed endless patience. My thanks go to Philip Marshall, Annette and Oscar de la Renta, Daniel Billy, Jr., Susan Robbins, Alec Marshall, Elizabeth Wheaton-Smith, Nan Starr, Paul Gilbert, Sam Peabody, Linda Gillies, Fraser Seitel, Vartan Gregorian, Ashton Hawkins, Minnette Christie, Pearline Noble, Suzanne Kuser, Emily Harding, Ira Salzman, Harvey Corn, Barbara Thompson, Liz Smith, Alicia Johnson, Ivan Obolensky, Alice Victor, Louis Auchincloss, Marilyn Berger, Randy Bourscheidt, John Dobkin, Barbara Goldsmith, Steve Hamor, John Hart, Naomi Packard-Koot, Mary Lou Scott, Patricia Roberts, Viscount William Astor, and Alice Perdue.

Frances Kiernan, the author of *The Last Mrs. Astor,* has been generous with research help and advice. As for my journalistic colleagues on the Astor beat, I have benefited from their reporting and guidance, with special thanks to Stefanie Cohen, Neil Weinberg, Serge Kovaleski, Dareh Gregorian, Helen Peterson, and Barbara Ross.

I have been blessed with wonderfully supportive friends. I am grateful to Jane Hartley, Ralph Schlosstein, Mary Macy, Michelle and Stephen Stoneburn, Suzanna Andrews, Christine Doudna, Rick Grand-Jean, Tom Curley, Patricia Bauer, Ed Muller, Gail Gregg, Tamar Lewin, Swoosie Kurtz, Jim Wetzler, Rita Jacobs, Jenny Allen, Jules Feiffer, Charles Tolk, Ron Silver, Elaine and Tino Kamarck, Louise Grunwald, Mandy Grunwald, Matt Cooper, Benjamin Cooper, Rachel Gotbaum, Betsy and Victor Gotbaum, Josh Gotbaum, Joyce Thornhill, Susan Chira, Michael Shapiro, Judy Miller, Jason Epstein, Susan Birkenhead, Jere Couture, Julie Glass, Joanna Coles, Joe Klein, Victoria Kaunitz, Stone and Betsey Roberts, Gale Epstein, Paula Sweet, Toni Goodale, Elizabeth Rohatyn, Maralee Schwartz, Jonathan Alter, Emily Lazar, Garrett Epps, Gwen Feder, Caroline Miller, Eric Himmel, Lindi Oberon, Jodie-Beth Galos, Jane Stanton Hitchcock, Nancy Leonard, and Urban Lehner.

My husband, Walter Shapiro, has been terrific during this exhilarating and exhausting marathon. Champion editor of boring sentences, comforting presence at 3 A.M., ever-vigilant and curious journalist, stand-up comedian who keeps me laughing, closest friend after thirty years together — I am so lucky that we found each other.

My parents, David and Adelle Gordon, have cheered me on all through life and read every draft of this book. My father is a marvelous descriptive writer; my mother, a social worker, has a talent for drawing people out. I'm grateful for their love and the skills they have sought to pass on.

My nephews, Jesse Gordon and Nate Gordon, are the lights of my life, and it has been a pleasure to welcome to our family Meghan Wolf and Victoria Clark. A special thanks is due to Nate, the baseball photo editor at *Sports Illustrated,* for his professional help in coordinating the photos for this book. My two sisters-in-law, Sarah Cooper-Ellis and Amy Shapiro, have been consistently warm and wise and fun. My brother, Bart Gordon, taught me how to read without speaking the words out loud, and remains always in my thoughts. I miss him every day.

This book evolved from a story I wrote for *New York* magazine, and I remain grateful to Bruce Wasserstein and the editors — Adam Moss,

John Homans, Jon Gluck, Hugo Lindgren, Lauren Kern, and Emily Nussbaum — for this assignment and many others. Wendy Wasserstein, Bruce's sister, repeatedly urged me to put aside magazine stories to do my own work, saying, "Seize the means of production." Her friendship and encouragement meant a great deal.

At Houghton Mifflin, Jane Rosenman, the acquiring editor of this book, was a dream to work with, and I regret that she was unable to see the book through for reasons beyond our control. George Hodgman, who took over the editing of the manuscript, came up with a terrific title and offered many smart insights. Lois Wasoff turned the legal vetting into a surprisingly pleasant experience. Liz Duvall provided thorough manuscript editing.

I am grateful for the support and enthusiasm of Rebecca Saletan, the publisher of Houghton Mifflin Harcourt, Andrea Schulz, the editor in chief, Lori Glazer, executive director of publicity, Bridget Marmion, senior vice president of marketing, Becky Saikia-Wilson, executive director of editorial operations, publicity manager Alia Hanna Habib, and Sasheem Silkiss-Hero. Julia Dahl, who provided research assistance, and Bob Hammond, who fact-checked the book, made invaluable contributions, but any mistakes in the manuscript are mine.

Notes

This book evolved from a story I wrote for *New York* magazine in August 2006. I began the research that led to that story a year earlier, in September 2005, before the legal fight began. Although I had contacts in Mrs. Astor's world from previous magazine assignments, I did not come to this subject with any special arrangements or access, just an intense desire to understand what happened to this family.

Ultimately, I was able to speak to every major figure involved in this controversy. I interviewed more than 230 people, including Mrs. Astor's family members, close friends, and former staffers. Many were initially reluctant to grant full cooperation. Only after ten months of phone calls did Philip Marshall agree to meet me in person and describe in detail the events that led him to sue his father. In her role as Mrs. Astor's guardian, Annette de la Renta refused all press requests for a year, but six months after Mrs. Astor's death, she spoke with me at length. David Rockefeller and Henry Kissinger also discussed the lawsuit and their friendship with Mrs. Astor in conversations at their respective offices.

Tony and Charlene Marshall, who met with me at their home in 2005 for my story in *New York*, declined to schedule a formal interview for this book but were nonetheless accessible. Tony granted me a half-hour phone interview in June 2007, and during a break in the surrogate's court proceedings in Westchester in October 2007, the Marshalls sat and spoke to me for nearly an hour. Whenever I went up to them at events and asked questions, they took the time to answer. They graciously provided family photographs for the book.

The majority of my interviews were taped. When taping was not possible, for various reasons (such as the ban on tape recorders at courthouses or requests by individuals that I not record them), I relied on my notes. Most conversations were on the record, but a few people would agree to speak only on a background basis. During two years of reporting, I did multiple interviews with many sources.

In researching this book, I read numerous newspaper clippings and books, especially Brooke Astor's two autobiographies, *Patchwork Child* (1962) and *Footprints* (1980), and Frances Kiernan's invaluable *The Last Mrs. Astor* (2007). I relied on, and derived insights from, several types of documents not available to the general public:

- The nurses' notes written by Mrs. Astor's caregivers from September 2003 to March 2004. As indicated in the text, these notes are far more than medical notations, since they include descriptions of Mrs. Astor's state of mind and running commentary on the events that occurred at her two homes, Holly Hill in Westchester and 778 Park Avenue in Manhattan.
- Schedules and phone message logs prepared for Mrs. Astor. These documents, some of which date back to 1990 and which conclude in 2005, have been verified for accuracy by members of Mrs. Astor's household.
- Letters written by Mrs. Astor and her family members to one another. Several of her close friends, including Vartan Gregorian, Liz Smith, and Annette de la Renta, shared personal notes that they received from Mrs. Astor.
- Documents related to the 2006 guardianship lawsuit. Some documents were part of the New York State Supreme Court files (index no. 500095/06; the public files have been redacted). Others derived from legal discovery in that case but were never formally filed with the court; these documents subsequently became part of the proceedings in Westchester County Surrogate's Court and New York County criminal court. Though some of these materials have been quoted in newspaper stories, I was able to make greater use of them at book length. In the chapter notes, for simplicity, I list these documents as related to the guardianship case.

Philip Graham, who acquired *Newsweek* with Brooke Astor's blessing from the Vincent Astor Foundation in 1961, famously described weekly journalism as "the first draft of history." A book like *Mrs. Astor Regrets* aspires to a higher level of accuracy than a news story written under unrelenting deadlines. But I also know something about the limitations of even the most careful reporter, and I make no claims to omniscience. That said, I have done my best to be meticulously accurate and fair-minded in telling the story that became *Mrs. Astor Regrets.*

page PROLOGUE: TRIAL BY TABLOID

4 "She could make her will known": Author phone interview with Lois Orlin, Jan. 24, 2008.

"She really loved": Author phone interview with Sandra Foschi, Jan. 31, 2008.

6 The *New York Times* later took the unusual step: Alex Kuczynski, "100 Candles for a Darling of Society and Charity," *New York Times,* Mar. 30, 2002. p. B1.

"She took on the Astor Foundation": Author phone interview with Viscount William Astor, July 30, 2006.

7 "a very material-minded woman": Author interview with Louis Auchincloss at his Park Avenue home, Nov. 16, 2008.

"Buddie was the love of her life": Author phone interview with Nancy Reagan, Apr. 25, 2007.

"She always said Vincent was difficult": Author phone interview with Barbara Walters, Jan. 18, 2008.

Her forty-two person staff: Judith Miller, "Old Money, New Needs," *New York Times Magazine,* Nov. 17, 1991.

8 "She always wanted to be in the limelight": Author interview with Philippe de Montebello at the Metropolitan Museum, Mar. 12, 2008.

"It always really helped": Author interview with Peg Breen at New York Landmarks Conservancy office, Jan. 25, 2007.

"Once Brooke began giving": Author interview with Howard Phipps at his Rockefeller Plaza office, June 12, 2007.

9 Vernon Jordan, the civil rights leader: Author interview with Vernon Jordan at his Rockefeller Plaza office, Apr. 9, 2007.

"The worst thing she could say": Author interview with Linda Gillies, multiple interviews by phone and in person, Sept. 2005–Apr. 2008.

"Tony was always very nice": Author interview with Nancy Kissinger at the Kissinger Associates office, Mar. 13, 2007.

"She didn't like the same people": Author interview with Vartan Gregorian at the Carnegie Corporation of New York office, Mar. 24, 2007.

"She was determined": Author interview with Freddy Melhado at his Park Avenue home, June 13, 2007.

10 "to look like ballgowns": Author interview with Albert Hadley at his office, Sept. 2005.

"She was talking so nicely": Author interview with Robert Caravaggi at Swifty's, Apr. 12, 2008.

"Brooke loved dressing up": Author interview with Annette de la Renta at her Park Avenue home, Jan. 29, 2008.

"It was kind of genetic": Author phone interview with Tom Brokaw, Mar. 27, 2007.

11 *Forbes* estimated Jane Engelhard's fortune: "The Forbes Four Hundred," *Forbes,* Oct. 28, 1985, p. 148.

"Brooke looked upon Annette": Philippe de Montebello interview.

Brooke was wintering: Author phone interview with Brooke Astor's landlords, Don and Ann Carmichael, Oct. 2006.

"Brooke always felt it was her duty": Author phone interview with Oscar de la Renta, Feb. 2008.

12 Birthdays could be a dilemma: Vartan Gregorian interview.

Ten years later: "Marines Making Music, Cannon Firing Confetti," *New York Times,* Mar. 8, 1992. p. 58.

"She had a ball": Author phone interview with Oz Elliott, Nov. 2006.

"I ran back and threw my arms": Videotaped Brooke Astor ninetieth birthday tribute, collection of Susan Trescher.

13 "I don't feel old": James Barron, "All This and Brooke Astor Too," *New York Times,* Mar. 6, 1992, p. B3.

it netted $892,741: Citizens Committee of New York press office.

She sent a note: Author interview with Vincent Stefan at the Sea Grill, Mar. 14, 2007.

On New Year's Eve: Author interview with David Rockefeller at his office, Dec. 18, 2007.

14 Several months before: Written description provided by David Rockefeller.

15 "There were rotating men": Author interview with John Hart in Manhattan, Sept. 26 2006.

When the historian: Author interview with Barbara Goldsmith at her home, Mar. 15, 2007.

"When I got Linda to come": Brooke Astor videotaped interview with Peg Breen, president of New York Landmarks Conservancy, Nov. 7, 1996. Courtesy of Landmarks Conservancy.

"Brooke was human": Author interview with John Dobkin at his home, Sept. 15, 2005.

16 "Once something was over": Author interview with Linda Gillies at her home, Sept. 12, 2005.

"We walked in": Author interview with Marshall Rose at his office, Apr. 10, 2007.

"Brooke was a big flirt": Nancy Reagan interview.

"She had an infatuation": Tom Brokaw interview.

Peter Jennings was among: Party guests who predeceased Brooke Astor include Eleanor Elliott, Andrew Heiskell, Peter Jennings, Nancy Pierrepont, George Plimpton, Eben Pyne, Laurance Rockefeller, Abe Rosenthal, Bobby Short, and George Trescher.

17 "She could have kept"; Author phone interview with Naomi Packard-Koot, Feb. 8, 2007.

"We had a little game": Author interview with Gregory Long at the Knickerbocker Club, Mar. 5, 2007.

She recalled playing tennis: Craig Wilson, "Astor's Good Fortune," *USA Today,* Dec. 3, 1993, p. 1D.

18 "Darn, I can't": Alex Kuczynski, "100 Candles for a Darling of Society and Charity," *New York Times,* Mar. 30, 2002, p. B1.

"maybe just a little": Author interview with Marian Heiskell at her home, Feb. 6, 2007.

"She was pretty much": Author interview with Alex Kuczynski at her home, Apr. 3, 2007.

"beeswax and money"; Janine di Giovanni, "Party Girl of the Century," *Toronto Globe and Mail,* Jan. 1, 2000, p. R9.

19   Tony Marshall had a secret: Anthony Dryden Marshall letter to Dr. Howard Fillit,
       Dec. 26, 2000, New York State Supreme Court, index no. 500095/06.

20   "It was obvious"; Author interview with Alec Marshall at his home, Dec. 12, 2007.
       "My father took me": Author interview with Philip Marshall, multiple interviews,
       July 28, 2006–June 2008.
       "Her health is pretty good": Mary Voboril, "100 Reasons to Celebrate," *Newsday,*
       Mar. 28, 2002, p B8.

21   "Nixon didn't know": Author interview with Ashton Hawkins at his office, July 16,
       2007.
       "I've got to go get my son": Author interview with Steve Hamor, July 19, 2007.
       Tony would later boast: New York State Supreme Court, index no. 50095/06, An-
       thony Marshall verification answer and cross petition, Sept. 19, 2006, p. 12.
       Compound growth rate of 5.9 percent: Selena Maranjian, "105 Years Old, with $816
       in the Bank," *Motley Fool,* www.fool.com, Apr. 11, 2007.

22   reached $450,000: New York State Supreme Court, index no. 500095/06, p. 39.
       "I think I'll talk": Alex Kuczynski. "100 Candles for a Darling of Society and Char-
       ity," *New York Times,* Mar. 30, 2002, p. B1.

23   "I came up at lunchtime": Author interview with Viscount William Astor, Dec. 26,
       2007.
       Brooke had never gushed: Author interview with Vartan Gregorian at the Carnegie
       Corporation, Mar. 24, 2007.

25   What a famous cast: Kuczynski, "100 Candles," p. B1.

26   "The three aunties": Author interview with Emily Harding at her home, Oct. 5,
       2006.
       "We always took a walk": Author interview with Henry Kissinger at his office, Sept.
       19, 2007.

27   personal assets of $120 million: Brooke Astor's will, Jan. 30, 2002, Surrogate's Court
       of the State of New York, County of Westchester, file no. 2127/2007.
       suspended from practicing law: Supreme Court, Appellate Division, First Depart-
       ment, N.Y. 217 A.D.2d 74, 634 N.Y.S. 2d. 51, Nov. 16, 1995.

28   "She lived with that painting": Author phone interview with Florence Irving, Apr.
       2008.
       now the artwork was on display: Author interview with George Soros, Mar. 26,
       2008.
       "I didn't want to sell it": Author interview with confidential source.
       "We did not grow up": Author interview with Alec Marshall at his home, Dec. 12,
       2007.
       "Brooke was fond of them": Interview with Ashton Hawkins at his office, July 16
       2007.
       "Philip was very nice": Author interview with John Hart in Manhattan, Sept. 26,
       2006.
       "They could not be": Author interview with Suzanne Kuser in Washington, D.C.,
       June 28, 2007.

29   "Philip's courses": Author interview with Kevin Clark in Manhattan, Dec. 2, 2007.

Her clothes were couture: Author phone interview with Elizabeth Corbett, of Chez Ninon, July 2007.

30   "She wasn't a grandmother": Author interview with Gregory Long at the Knickerbocker Club, Mar. 5, 2007.

"I liked Tony": Author phone interview with Barbara Walters, Jan. 18, 2008.

"She wasn't totally there": Henry Kissinger interview.

"Oscar did this phenomenal dress": Author interview with Paul LeClerc at the New York Public Library, May 17, 2007.

31   The waiters served: Alex Kuczynski, "Grandest of Dames Turns 100 in Style," *New York Times,* Apr. 1, 2002, p. B3.

"Everybody knew that Brooke": Author phone interview with Robert Pirie, Sept. 2007.

"Charlene brought over the flowers": Barbara Walters interview.

"Brooke had some kind of altercation": Author interview with Liz Smith in Manhattan, Jan. 23, 2007.

32   Tony Marshall had prepared: Author phone interview with Tony Marshall, June 21, 2007.

33   "It was a magical night": Vartan Gregorian interview.

"You looked around": Author interview with John Dobkin in Manhattan, Sept. 19, 2006.

"precious asset": "Brooke Astor: A Precious Asset," *Hartford Courant,* Apr. 5, 2002, p. A16.

"she has had everything": "Brooke Astor's Century," *New York Times,* Mar. 30, 2002, p. 14.

"On Saturday": Nicholas Wapshott, "The So-Called 'Melting pot' of New York Is No Such Thing." *Times (London),* Apr. 5, 2002, p. 14.

3. DISASTER FOR MRS. ASTOR

34   At Holly Hill the morning after: Author interview with Philip Marshall, multiple interviews, July 28, 2006–June 2008.

36   "I'll never forget": Author phone interview with Nan Starr, Feb. 2008.

"He said he did not intend": Author phone interview with Alec Marshall, Feb. 2008.

gardeners had plowed: Author phone interview with Steve Hamor, Feb. 2007.

37   On Monday morning: Philip Marshall interview.

38   "I offered to barricade myself": Author interview with Daniel Billy, Jr., in Manhattan, Apr. 10, 2007.

39   "Tony asked me": Steve Hamor interview.

"I drove up the driveway": Author interview with Sam Peabody at his home, Apr. 17, 2007.

Three days earlier: Author interview with Ira Salzman at his office, Dec. 4, 2006.

40   On Monday afternoon: Author phone interview with Helen Peterson, Jan. 2008.

41   "I knew that Philip": Author interview with Tenzing Chadotsang in Manhattan, Dec. 14, 2007.

"At that point": Philip Marshall interview.

41   Annette is an early riser: Author interview with Annette de la Renta at her home,
       Jan. 29, 2008.
       Annette was horrified: Helen Peterson, "Battle of N.Y. Blue Bloods!," *Daily News,*
       July 26, 2006, p. 1.
       "sad and deplorable": Ibid., p. 6.

42   "The apartment is shabby": Annette de la Renta affidavit, New York State Supreme
       Court, Philip Marshall application of "Guardians of the Person and Property of
       Brooke Astor," order to show cause, index 500095/06.
       "That's when I knew": Nan Starr interview.

43   "Reporters were outside": Author interview with Sandra Gelbard in Manhattan,
       Oct. 3, 2007.
       "we had to pull down the shades": Author interview with Bob Pyle in Northeast
       Harbor, July 19, 2007.
       "I thought the *New York Post*": Author interview with Charlene Marshall at the
       Metropolitan Museum of Art, Sept. 29, 2007.
       "I thought he had a case": Author interview with Suzanne Kuser in Washington,
       D.C., June 28, 2007.
       "I felt terrible": Author phone interview with Nancy Reagan, Apr. 25, 2007.
       "I'm just appalled": Author interview with Viscount Astor, July 30, 2006.
       They were accused of finagling millions: Serge Kovaleski and Mike McIntire. "A
       Former Aide tells How Spending Habits Changed," *New York Times,* Aug. 1, 2006,
       p. 1; Serge Kovaleski, "Mrs. Astor's Son Is Accused of Mishandling Millions," *New
       York Times,* Sept. 7, 2006, p. A1; Serge Kovaleski and Mike McIntire, "Mrs. Astor's
       Guardians Question Legitimacy of Will's Amendments," *New York Times,* Sept. 13,
       2006, p. B1.

44   there was an uproar: Serge Kovaleski, "Major Error is Reported in Tax paid by Mrs.
       Astor on Sale of Painting," *New York Times,* Sept. 24, 2006, p. 37.
       "My mother has always": Anthony D. Marshall press release, July 31, 2006.
       "I thought they were all friends": Author phone interview with Tony Marshall, June
       21, 2007.
       "I don't know Philip": Author interview with David Rockefeller at his office, Dec.
       18, 2007.
       "Nobody said": Author interview with Henry Kissinger at his office, Sept. 19, 2007.

45   "a disturbed attention-getting": Author phone interview with David Richenthal,
       July 2006.
       "I am perplexed": Mike Wallace statement, July 31, 2006, issued by Kenneth War-
       ner, attorney for Tony Marshall.
       "When I read about it": Author phone interview with Mike Wallace, Nov. 8, 2006.
       "I was dumbfounded": Author interview with Brenda Husson at St. James' Church,
       July 2, 2007.
       "If David Rockefeller": Author phone interview with Oz Elliott, Nov. 2006.
       "parricidal intervention": William F. Buckley, Jr., "Sonnytime," Universal Press Syn-
       dicate, Aug. 8, 2006.
       "What they've done": Author interview with Daniel Billy Jr. in Manhattan, Mar. 3,
       2008.

46 "As we have learned": U.S. Senate Special Committee on Aging, Chairman Gordon H. Smith, Sept. 7, 2006.

"She never went out": Author interview with Louis Auchincloss at his home, Nov. 16, 2006.

47 "Look at the marvelous sauces": Marilyn Berger, "Being Brooke Astor," *New York Times,* May 20, 1984.

"The American Astor Family": Cleveland Amory, *Who Killed Society?* (New York: Harper & Brothers, 1960), p. 468.

"She loved to get to know": Author interview with Gregory Long at the Knickerbocker Club, Mar. 5, 2007.

4. "I MARRIED A TERRIBLE MAN"

49 "She took books": Author phone interview with Linda Gillies, Apr. 2008.

50 "My mother used to say": Videotape of Andrew Carnegie Medals of Philanthropy awards ceremony, Dec. 10, 2001, courtesy of Carnegie Corporation.

"No one knew what to do": Author interview with Annette de la Renta at her home, multiple interviews, Jan. 29, 2008–July 2008.

51 "Keep in mind": Author phone interview with Robert Pirie, Sept. 2007.

"Part of the problem": Author interview with Ashton Hawkins at his office, July 16, 2007.

On April 27: "Elaborate Weddings Mark the Spring Season," *Washington Post,* Apr. 27, 1919, p. S6.

52 Brooke would later tear up: Brooke Astor, *Footprints* (New York: Doubleday, 1980), p. 38.

Brooke's paternal grandfather: "Admiral Russell's Services," *New York Times,* Mar. 22, 1896.

"extraordinarily able": Arthur Krock, "Russell of the Marines Justifies Cleveland's Faith," *New York Times,* Feb. 22, 1934.

"Mrs. Russell was jolly": Author interview with Ivan Obolensky in Manhattan, Oct. 11, 2007.

53 "I revered Miss Madeira": Mort Sheinman and Lorna Koski, "The Last Queen," *Women's Wear Daily,* Aug. 14, 2007, p. 1 (excerpts from 1991 interview).

54 "We were a totally miscast pair": Astor, *Footprints,* p. 39.

"She told me that she ran": Author interview with Liz Smith in Manhattan, Jan. 23, 2007.

"She was naughty": Author interview with Philippe de Montebello at the Metropolitan Museum, Mar. 12, 2008.

"When I can't sleep": Brooke Astor, *The Bluebird Is at Home* (New York: Harper & Row, 1965), p. 17.

55 "If only I were younger": Author interview with Vernon Jordan at his office, Apr. 9, 2007.

Faircourt, the family's grandiose: John Turpin and W. Barry Thomson, *New Jersey Country Houses: The Somerset Hills,* vol. I (Far Hills, N.J.: Mountain Colony Press, 2004); author visit to Faircourt, July 2007.

55 notorious robbery: "Adroit Thief Drugs Then Robs Kuser," *New York Times,* Nov. 2, 1921; Astor, *Footprints,* pp. 57–58.

56 "Dryden was fast-drinking": Author phone interview with Andrew Kravchenko, July 2007.

"Having not participated": Astor, *Footprints,* p. 51.

"Now, Bob dear": Author interview with Bob Pyle in Northeast Harbor, Maine, July 19, 2007.

"She wanted to talk": Author phone interview with Sandra Graves, Sept. 2007.

57 "One day he knocked me down": Marilyn Berger, "Being Brooke Astor," *New York Times Magazine,* May 20, 1984.

"a trust fund": Mrs. Lester Perrin to Suzanne Kuser, n.d. Courtesy of Suzanne Kuser.

58 "I hardly ever saw": Author interview with Suzanne Kuser in Washington, D.C., June 28, 2007.

"He once created": Kravchenko interview.

"I had an affair:" Eileen Simpson interview with Brooke Astor, June 15, 1996, New York Public Library, Vincent Astor Foundation collection.

Buddie Marshall finally left: Frances Kiernan, *The Last Mrs. Astor* (New York: W. W. Norton, 2007), p. 73.

"I was quite shocked": Mrs. Lester Perrin to Suzanne Kuser.

59 "I didn't like it": Author interview with Tony Marshall at his home, Sept. 16, 2005.

"At the age of six": Tony Marshall, speech to U.S. Marine Corps University Foundation, Russell Leadership Award ceremonies, Oct. 26, 2005, transcript.

"I'm totally for abortion": Regina Nadelson, "Wednesday Women: Dollar Duchess," *Guardian,* June, 8, 1988.

"In my day": Author interview with confidential source.

"He was very shy": Author interview with Samuel Peabody at his home, Apr. 17, 2007.

60 "My grandfather said": Author interview with Tony Marshall at Westchester County Surrogate's Court, Oct. 19, 2007.

General Russell also called the Brooks School: Astor, *Footprints,* p. 232.

Tony went to war: Marshall, speech to U.S. Marine Corps University Foundation.

When his father learned: Astor, *Footprints,* p. 232.

"I led a platoon": Tony Marshall interview, Oct. 19, 2007.

61 "Brooke was in a dither": Louis Auchincloss interview.

"I didn't really want": Tony Marshall interview, Sept. 16, 2005.

62 "She got a lot of money out of him": Author interview with confidential source.

Dryden finally took Tony to court: Astor, *Footprints,* p. 232.

"The boy was another": Brooke Astor, *The Last Blossom on the Plum Tree* (New York: Random House, 1986), p. 5.

"From his first spanking": Anthony D. Marshall, *Dash* (New York: Vantage, 2001), p. 15.

"Dryden used to call": Author phone interview with Elizabeth Wheaton-Smith, May 17, 2007.

63 "Brooke was supporting him": Louis Auchincloss interview.

64 "Who the hell": Author phone interview with Cynthia Meanwell, July 2007.

"They've changed things around": Tony Marshall interview, Westchester County Surrogate's Court, Sept. 5, 2007.

5. AN AMERICAN ROMANCE

66 Brooke was left with: Frances Kiernan, *The Last Mrs. Astor* (New York: W. W. Norton, 2007), p. 102.

"She was feeling": Author interview with confidential source.

67 Astor's sprawling real estate empire: "Son is Chief Heir," *Washington Post,* May 7, 1912.

memory of being locked: Brooke Astor, *Footprints* (New York: Doubleday, 1980), pp. 303, 278–79.

"Always Kept Under Guard," *Washington Post,* July 17, 1904.

product of Ava Astor's illicit affair: Justin Kaplan, *When the Astors Owned New York* (New York: Viking, 2006) p. 150.

"She was a tigress": Interview with Ivan Obolensky in Manhattan, Oct. 11, 2007.

68 "The perils of being young": "Good Mate for Astor," *Washington Post,* May 23, 1913

"She is a typical": "Vincent Astor Is Wed," *Washington Post,* Nov. 8, 1913.

"Mr. Astor was shocked": "Vincent Astor Dies in his Home at 67," *New York Times,* Feb. 4, 1959.

69 "Any crank": Jonathan Alter, *The Defining Moment* (New York: Simon & Shuster, 2006), pp. 168–71.

"Fun with Friends," *Time,* Apr. 9, 1934.

At a Washington dinner party: David Grafton, *The Sisters* (New York: Villard, 1992), p. 39.

70 "The word got out": Ivan Obolensky interview.

"I was terrified": Author interview with Reinaldo Hererra at his home, May 2007.

"If you have the slightest doubt": Vincent Astor to Brooke Astor, bound volume for Brooke Astor's one hundredth birthday party. Courtesy of David Rockefeller.

71 "It was important": Author interview with Barbara Goldsmith at her home, Mar. 15, 2007.

"Vincent would to go this sanitorium": Ivan Obolensky interview.

"If she married him": Author interview with Louis Auchincloss at his home, Nov. 16, 2007.

"only a few relatives": "Mrs. Marshall Wed to Vincent Astor," *New York Times,* Oct. 9, 1953.

72 "I asked him what I should do": Author interview with Tony Marshall, Westchester County Surrogate's Court, Oct. 17, 2007.

73 "Tony clearly loved those days": Author interview with Frances Fitzgerald at her home, Apr. 11, 2007.

"She did not approve": Author phone interview with Winthrop Aldrich, Feb. 2008. (This is not the same Winthrop Aldrich mentioned by David Rockefeller in Chapter 1.)

"I saw very little of Tony": Astor, *Footprints,* pp. 303–4.

74 "At ten-thirty A.M.": Author phone interview with Elizabeth Wheaton-Smith, multiple interviews, May 17, 2007–Mar. 2008.

74 "Vincent had a boat": Author phone interview with James McCabe, July 20, 2007.
"He was tall and gruff": Author phone interview with Emily Harding, Feb. 2008.
"Vincent had one of the early VWs": Author interview with Philip Marshall, multiple interviews, July 31, 2006–June 2008.
he revised his will: Vincent Astor will, May 15, 1957.

75 "I don't think I can stand": Elizabeth Wheaton-Smith interview.
"You are the luckiest": Barbara Goldsmith interview.

76 "I've had it": Ivan Obolensky interview; Kiernan, *The Last Mrs. Astor,* pp. 144–45.
"He used to change": Astor, *Footprints,* pp. 323–24.

77 "'Vincent drank so much'": Astor, *Footprints,* pp. 323–25; Kiernan, *The Last Mrs. Astor,* pp. 139–45.
"Please Help": "Please Help Poor John Jacob Astor," *Washington Post,* June 21, 1959.
"Vincent Astor had died": Author phone interview with Albert Hadley, Apr. 2008.

6. WHITE-GLOVE PHILANTHROPY

78 "Vincent told me": Videotaped interview with Brooke Astor by Peg Breen, president of the Landmarks Conservancy, Nov. 1984. Collection of the Landmarks Conservancy.

79 "Brooke was perfectly aware": Author interview with Philippe de Montebello at the Metropolitan Museum, Mar. 12, 2008.
During the city's newspaper strike: Author interview with Robert Silvers, June 2008.
"outdoor living rooms": "Mrs. Astor Sponsors Outdoor Living Rooms," *Washington Post,* Mar. 6, 1966.
"Brooke really came into her own": Author interview with Howard Phipps at his office, June 12, 2007.

80 "Mrs. Astor came frequently": Author phone interview with Marie Ridder, June 2007.
"She had this wonderful personality": Author phone interview with Elizabeth Corbett, July 2007.
"I thought it was wonderful": Author phone interview with Nancy Reagan, Apr. 25, 2007.
"If I go up to Harlem": Marilyn Berger, "Being Brooke Astor," *New York Times,* May 20, 1984.

81 "Brooke, to her ever-loving credit": Author interview with Peter Duchin, Nov. 1, 2006.
"There was consternation": Author interview with Ashton Hawkins at his office, Sept. 2005.
"She was not a snob": Philippe de Montebello interview.

82 "I went to things": Author interview with Liz Smith in Manhattan, Jan. 23, 2007.
"If you are an Astor": "Mrs. Astor Sponsors Outdoor Living Rooms."
"Vincent was a very suspicious man": Dana Kennedy, Associated Press; "The Grand Mrs. Astor, a Young 90, Works Hard at Giving Away Money," *Los Angeles Times,* Mar. 22, 1992, p. A3.

I knew he was hard up": Caroline Seebohm, *No Regrets* (New York: Simon & Schuster, 1997), p. 280.

83 "Hiring the actor Frederic Bradlee": Author interview with Alexandra Schlesinger, Feb. 1, 2007; "Mrs. J. H. Russell, Mother of Mrs. Vincent Astor, Dies," *New York Times,* Apr. 1, 1967.

"She made a big effort": Author phone interview with James McCabe, July 20, 2007.

"bathed in a glow": Enid Nemy, "Emeralds Cast Their Glow on a Night of Oriental Splendor," *New York Times,* Dec. 2, 1976, p. 58.

"I was invited": Brooke Astor, "Not at the Party," *New York Times,* Mar. 2, 1970.

84 "I was desperately upset": Author phone interview with Elizabeth Wheaton-Smith, multiple interviews, May 17, 2007–Mar. 2008.

"I don't think we saw it coming": Author phone interview with Philip Marshall, multiple interviews, July 28, 2006–June 2008.

85 "Visiting my father and grandmother": Author interview with Alec Marshall at his home, Dec. 12, 2007.

"Philip was artistic": Author phone interview with Toby Hilliard, Aug. 2007.

86 "I've got to give my father credit": Philip Marshall interview.

"svelte, sixtyish": Judy Klemesrud, "The Goal of Brooke Astor: Easing the Misery of Others," *New York Times,* June 16, 1968.

87 "I'm sure that her contributions": Author interview with Henry Kissinger at his office, Sept. 19, 2007.

"Brooke bought": Author interview with Suzanne Kuser in Washington, D.C., June 28, 2007.

"Anybody who wants to be an ambassador": Richard Reeves, *President Nixon: Alone in the White House* (New York: Simon & Schuster, 2001), p. 462.

"Brooke used to say": Author interview with Louis Auchincloss at his home, Nov. 16, 2006.

"I was a friend of Dick Nixon": Author interview with Tony Marshall at his home, Sept. 16, 2005.

Marshall contributed $20,000: Morton Mintz, "Nixon Got $1 Million Donation," *Washington Post,* Nov. 3, 1972.

"Anthony [Tony] Marshall": "Suzy Says," *Chicago Tribune,* Dec. 16, 1969.

"You can make it": Senate Foreign Relations Committee, Dec. 12, 1969, transcript.

88 "Madagascar was not one": Author phone interview with David Newsom, July 3, 2007.

"We wondered": Author phone interview with Pamela Walker, Nov. 2007.

"I had brought my ratty clothes": Philip Marshall interview.

"He was persona non grata": Suzanne Kuser interview.

89 "in a supposed coup": "Little Black Lies: Spy Groups Increase Use of False Material to Put Enemy on the Spot," *Wall Street Journal,* Sept. 25, 1971.

"aggressively attempted": Jim Hoagland, "Malagasy Demonstrators Quietened After Power Is Transferred to Army," *Washington Post,* May 22, 1972.

Languishing in the tropics: Mintz, "Nixon got $1 Million Donation."

"I suspect the influence": David Newsom interview.

89 "Tony was competent": Henry Kissinger interview.

90 He did some consulting work: Author interview with Tony Marshall, Sept. 16, 2005.

his rate of return lagged: Selena Maranjian, "105 Years Old, with $816 in the Bank," *Motley Fool*, www.fool.com, Apr. 11, 2007.

"You could often": Author interview with Linda Gillies, Oct. 2007.

"My father had plenty of room": Alec Marshall interview.

91 "The wives couldn't get along": Suzanne Kuser interview.

"lots of proposals": Judy Klemesrud, "The Private Moments of a Public Benefactor," *New York Times*, June 14, 1980.

"delightful": Eden Ross Lipson, "Fairy Godmother," *New York Times Book Review*, Sept. 7, 1980, p. 14.

"A lot of us knew": Howard Phipps interview.

92 "She asked all of the boards": Author interview with Ashton Hawkins at his office, July 16, 2007.

"Ronnie was under the table": Author phone interview with Nancy Reagan, Apr. 25, 2007; John Duka, "The Elite Welcome Reagan, Who Offers Toast to the City," *New York Times*, Dec. 10, 1980.

93 "She could talk": Author interview with Vartan Gregorian at his office, Mar. 24, 2007.

"By virtue of her prestige": Author interview with Paul LeClerc at the New York Public Library, May 17, 2007.

"You had to be tough": Author phone interview with John Meaney, June 2008.

94 "It was Brooke's way of saying": Author interview with John Hart in Manhattan, Sept. 26, 2006.

"It was traffic": Nancy Reagan interview.

95 "How am I going to find": Author phone interview with Oscar de la Renta, Mar. 2008.

"Brooke was always": Author interview with Annette de la Renta at her home, Jan. 29, 2008.

"She was a hellion": Author interviews with Betsy and Victor Gotbaum at their home, Jan. 13, 2008.

96 Jane Pinto-Reis Brian: Douglas Martin, "Jane Engelhard, 86, Fixture in Society and Philanthropy," *New York Times*, Mar. 3, 2004.

His death, on the cusp: "Fritz Mannheimer, Financier, Is Dead," *New York Times*, Aug. 11, 1939, p. 19; "Action Follows Shortly after Mannheimer's Death," *New York Times*, Aug. 12, 1939, p. 3.

"cigar-smoking German Jew": "Post-War Story," *Time*, Aug. 21, 1939.

97 "pure-gold bracelets": Stephen Grover, "C. W. Engelhard, Industrialist, Dies at 54," *Wall Street Journal*, Mar. 3, 1971, p. 8.

"I didn't know": Author phone interview with Susan O'Connor, Mar. 2008.

"People think Annette": Oscar de la Renta interview.

"one could not infer": John Heminway, "At Home on the Range," *Town & Country*, Aug. 1997, p. 78.

98 "Brooke admired Jane": Author phone interview with Robert Silvers, Mar. 2008.

"Her stepfather adored her": Betsy Gotbaum interview.

"We had the nannies": Susan O'Connor interview.

"She'd make everybody laugh": Author phone interview with Elise Lufkin, Mar. 2008.

99 "People practically committed suicide": Liz Smith, *Dishing* (New York: Simon & Schuster, 2005), pp. 67–71.

"I loved her": Annette de la Renta interview (multiple interviews).

"enormous chocolate cake": Oscar de la Renta interview (multiple interviews).

"They are among": Enid Nemy, "They Look Alike, They Dress Alike, They Like Each Other Very Much," *New York Times,* Apr. 1, 1967, p. 16.

100 "Annette was unquestionably": Author interview with John Richardson at his home, June 5, 2007.

"Brooke was a better mother": Author phone interview with Florence Irving, Apr. 2008.

"They could be unguarded": Author interview with Randy Bourscheidt in Manhattan, June 8, 2007.

"Jane gathered into herself": Robert Silvers interview.

"When my mother moved": Susan O'Connor interview.

101 "My wife died": Oscar de la Renta interview.

"Astor herself": Julia Reed, "Brooke Astor. The Last Empress," *Manhattan Inc.,* Sept. 1988.

"It was unpleasant": Annette de la Renta interview.

Oscar and Annette: "Mrs. Reed Weds Oscar de la Renta," *New York Times,* Dec. 28, 1989.

"I was a little nervous": Betsy Gotbaum interview.

"Brooke was clinging": Oscar de la Renta interview.

102 "They were playing": Robert Silvers interview.

"She leaned over": Author phone interview with Tom Brokaw, Mar. 27, 2007.

"Why couldn't Mr. Clinton": Arthur Schlesinger, Jr., *Journals: 1952–2000* (New York: Penguin, 2007), p. 719.

"I think there was a moment": Howard Phipps interview.

"Tony was always trying": Author interview with Viscount William Astor, Dec. 26, 2007.

"She unraveled to the point": John Meaney interview.

103 "Brooke said, 'Go out'": Philippe de Montebello interview.

But that autumn: Linda Gilles interview.

"My son is not an Astor": Geraldine Fabrikant, "Brooke Astor Has a Year's Worth of Giving Left," *New York Times,* Dec. 18. 1996, p. A1.

104 "I'd see her pull herself:" Author interview with confidential source.

"He was always giving her grief": Author interview with Robert Pirie, Sept. 2007.

7. THE PERILS OF CHARLENE

105 When Mrs. Astor awoke: Author interview with Alicia Johnson in Northeast Harbor, Maine, July 17, 2007.

106 "Maine was perfect": Author interview with Judy Miller in Manhattan, Apr. 2007.

"The house in Maine": Author phone interview with Barbara Walters, Jan. 18, 2008.

106　"They were fighting": Author interview with Betty Halpern in Northeast Harbor, Maine, July 19, 2007.

"This party was not": Author interview with Bob Pyle in Northeast Harbor, Maine, July 19, 2008.

107　"She was hell on wheels": Judy Miller interview.

"She was terrible": Author interview with Freddy Melhado at his home, June 4, 2007.

"They wanted me to dissuade her": Author phone interview with Naomi Packard-Koot, Mar. 2008.

"She would be sitting there": Alicia Johnson interview.

108　"Mrs. de la Renta": Brooke Astor phone logs, 1990–92; Brooke Astor summer calendar schedules, 2000–2002.

"George went every summer": Author phone interview with Susan Trescher, Jan. 2007.

"By the time I left": Author interview with Paul Pearson in Manhattan, Mar. 21, 2007.

"Christopher is outstanding": Joel Schumacher, Jan. 22, 1990.

109　"Brooke read it": Author interview with John Hart in Manhattan, Sept. 26, 2006.

"She would get into": Alicia Johnson interview.

"Brooke couldn't talk on the phone": Author phone interview with Emily Harding, Mar. 2008.

110　"We were both nutty": Author interview with Nancy Pyne in Northeast Harbor, Maine, July 19, 2007.

"Is this another thing": Author phone interview with James McCabe, July 20, 2007.

"I don't know why": Author interview with Gerrit Lansing in Northeast Harbor, Maine, July 18, 2007.

"She'd be right on top": Author interview with Steve Hamor in Northeast Harbor, Maine, July 18, 2007.

"'You'll have a job here'": Author interview with Steve Hamor Jr. in Northeast Harbor, Maine, July 18, 2007.

111　"The high point came": Author interview with Robert Pirie, Sept. 2007.

"Sometimes I lie down": Marilyn Berger. "Being Brooke Astor," *New York Times,* May 20, 1984.

"Brooke told me": Author interview with Marshall Rose at his office, Apr. 10, 2007.

"I didn't understand": Author interview with Peggy Pierrepont, May 11, 2007.

113　"You have to provide": Author interview with Frances Fitzgerald at her office, Apr. 11, 2007

"I liked the fact": Author phone interview with Paul Gilbert, Jan. 6, 2008.

"We admitted later": Author interview with Tony Marshall at Westchester County Surrogate's Court, Oct. 19, 2007.

114　"He could walk": Author phone interview with Oscar Johnson Small, Jr., Jan. 2008.

"The father and mother": Author phone interview with confidential source.

"He was a born salesman": Paul Gilbert interview.

"Charlene had a childhood": Author interview with confidential source.

115　"What happened in that house": Author interview with confidential source.

"Charlene would come by": Oscar Small interview.

"The grandmother saved Charlene": Author interview with confidential source.

"Charlene was very funny": Author phone interview with Anne Miller Moises, Jan. 2008.

116 "I remember sitting": Author phone interview with Gail Townsend Bailey, Jan. 2008.

117 "She was very outgoing": Paul Gilbert interview.

"There was no air conditioning": Author interview with Mary Lou Scott in Manhattan, Oct. 9, 2007.

"Charlene and Paul were warmly received": Bob Pyle interview.

"Charlene was more talkative": Author interview with Gunnar Hansen in Northeast Harbor, Maine, July 19, 2007.

118 "My mother died in Charlene's arms": Author phone interview with Pattie O'Brien, Jan. 17, 2008.

"We converted our living room": Paul Gilbert interview.

"We had them to dinner": Frances Fitzgerald interview.

"Francis is very charming": Paul Gilbert interview.

119 "It was a renewal": Tony Marshall interview, Oct. 19, 2007.

"I got to work": Author interview with Sandra Graves in Northeast Harbor, Maine, July 19, 2007.

"If you're a minister's wife": Author interview with Dot Renaud in Northeast Harbor, Maine, July 19, 2007.

120 "I was telling everyone": Author interview with Philip Marshall, multiple interviews, July 28, 2006–June 2008.

"I was very much in love": Author phone interview with Nan Starr, Mar. 2008.

"We were broke": Paul Gilbert interview.

"Charlene's husband": Sandra Graves interview.

121 "Quick? You moved out": Paul Gilbert interview.

"This winter was": Paul E. Gilbert, *Personally Speaking* (Maine: Horizon, 1996), p. 72.

"She has said the marriage": Author interview with Sam Peabody at his home, Apr. 17, 2007.

"One of the sad things": Author phone interview with Pamela Walker, Nov. 2007.

"I'd talk to her": Author interview with Alec Marshall, Jan. 2008.

"It was hard": Philip Marshall interview.

122 "She didn't go to her parish": Author interview with Ashton Hawkins, July 16, 2007.

"Charlene was talking about": Philip Marshall interview.

"Was she a gold digger": Author phone interview with Nan Lincoln, July 2006.

123 Living in a studio apartment: Vicky Ward, "In Mrs. Astor's Shadow," *Vanity Fair*, Dec. 2007, p. 240.

"She had a miserable beginning": Author interview with confidential source.

"I was not invited": Alec Marshall interview.

"When Tony and Charlene married": Written description from Suzanne Harbour Kahanovitz, July 2006.

124 "Brooke was never hostile": Freddy Melhado interview.

"My impression was": Author interview with Henry Kissinger at his office, Sept. 19, 2007

124 "Charlene is one of those people": Author phone interview with Viscount William Astor, Dec. 26, 2007.

"Tony and Charlene would be staying": Author interview with John Dobkin in Manhattan, Sept. 19, 2006.

125 "Mrs. Astor used to tell": Alicia Johnson interview.

"Brooke assigned them": Ashton Hawkins interview.

"She thought Charlene was taking": Author interview with Liz Smith in Manhattan, Jan. 23, 2007.

"I loved sitting next to": Author interview with Patricia Roberts at her home, Sept. 25, 2007.

"She behaved like a summer person": Gunnar Hansen interview.

126 "Chris said": John Hart interview.

"My grandson, Philip Marshall": Brooke Astor's will, Jan. 30, 2002, Westchester County Surrogate's Court, file no. 2127/2007.

127 "We went by": Nancy Pyne interview.

8. THE PAINTING VANISHES

128 "An exhilarating picture": Brendan Gill, "A Party for Brooke," *New Yorker*, Apr. 21, 1997.

Hassam, America's best-known: Ilene Susan Fort, "The Flag Paintings of Childe Hassam," Los Angeles County Museum of Art, 1988.

129 "The curator felt": Author interview with Ashton Hawkins at his office, July 16, 2007.

"Every time I went": Author interview with Philippe de Montebello at the Metropolitan Museum, Mar. 12, 2008.

Dating from 1992: Brooke Astor wills, 1992, 1993, 2001.

130 "It was a picture": Author interview with David Rockefeller at his office, Dec. 18, 2007.

"I didn't even have to ask": Author interview with Annette de la Renta at her home, multiple interviews, Jan. 29, 2008–June 2008.

"'Tony says'": Author phone interview with Viscount William Astor, Dec. 26, 2007.

"At the time the exhibition was arranged": Anthony Marshall Verified Answer and Cross-Petition, New York State Supreme Court, file no. 500095/06, Sept. 19, 2006, p. 35.

131 "I remember her delight": Author phone interview with Peggy Pierrepont, May 11, 2007.

"Tony Marshall was at a dinner": Author phone interview with Gerald Peters, Aug. 13, 2007.

"It worked out well": Ibid.

"I was touched": Annette de la Renta interview.

132 "I want to see you": Author interview with Everett Fahy at the Metropolitan Museum, Apr. 12, 2007.

"What can I do for you": Author interview with Vartan Gregorian at his office, Mar. 24, 2007.

"He stressed": Brooke Astor phone logs, Oct. 22, 2002.

"She really didn't know": Author phone interview with Louise Grunwald, Apr. 2007.

"She always looked wonderful": Author phone interview with Oscar de la Renta, Mar. 2008.

"You told Mr. Rockefeller": Brooke Astor phone logs, Oct. 21, 2002.

133 "A cook had fallen down": Author phone interview with Naomi Packard-Koot, Feb. 8, 2007.

"When Mrs. Astor began to lose": Author phone interview with Marciano Amaral, Jan. 2007.

134 Relatives of that Park Avenue widow: The estate of Elisabeth Von Knapitsch, Surrogate's Court of the State of New York, New York County, file no. 299/00, settlement stipulation, Jan. 27, 2003.

A similar case involving another: The estate of Sam Schurr, Surrogate's Court of the State of New York, New York County, file no. 1121/P2002.

135 "Young Frank is a charming man": Author interview with Arthur M. Schlesinger, Jr., at his home, Feb. 1, 2007.

"Frank appeared one day": Author phone interview with Frederic Kass, June 2008.

limitations of connections: Arthur M. Schlesinger, Jr., *Robert Kennedy and His Times* (Boston: Houghton Mifflin, 1978), pp. 375–376, 683–685.

136 was later censured and fined: Edgar J. Driscoll, Jr., and David Abel, "Francis X. Morrissey, at 97, was Judge, Longtime Kennedy Confidant," *Boston Globe,* Jan. 2, 2008, p. B9.

"I'm one of the people": Author phone interview with Nancy Colhoun, Aug. 2007.

137 "It's blatantly improper": Author phone interview with Stephen Gillers, Apr. 2008.

stack of character references: Supreme Court of New York, Appellate Division, First Department, Lexis 11762, Nov. 16, 1995.

138 yearly income of around $150,000: New York State Department Disciplinary Committee, First Judicial Department, Supreme Court Appellate Division, Apr. 9, 1998.

"He was devastated": Author phone interview with Chuck Merten, Nov. 2006.

Morrissey claimed that: New York State Departmental Disciplinary Committee, First Judicial Department, Supreme Court Appellate Division, Apr. 9, 1998, transcript, pp. 83–84.

"my name is the same": Ibid., pp. 113–14.

139 embroiled in other legal controversies: Serge Kovaleski, "Lawyer Charged with Astor Case Has Been Accused of Other Improprieties," *New York Times,* Dec. 1, 2007, p. B1; Serge Kovaleski, "Many Clients of Astor Lawyer Left Him Bequests in Their Wills," *New York Times,* Jan. 4, 2008, p. B1.

"Frank can read": Author phone interview with Peter J. Kelley, Dec. 26, 2007.

140 Sam Schurr, an economist: The estate of Sam Schurr, Surrogate's Court of the State of New York, file no. 1121 P2002, affidavit of Donald Novick, Nov. 19, 2003,; affidavit of Stephen Rubin, June 27, 2003.

The Renoirs were actually: Brasswell Galleries, sales inquiry listing.

"There was no one": Author phone interview with Margot Adler, July 2007.

141 "Dearest, Darling Annette": Brooke Astor to Annette de la Renta, Nov. 2002. Collection of Annette de la Renta.

142 She scheduled her annual: Brooke Astor's schedule, Jan. 28, 2003; "Mrs. Astor leaves

Holly Hill for Westchester Airport. Virginia Melhado and Bunny du Pont will meet you at the Palm Beach Airport."

142   Four days before: "Dinner in Mrs. Astor's honor at the home of Mr. and Mrs. Anthony Marshall." Feb. 1, 2003.

"miles of scenery": Walter Kerr, "Theatre: Electric 'Extremities' and a Muffled 'Alice,'" *New York Times*, Jan. 2, 1983.

"I swore I'd never": Jesse McKinley, "He Is His Own Producer and Much More," *New York Times*, Dec. 17, 2003.

143   "Charlene's a delightful person": Author phone interview with Mary Rodgers Guettel, Mar. 20, 2007.

Tony also had a real fear: Anthony Marshall to Terry Christensen, Oct. 3, 2001, guardianship files.

144   "I always saw them bristle": Naomi Packard-Koot interview.

"At Holly Hill, we'd sit in the library": Author phone interview with Sophie Marshall, Apr. 2008.

145   "I didn't give her important jewelry": Author interview with David Rockefeller at his office, Dec. 18, 2007.

"Would you take": Naomi Packard-Koot interview.

"What can I do for Tony?": Francis X. Morrissey, Jr., to Anthony Marshall, Mar. 4, 2004, guardianship files.

146   informed Tony by letter: Henry Christensen III to Anthony D. Marshall, Apr. 28, 2003, guardianship files.

"I was very keen": Anthony D. Marshall memorandum, "Meeting with Terry Christensen," Feb. 11, 2004, guardianship files.

"It was really sudden": Naomi Packard-Koot interview.

148   "I wasn't expecting": Philip Marshall interview.

"It felt to Philip": Author phone interview with Nan Starr, Mar. 2008.

149   "Dear Tony": New York State Supreme Court, file no. 500095/06, Brooke Astor to her son, Aug. 12, 2003.

150   "rift between the Marshalls and Mrs. Astor": Christopher Ely notes, guardianship files.

"seemed to want me": Ibid.

"I told her": Ibid.

151   "John, I'm gaga": Author interview with John Hart in Manhattan, Sept. 26, 2006.

9. THE TREACHEROUS CODICILS

152   "He used to go visit Brooke": Author interview with Catia Chapin at her home, Mar. 19, 2007.

153   Vincent Astor had so disliked: Author phone interview with Linda Gillies, Apr. 2008.

"Everything was fine:" Author interview with Alice Perdue in Manhattan, Oct. 3, 2007.

Alicia Johnson . . . noticed: Author interview with Alicia Johnson, July 2007.

"I knew there was no way": Author interview with Philip Marshall, multiple interviews, July 28, 2006–June 2008.

154   "I did think it was odd": Alice Perdue interview.

"All the nurses got dressed up": Author interview with Minnette Christie in Manhattan, Jan. 14, 2008.

"Suppose I'm taking her": Author interview with Pearline Noble in Manhattan, Jan. 14, 2008.

"I started in Holly Hill": Author phone interview with Beverly Thomson, Aug. 29, 2007.

155   "I just wanted to put down": Pearline Noble interview.

"She is dead set": Pearline Noble, nurses' notes, Sept. 25, 2003.

"A very restless night": Minnette Christie, nurses' notes, Sept. 28, 2003.

"Mrs. Astor would tell me:" Minnette Christie interview.

156   "Mrs. A. curtsied": Pearline Noble, nurses' notes, Sept. 30, 2003.

"This is how you do it": Ibid.

"The first thing that struck me": Author interview with Moises Kaufman at his office, Apr. 5, 2007.

"The theatre is a little like": Robert Hofler, "Delphi Predictions," *Variety*, Dec. 15, 2003.

157   the ultimate civilian medal: Jesse McKinley, "He Is His Own Producer, and Much More," *New York Times*, Dec. 17, 2003.

"periods of confusion and illusions": Minnette Christie, nurses' notes, Dec. 13, 2003.

"Periods of confusion": Minnette Christie, nurses' notes, Dec. 14, 2003.

"Paranoia, undecipherable words": Pearline Noble, nurses' notes, Dec. 17, 2003.

"She was on automatic pilot": Author phone interview with Barbara Goldsmith, Mar. 2008.

158   "I have enjoyed": First codicil of Brooke Astor's will, Dec. 18, 2003, Westchester County Surrogate's Court, file no. 2127/2007.

"Wanted to know who": Pearline Noble, nurses' notes, Dec. 18, 2003.

"they are putting her away": Minnette Christie, nurses' notes, Dec. 19, 2003.

159   "She knew me": Author interview with Louis Auchincloss, Nov. 2006.

"I'm sorry, but I don't believe": Vartan Gregorian, *The Road to Home* (New York: Simon & Schuster, 2003), p. 277.

160   "She extended her arm": Francis X. Morrissey, Jr., memo, Jan. 19, 2004, guardianship files.

161   He met with Mrs. Astor: G. Warren Whitaker memo, "Re: Brooke Russell Astor Codicil execution date," Jan. 12, 2004, guardianship files.

162   "Golden boy & tutor": Pearline Noble, nurses' notes, Jan. 12, 2004, 4 P.M.

"They started to pull": Pearline Noble interview.

"four men are in the house": Minnette Christie, nurses' notes, Jan. 12, 2004.

"It has not been easy": New York State Supreme Court, file no. 500095/06.

163   But Dr. Pritchett later stated: Court evaluator's report, Dec. 2006, guardianship files.

The experience was so traumatic: Pearline Noble interview.

"On entering our apartment": Anthony D. Marshall, "Subject: Meeting with Terry Christensen," Feb. 11, 2004, guardianship files.

163   "I did not describe": Author phone interview with Terry Christensen, Feb. 2008.

164   "Presumably you determined": G. Warren Whitaker to Terry Christensen, Feb. 13, 2004, guardianship files.

Worried about what: Anthony D. Marshall, "Memorandum to files. Re: Terry Christensen. Subject: Brooke Astor. Can the situation be resolved without litigation? Even if the opinion that it could be, would it be good judgement to prepare documents with which to proceed if Terry Christensen does not cooperate? Who/how should Terry Christensen be faced with the issue? (In a friendly manner: by Francis Morrissey? By Warren Whitaker, who has acted as BA's lawyer? By Ken Warner?)"

"I considered publicly": Terry Christensen interview.

Executors' fees: "Brooke Russell Astor Estate Planning," G. Warren Whitaker to Anthony D. Marshall, Mar. 2, 2006, guardianship files.

165   Two years later: Serge Kovaleski, "Recollections of Witnesses to Astor Wills Are Cloudy," *New York Times,* Nov. 1, 2006.

"I agree with Charlene": Francis X. Morrissey to Anthony Marshall, Mar. 4, 2004, guardianship files.

"Her son arrive": Pearline Noble, nurses' notes, Mar. 2, 2004.

"me and the driver will protect": Pearline Noble, nurses' notes, Mar. 4, 2004.

166   "She wouldn't get out of the car": Author interview with Nancy Kissinger at Kissinger Associates, Mar. 13, 2008.

"David Rockefeller told me": Author interview with Henry Kissinger at his office, Sept. 19, 2007. (Note: David Rockefeller does not recall this story.)

167   "She looked like a deer": Author phone interview with Nan Starr, Mar. 2008.

Charlene later insisted: Vicky Ward, "In Mrs. Astor's Shadow," *Vanity Fair,* Dec. 2006, p. 243.

"She played possum": Author phone interview with Marciano Amaral, Jan. 2007.

168   "She was always frail": Author phone interview with Sandra Foschi, Jan. 31, 2008.

"Ever since I was a little girl": Minnette Christie interview.

"To me, just writing this": Philip Marshall interview.

169   grandmother's many wills: Brooke Astor's wills, 1992–2002, Westchester County Surrogate's Court, file no. 2127/2007.

Philip "acted strangely": Ward, "In Mrs. Astor's Shadow," p. 235.

"A man": Pearline Noble interview.

170   "Pearline, I'm toast": Annette de la Renta interview.

"Mrs. Astor would stroke her hair": Minnette Christie interview.

"She was like a child": Pearline Noble interview.

"I went to see her": Author interview with Vartan Gregorian at his office, Mar. 24, 2007.

"I would go to have tea": Author interview with Philippe de Montebello at the Metropolitan Museum, Mar. 12, 2008.

171   "Chris was wonderful": Author interview with David Rockefeller at his office, Dec. 18, 2007.

"After Chris was fired": Author phone interview with Barbara Goldsmith, Mar. 2008.

"During the past two years": Anthony D. Marshall letter of recommendation for Christopher Ely.

Mrs. Astor had left Ely: Brooke Astor will, Jan. 30, 2002, Westchester County Surrogate's Court, file no. 2127/2007.

"I thought it was a little late": Philip Marshall interview.

172 "We showed her a picture": Minnette Christie interview.

10. "I DIDN'T KNOW IT WOULD BE ARMAGEDDON"

174 "I remember going": Author interview with Annette de la Renta at her home, multiple interviews, Jan. 29, 2007–July 2008.

"Brooke was sitting there": Author phone interview with Bob Silvers, Mar. 2007.

"I started saying": Author interview with John Richardson at his home, June 5, 2007.

"She didn't recognize me": Author phone interview with Viscount William Astor, July 2006.

175 "We had a perfectly cordial:" Author interview with David Rockefeller at his office, Dec. 18, 2007.

"We were upset": Annette de la Renta interview.

176 "What I said": David Rockefeller interview.

"If I had not heard": Author interview with Philip Marshall, multiple interviews, July 28, 2006–June 2008.

"We were told": Author phone interview with Beverly Thomson, Aug. 29, 2007.

"She did not leave": Author interview with Pearline Noble in Manhattan, Apr. 10, 2008.

177 "When I die": Ibid.

Brooke Astor's mortality: Francis Morrissey/G. Warren Whitaker letter to files, Aug. 23, 2005, guardianship files.

"I was a driver": Author phone interview with Marciano Amaral, Jan. 2007.

"Tony said that he was terribly sorry": Author interview with Alice Perdue in Manhattan, Oct. 3, 2007.

178 "Ambassador Marshall": Author interview with Daniel Billy, Jr., in Manhattan, Mar. 3, 2008.

"You'd make an appointment": Author phone interview with Robert Pirie, Oct. 22, 2007.

182 "I think of my grandfather": Tony Marshall speech to Marine Corps University Foundation, Oct. 25, 2005, transcript.

"NO ONE is to be": Daniel Billy, Jr., memo to staff, Dec. 9, 2005, guardianship files.

183 "If you put me": Marciano Amaral interview.

"They said there's no way": Pearline Noble interview.

"heartfelt thanks": Charlene Marshall to Brooke Astor, Dec. 20, 2005, guardianship files.

"They could see that she was declining": Author phone interview with Peter J. Kelley, Dec. 26, 2007.

184 the Juilliard school received: Serge Kovaleski. "In-Law's Charity Has One Donor, Astor, and Few Public Details," *New York Times,* Aug. 8, 2006, p. B1.

184 "If I want to see my father": Author interview with Tenzing Chadotsang in Manhattan, Dec. 14, 2007.

"I did not want my father": Philip Marshall interview.

186 "We weren't saying anything": Author interview with Pearline Noble in Manhattan, Jan. 14, 2008.

"Chris egged me on;" Philip Marshall interview.

"I thought, 'Oh, good'": Alice Perdue interview.

"It was really tearing Philip up": Author phone interview with Toby Hilliard, Aug. 2007.

187 "Dear Mr. Rockefeller": Philip Marshall to David Rockefeller, Mar. 6, 2006. With permission of Philip Marshall.

188 "I talked to Annette": David Rockefeller interview.

189 "I was amazed at how much;" Annette de la Renta interview.

"I wasn't going to fake it": Philip Marshall interview.

"I guess it was a fantasy": Author phone interview with Nan Starr, Mar. 2008.

190 "No one wanted him": Tenzing Chadotsang interview.

"Philip is mild-mannered": Author phone interview with Sam Adams, July 2006.

"People ask me:" Philip Marshall interview.

"He spent a long time": Author phone interview with Marta Grabowska, Sept. 12, 2007.

Invoices from CodeShred: Leslie Gordon Fagen, for JP Morgan Chase Bank, Reply Affirmation in Support of Temporary Guardian's Application, Supreme Court of the State of New York, file no. 5000095/06, Sept. 12, 2006, p. 9.

"If you consider a scrap": Daniel Billy, Jr., interview.

191 "It was very traumatic": Author phone interview with Oscar de la Renta, Mar. 2008.

"In a way it was a good thing": Author interview with John Richardson at his home, June 5, 2007.

"I thought I was doing": Annette de la Renta interview.

192 "We knew the trickiest part": Philip Marshall interview.

"I want to visit": Ibid.

"Philip was the most stressed out": Nan Starr interview.

"I had to believe": Author interview with Henry Kissinger at his office, Sept. 19, 2007.

"I was freaking": Philip Marshall interview.

193 "I said, 'Let's call a meeting'": Author interview with Beverly Thomson, Aug. 29, 2007.

"I saw two big plastic containers": Marta Grabowska interview.

"It was hot and stuffy": Author phone interview with Sandra Foschi, Jan. 3, 2008.

"Make no mistake": Author interview with Ira Salzman at his office, Dec. 4, 2007.

The lawsuit would charge: In the Matter of the Application of PHILIP MARSHALL for the Appointment of Guardians of the Person and Property of BROOKE ASTOR, an alleged Incapacitated Person, Supreme Court of the State of New York, file no. 500095/06, index.

194 "Dr. Pritchett later stated": Court evaluator's report, 2006, guardianship files.

"When she was feeling well": Author phone interview with Sam Karalis, July 2007.

195   "All the money stuff": Ira Salzman interview.

      "Her diet is inadequate: Guardianship lawsuit, ibid.

      "If we weren't effective": Philip Marshall interview.

196   "I knew it was something weird": Author interview with Susan Robbins, Oct. 2006.

197   "I thought it would be taken care of": Annette de la Renta interview.

      "I'm worried": Philip Marshall interview

      "No, Philip": Ira Salzman interview.

11. BLUE-BLOOD BATTLE

199   "She was perfectly fine": Author phone interview with Marta Grabowska, Sept. 12, 2007.

      "I worked with Mrs. Astor": Author phone interview with Beverly Thomson, Aug. 29, 2007. (Note: Thomson originally signed an affidavit supporting Philip Marshall's lawsuit. But after she lost her job as one of Brooke Astor's nurses, she filed a new affidavit on behalf of Tony Marshall.)

      "I thought she had fluid": Author interview with Minnette Christie in Manhattan, Jan. 14, 2008.

      "For a person": Author interview with Dr. Sandra Gelbard in Manhattan, Oct 3, 2007.

      "very elderly people": Author interview with Susan Robbins at her office, Oct. 2006.

200   "Mrs. Marshall burst in": Author interview with Pearline Noble in Manhattan, Apr. 10, 2008.

      "This was like nothing": Sandra Gelbard interview.

      "She weighs seventy-three pounds": Adam Lisberg, Julian Kesner, and Nancy Dillon, 'Emaciated Brooke's Chart," *Daily News*, July 31, 2006, p. 3.

201   "Winslow went out": Author interview with Nan Starr, Mar. 2008.

      They had to endure: Todd Venezia, Jana Winter, and Ayesha Akram, "'Evil' Son Sees Astor in the Hospital," *New York Post*, July 29, 2006, p. 7.

      "I thought, oh my God": Author interview with Moises Kaufman at his office, May 15, 2007.

202   "shocked and deeply hurt": Anthony D. Marshall statement, July 27, 2006, issued by Stephanie Pillersdorf, Citigate Sard Verbinnen.

      When the *Daily News:* Helen Peterson, "I Am Son Kind of Wonderful," *Daily News*, July 28, 2006, p. 7.

      "In these family fights": Author phone interview with Harvey Corn, Nov. 2006.

203   "Are you kidding?": Susan Robbins interview.

      "There was a guard": Ibid.

204   "She was stable to go": Sandra Gelbard interview.

      No one had the courtesy: Timothy Williams, "Son Not Notified as Mrs. Astor Goes to Westchester," *New York Times*, July 30, 2006.

      "I touched him on the knee": Author interview with Philip Marshall, multiple interviews, July 28, 2006–June 2008.

205   "Ordinarily, it would have been": Vicky Ward, "In Mrs. Astor's Shadow," *Vanity Fair*, Dec. 2006.

205   "Charlene was seething": Philip Marshall interview.

"Mrs. Marshall was trying": Pearline Noble interview.

"Charlene is a Leo": Author interview with Daniel Billy, Jr., in Manhattan, Mar. 3, 2008.

206   "I know that I am right": Anthony Marshall statement, July 30, 2006.

"Oh, I couldn't possibly answer": Cara Buckley, "Socialite's Son Pays a Visit, Then Lashes Out at Those Accusing Him of Mistreatment," *New York Times,* July 31, 2006.

"No protégée of Brooke Astor": Joseph Goldstein, "The Melodrama over Mrs. Astor Enters a Second Bitter Act," *New York Sun,* July 31, 2006.

"I understood that Charlene": Author interview with Paul Saunders, Jan. 29, 2008.

207   "When you go to see her": Justice Stackhouse's remarks, court file, transcript.

208   "Someone got in there": Susan Robbins interview..

"The couch referred to": Harvey Corn legal papers filed in guardianship lawsuit.

"We don't know who did it": Adam Lisberg, "Sofa from Truth Say Astor Kin," *Daily News,* Sept. 13, 2006, p. 6.

209   "I was on Philip's side": Author interview with Suzanne Kuser in Washington, D.C., June 28, 2007.

"Mr. Marshall told me": Author interview with Steve Hamor in Northeast Harbor, Maine, July 19, 2007.

210   "philanthropist now appears": "The Brooke Astor Effect," *New York Times,* Aug. 7, 2006, p. A14.

"Mr. Marshall has been lovingly devoted": Kenneth Warner and Harvey Corn, letter to the editor, *New York Times,* Aug. 11, 2006, p. A14.

12. THE ART OF SHUNNING

214   "I debated": Author phone interview with Tony Marshall, June 16, 2007.

"I averted my eyes": Author interview with Philippe de Montebello at the Metropolitan Museum, Mar. 12, 2008.

"It was an unpleasant situation": Author interview with Annette de la Renta at her home, Jan. 29, 2008.

"By my being there": Tony Marshall interview.

215   "She certainly came to me": Author interview with Brenda Husson at St. James' Church, July 2, 2007.

"She'd sit in the back of the church": Author interview with Sam Peabody at his home, Apr. 17, 2007.

216   "You would think that people": Author phone interview with Christopher Meigher, Mar. 2008.

"Was Mrs. Astor competent": Leslie Gordon Fagen for J. P. Morgan Chase, Reply Affirmation in Support of the Temporary Guardian's Application, Supreme Court of the State of New York, index no. 500095/06, Sept. 12, 2006, p. 5.

As part of the ongoing blizzard: Anthony Marshall, Verified Answer and Cross-Petition, Supreme Court of the State of New York, Sept. 19, 2006.

217 "were furious at me": Author interview with Freddy Melhado at his home, June 13, 2007.

218 "If anyone deserved a painting": Author phone interview with Viscount William Astor, Dec. 26, 2007.

Tony abruptly admitted: Harvey Corn to J. P. Morgan Chase, Aug. 28, 2006, Supreme Court of the State of New York, index no. 500095/06.

"My client was outraged": Author phone interview with Alan Pollack, Dec. 21, 2007.

"I consider Chris and Philip": Annette de la Renta interview.

219 "I loved him": Susan Robbins interview.

"She was so great": Author interview with Philip Marshall, multiple interviews, July 28, 2006–June 2008.

220 "was a smoking cannon": Susan Robbins interview.

"It was an oh-my-God moment": Author phone interview with Ira Salzman, Mar. 2008.

"I don't know what's the matter": Anthony D. Marshall to Dr. Howard Fillit, Dec. 26, 2000, Supreme Court of the State of New York, index no. 500095/06.

222 "We knew it was": Paul Saunders interview.

"on a witch hunt": Kenneth Warner, Attorney's Affirmation in Response, Supreme Court of the State of New York, index no. 500095/06, Sept. 22, 2006, p. 7.

"Mrs. Astor was obviously": Harvey Corn, Affirmation in Opposition to the Motion of Susan Robbins, Sept. 14, 2006, p. 7.

During the three emotional hours: Neil Weinberg, "The Father, the Son and High Society," *Forbes*, Oct. 9, 2006, p. 46.

223 In the full transcript: Courtesy of Neil Weinberg.

224 "The term I would use": Author interview with David Rockefeller at his office, Dec. 18, 2007.

"Every time there was something": Author phone interview with Barbara Walters, Jan. 18, 2008.

"They were deathly afraid": Author interview with Paul Saunders in Manhattan, Jan. 29, 2008.

"I wanted a standstill": Author phone interview with Harvey Corn, Feb. 2008.

225 "That's when I said": Susan Robbins interview.

"Susan didn't want": Paul Saunders interview.

"I have known Mrs. Astor": Stefanie Cohen, "Astor Great Society War Ends as Son Cedes Fight for Brooke," *New York Post*, Oct. 14, 2006, p. 9.

226 Yet the actual legal agreement: Supreme Court of the State of New York, file no. 500095/06, stipulation and settlement order, Oct. 13, 2006.

"There will be a battle royal": Vicky Ward, "In Mrs. Astor's Shadow," *Vanity Fair*, Dec. 2006, p. 230.

"Tony said those had been gifts": Author phone interview with Grace Richardson, May 2007.

227 "due to the deterioration": Serge Kovaleski; "Expert Says Mrs. Astor's Signature Was Forged," *New York Times*, Oct. 20, 2006, p. B1.

"I thought he was brilliant": Susan Robbins interview.

228 "When I spoke to the doctor": Author phone interview with Lois Orlin, Jan. 24, 2008.

"I kept telling everyone": Author interview with Minnette Christie in Manhattan, Jan. 14, 2008.

"Come on, Mrs. A.": Author interview with Pearline Noble in Manhattan, Jan. 14, 2008.

229 "I recited it every time": Author phone interview with Sandra Foschi, Jan. 31, 2007.

"They'd wheel her": Author phone interview with Alec Marshall, Mar. 2008.

"You could see her eyes light up": Author phone interview with Naomi Packard-Koot, Mar. 2008.

230 "Fortunately, I really don't think": Author interview with David Rockefeller in Manhattan, Dec. 18, 2007.

"Mr. Rockefeller would hold her hand": Author phone interview with Noreen Nee, Jan. 2008.

"When I would give her communion": Author phone interview with Rev. Charles Pridemore, Aug. 2007.

"It was tense": Noreen Nee interview.

"All the staff came to him": Author interview with Sam Peabody at his home, Apr. 17, 2007.

231 "They sang for her like a band": Pearline Noble interview.

"We didn't have to be so formal": Author interview with Sophie Marshall, Apr. 2008.

"If I knew that things": Minnette Christie and Pearline Noble interviews.

232 On December 4, 2006: Justice John Stackhouse ruling on legal fees, Dec. 4, 2006, Supreme Court of the State of New York, index no. 50095/06, court evaluator Sam Liebowitz report; guardianship files.

233 "My understanding is": Author interview with Henry Kissinger at his office, Sept. 19, 2008.

234 "She threw herself": Author interview with Louis Auchincloss, May 2007.

"As you may know": Charlene Marshall, "A Letter to the People of St. James," *St. James Epistle,* Dec. 2006.

"We went, we made our excuses": Author interview with Paul Gilbert, Jan. 6, 2008.

235 "It has nearly destroyed him": Author interview with Catia Chapin at her home, Mar. 18, 2007.

"I don't know Tony Marshall": Author phone interview with Chuck Merten, Nov. 2006.

"I've never had a lot": Author phone interview with Richard Estes, July 19, 2007.

236 "So much has changed": Philip Marshall to Tony Marshall, Mar. 18, 1993. Collection of Philip Marshall.

237 "I said no": Paul Saunders interview.

238 "She does spend a lot of time sleeping.": Associated Press, "Quiet 105th Birthday for Socialite Astor," Mar. 30, 2007; Ethan Rouen and Celeste Katz, "Mrs. Astor Snoozes Thru B'day Visit by Embattled Son," *Daily News,* Mar. 31, 2007, p. 10; Jill Culora. "A High 105 for Brooke," *New York Post,* Mar. 25, 2007, p. 21. Jill Culora, "A High 105 for Brooke," *New York Post,* Mar. 25, 2007, p. 21.

David Rockefeller carried: Serge Kovaleski, "Flowers, Not Fanfare for Brooke Astor's 105th," *New York Times*, Mar. 31, 2007, p. B2.

"She knew that everyone": Annette de la Renta interview.

"My grandmother was taking it all in": Philip Marshall interview.

13. A WONDERFUL LIFE

239   "I am very distressed": Alec Marshall to Tony Marshall, May 2007. Quoted with permission from Alec Marshall.

240   "I thought this was the only chance": Author interview with Alec Marshall at his home, Dec. 12, 2007.

"Trust me, they're shunned": Author interview with Clare Stone in Northeast Harbor, Maine, July 18, 2007.

"It was almost like": Author interview with Betty Halpern in Northeast Harbor, Maine, July 2007.

241   "They have a lot of nerve": Author interview with Dot Renaud in Northeast Harbor, Maine, July 2007.

"We came up the day before yesterday": Author phone interview with Tony Marshall, June 16, 2007.

"When the Marshalls came up": Author phone interview with William Bigelow, July 2007.

"She grabbed my hand": Author interview with Noreen Nee, Mar. 2008.

"When I first went in the room": Author interview with David Rockefeller at his office, Dec. 18, 2007.

242   "I was there": Author phone interview with Charles Pridemore, Aug. 2007.

"heartless and hostile": Tony Marshall, affidavit filed in Westchester County Surrogate's Court, file no. 21227/2007, Aug. 2007.

"I told Tony": Author interview with Annette de la Renta, multiple interviews, Jan. 29, 2008–July 2008.

"He glared at us": Author interview with Minnette Christie in Manhattan, Apr. 10, 2008.

243   "There was a bit of a scare": Author phone interview with Philip Marshall, Aug. 12, 2007.

"She was sweating": Author interview with Minnette Christie in Manhattan, Jan. 14, 2008.

"I will never forget": Author interview with Pearline Noble in Manhattan, Jan. 14, 2008.

244   "She's traveling" Minnette Christie interview.

"I have lost": www.nytimes.com, Aug. 13, 2008.

"Brooke left the world": Ibid.

"He was able to cradle her": Corky Siemaszo, "Socialite and Philanthropist Brooke Astor Dead at 105," *Daily News,* online ed., Aug. 13, 2007.

"The Marshalls got there": Charles Pridemore interview.

245   The *New York Times* immortalized: Marilyn Berger, "Brooke Astor, Wry Aristocrat of the People, Is Dead at 105," Aug. 14, 2007, p. 1.

245 "The accusation of": Barbara Ross, Adam Lisberg, and Corky Siemaszo. "Fight over Brooke Fortune," Aug 15, 2007, p. 8.

Mrs. Astor "was not competent": Serge Kovaleski, "Astor's Guardians Challenge Her Last Wills, Citing Incompetence," *New York Times,* Aug. 16, 2007, p. B1.

246 "For someone who is supposed to": Barbara Ross, Peter Kadushin, and Corky Siemaszo, "Astor Family Feud Heats Up as City Buries a Legend," *Daily News,* Aug. 17, 2006, p. 5.

I was at my mother's bedside": Author interview with Tony Marshall, Westchester County Surrogate's Court, Sept. 5, 2007.

"I thought it was tacky": Author phone interview with Philip Marshall, Aug. 2008.

"It was unclear": Author interview with Paul Saunders in Manhattan, Jan. 29, 2007.

247 "In a perfect world": Author phone interview with Annette de la Renta, May 2008.

"There was no need": Author phone interview with Susan Robbins, Aug. 2007.

list of guests: Eric Konigsberg and Serge Kovaleski, "Funeral A-List: New Version of Mrs. Astor's 400," *New York Times,* Aug. 15, 2007, p. B1.

248 "Our side didn't leak": Author phone interview with Daniel Billy, Jr., Aug. 2007.

"It was a roomful of people": Author interview with Henry Kissinger at his office, Sept. 19, 2007.

"I was pretty much planning": David Rockefeller interview.

249 "I suggest maybe": Cindy Adams. "Victim's Sister Rips Planned O.J. Book," *New York Post,* Aug. 22, 2007, p. 14.

250 "My father walked over": Author interview with Alec Marshall at his home, Dec. 12, 2007.

"I couldn't be more honored": Author phone interview with John Hart, Aug. 2007.

252 "It was as if": Author interview with confidential source.

253 "It was perfectly pleasant": Author phone interview with Emily Harding, Aug. 2007.

"It's as if Tony": Author interview with confidential source.

"We just stopped by": Lorena Mongelli and Lukas Alpert, "Secret Burial for Brooke," *New York Post,* Aug. 19, 2007, p. 15.

"I never thought": Author interview with Ramon Acosta, Dec. 12, 2007.

14. FAMILY PLOT

255 "We connected straight up": Author interview with Philip Marshall, multiple interviews, July 28, 2006–June 2008.

"I feel a bit like": Author interview with Susan Robbins, multiple interviews, Sept. 5, 2007.

"This is a nightmare": Westchester County Surrogate's Court, Sept. 5, 2007, transcript.

258 "Brooke specifically didn't want them": Author phone interview with Robert Pirie, Sept. 2007.

"Torturous": Author interview with Charlene Marshall at Westchester County Surrogate's Court, Sept. 5, 2007.

259 "I'm eighty-three": Author interview with Tony Marshall at Westchester County Surrogate's Court, Sept. 5, 2007.

"I didn't think he looked well": Author interview with Philip Marshall, Sept. 5, 2007.

260 "We were not invited"; Author interview with Tony Marshall at the Metropolitan Museum, Sept. 28, 2007.

261 "Brooke said, 'Oh'"; Author eyewitness account, New York Public Library, Sept. 11, 2007.

"All we do is": Author interview with Charlene Marshall at the Metropolitan Museum, Sept. 28, 2007.

"the most extraordinary thing": Author phone interview with Viscount William Astor, Dec. 26, 2007.

262 "All the help"; Author interview with Alice Perdue at the Metropolitan Museum, Sept. 28, 2007.

"I'd rather say things": Author interview with Chris Ely at the Metropolitan Museum, Sept. 28, 2007.

263 the couple had attended: "Sightings," *New York Post,* Dec. 31, 2007, p. 11.

"If one didn't know": Author interview with Marilyn Berger at her home, Nov. 14, 2007.

"They are the death of civilization": Author interview with Tony Marshall at Westchester County Surrogate's Court, Oct. 18, 2007.

264 "I adore him": Author interview with Charlene Marshall at Westchester County Surrogate's Court, Oct. 18, 2007.

"That was perfectly acceptable": Author interview with Paul Saunders in Manhattan, Jan. 29, 2007.

265 "If it wasn't for Philip": Author interview with Dan Castleman in Manhattan, Jan. 8, 2008.

266 "When I had a terrible nosebleed": Steve Fishman, "The Curse of Mrs. Astor," *New York,* Nov. 19, 2007, pp. 22–27, 106–9.

267 "Philip has not looked": Author phone interview with Nan Starr, Mar. 2008.

"I thought of going downstairs": Author phone interview with Alec Marshall, Mar. 2008.

268 "I sincerely hope": Melinda Grace, "Astor Grandson: Show Dad Mercy," *Daily News,* Nov. 28, 2007, pp. 5–6.

"swindling Mrs. Astor": Robert M. Morgenthau press conference, Nov. 27, 2007, author eyewitness account and transcript.

270 "Whose suit is that?": Author interview with Shirley Shepard in Manhattan, Nov. 27, 2007.

271 "They may have arrested": Author phone interview with Viscount William Astor, Dec. 26, 2007.

"He was ashen": Author interview with confidential source.

272 "I can argue": Author phone interview with Philip Marshall, Dec. 1, 2007.

"I think that Tony": Author phone interview with Paul Gilbert, Jan. 6, 2008.

"Charlene was so hostile": Author phone interview with Frances Kiernan, Dec. 2007.

273 "Girlsie is a total princess": Author phone interview with Molly Flint, July 1, 2008.

274 "My grandmother used to": Author interview with Alec Marshall, Dec. 12, 2007.

277 Opris "was upset": Laura Italiano, "Battle 'Royal,'" *New York Post*, Feb. 26, 2008, p. 15.

EPILOGUE: A SUNSET IN MAINE

278 "We were freer": Author phone interview with Nan Starr, Apr. 2008.

279 "She had all these trinkets": Author interview with Philip Marshall, multiple interviews, July 28, 2006–June 2008.

"Every time we went to see Gagi": Author interview with Sophie Marshall, Apr. 2008.

"And not drink:" Winslow Marshall e-mail to author, Apr. 2008.

"She loved the little girl": Author interview with Alicia Johnson in Northeast Harbor, Maine, July 2007.

280 "I'd never met any of them": Author interview with Annette de la Renta, multiple interviews, Jan. 29, 2008–July 2008.

"Brooke and I": Nan Starr interview.

"She was a little offended": Author interview with David Rockefeller in his office, Dec. 18, 2007.

"She was impressed": Sophie Marshall interview.

281 "It was really, really important": Nan Starr interview.

Bibliography

Alter, Jonathan. *The Defining Moment.* New York: Simon & Schuster, 2007.

Amory, Cleveland. *Who Killed Society?* New York: Harper and Brothers, 1960.

Astor, Brooke. *The Bluebird Is at Home.* New York: Harper & Row, 1965.

———. *Footprints.* New York: Harper & Row, 1980.

———. *The Last Blossom on the Plum Tree.* New York: Random House, 1986.

———. *Patchwork Child.* New York: Random House, 1993.

Duchin, Peter. *Ghost of a Chance.* New York: Random House, 1998.

Fort, Ilene Susan. *The Flag Paintings of Childe Hassam.* Los Angeles: Los Angeles County Museum of Art, 1988.

Gilbert, Paul E. *Personally Speaking.* Maine: Horizon, 1996.

Grafton, David. *The Sisters: The Lives and Times of the Fabulous Cushing Sisters.* New York: Villard, 1992.

Gregorian, Vartan. *The Road from Home.* New York: Simon & Schuster, 2003.

Hays, Charlotte. *The Fortune Hunters: Dazzling Women and the Men They Married.* New York: St. Martin's, 2007.

Hoving, Thomas. *Making the Mummies Dance.* New York: Touchstone/Simon & Schuster, 1994.

Kaplan, Justin. *When the Astors Owned New York.* New York: Viking, 2006.

Kiernan, Frances. *The Last Mrs. Astor.* New York: W. W. Norton, 2007.

Lewis, Adam. *Albert Hadley: The Story of America's Preeminent Interior Designer.* New York: Rizzoli, 2005.

Marshall, Anthony D. *Dash.* New York: Vantage, 2001.

Okrent, Daniel. *Great Fortune: The Epic of Rockefeller Center.* New York: Viking, 2003.

Rockefeller, David. *Memoirs.* New York: Random House, 2002.

Schlesinger, Arthur M., Jr. *Journals: 1952–2000.* New York: Penguin, 2007.

———. *Robert Kennedy and His Times.* Boston: Houghton Mifflin, 1978.

Seebohm, Caroline. *No Regrets.* New York: Simon & Schuster, 1997.

Smith, Liz. *Dishing: Great Dishes* — and Dishes — from America's Most Beloved Gossip Columnist. New York: Simon & Schuster, 2005.

——. *Natural Blonde.* New York: Hyperion, 2000.

Sterba, Jim. *Frankie's Place: A Love Story.* New York: Grove, 2003.

Turpin, John K., and W. Barry Thomson. *The Somerset Hills. New Jersey Country Houses,* vol. II. Far Hills, N.J.: Mountain Colony, 2005.

The Vincent Astor Foundation 1948–1997. New York: Vincent Astor Foundation, c. 1998.

Weinberg, H. Barbara. *Childe Hassam, American Impressionist.* New York: Metropolitan Museum of Art, 2004.